CASE CLOSED

V O L U M E   71

Gosho Aoyama

Case Briefing:

Subject:
Occupation:
Special Skills:
Equipment:

Jimmy Kudo, a.k.a. Conan Edogawa
High School Student/Detective
Analytical thinking and deductive reasoning, Soccer
Bow Tie Voice Transmitter, Super Sneakers,
Homing Glasses, Stretchy Suspenders

The subject is hot on the trail of a pair of suspicious men in black when he is attacked from behind and administered a strange substance which physically transforms him into a first grader. When the subject confides in the eccentric inventor Dr. Agasa, they decide to keep the subject's true identity a secret for the safety of everyone around him. Assuming the new identity of first-grader Conan Edogawa, the subject continues to assist the police force on their most baffling cases. The only problem is that most crime-solving professionals won't take a little kid's advice!

Table of Contents

CONFIDEN

CASE CLOSED

Volume 71
Shonen Sunday Edition

Story and Art by **GOSHO AOYAMA**

MEITANTEI CONAN Vol. 71
by Gosho AOYAMA
© 1994 Gosho AOYAMA
All rights reserved.
Original Japanese edition published by SHOGAKUKAN.
English translation rights in the United States of America, Canada,
the United Kingdom, Ireland, Australia and New Zealand arranged with SHOGAKUKAN.

Translation
Tetsuichiro Miyaki

Touch-up & Lettering
Freeman Wong

Cover & Graphic Design
Andrea Rice

Editor
Shaenon K. Garrity

Printed in the U.S.A.

Published by VIZ Media, LLC
P.O. Box 77010
San Francisco, CA 94107

10 9 8 7 6 5 4 3 2 1
First printing, July 2019

WWW.SHONENSUNDAY.COM

viz.com

VIDEO MEMORY

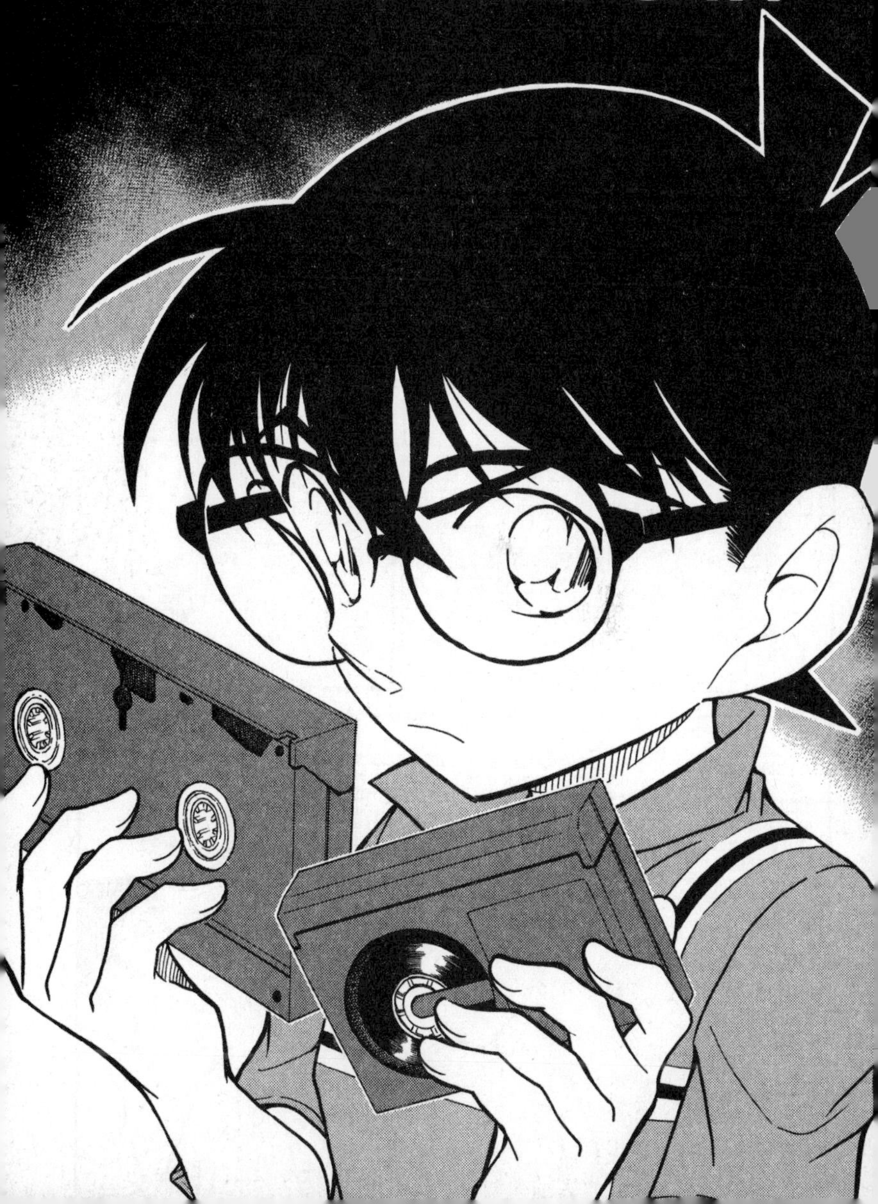

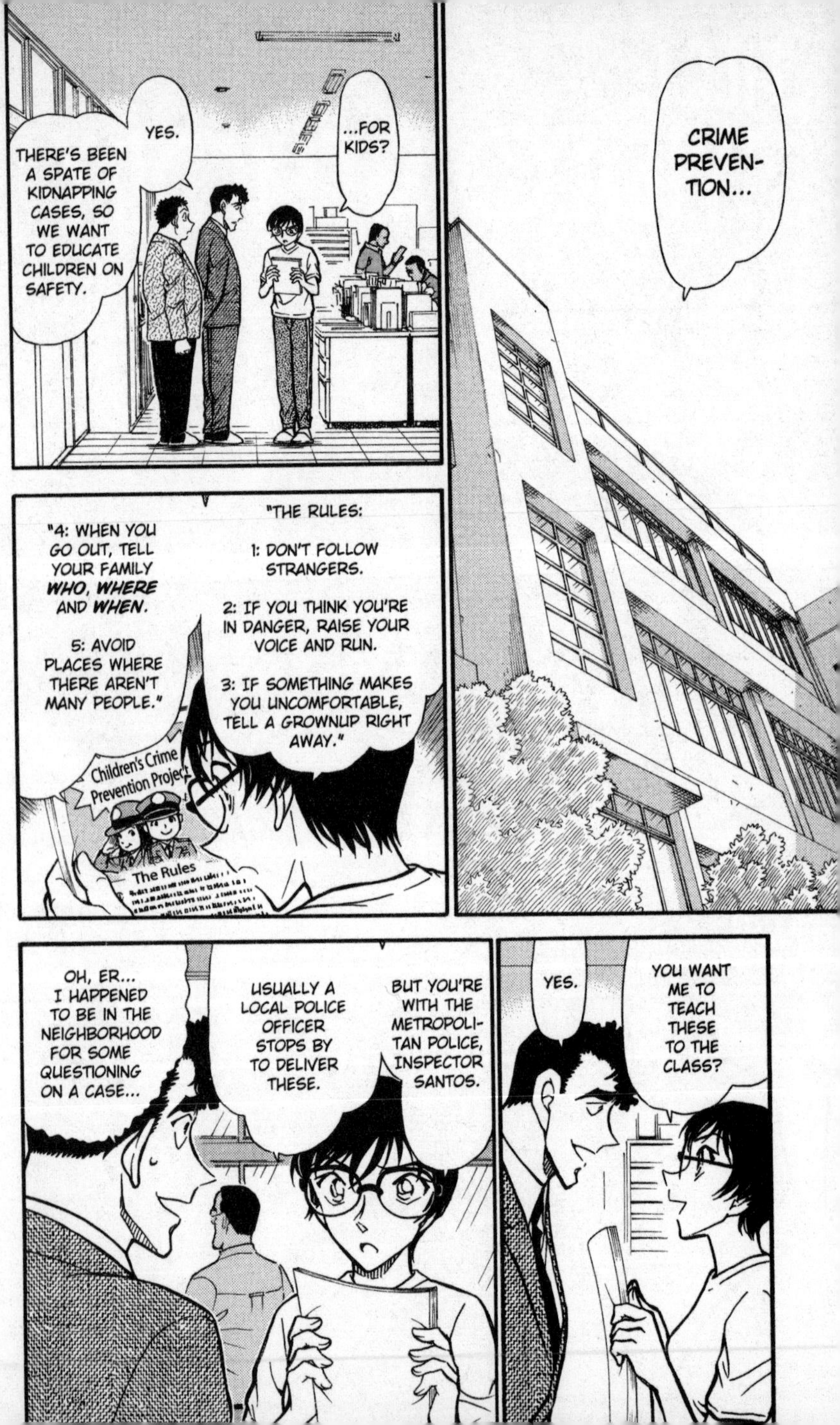
CRIME PREVENTION...
...FOR KIDS?
YES.
THERE'S BEEN A SPATE OF KIDNAPPING CASES, SO WE WANT TO EDUCATE CHILDREN ON SAFETY.
"THE RULES:
1: DON'T FOLLOW STRANGERS.
2: IF YOU THINK YOU'RE IN DANGER, RAISE YOUR VOICE AND RUN.
3: IF SOMETHING MAKES YOU UNCOMFORTABLE, TELL A GROWNUP RIGHT AWAY."
"4: WHEN YOU GO OUT, TELL YOUR FAMILY ***WHO, WHERE*** AND ***WHEN***.
5: AVOID PLACES WHERE THERE AREN'T MANY PEOPLE."
Children's Crime Prevention Project
The Rules
YOU WANT ME TO TEACH THESE TO THE CLASS?
YES.
BUT YOU'RE WITH THE METROPOLITAN POLICE, INSPECTOR SANTOS.
USUALLY A LOCAL POLICE OFFICER STOPS BY TO DELIVER THESE.
OH, ER... I HAPPENED TO BE IN THE NEIGHBORHOOD FOR SOME QUESTIONING ON A CASE...

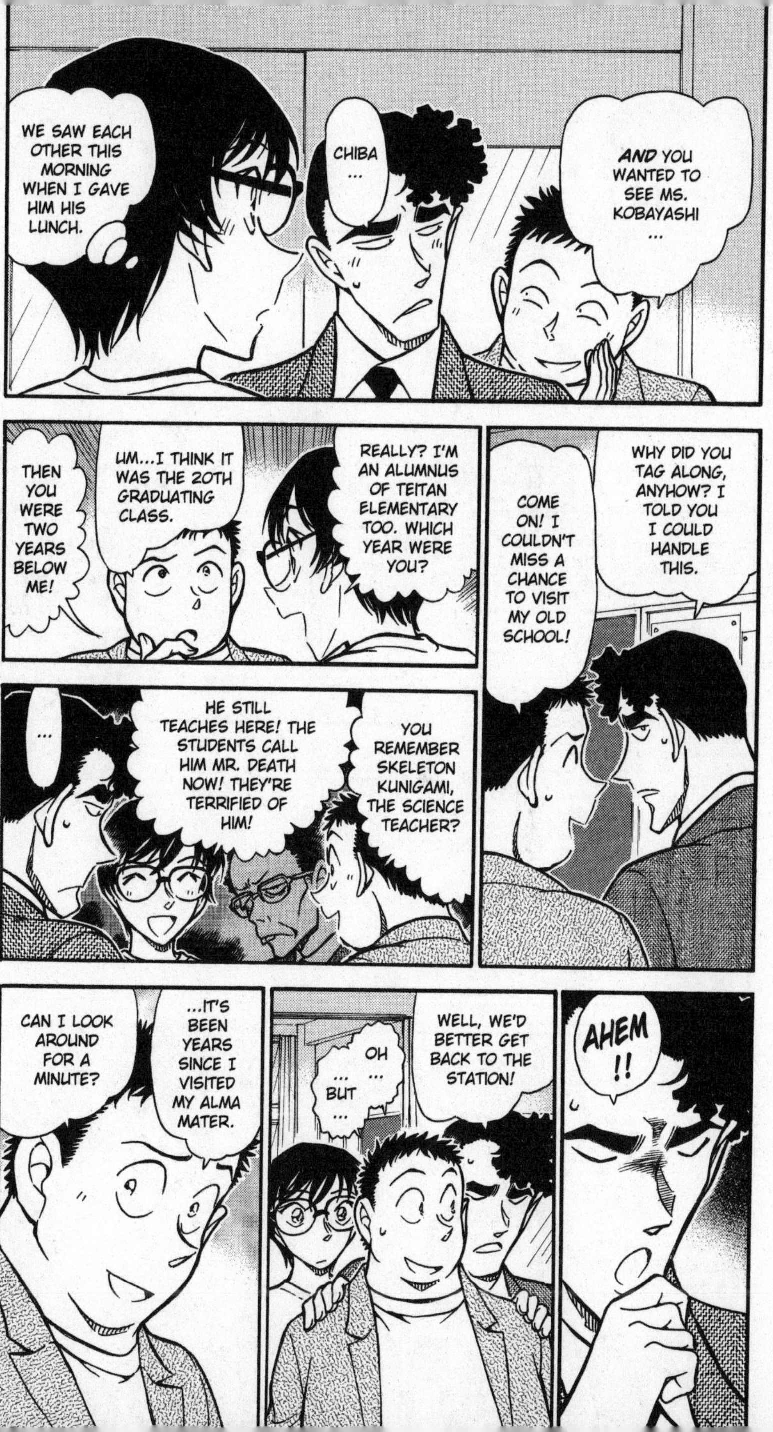
AND YOU WANTED TO SEE MS. KOBAYASHI ...
CHIBA ...
WE SAW EACH OTHER THIS MORNING WHEN I GAVE HIM HIS LUNCH.
WHY DID YOU TAG ALONG, ANYHOW? I TOLD YOU I COULD HANDLE THIS.
COME ON! I COULDN'T MISS A CHANCE TO VISIT MY OLD SCHOOL!
REALLY? I'M AN ALUMNUS OF TEITAN ELEMENTARY TOO. WHICH YEAR WERE YOU?
UM...I THINK IT WAS THE 20TH GRADUATING CLASS.
THEN YOU WERE TWO YEARS BELOW ME!
YOU REMEMBER SKELETON KUNIGAMI, THE SCIENCE TEACHER?
HE STILL TEACHES HERE! THE STUDENTS CALL HIM MR. DEATH NOW! THEY'RE TERRIFIED OF HIM!
...
AHEM !!
WELL, WE'D BETTER GET BACK TO THE STATION!
OH ... ... BUT ...
...IT'S BEEN YEARS SINCE I VISITED MY ALMA MATER.
CAN I LOOK AROUND FOR A MINUTE?

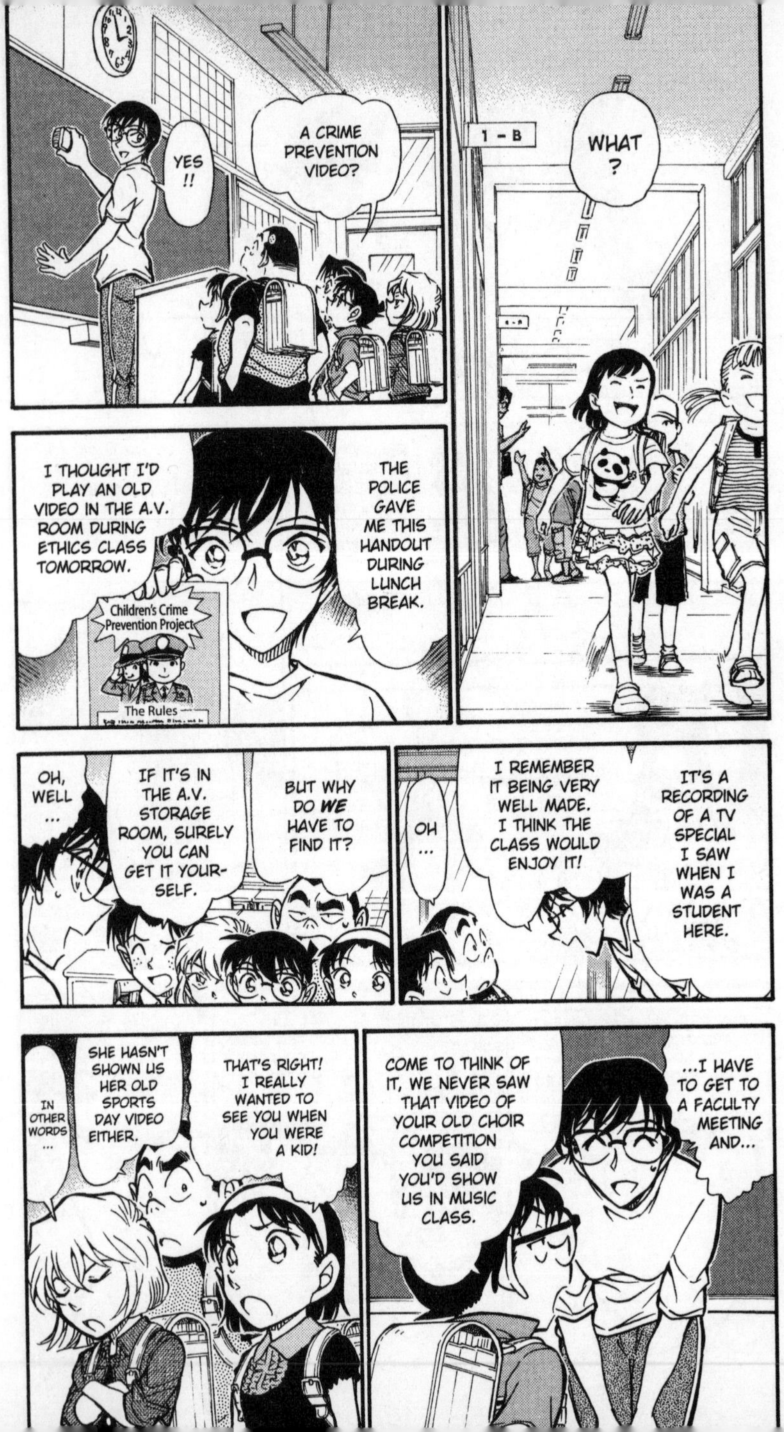
1 – B
WHAT?
A CRIME PREVENTION VIDEO?
YES!!
THE POLICE GAVE ME THIS HANDOUT DURING LUNCH BREAK.
I THOUGHT I'D PLAY AN OLD VIDEO IN THE A.V. ROOM DURING ETHICS CLASS TOMORROW.
Children's Crime Prevention Project
The Rules
IT'S A RECORDING OF A TV SPECIAL I SAW WHEN I WAS A STUDENT HERE.
I REMEMBER IT BEING VERY WELL MADE. I THINK THE CLASS WOULD ENJOY IT!
OH...
BUT WHY DO WE HAVE TO FIND IT?
IF IT'S IN THE A.V. STORAGE ROOM, SURELY YOU CAN GET IT YOURSELF.
OH, WELL...
...I HAVE TO GET TO A FACULTY MEETING AND...
COME TO THINK OF IT, WE NEVER SAW THAT VIDEO OF YOUR OLD CHOIR COMPETITION YOU SAID YOU'D SHOW US IN MUSIC CLASS.
THAT'S RIGHT! I REALLY WANTED TO SEE YOU WHEN YOU WERE A KID!
SHE HASN'T SHOWN US HER OLD SPORTS DAY VIDEO EITHER.
IN OTHER WORDS...

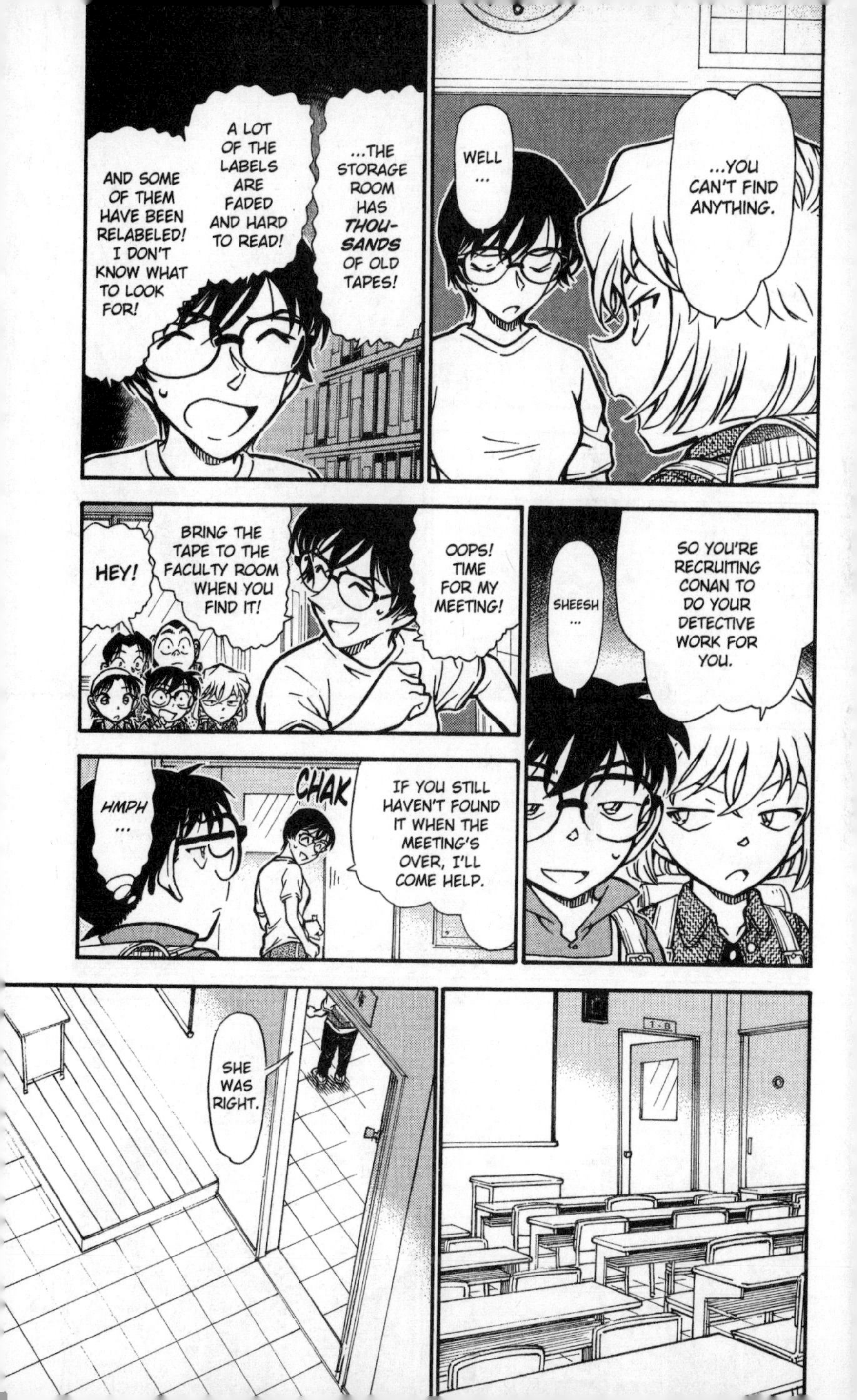
...YOU CAN'T FIND ANYTHING.
WELL ...
...THE STORAGE ROOM HAS *THOUSANDS* OF OLD TAPES!
A LOT OF THE LABELS ARE FADED AND HARD TO READ!
AND SOME OF THEM HAVE BEEN RELABELED! I DON'T KNOW WHAT TO LOOK FOR!
SO YOU'RE RECRUITING CONAN TO DO YOUR DETECTIVE WORK FOR YOU.
SHEESH ...
OOPS! TIME FOR MY MEETING!
BRING THE TAPE TO THE FACULTY ROOM WHEN YOU FIND IT!
HEY!
IF YOU STILL HAVEN'T FOUND IT WHEN THE MEETING'S OVER, I'LL COME HELP.
CHAK
HMPH ...
SHE WAS RIGHT.

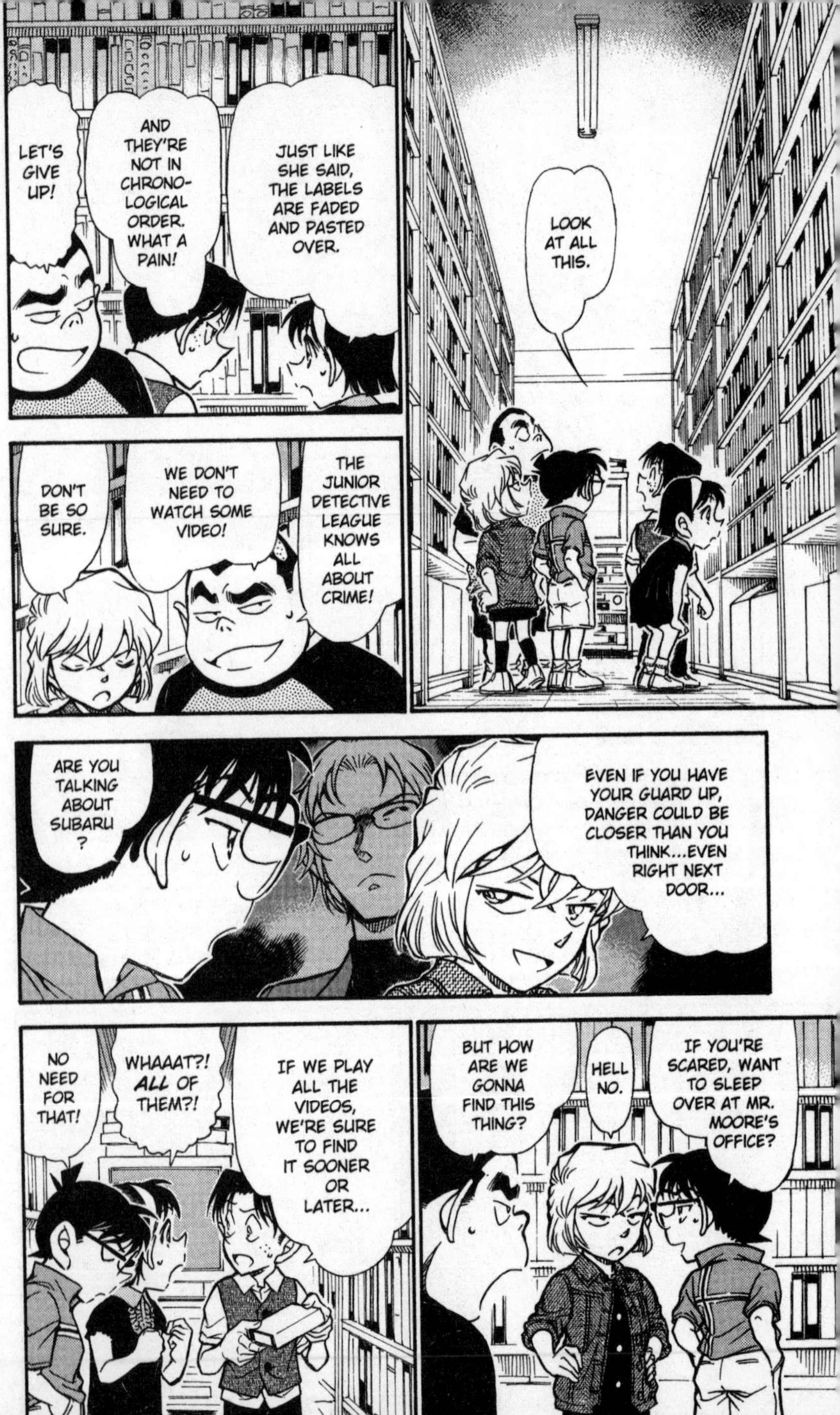
LOOK AT ALL THIS.
JUST LIKE SHE SAID, THE LABELS ARE FADED AND PASTED OVER.
AND THEY'RE NOT IN CHRONO-LOGICAL ORDER. WHAT A PAIN!
LET'S GIVE UP!
THE JUNIOR DETECTIVE LEAGUE KNOWS ALL ABOUT CRIME!
WE DON'T NEED TO WATCH SOME VIDEO!
DON'T BE SO SURE.
EVEN IF YOU HAVE YOUR GUARD UP, DANGER COULD BE CLOSER THAN YOU THINK...EVEN RIGHT NEXT DOOR...
ARE YOU TALKING ABOUT SUBARU?
IF YOU'RE SCARED, WANT TO SLEEP OVER AT MR. MOORE'S OFFICE?
HELL NO.
BUT HOW ARE WE GONNA FIND THIS THING?
IF WE PLAY ALL THE VIDEOS, WE'RE SURE TO FIND IT SOONER OR LATER...
WHAAAT?! *ALL* OF THEM?!
NO NEED FOR THAT!

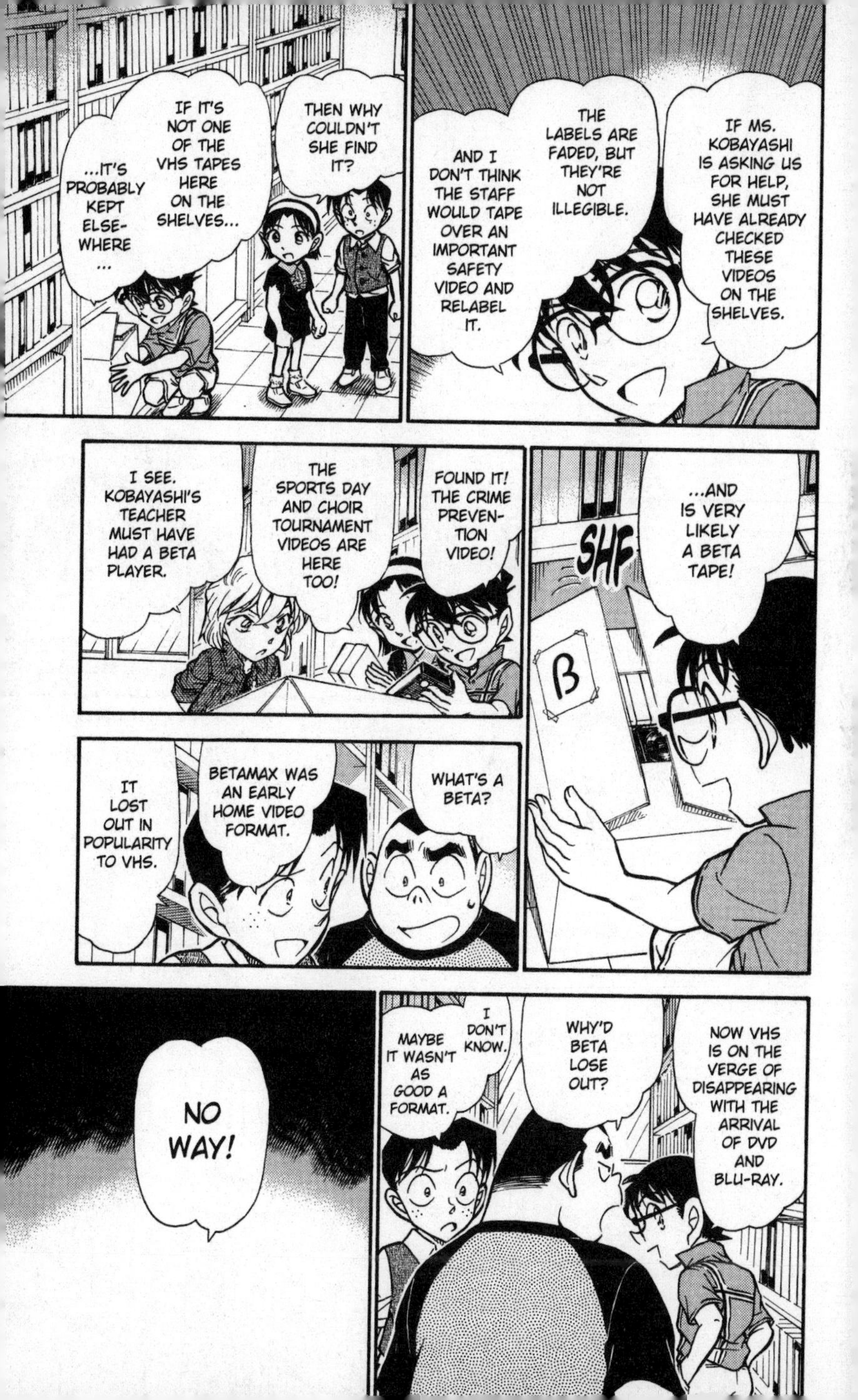
IF MS. KOBAYASHI IS ASKING US FOR HELP, SHE MUST HAVE ALREADY CHECKED THESE VIDEOS ON THE SHELVES.
THE LABELS ARE FADED, BUT THEY'RE NOT ILLEGIBLE.
AND I DON'T THINK THE STAFF WOULD TAPE OVER AN IMPORTANT SAFETY VIDEO AND RELABEL IT.
THEN WHY COULDN'T SHE FIND IT?
IF IT'S NOT ONE OF THE VHS TAPES HERE ON THE SHELVES...
...IT'S PROBABLY KEPT ELSE-WHERE ...
...AND IS VERY LIKELY A BETA TAPE!
SHF
β
FOUND IT! THE CRIME PREVEN-TION VIDEO!
THE SPORTS DAY AND CHOIR TOURNAMENT VIDEOS ARE HERE TOO!
I SEE. KOBAYASHI'S TEACHER MUST HAVE HAD A BETA PLAYER.
WHAT'S A BETA?
BETAMAX WAS AN EARLY HOME VIDEO FORMAT.
IT LOST OUT IN POPULARITY TO VHS.
NOW VHS IS ON THE VERGE OF DISAPPEARING WITH THE ARRIVAL OF DVD AND BLU-RAY.
WHY'D BETA LOSE OUT?
I DON'T KNOW.
MAYBE IT WASN'T AS GOOD A FORMAT.
NO WAY!

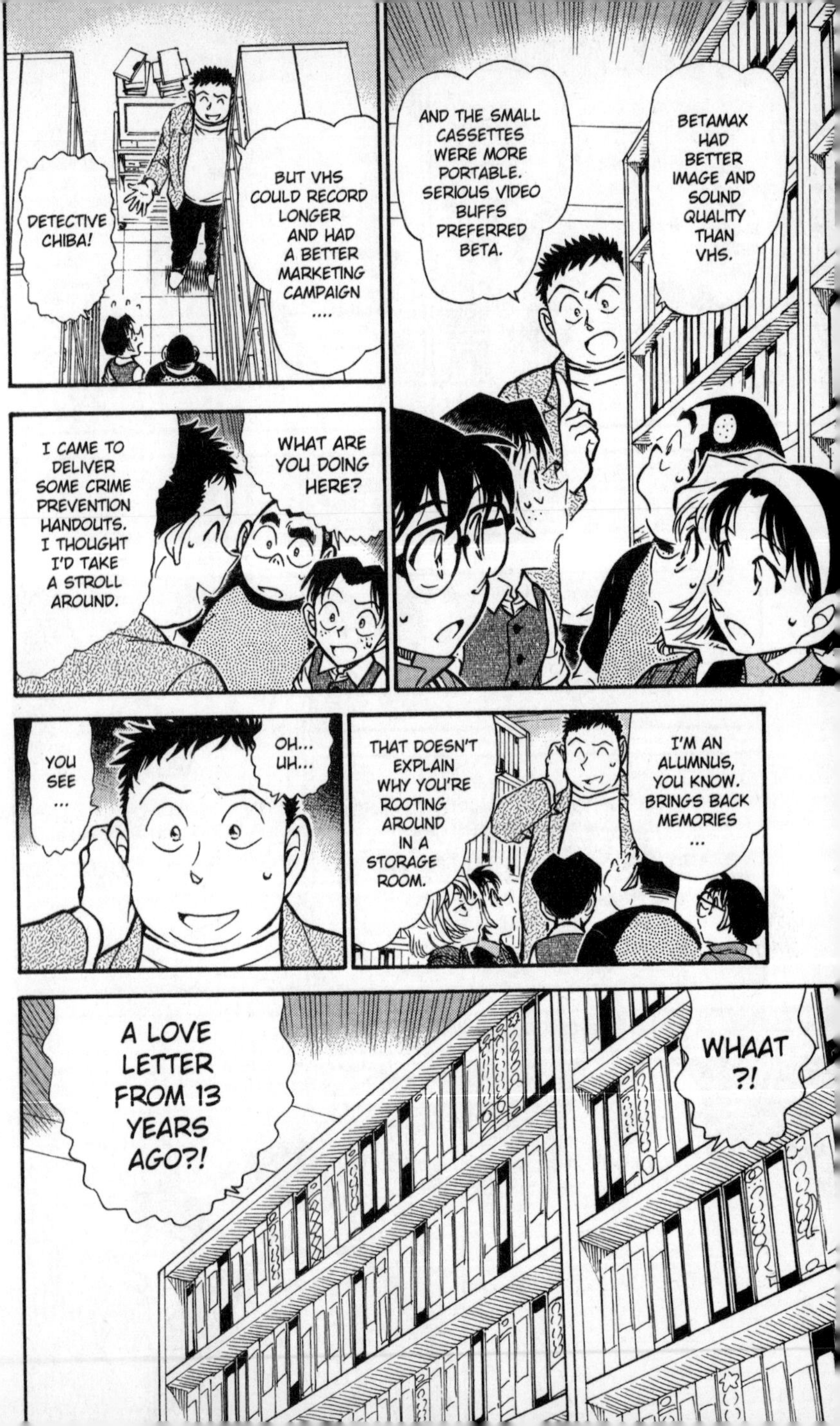
BETAMAX HAD BETTER IMAGE AND SOUND QUALITY THAN VHS.
AND THE SMALL CASSETTES WERE MORE PORTABLE. SERIOUS VIDEO BUFFS PREFERRED BETA.
BUT VHS COULD RECORD LONGER AND HAD A BETTER MARKETING CAMPAIGN ....
DETECTIVE CHIBA!
WHAT ARE YOU DOING HERE?
I CAME TO DELIVER SOME CRIME PREVENTION HANDOUTS. I THOUGHT I'D TAKE A STROLL AROUND.
I'M AN ALUMNUS, YOU KNOW. BRINGS BACK MEMORIES ...
THAT DOESN'T EXPLAIN WHY YOU'RE ROOTING AROUND IN A STORAGE ROOM.
OH... UH...
YOU SEE ...
WHAAT ?!
A LOVE LETTER FROM 13 YEARS AGO?!

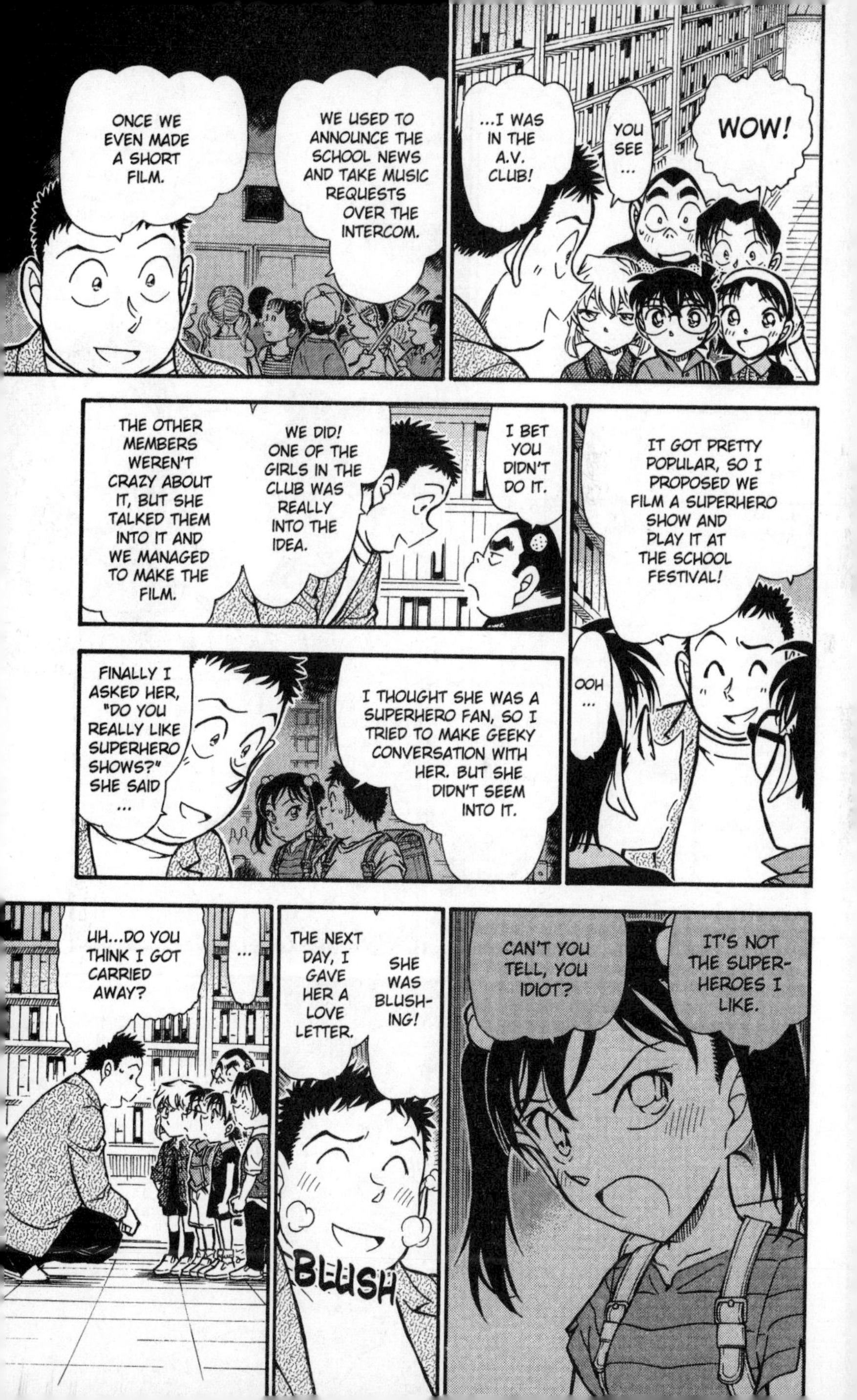
WOW!
YOU SEE ...
...I WAS IN THE A.V. CLUB!
WE USED TO ANNOUNCE THE SCHOOL NEWS AND TAKE MUSIC REQUESTS OVER THE INTERCOM.
ONCE WE EVEN MADE A SHORT FILM.
IT GOT PRETTY POPULAR, SO I PROPOSED WE FILM A SUPERHERO SHOW AND PLAY IT AT THE SCHOOL FESTIVAL!
OOH ...
I BET YOU DIDN'T DO IT.
WE DID! ONE OF THE GIRLS IN THE CLUB WAS REALLY INTO THE IDEA.
THE OTHER MEMBERS WEREN'T CRAZY ABOUT IT, BUT SHE TALKED THEM INTO IT AND WE MANAGED TO MAKE THE FILM.
I THOUGHT SHE WAS A SUPERHERO FAN, SO I TRIED TO MAKE GEEKY CONVERSATION WITH HER. BUT SHE DIDN'T SEEM INTO IT.
FINALLY I ASKED HER, "DO YOU REALLY LIKE SUPERHERO SHOWS?" SHE SAID ...
IT'S NOT THE SUPER-HEROES I LIKE.
CAN'T YOU TELL, YOU IDIOT?
THE NEXT DAY, I GAVE HER A LOVE LETTER.
SHE WAS BLUSH-ING!
BLUSH
...
UH...DO YOU THINK I GOT CARRIED AWAY?

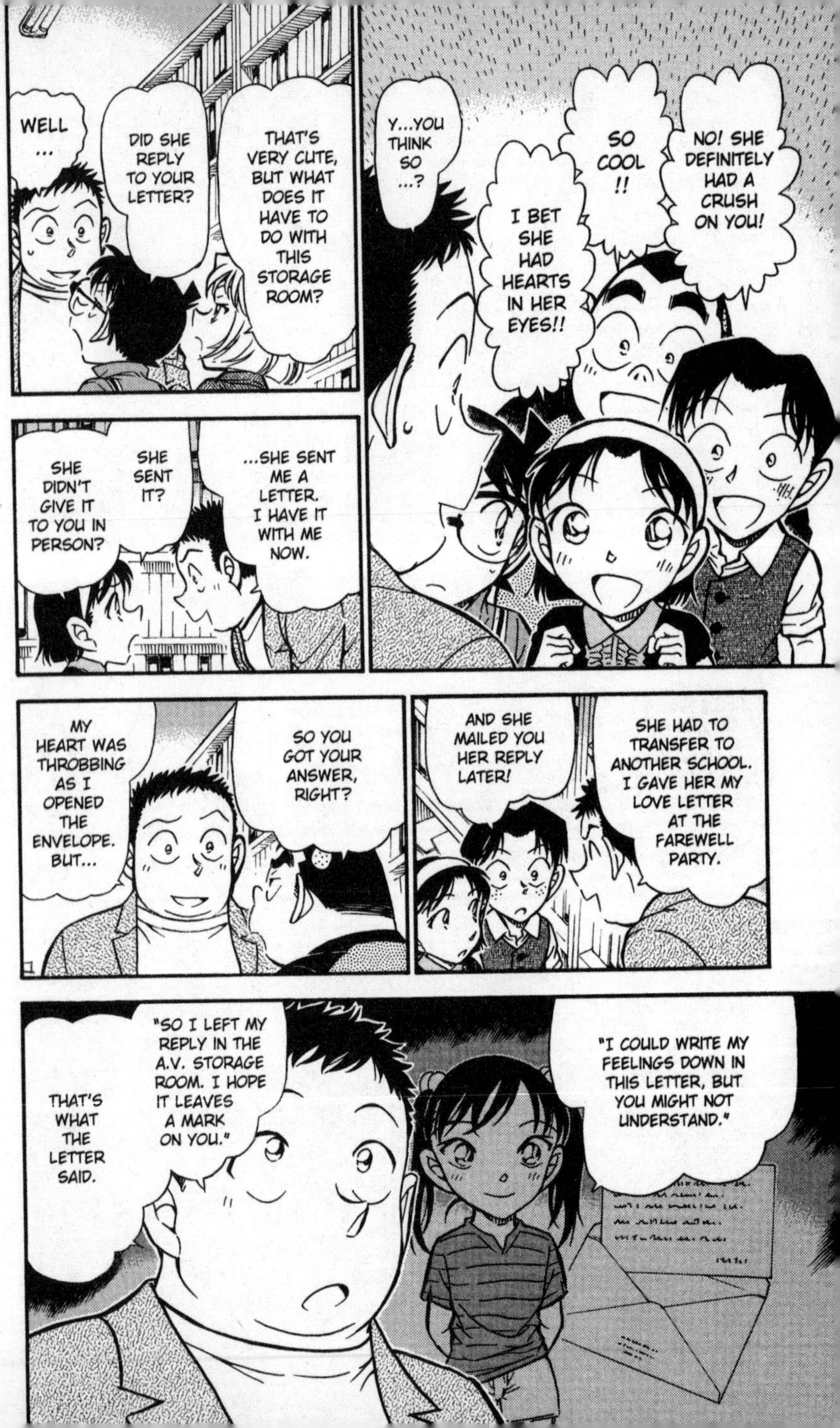
NO! SHE DEFINITELY HAD A CRUSH ON YOU!
SO COOL!!
Y...YOU THINK SO ...?
I BET SHE HAD HEARTS IN HER EYES!!
THAT'S VERY CUTE, BUT WHAT DOES IT HAVE TO DO WITH THIS STORAGE ROOM?
DID SHE REPLY TO YOUR LETTER?
WELL ...
...SHE SENT ME A LETTER. I HAVE IT WITH ME NOW.
SHE SENT IT?
SHE DIDN'T GIVE IT TO YOU IN PERSON?
SHE HAD TO TRANSFER TO ANOTHER SCHOOL. I GAVE HER MY LOVE LETTER AT THE FAREWELL PARTY.
AND SHE MAILED YOU HER REPLY LATER!
SO YOU GOT YOUR ANSWER, RIGHT?
MY HEART WAS THROBBING AS I OPENED THE ENVELOPE. BUT...
"I COULD WRITE MY FEELINGS DOWN IN THIS LETTER, BUT YOU MIGHT NOT UNDERSTAND."
"SO I LEFT MY REPLY IN THE A.V. STORAGE ROOM. I HOPE IT LEAVES A MARK ON YOU."
THAT'S WHAT THE LETTER SAID.

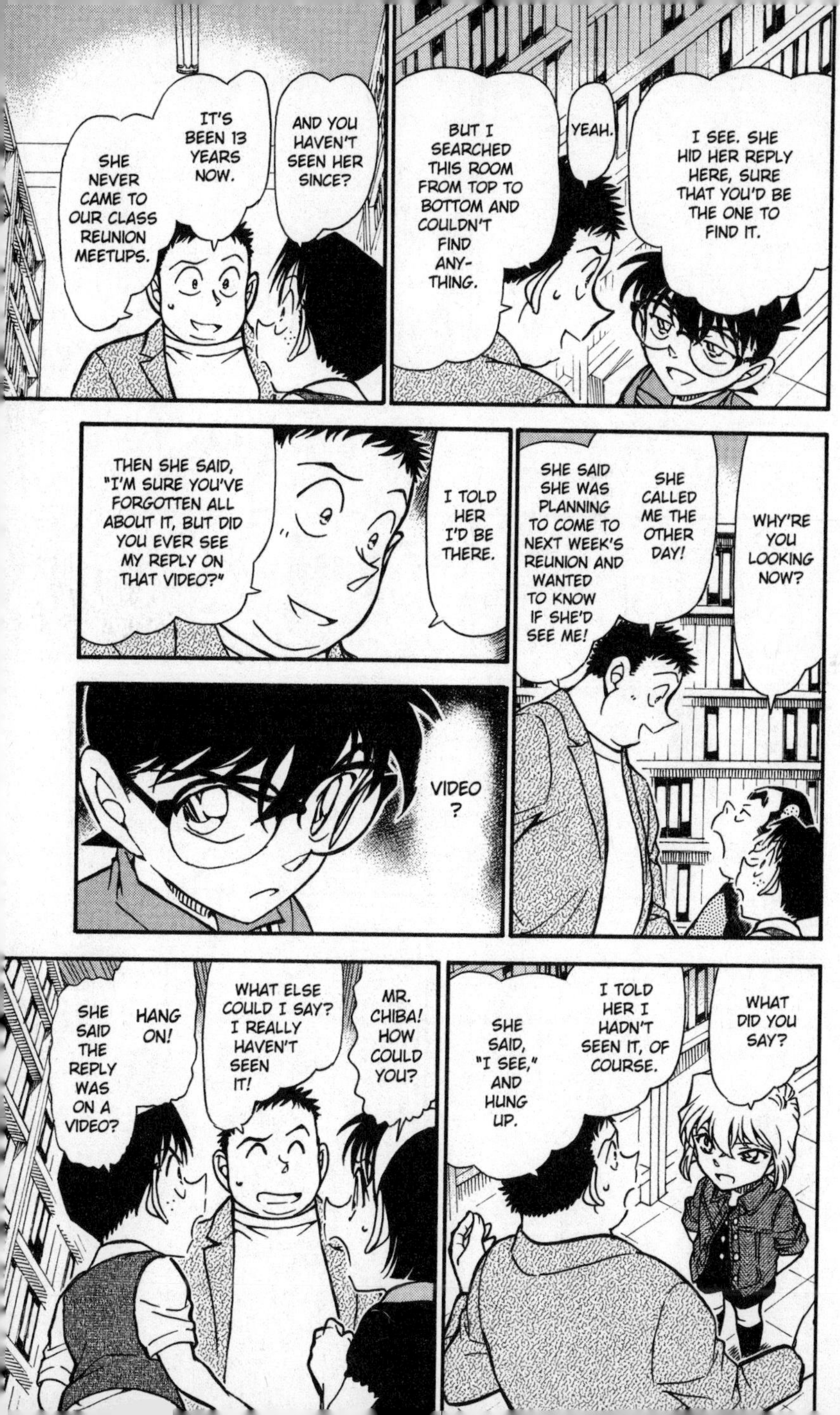
I SEE. SHE HID HER REPLY HERE, SURE THAT YOU'D BE THE ONE TO FIND IT.
YEAH.
BUT I SEARCHED THIS ROOM FROM TOP TO BOTTOM AND COULDN'T FIND ANYTHING.
AND YOU HAVEN'T SEEN HER SINCE?
IT'S BEEN 13 YEARS NOW.
SHE NEVER CAME TO OUR CLASS REUNION MEETUPS.
WHY'RE YOU LOOKING NOW?
SHE CALLED ME THE OTHER DAY!
SHE SAID SHE WAS PLANNING TO COME TO NEXT WEEK'S REUNION AND WANTED TO KNOW IF SHE'D SEE ME!
I TOLD HER I'D BE THERE.
THEN SHE SAID, "I'M SURE YOU'VE FORGOTTEN ALL ABOUT IT, BUT DID YOU EVER SEE MY REPLY ON THAT VIDEO?"
VIDEO?
WHAT DID YOU SAY?
I TOLD HER I HADN'T SEEN IT, OF COURSE.
SHE SAID, "I SEE," AND HUNG UP.
MR. CHIBA! HOW COULD YOU?
WHAT ELSE COULD I SAY? I REALLY HAVEN'T SEEN IT!
HANG ON!
SHE SAID THE REPLY WAS ON A VIDEO?

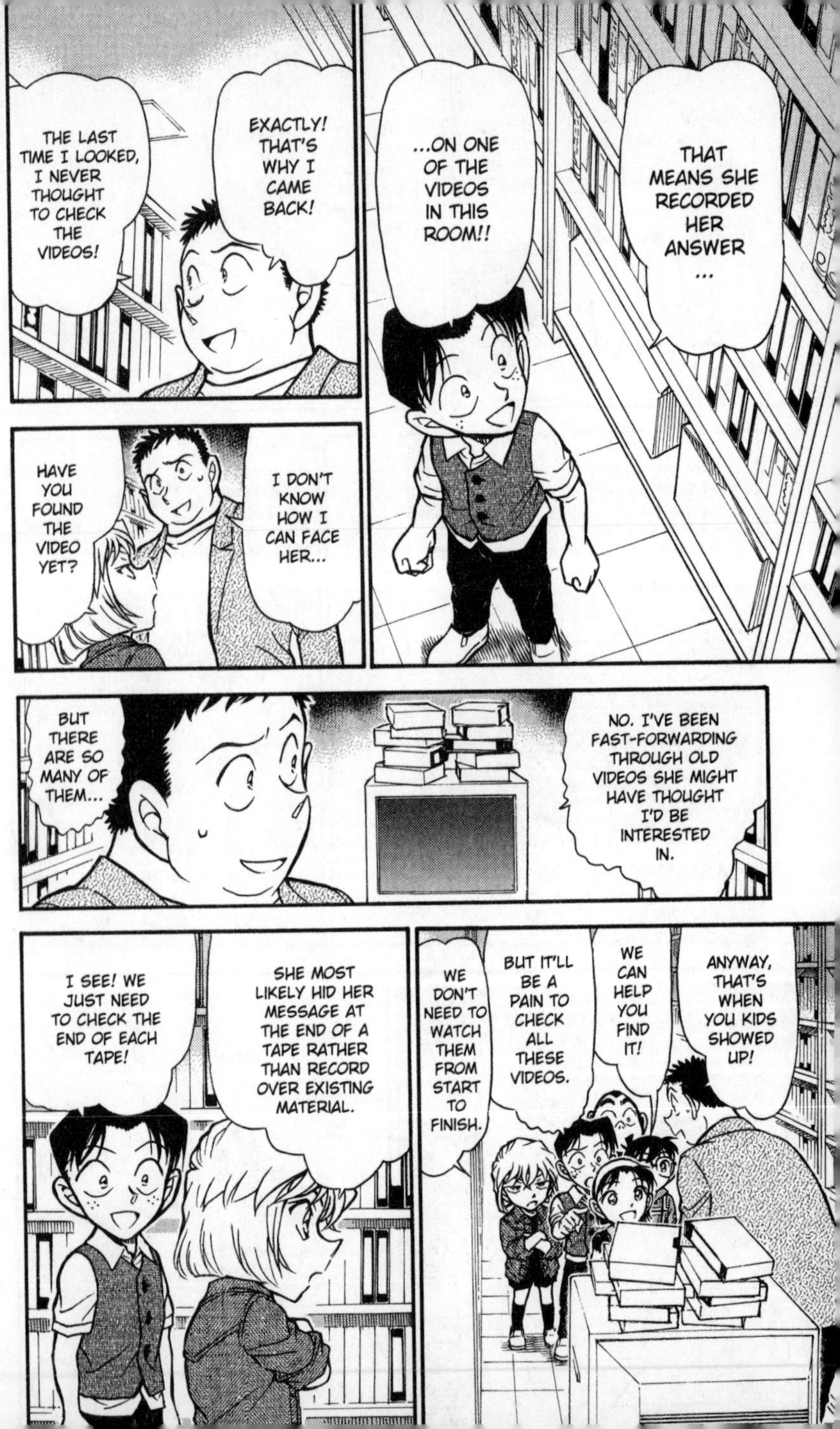
THAT MEANS SHE RECORDED HER ANSWER ...
...ON ONE OF THE VIDEOS IN THIS ROOM!!
EXACTLY! THAT'S WHY I CAME BACK!
THE LAST TIME I LOOKED, I NEVER THOUGHT TO CHECK THE VIDEOS!
I DON'T KNOW HOW I CAN FACE HER...
HAVE YOU FOUND THE VIDEO YET?
NO. I'VE BEEN FAST-FORWARDING THROUGH OLD VIDEOS SHE MIGHT HAVE THOUGHT I'D BE INTERESTED IN.
BUT THERE ARE SO MANY OF THEM...
ANYWAY, THAT'S WHEN YOU KIDS SHOWED UP!
WE CAN HELP YOU FIND IT!
BUT IT'LL BE A PAIN TO CHECK ALL THESE VIDEOS.
WE DON'T NEED TO WATCH THEM FROM START TO FINISH.
SHE MOST LIKELY HID HER MESSAGE AT THE END OF A TAPE RATHER THAN RECORD OVER EXISTING MATERIAL.
I SEE! WE JUST NEED TO CHECK THE END OF EACH TAPE!

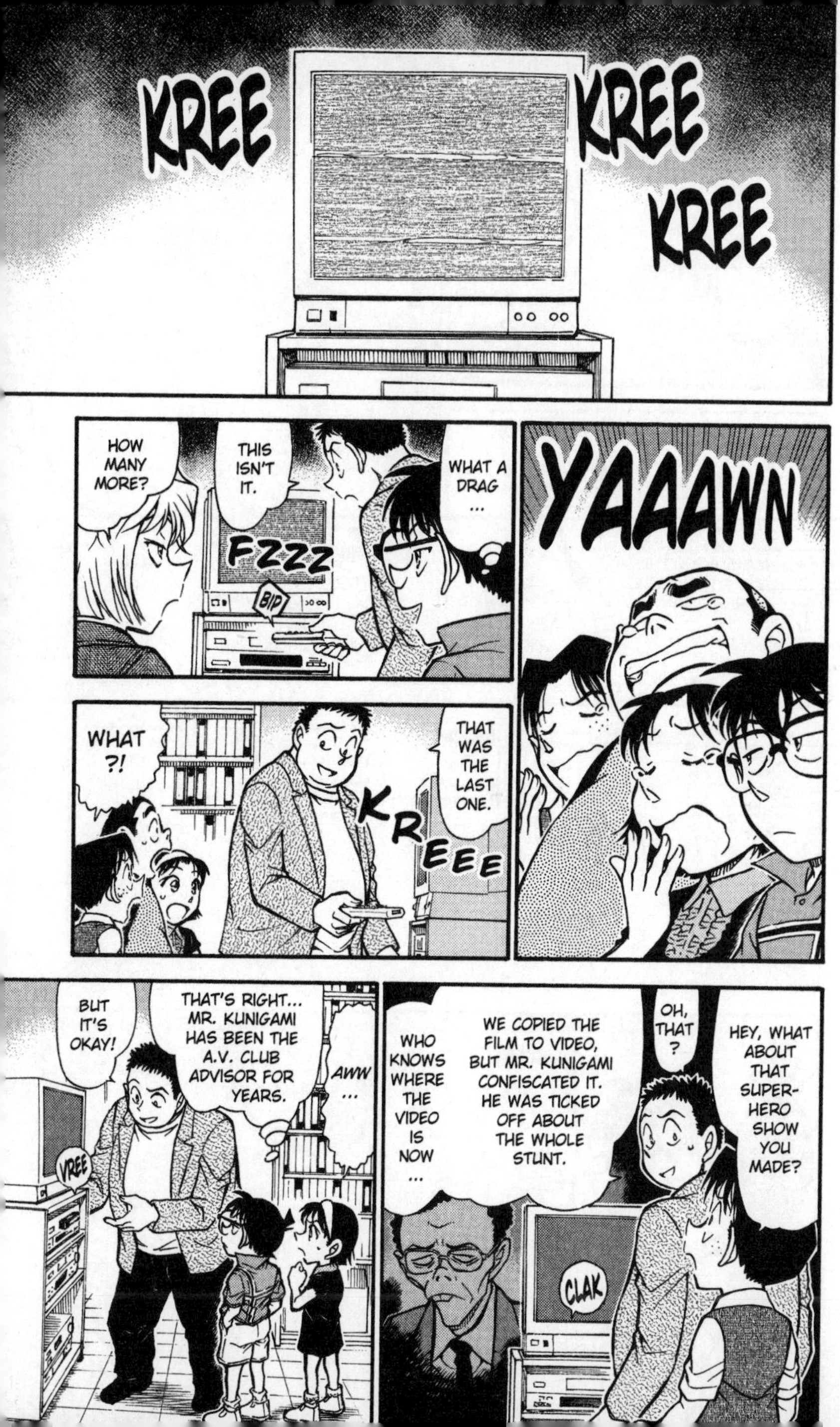
KREE
KREE
KREE
YAAAWN
WHAT A DRAG ...
THIS ISN'T IT.
HOW MANY MORE?
FZZZ
BIP
THAT WAS THE LAST ONE.
KREEEE
WHAT ?!
HEY, WHAT ABOUT THAT SUPER-HERO SHOW YOU MADE?
OH, THAT ?
WE COPIED THE FILM TO VIDEO, BUT MR. KUNIGAMI CONFISCATED IT. HE WAS TICKED OFF ABOUT THE WHOLE STUNT.
WHO KNOWS WHERE THE VIDEO IS NOW ...
CLAK
AWW ...
THAT'S RIGHT... MR. KUNIGAMI HAS BEEN THE A.V. CLUB ADVISOR FOR YEARS.
BUT IT'S OKAY!
VREE

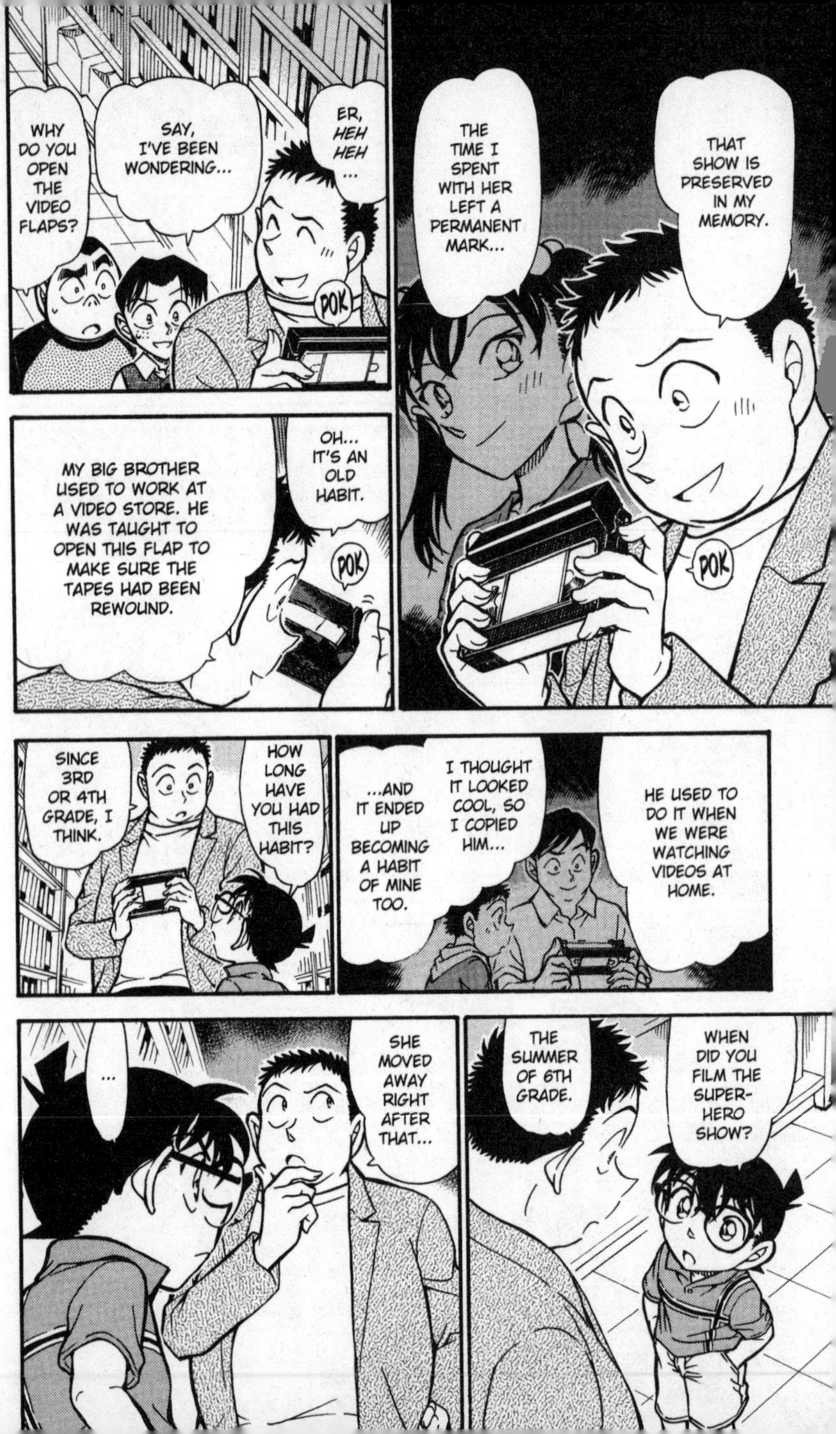
THAT SHOW IS PRESERVED IN MY MEMORY.
THE TIME I SPENT WITH HER LEFT A PERMANENT MARK...
POK
ER, HEH HEH...
SAY, I'VE BEEN WONDERING...
WHY DO YOU OPEN THE VIDEO FLAPS?
POK
OH... IT'S AN OLD HABIT.
MY BIG BROTHER USED TO WORK AT A VIDEO STORE. HE WAS TAUGHT TO OPEN THIS FLAP TO MAKE SURE THE TAPES HAD BEEN REWOUND.
POK
HE USED TO DO IT WHEN WE WERE WATCHING VIDEOS AT HOME.
I THOUGHT IT LOOKED COOL, SO I COPIED HIM...
...AND IT ENDED UP BECOMING A HABIT OF MINE TOO.
HOW LONG HAVE YOU HAD THIS HABIT?
SINCE 3RD OR 4TH GRADE, I THINK.
WHEN DID YOU FILM THE SUPER-HERO SHOW?
THE SUMMER OF 6TH GRADE.
SHE MOVED AWAY RIGHT AFTER THAT...
...

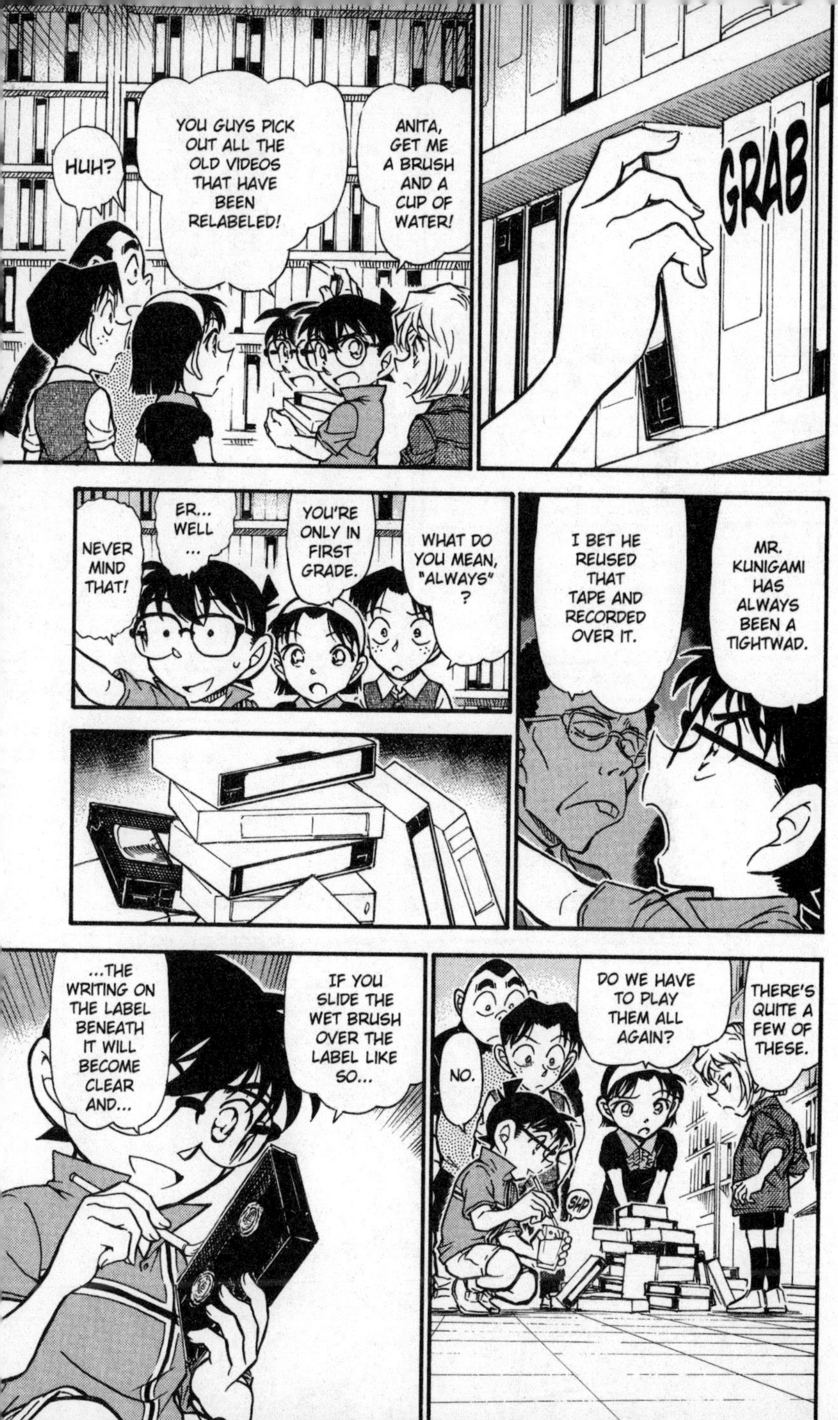
GRAB
ANITA, GET ME A BRUSH AND A CUP OF WATER!
YOU GUYS PICK OUT ALL THE OLD VIDEOS THAT HAVE BEEN RELABELED!
HUH?
MR. KUNIGAMI HAS ALWAYS BEEN A TIGHTWAD.
I BET HE REUSED THAT TAPE AND RECORDED OVER IT.
WHAT DO YOU MEAN, "ALWAYS"?
YOU'RE ONLY IN FIRST GRADE.
ER... WELL ...
NEVER MIND THAT!
THERE'S QUITE A FEW OF THESE.
DO WE HAVE TO PLAY THEM ALL AGAIN?
NO.
SHP
IF YOU SLIDE THE WET BRUSH OVER THE LABEL LIKE SO...
...THE WRITING ON THE LABEL BENEATH IT WILL BECOME CLEAR AND...

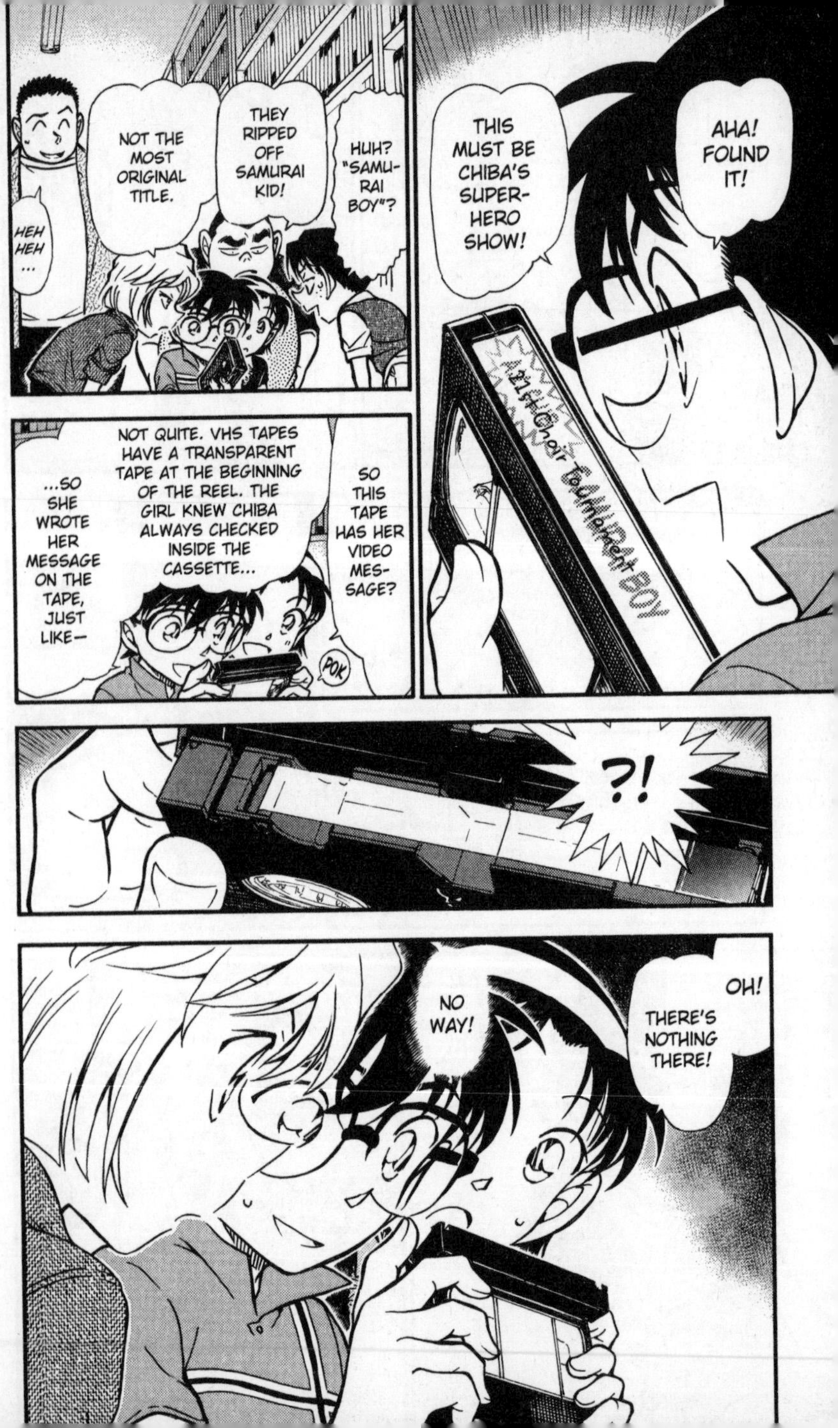
AHA! FOUND IT!
THIS MUST BE CHIBA'S SUPER-HERO SHOW!
HUH? "SAMURAI BOY"?
THEY RIPPED OFF SAMURAI KID!
NOT THE MOST ORIGINAL TITLE.
HEH HEH ...
SO THIS TAPE HAS HER VIDEO MESSAGE?
POK
NOT QUITE. VHS TAPES HAVE A TRANSPARENT TAPE AT THE BEGINNING OF THE REEL. THE GIRL KNEW CHIBA ALWAYS CHECKED INSIDE THE CASSETTE...
...SO SHE WROTE HER MESSAGE ON THE TAPE, JUST LIKE—
?!
OH!
THERE'S NOTHING THERE!
NO WAY!

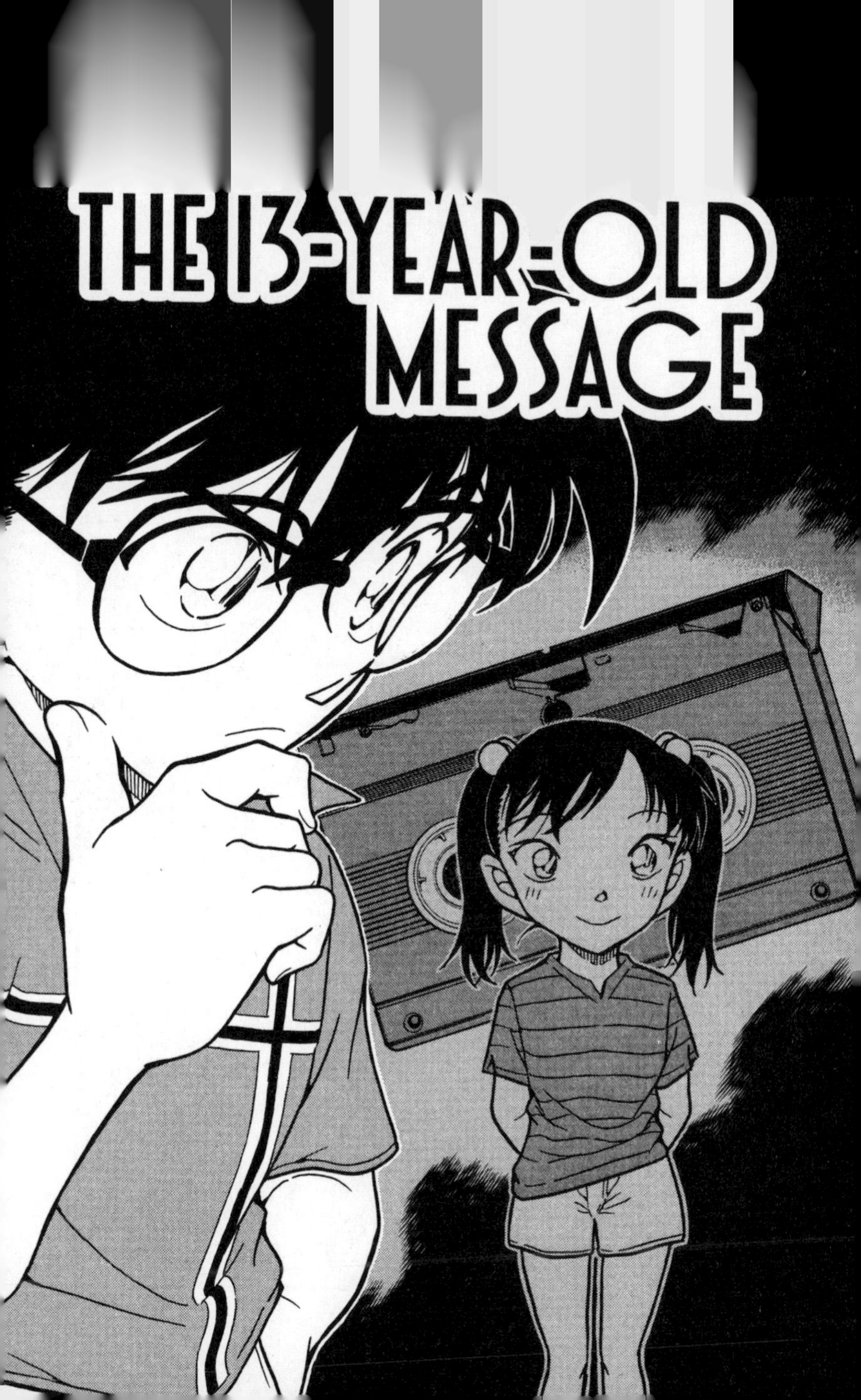
THE 13-YEAR-OLD MESSAGE

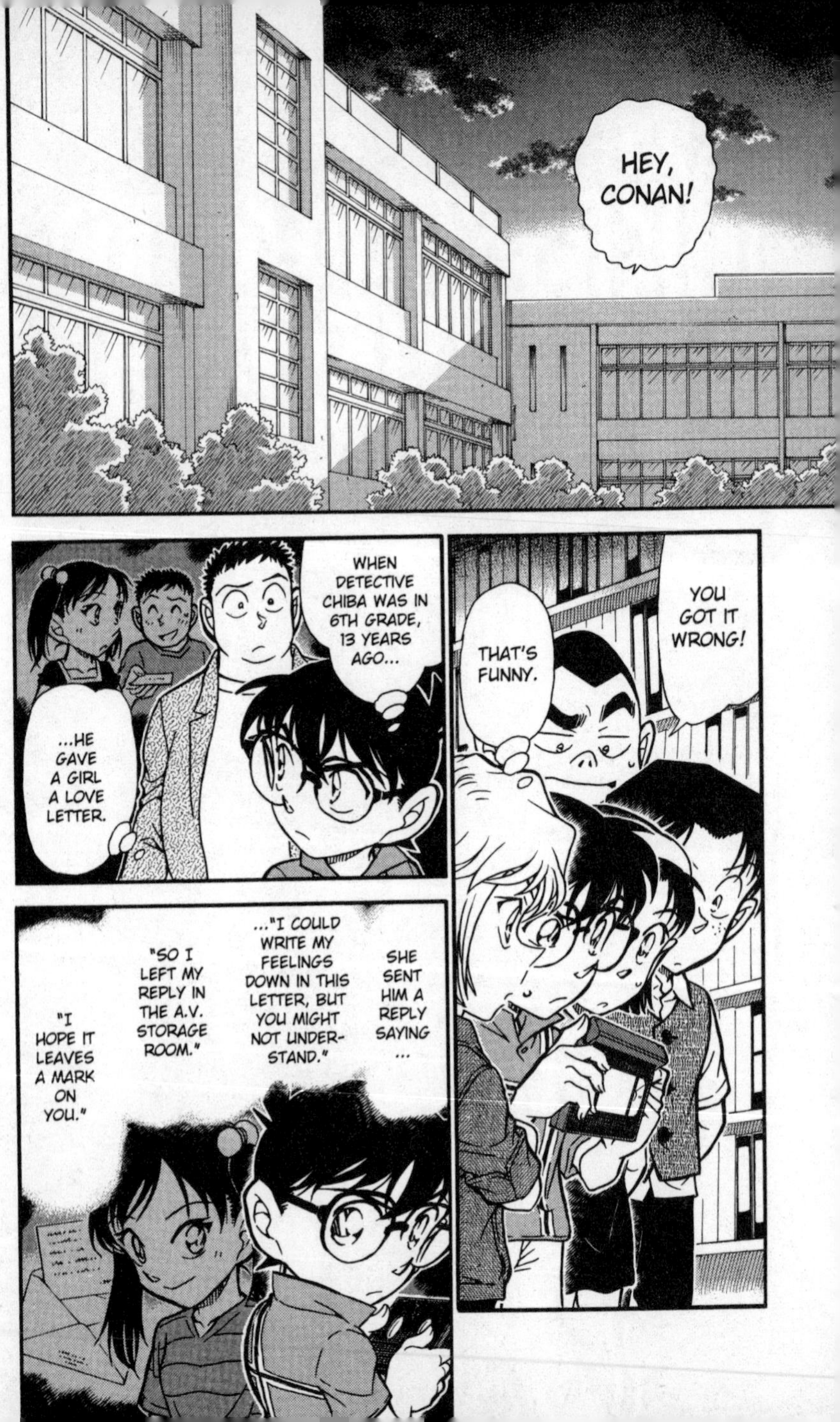
HEY, CONAN!
YOU GOT IT WRONG!
THAT'S FUNNY.
WHEN DETECTIVE CHIBA WAS IN 6TH GRADE, 13 YEARS AGO...
...HE GAVE A GIRL A LOVE LETTER.
SHE SENT HIM A REPLY SAYING...
..."I COULD WRITE MY FEELINGS DOWN IN THIS LETTER, BUT YOU MIGHT NOT UNDER-STAND."
"SO I LEFT MY REPLY IN THE A.V. STORAGE ROOM."
"I HOPE IT LEAVES A MARK ON YOU."

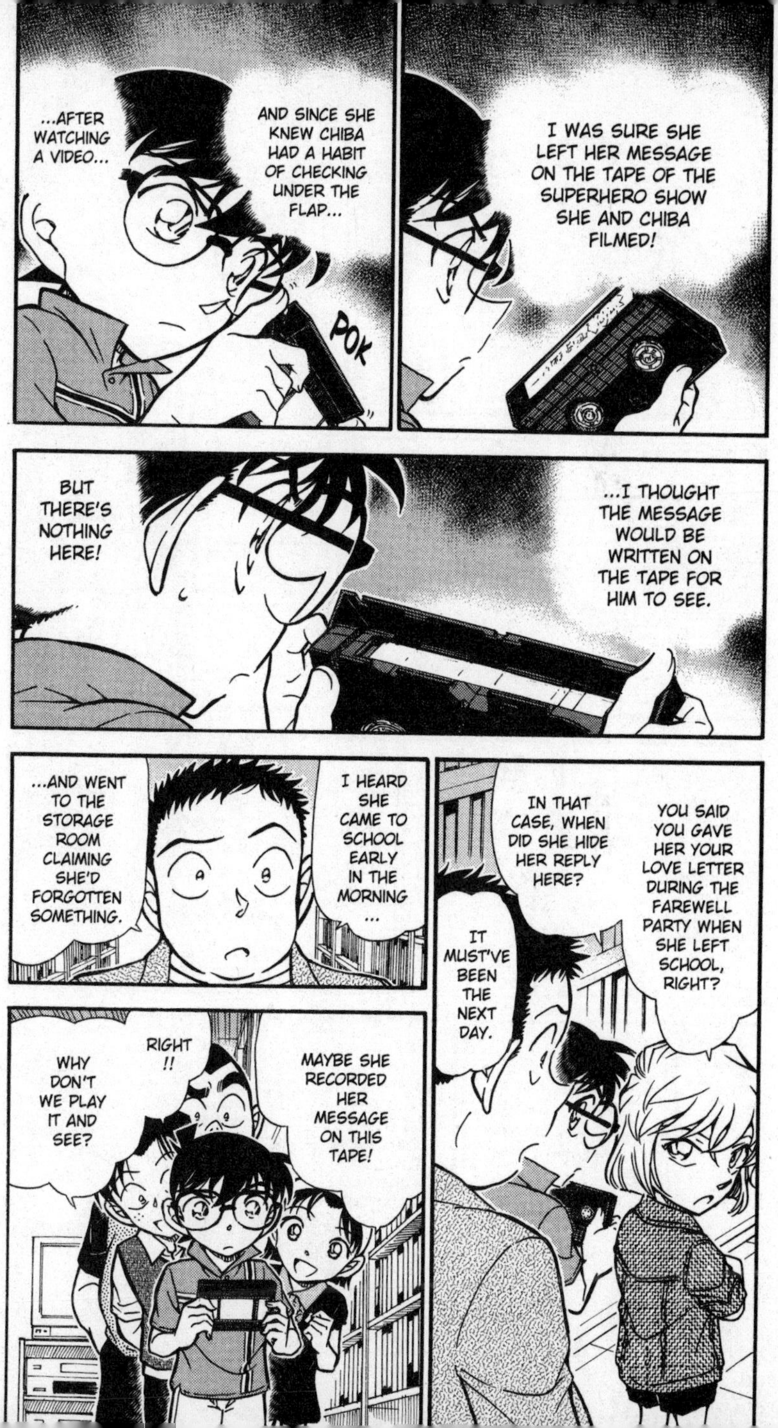
I WAS SURE SHE LEFT HER MESSAGE ON THE TAPE OF THE SUPERHERO SHOW SHE AND CHIBA FILMED!
AND SINCE SHE KNEW CHIBA HAD A HABIT OF CHECKING UNDER THE FLAP...
...AFTER WATCHING A VIDEO...
POK
...I THOUGHT THE MESSAGE WOULD BE WRITTEN ON THE TAPE FOR HIM TO SEE.
BUT THERE'S NOTHING HERE!
YOU SAID YOU GAVE HER YOUR LOVE LETTER DURING THE FAREWELL PARTY WHEN SHE LEFT SCHOOL, RIGHT?
IN THAT CASE, WHEN DID SHE HIDE HER REPLY HERE?
IT MUST'VE BEEN THE NEXT DAY.
I HEARD SHE CAME TO SCHOOL EARLY IN THE MORNING ...
...AND WENT TO THE STORAGE ROOM CLAIMING SHE'D FORGOTTEN SOMETHING.
MAYBE SHE RECORDED HER MESSAGE ON THIS TAPE!
RIGHT !!
WHY DON'T WE PLAY IT AND SEE?

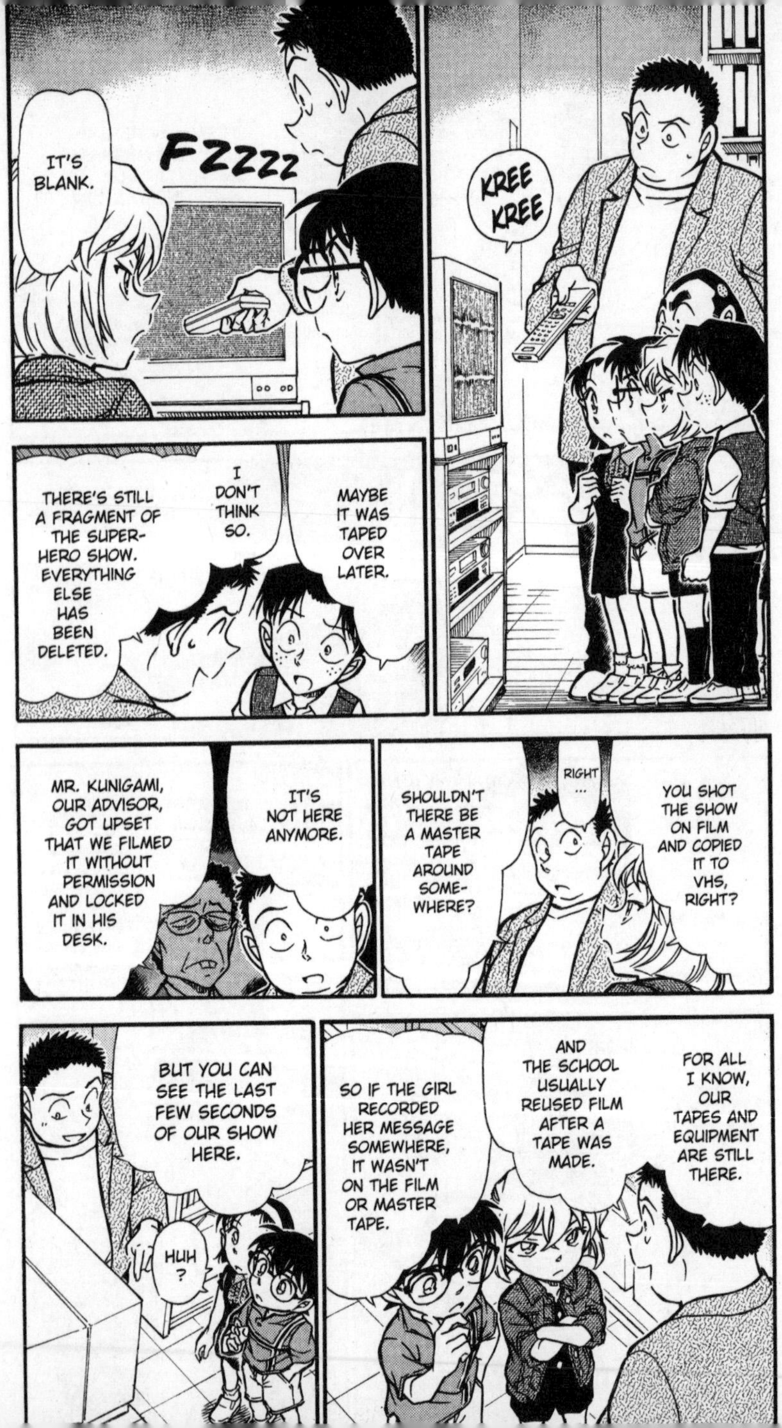
KREE KREE
FZZZZZ
IT'S BLANK.
MAYBE IT WAS TAPED OVER LATER.
I DON'T THINK SO.
THERE'S STILL A FRAGMENT OF THE SUPER-HERO SHOW. EVERYTHING ELSE HAS BEEN DELETED.
YOU SHOT THE SHOW ON FILM AND COPIED IT TO VHS, RIGHT?
RIGHT ...
SHOULDN'T THERE BE A MASTER TAPE AROUND SOME-WHERE?
IT'S NOT HERE ANYMORE.
MR. KUNIGAMI, OUR ADVISOR, GOT UPSET THAT WE FILMED IT WITHOUT PERMISSION AND LOCKED IT IN HIS DESK.
FOR ALL I KNOW, OUR TAPES AND EQUIPMENT ARE STILL THERE.
AND THE SCHOOL USUALLY REUSED FILM AFTER A TAPE WAS MADE.
SO IF THE GIRL RECORDED HER MESSAGE SOMEWHERE, IT WASN'T ON THE FILM OR MASTER TAPE.
BUT YOU CAN SEE THE LAST FEW SECONDS OF OUR SHOW HERE.
HUH ?

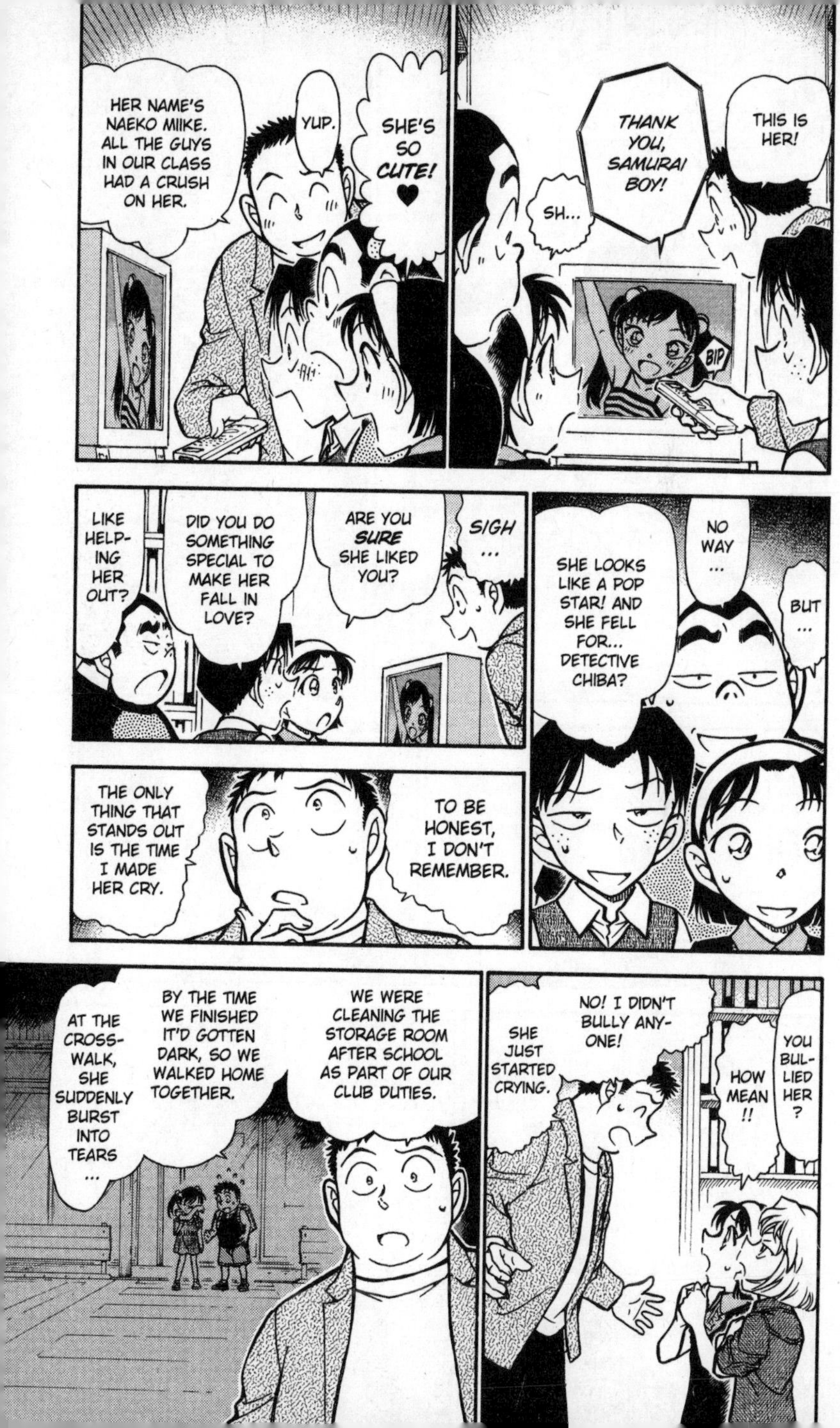
THIS IS HER!
THANK YOU, SAMURAI BOY!
SH...
BIP
SHE'S SO CUTE! ♥
YUP.
HER NAME'S NAEKO MIIKE. ALL THE GUYS IN OUR CLASS HAD A CRUSH ON HER.
BUT...
NO WAY...
SHE LOOKS LIKE A POP STAR! AND SHE FELL FOR... DETECTIVE CHIBA?
SIGH...
ARE YOU SURE SHE LIKED YOU?
DID YOU DO SOMETHING SPECIAL TO MAKE HER FALL IN LOVE?
LIKE HELPING HER OUT?
TO BE HONEST, I DON'T REMEMBER.
THE ONLY THING THAT STANDS OUT IS THE TIME I MADE HER CRY.
YOU BULLIED HER?
HOW MEAN!!
NO! I DIDN'T BULLY ANYONE!
SHE JUST STARTED CRYING.
WE WERE CLEANING THE STORAGE ROOM AFTER SCHOOL AS PART OF OUR CLUB DUTIES.
BY THE TIME WE FINISHED IT'D GOTTEN DARK, SO WE WALKED HOME TOGETHER.
AT THE CROSSWALK, SHE SUDDENLY BURST INTO TEARS...

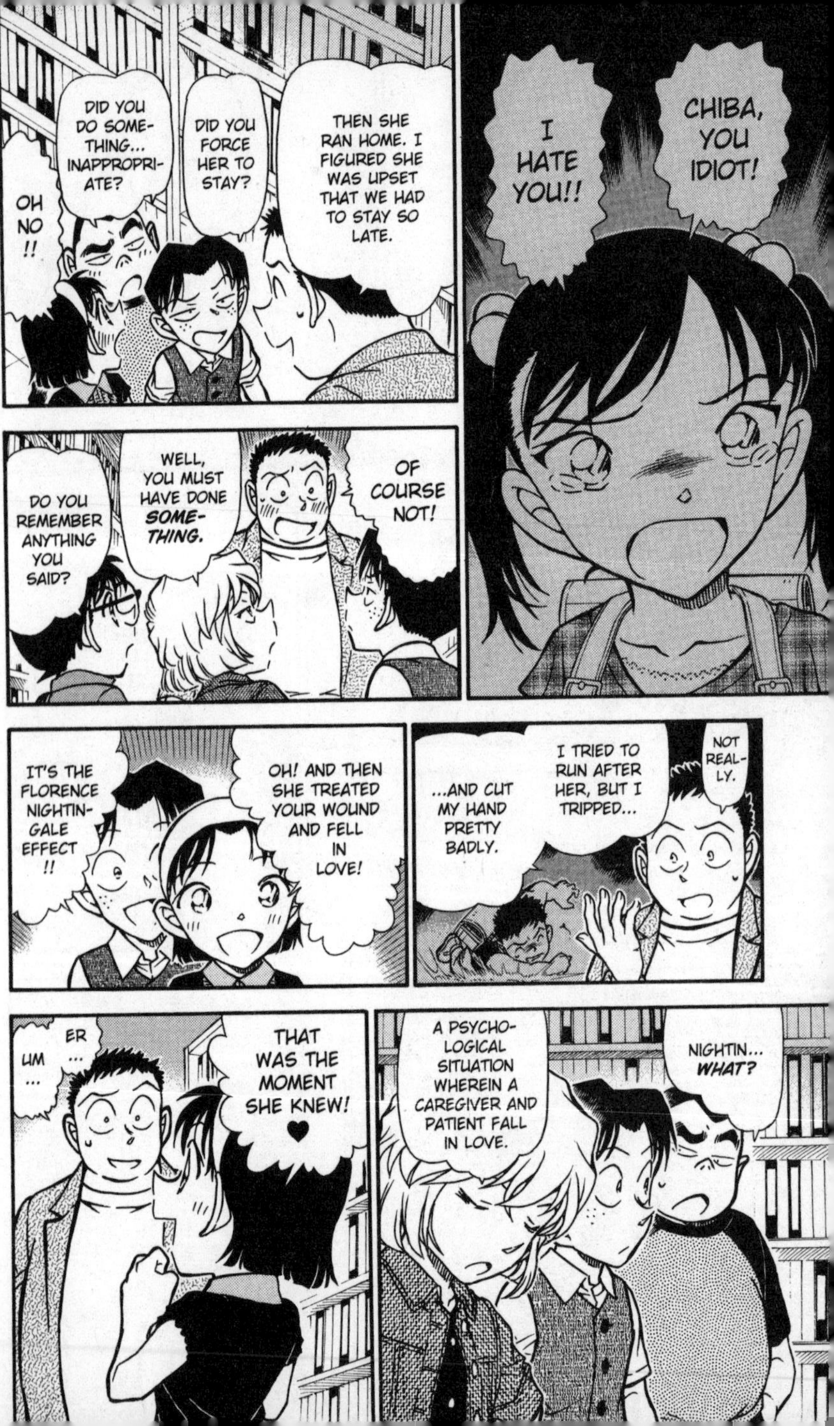
CHIBA, YOU IDIOT!
I HATE YOU!!
THEN SHE RAN HOME. I FIGURED SHE WAS UPSET THAT WE HAD TO STAY SO LATE.
DID YOU FORCE HER TO STAY?
DID YOU DO SOME-THING... INAPPROPRI-ATE?
OH NO !!
OF COURSE NOT!
WELL, YOU MUST HAVE DONE ***SOME-THING.***
DO YOU REMEMBER ANYTHING YOU SAID?
NOT REAL-LY.
I TRIED TO RUN AFTER HER, BUT I TRIPPED...
...AND CUT MY HAND PRETTY BADLY.
OH! AND THEN SHE TREATED YOUR WOUND AND FELL IN LOVE!
IT'S THE FLORENCE NIGHTIN-GALE EFFECT !!
NIGHTIN... ***WHAT?***
A PSYCHO-LOGICAL SITUATION WHEREIN A CAREGIVER AND PATIENT FALL IN LOVE.
THAT WAS THE MOMENT SHE KNEW! ♥
ER ...
UM ...

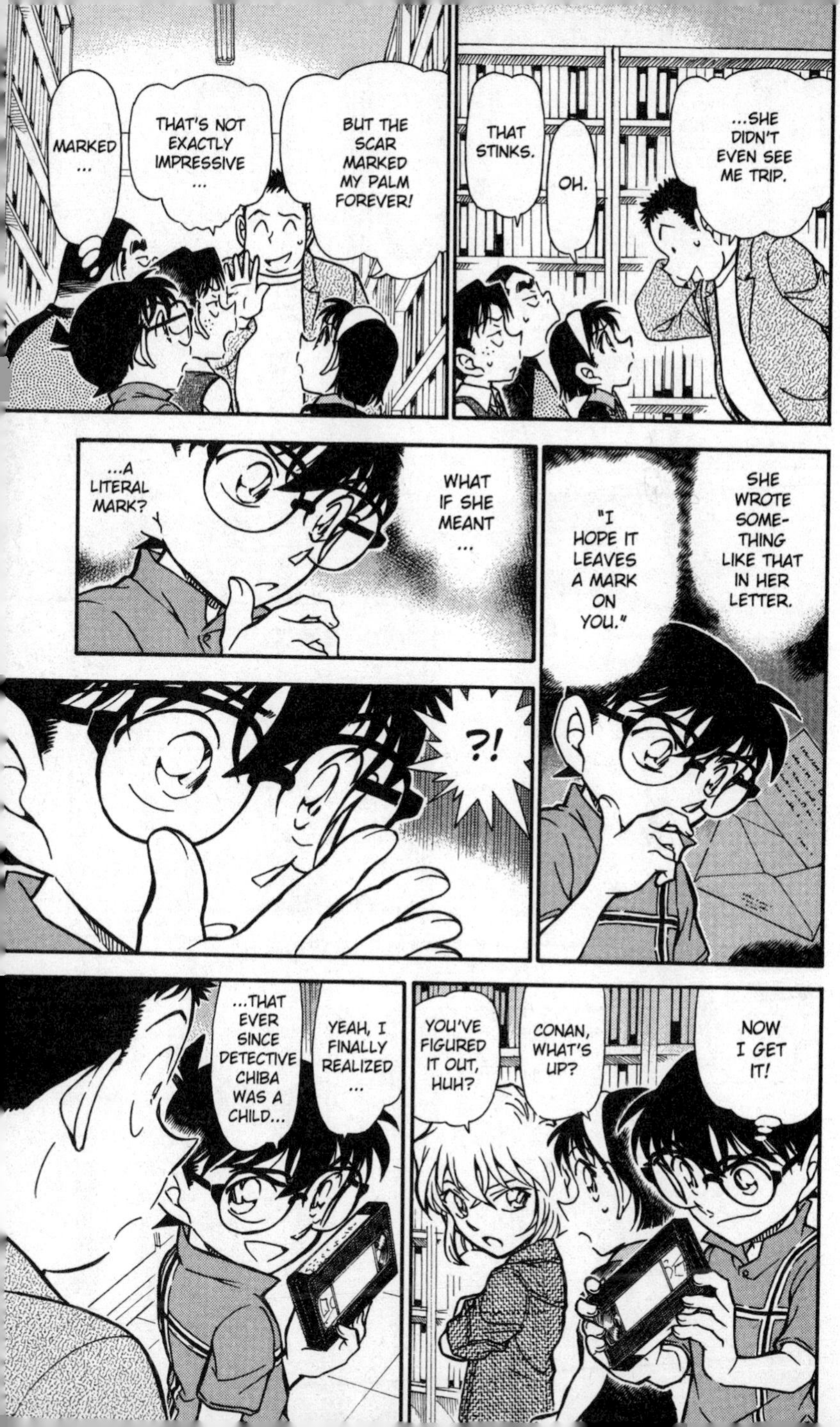
...SHE DIDN'T EVEN SEE ME TRIP.
OH.
THAT STINKS.
BUT THE SCAR MARKED MY PALM FOREVER!
THAT'S NOT EXACTLY IMPRESSIVE ...
MARKED ...
SHE WROTE SOMETHING LIKE THAT IN HER LETTER.
"I HOPE IT LEAVES A MARK ON YOU."
WHAT IF SHE MEANT ...
...A LITERAL MARK?
?!
NOW I GET IT!
CONAN, WHAT'S UP?
YOU'VE FIGURED IT OUT, HUH?
YEAH, I FINALLY REALIZED ...
...THAT EVER SINCE DETECTIVE CHIBA WAS A CHILD...

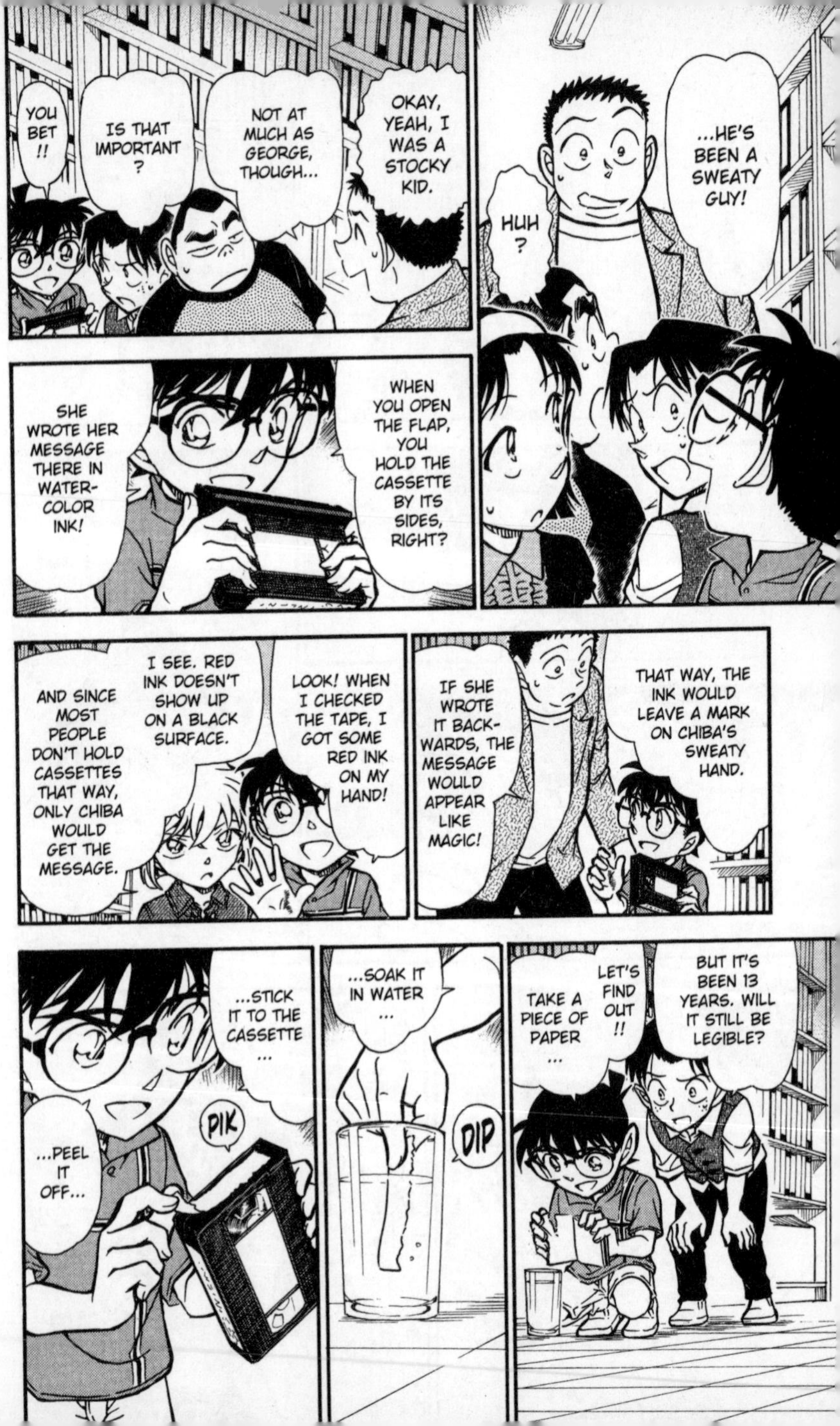
...HE'S BEEN A SWEATY GUY!
HUH?
OKAY, YEAH, I WAS A STOCKY KID.
NOT AT MUCH AS GEORGE, THOUGH...
IS THAT IMPORTANT?
YOU BET!!
WHEN YOU OPEN THE FLAP, YOU HOLD THE CASSETTE BY ITS SIDES, RIGHT?
SHE WROTE HER MESSAGE THERE IN WATER-COLOR INK!
THAT WAY, THE INK WOULD LEAVE A MARK ON CHIBA'S SWEATY HAND.
IF SHE WROTE IT BACK-WARDS, THE MESSAGE WOULD APPEAR LIKE MAGIC!
LOOK! WHEN I CHECKED THE TAPE, I GOT SOME RED INK ON MY HAND!
I SEE. RED INK DOESN'T SHOW UP ON A BLACK SURFACE.
AND SINCE MOST PEOPLE DON'T HOLD CASSETTES THAT WAY, ONLY CHIBA WOULD GET THE MESSAGE.
BUT IT'S BEEN 13 YEARS. WILL IT STILL BE LEGIBLE?
LET'S FIND OUT!!
TAKE A PIECE OF PAPER...
...SOAK IT IN WATER...
DIP
...STICK IT TO THE CASSETTE...
PIK
...PEEL IT OFF...

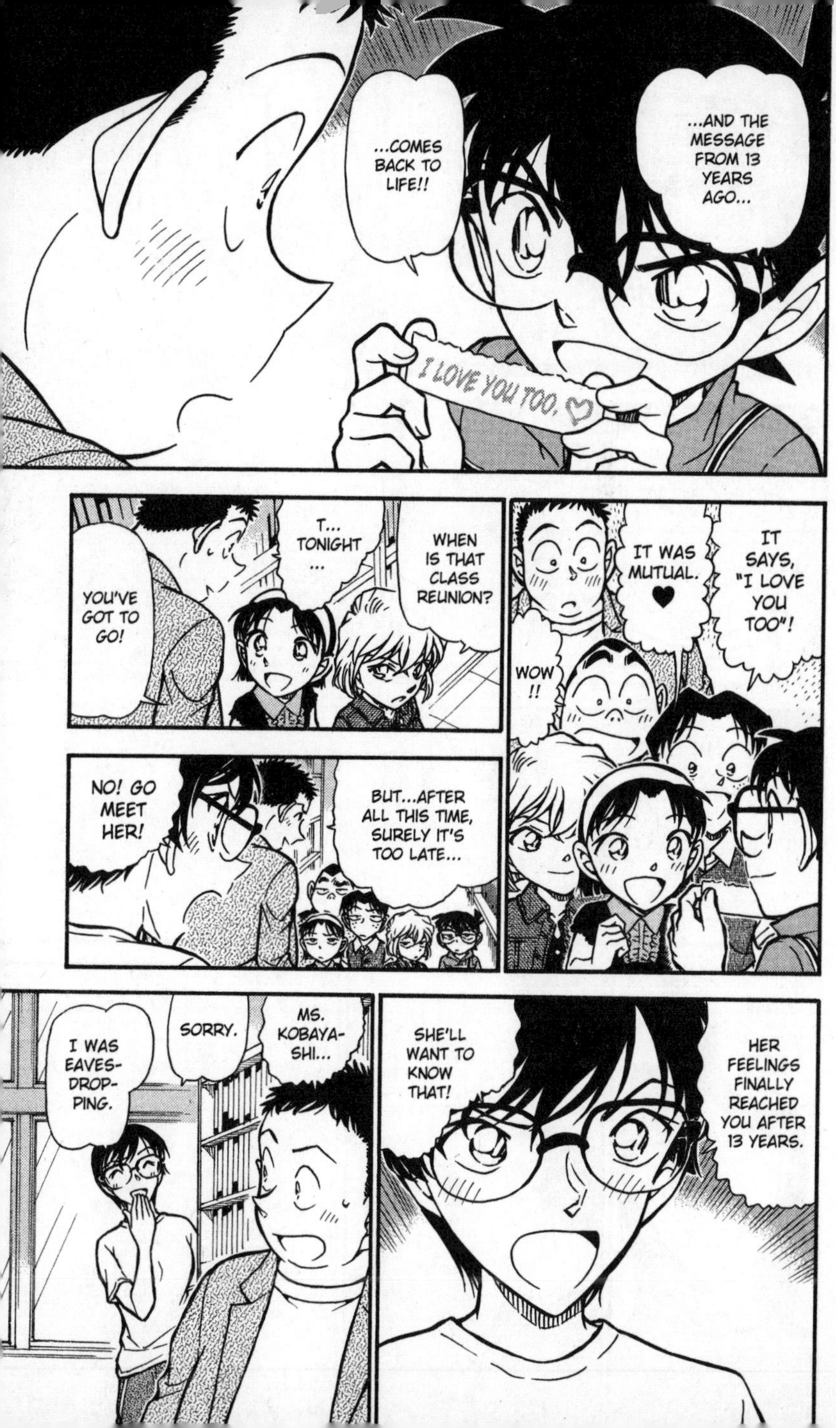
...AND THE MESSAGE FROM 13 YEARS AGO...
...COMES BACK TO LIFE!!
I LOVE YOU TOO, ♥
IT SAYS, "I LOVE YOU TOO"!
IT WAS MUTUAL. ♥
WOW!!
WHEN IS THAT CLASS REUNION?
T... TONIGHT...
YOU'VE GOT TO GO!
BUT...AFTER ALL THIS TIME, SURELY IT'S TOO LATE...
NO! GO MEET HER!
HER FEELINGS FINALLY REACHED YOU AFTER 13 YEARS.
SHE'LL WANT TO KNOW THAT!
MS. KOBAYA-SHI...
SORRY.
I WAS EAVES-DROP-PING.

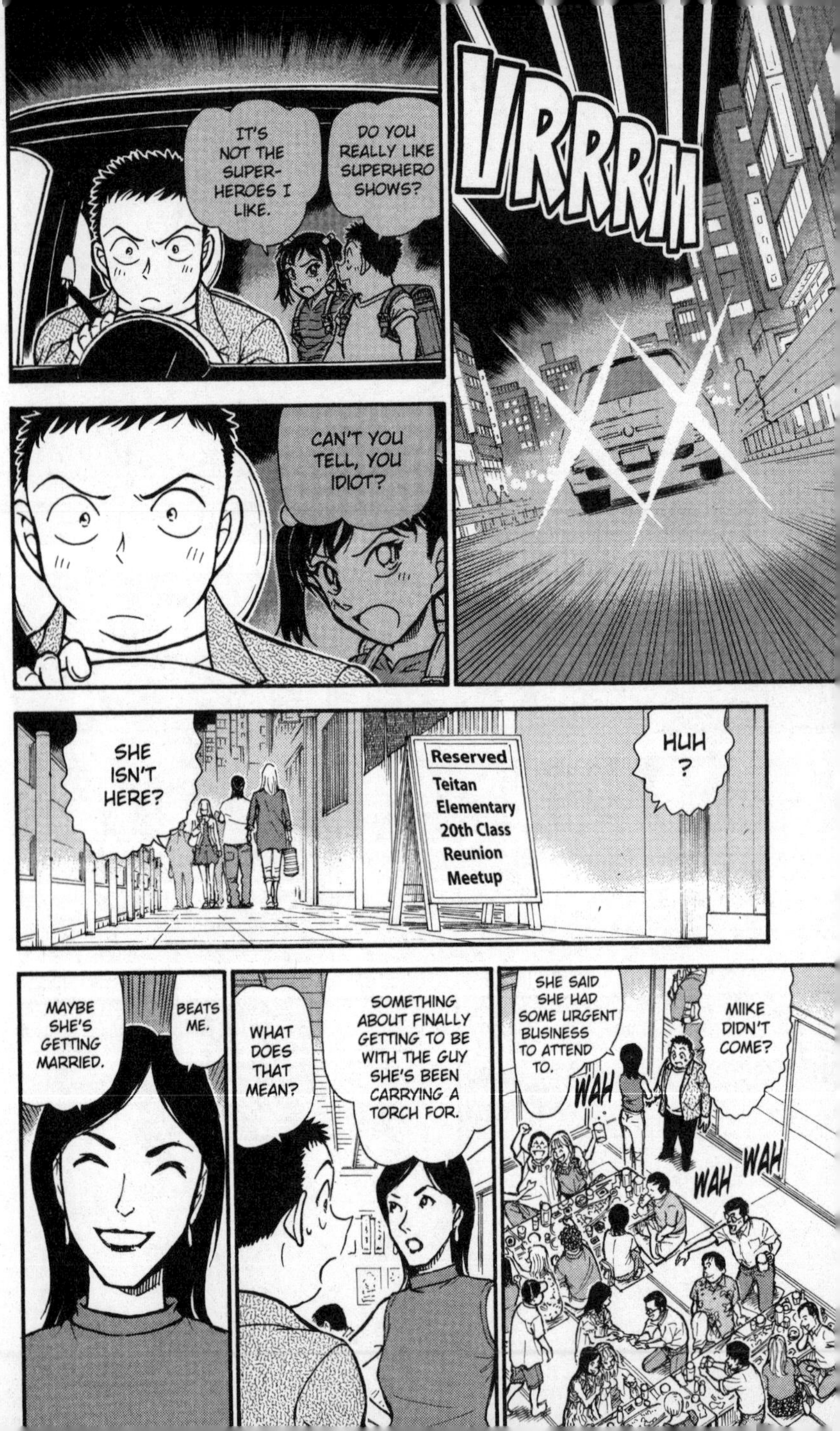
URRRM
DO YOU REALLY LIKE SUPERHERO SHOWS?
IT'S NOT THE SUPER-HEROES I LIKE.
CAN'T YOU TELL, YOU IDIOT?
HUH?
Reserved
Teitan Elementary 20th Class Reunion Meetup
SHE ISN'T HERE?
MIIKE DIDN'T COME?
SHE SAID SHE HAD SOME URGENT BUSINESS TO ATTEND TO.
WAH
WAH
WAH
SOMETHING ABOUT FINALLY GETTING TO BE WITH THE GUY SHE'S BEEN CARRYING A TORCH FOR.
WHAT DOES THAT MEAN?
BEATS ME.
MAYBE SHE'S GETTING MARRIED.

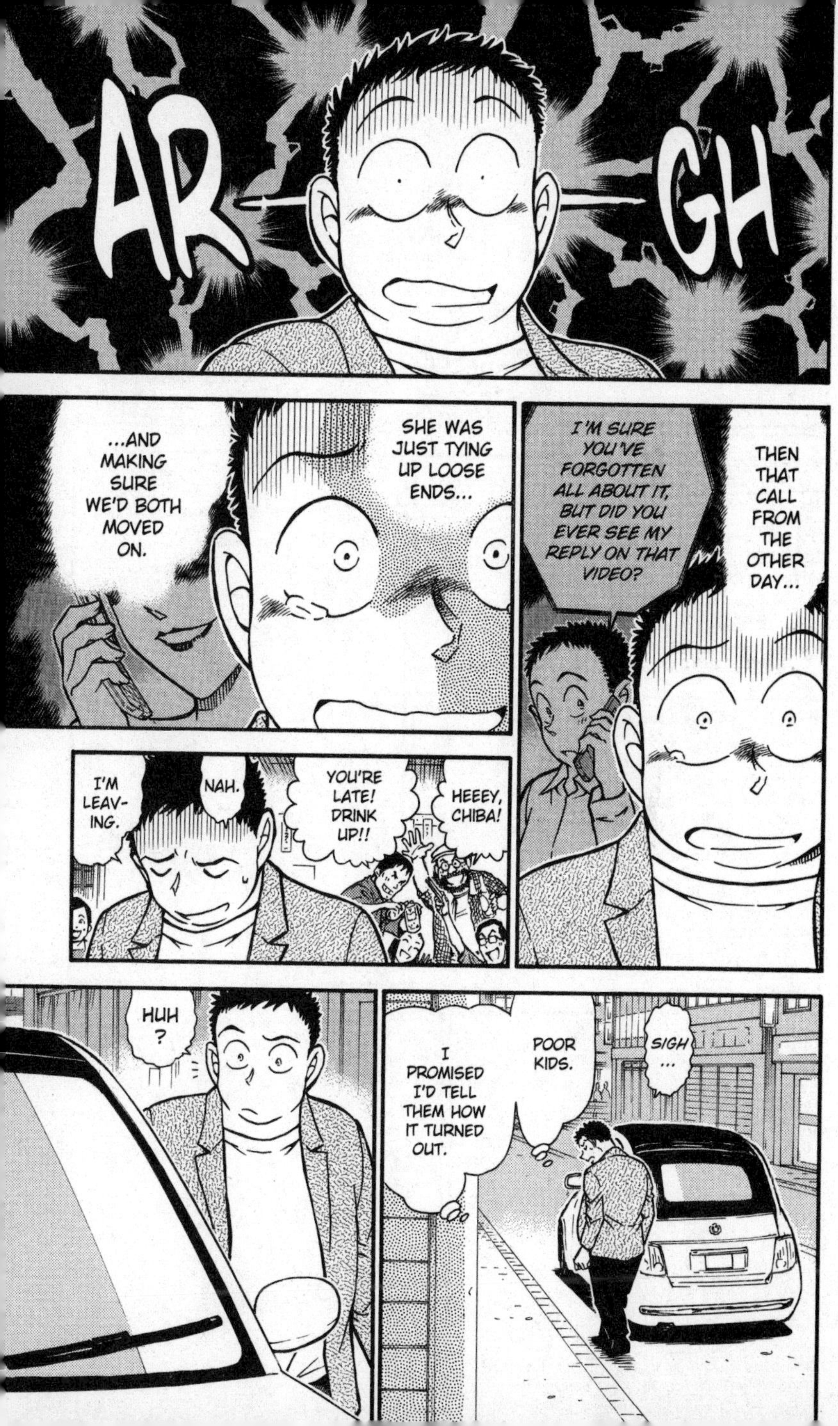
ARGH
THEN THAT CALL FROM THE OTHER DAY...
I'M SURE YOU'VE FORGOTTEN ALL ABOUT IT, BUT DID YOU EVER SEE MY REPLY ON THAT VIDEO?
SHE WAS JUST TYING UP LOOSE ENDS...
...AND MAKING SURE WE'D BOTH MOVED ON.
HEEEY, CHIBA!
YOU'RE LATE! DRINK UP!!
NAH.
I'M LEAVING.
SIGH...
POOR KIDS.
I PROMISED I'D TELL THEM HOW IT TURNED OUT.
HUH?

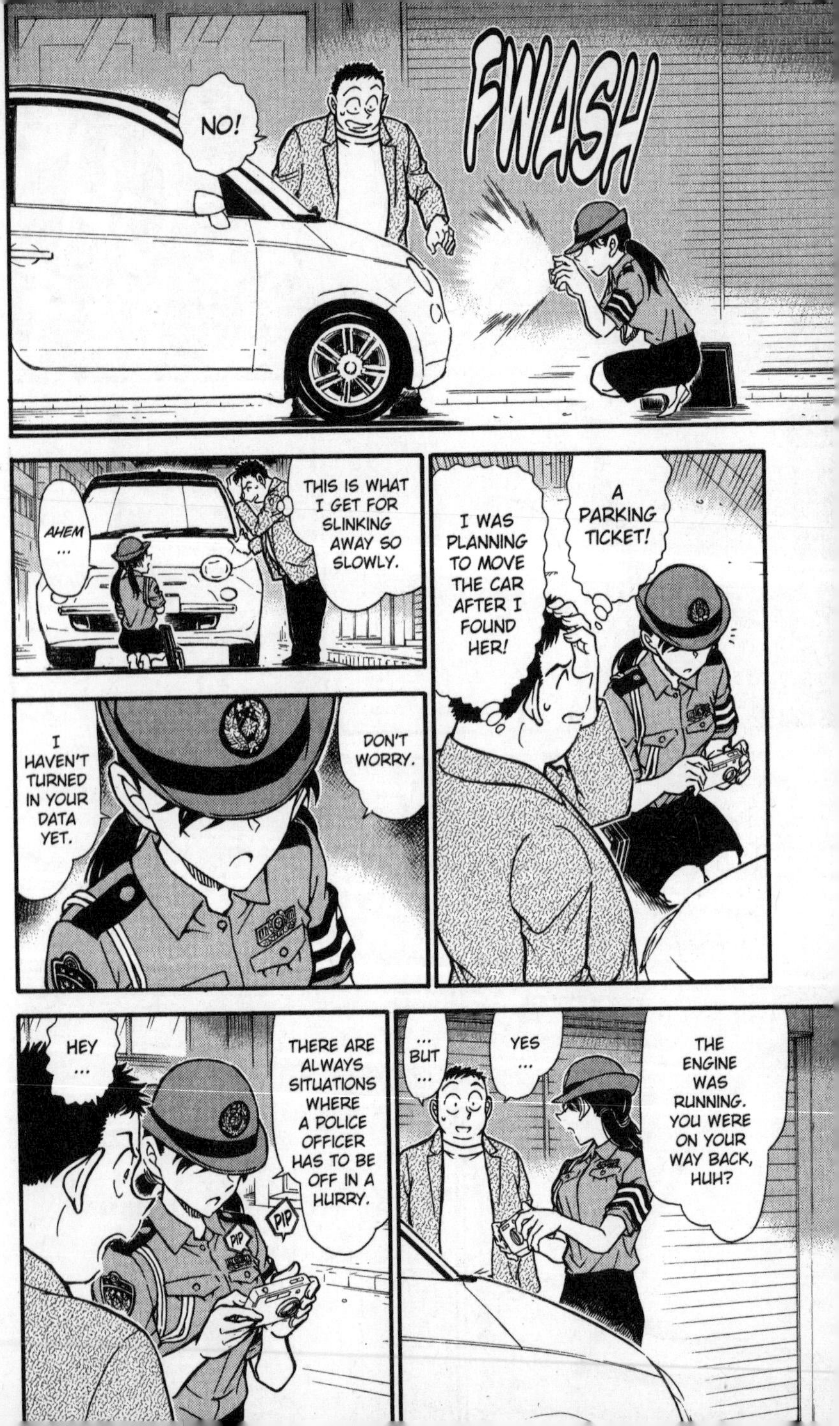
FWASH
NO!
A PARKING TICKET!
I WAS PLANNING TO MOVE THE CAR AFTER I FOUND HER!
THIS IS WHAT I GET FOR SLINKING AWAY SO SLOWLY.
AHEM ...
DON'T WORRY.
I HAVEN'T TURNED IN YOUR DATA YET.
THE ENGINE WAS RUNNING. YOU WERE ON YOUR WAY BACK, HUH?
YES ...
... BUT ...
THERE ARE ALWAYS SITUATIONS WHERE A POLICE OFFICER HAS TO BE OFF IN A HURRY.
HEY ...
PIP
PIP

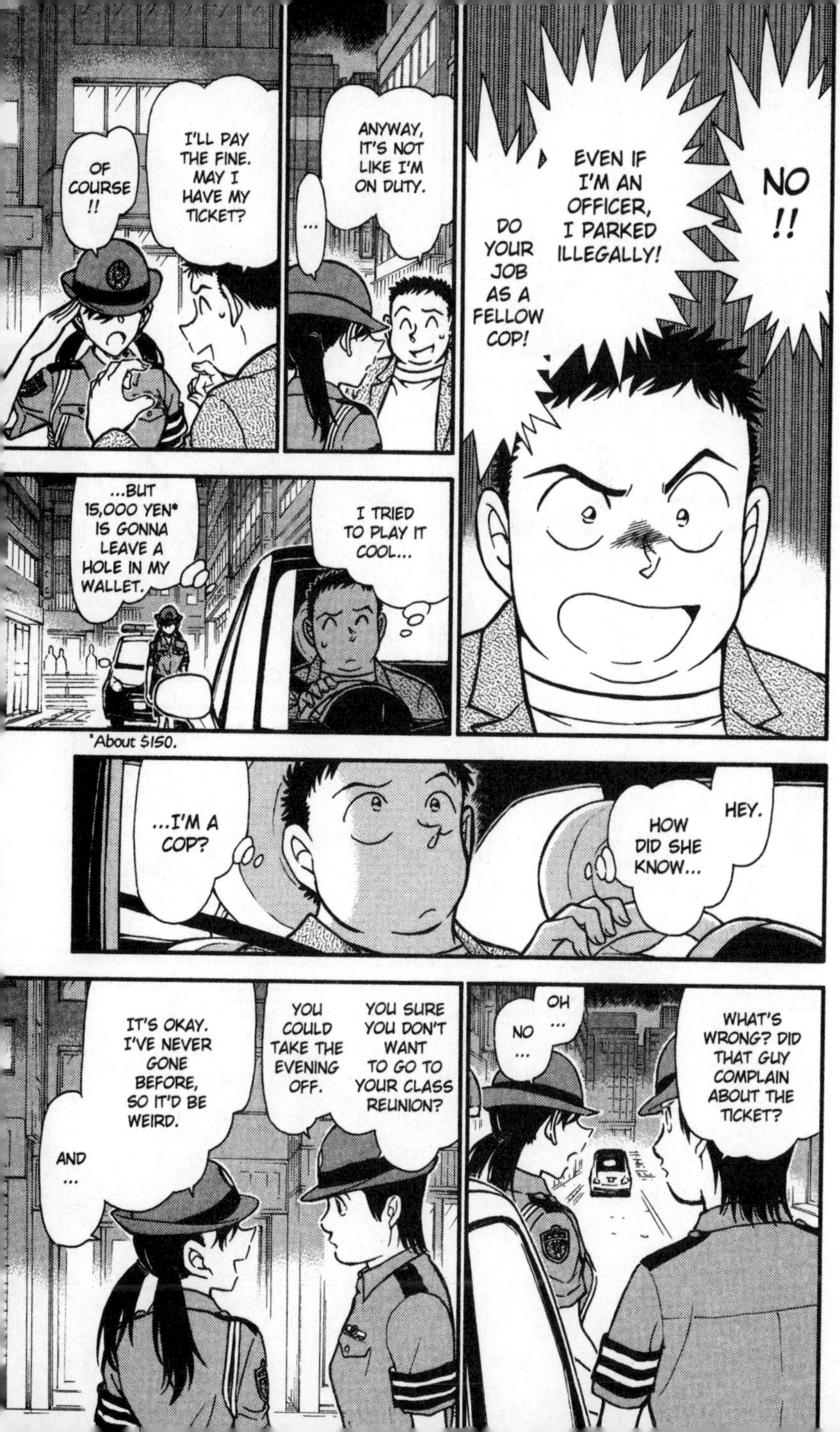
NO!!
EVEN IF I'M AN OFFICER, I PARKED ILLEGALLY!
DO YOUR JOB AS A FELLOW COP!
ANYWAY, IT'S NOT LIKE I'M ON DUTY.
...
I'LL PAY THE FINE. MAY I HAVE MY TICKET?
OF COURSE!!
I TRIED TO PLAY IT COOL...
...BUT 15,000 YEN* IS GONNA LEAVE A HOLE IN MY WALLET.
HEY.
HOW DID SHE KNOW...
...I'M A COP?
WHAT'S WRONG? DID THAT GUY COMPLAIN ABOUT THE TICKET?
OH...
NO...
YOU SURE YOU DON'T WANT TO GO TO YOUR CLASS REUNION?
YOU COULD TAKE THE EVENING OFF.
IT'S OKAY. I'VE NEVER GONE BEFORE, SO IT'D BE WEIRD.
AND...

*About $150.

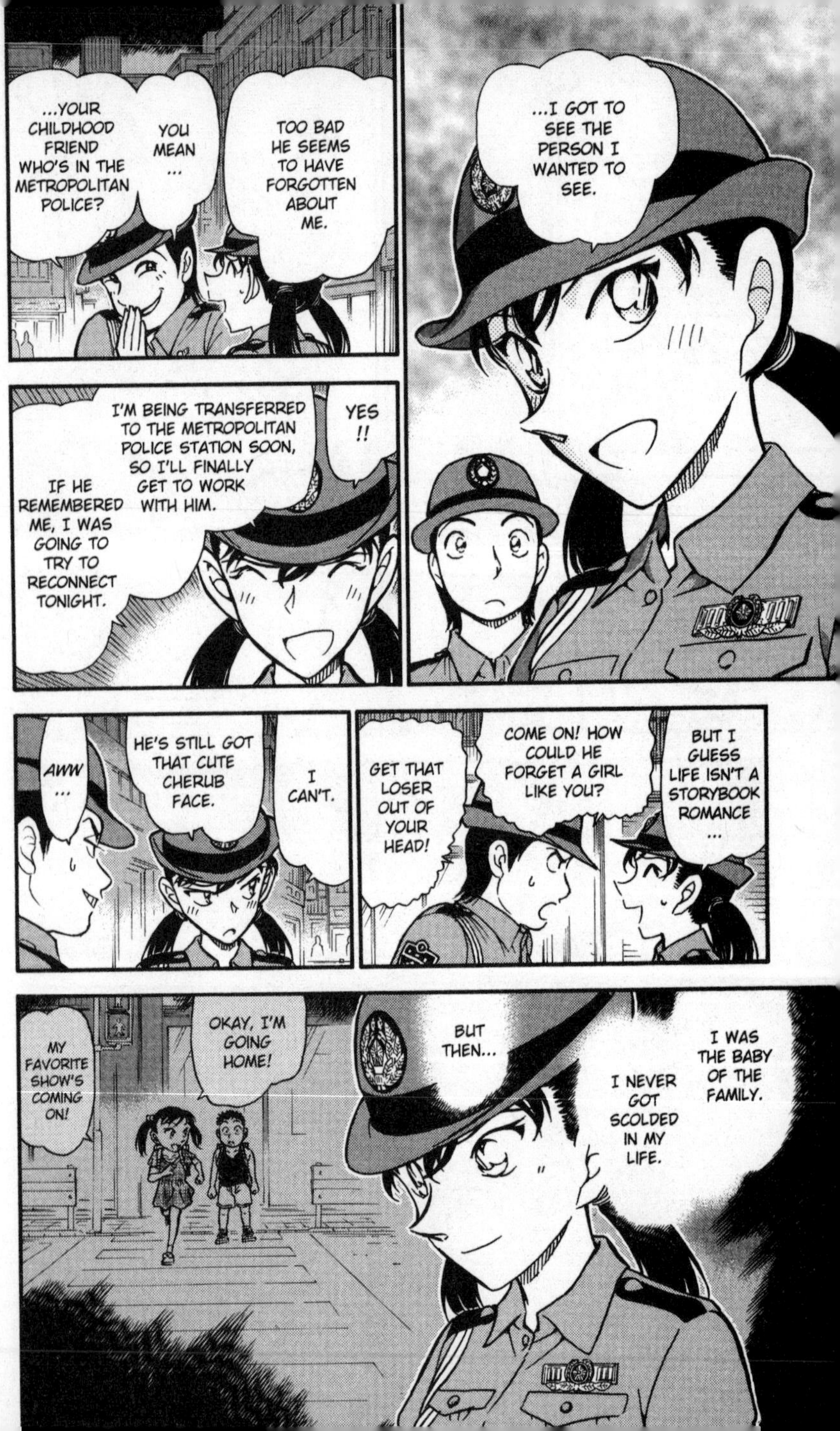
...I GOT TO SEE THE PERSON I WANTED TO SEE.
TOO BAD HE SEEMS TO HAVE FORGOTTEN ABOUT ME.
YOU MEAN ...
...YOUR CHILDHOOD FRIEND WHO'S IN THE METROPOLITAN POLICE?
YES !!
I'M BEING TRANSFERRED TO THE METROPOLITAN POLICE STATION SOON, SO I'LL FINALLY GET TO WORK WITH HIM.
IF HE REMEMBERED ME, I WAS GOING TO TRY TO RECONNECT TONIGHT.
BUT I GUESS LIFE ISN'T A STORYBOOK ROMANCE ...
COME ON! HOW COULD HE FORGET A GIRL LIKE YOU?
GET THAT LOSER OUT OF YOUR HEAD!
I CAN'T.
HE'S STILL GOT THAT CUTE CHERUB FACE.
AWW ...
I WAS THE BABY OF THE FAMILY.
I NEVER GOT SCOLDED IN MY LIFE.
BUT THEN...
OKAY, I'M GOING HOME!
MY FAVORITE SHOW'S COMING ON!

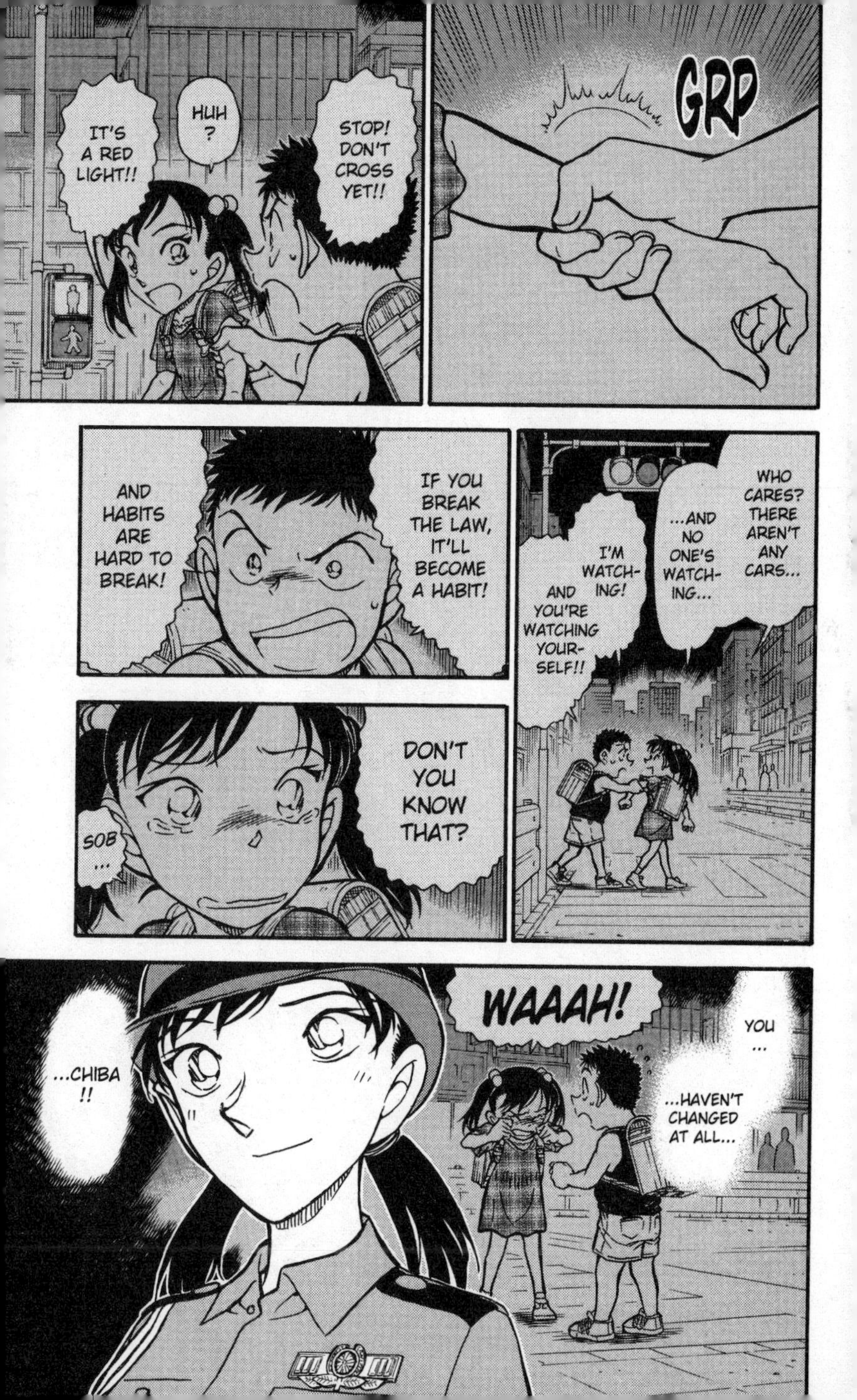
GRP
STOP! DON'T CROSS YET!!
HUH?
IT'S A RED LIGHT!!
WHO CARES? THERE AREN'T ANY CARS...
...AND NO ONE'S WATCHING...
I'M WATCHING!
AND YOU'RE WATCHING YOURSELF!!
IF YOU BREAK THE LAW, IT'LL BECOME A HABIT!
AND HABITS ARE HARD TO BREAK!
DON'T YOU KNOW THAT?
SOB...
YOU...
...HAVEN'T CHANGED AT ALL...
WAAAH!
...CHIBA!!

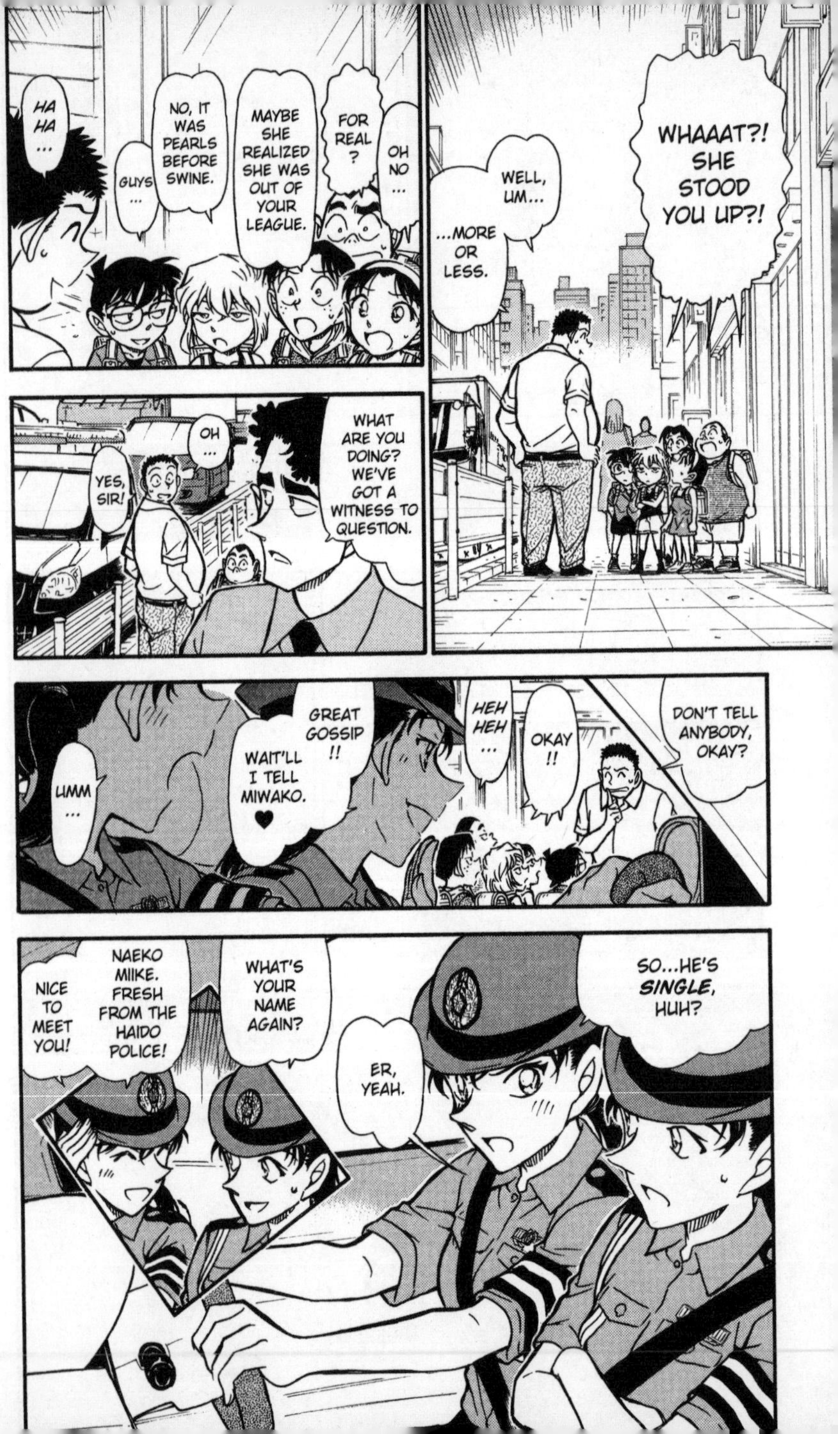
WHAAAT?! SHE STOOD YOU UP?!
WELL, UM...
...MORE OR LESS.
OH NO ...
FOR REAL ?
MAYBE SHE REALIZED SHE WAS OUT OF YOUR LEAGUE.
NO, IT WAS PEARLS BEFORE SWINE.
GUYS ...
HA HA ...
WHAT ARE YOU DOING? WE'VE GOT A WITNESS TO QUESTION.
OH ...
YES, SIR!
DON'T TELL ANYBODY, OKAY?
OKAY !!
HEH HEH ...
GREAT GOSSIP !!
WAIT'LL I TELL MIWAKO. ♥
UMM ...
SO...HE'S *SINGLE*, HUH?
ER, YEAH.
WHAT'S YOUR NAME AGAIN?
NAEKO MIIKE. FRESH FROM THE HAIDO POLICE!
NICE TO MEET YOU!

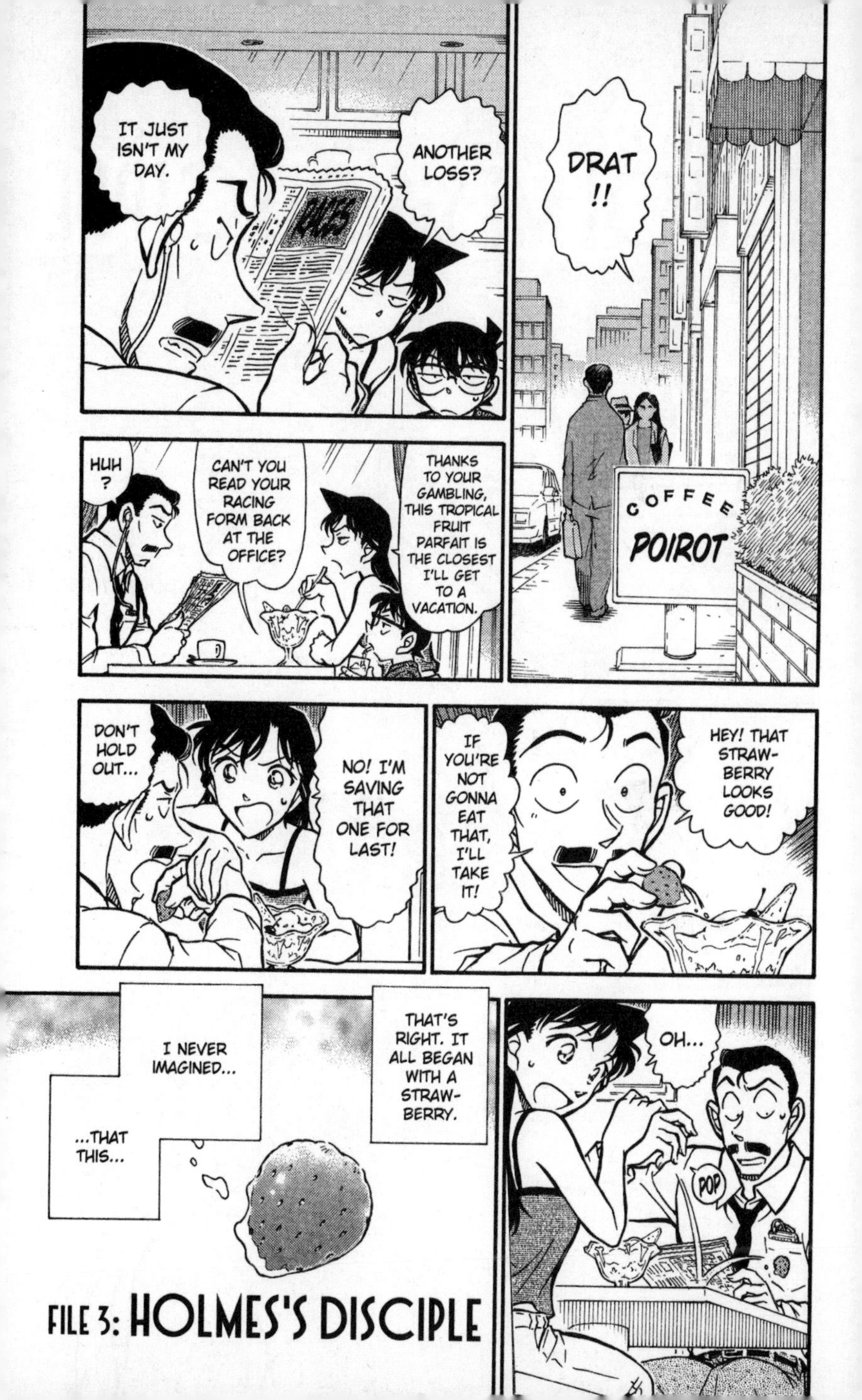

DRAT!!
COFFEE
POIROT
ANOTHER LOSS?
IT JUST ISN'T MY DAY.
THANKS TO YOUR GAMBLING, THIS TROPICAL FRUIT PARFAIT IS THE CLOSEST I'LL GET TO A VACATION.
CAN'T YOU READ YOUR RACING FORM BACK AT THE OFFICE?
HUH?
HEY! THAT STRAW-BERRY LOOKS GOOD!
IF YOU'RE NOT GONNA EAT THAT, I'LL TAKE IT!
NO! I'M SAVING THAT ONE FOR LAST!
DON'T HOLD OUT...
OH...
POP
THAT'S RIGHT. IT ALL BEGAN WITH A STRAW-BERRY.
I NEVER IMAGINED...
...THAT THIS...
FILE 3: HOLMES'S DISCIPLE

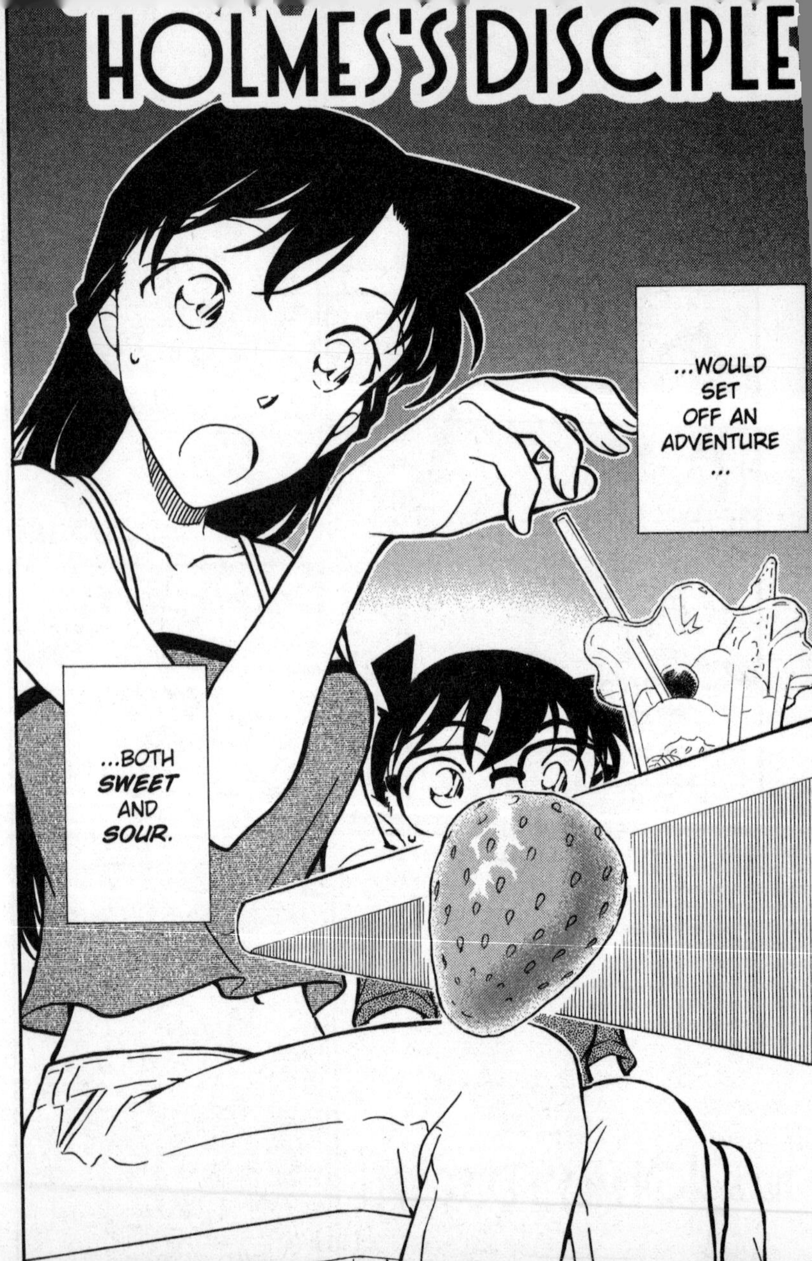
HOLMES'S DISCIPLE
...WOULD SET OFF AN ADVENTURE ...
...BOTH SWEET AND SOUR.

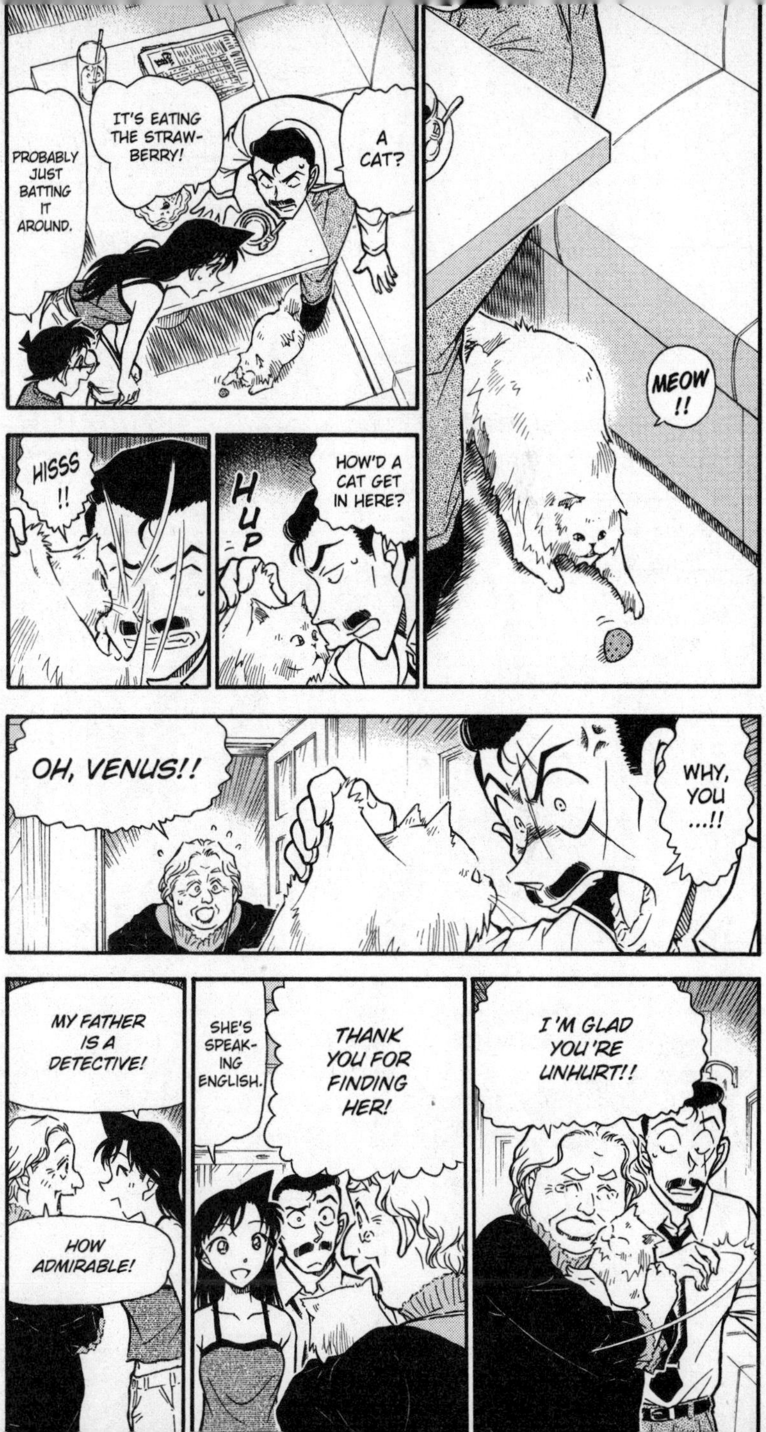
MEOW !!
A CAT?
IT'S EATING THE STRAW-BERRY!
PROBABLY JUST BATTING IT AROUND.
HOW'D A CAT GET IN HERE?
HUP
HISSS !!
WHY, YOU ...!!
OH, VENUS!!
I'M GLAD YOU'RE UNHURT!!
THANK YOU FOR FINDING HER!
SHE'S SPEAK-ING ENGLISH.
MY FATHER IS A DETECTIVE!
HOW ADMIRABLE!

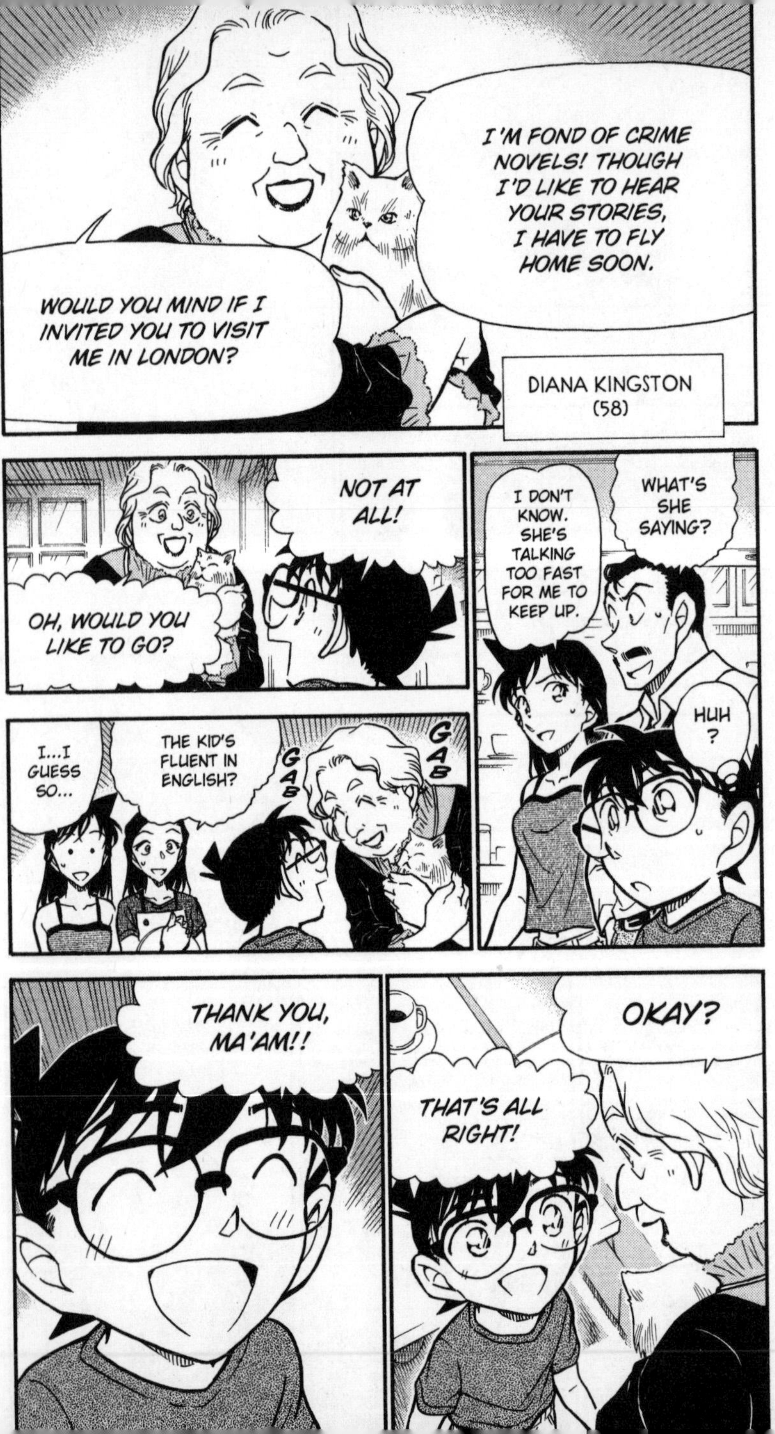
I'M FOND OF CRIME NOVELS! THOUGH I'D LIKE TO HEAR YOUR STORIES, I HAVE TO FLY HOME SOON.
WOULD YOU MIND IF I INVITED YOU TO VISIT ME IN LONDON?
DIANA KINGSTON (58)
WHAT'S SHE SAYING?
I DON'T KNOW. SHE'S TALKING TOO FAST FOR ME TO KEEP UP.
HUH?
NOT AT ALL!
OH, WOULD YOU LIKE TO GO?
GAB
GAB
THE KID'S FLUENT IN ENGLISH?
I...I GUESS SO...
OKAY?
THAT'S ALL RIGHT!
THANK YOU, MA'AM!!

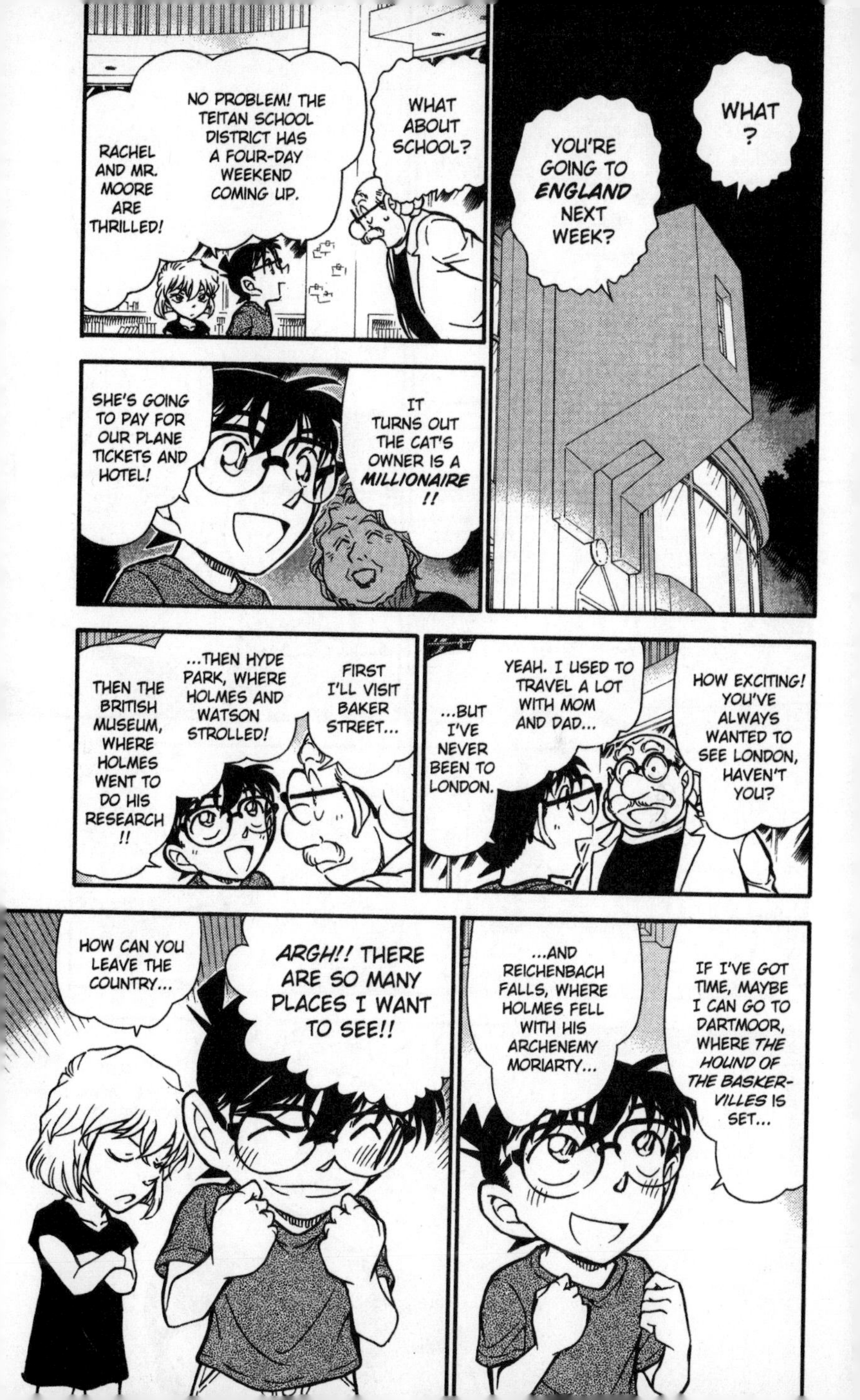
WHAT?
YOU'RE GOING TO *ENGLAND* NEXT WEEK?
WHAT ABOUT SCHOOL?
NO PROBLEM! THE TEITAN SCHOOL DISTRICT HAS A FOUR-DAY WEEKEND COMING UP.
RACHEL AND MR. MOORE ARE THRILLED!
IT TURNS OUT THE CAT'S OWNER IS A *MILLIONAIRE* !!
SHE'S GOING TO PAY FOR OUR PLANE TICKETS AND HOTEL!
HOW EXCITING! YOU'VE ALWAYS WANTED TO SEE LONDON, HAVEN'T YOU?
YEAH. I USED TO TRAVEL A LOT WITH MOM AND DAD...
...BUT I'VE NEVER BEEN TO LONDON.
FIRST I'LL VISIT BAKER STREET...
...THEN HYDE PARK, WHERE HOLMES AND WATSON STROLLED!
THEN THE BRITISH MUSEUM, WHERE HOLMES WENT TO DO HIS RESEARCH !!
IF I'VE GOT TIME, MAYBE I CAN GO TO DARTMOOR, WHERE *THE HOUND OF THE BASKERVILLES* IS SET...
...AND REICHENBACH FALLS, WHERE HOLMES FELL WITH HIS ARCHENEMY MORIARTY...
ARGH!! THERE ARE SO MANY PLACES I WANT TO SEE!!
HOW CAN YOU LEAVE THE COUNTRY...

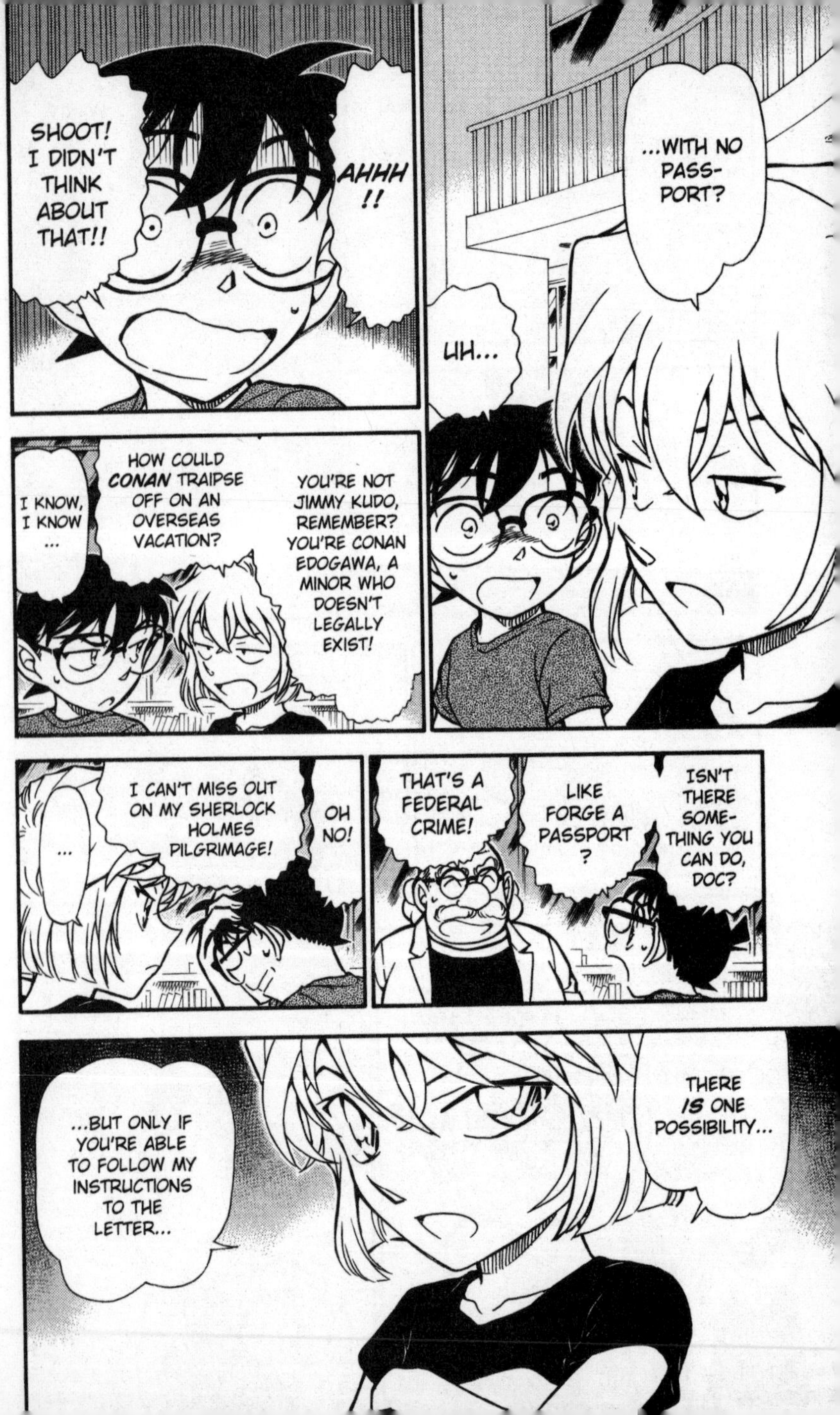
...WITH NO PASS-PORT?
UH...
AHHH!!
SHOOT! I DIDN'T THINK ABOUT THAT!!
YOU'RE NOT JIMMY KUDO, REMEMBER? YOU'RE CONAN EDOGAWA, A MINOR WHO DOESN'T LEGALLY EXIST!
HOW COULD *CONAN* TRAIPSE OFF ON AN OVERSEAS VACATION?
I KNOW, I KNOW ...
ISN'T THERE SOME-THING YOU CAN DO, DOC?
LIKE FORGE A PASSPORT?
THAT'S A FEDERAL CRIME!
OH NO!
I CAN'T MISS OUT ON MY SHERLOCK HOLMES PILGRIMAGE!
...
THERE *IS* ONE POSSIBILITY...
...BUT ONLY IF YOU'RE ABLE TO FOLLOW MY INSTRUCTIONS TO THE LETTER...

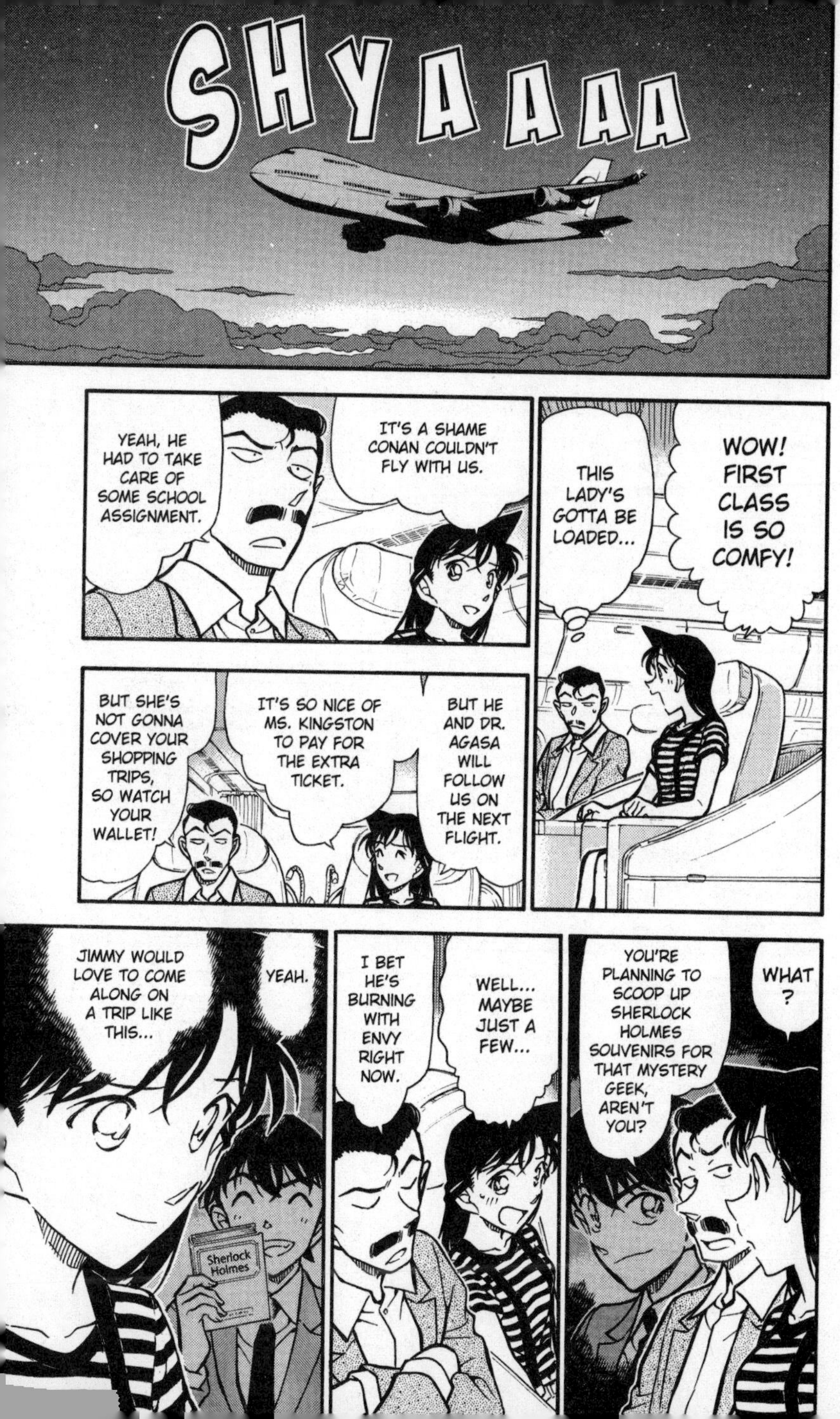
SHYAAAA
WOW! FIRST CLASS IS SO COMFY!
THIS LADY'S GOTTA BE LOADED...
IT'S A SHAME CONAN COULDN'T FLY WITH US.
YEAH, HE HAD TO TAKE CARE OF SOME SCHOOL ASSIGNMENT.
BUT HE AND DR. AGASA WILL FOLLOW US ON THE NEXT FLIGHT.
IT'S SO NICE OF MS. KINGSTON TO PAY FOR THE EXTRA TICKET.
BUT SHE'S NOT GONNA COVER YOUR SHOPPING TRIPS, SO WATCH YOUR WALLET!
WHAT?
YOU'RE PLANNING TO SCOOP UP SHERLOCK HOLMES SOUVENIRS FOR THAT MYSTERY GEEK, AREN'T YOU?
WELL... MAYBE JUST A FEW...
I BET HE'S BURNING WITH ENVY RIGHT NOW.
YEAH.
JIMMY WOULD LOVE TO COME ALONG ON A TRIP LIKE THIS...
Sherlock Holmes

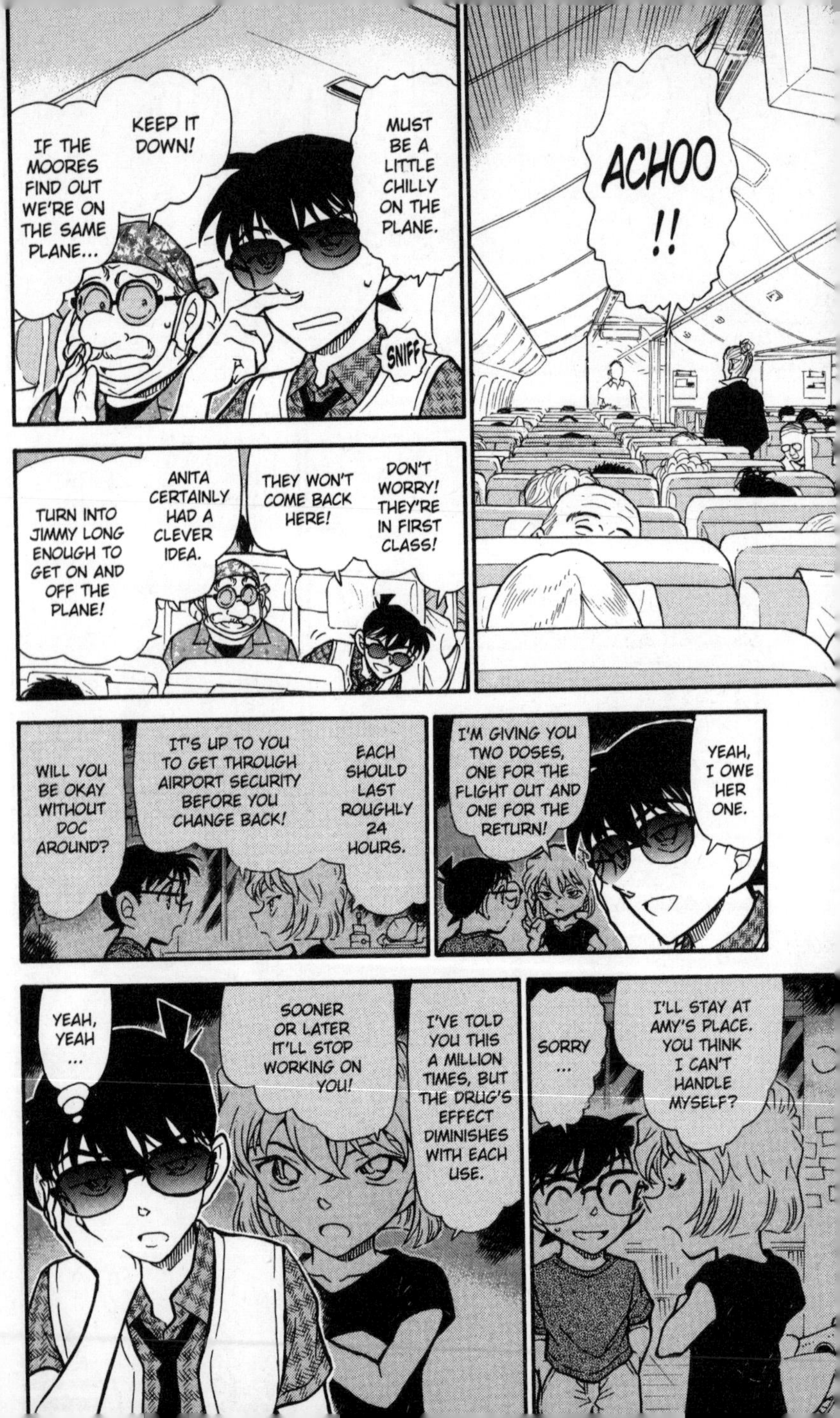
ACHOO !!
MUST BE A LITTLE CHILLY ON THE PLANE.
SNIFF
KEEP IT DOWN!
IF THE MOORES FIND OUT WE'RE ON THE SAME PLANE...
DON'T WORRY! THEY'RE IN FIRST CLASS!
THEY WON'T COME BACK HERE!
ANITA CERTAINLY HAD A CLEVER IDEA.
TURN INTO JIMMY LONG ENOUGH TO GET ON AND OFF THE PLANE!
YEAH, I OWE HER ONE.
I'M GIVING YOU TWO DOSES, ONE FOR THE FLIGHT OUT AND ONE FOR THE RETURN!
EACH SHOULD LAST ROUGHLY 24 HOURS.
IT'S UP TO YOU TO GET THROUGH AIRPORT SECURITY BEFORE YOU CHANGE BACK!
WILL YOU BE OKAY WITHOUT DOC AROUND?
I'LL STAY AT AMY'S PLACE. YOU THINK I CAN'T HANDLE MYSELF?
SORRY ...
I'VE TOLD YOU THIS A MILLION TIMES, BUT THE DRUG'S EFFECT DIMINISHES WITH EACH USE.
SOONER OR LATER IT'LL STOP WORKING ON YOU!
YEAH, YEAH ...

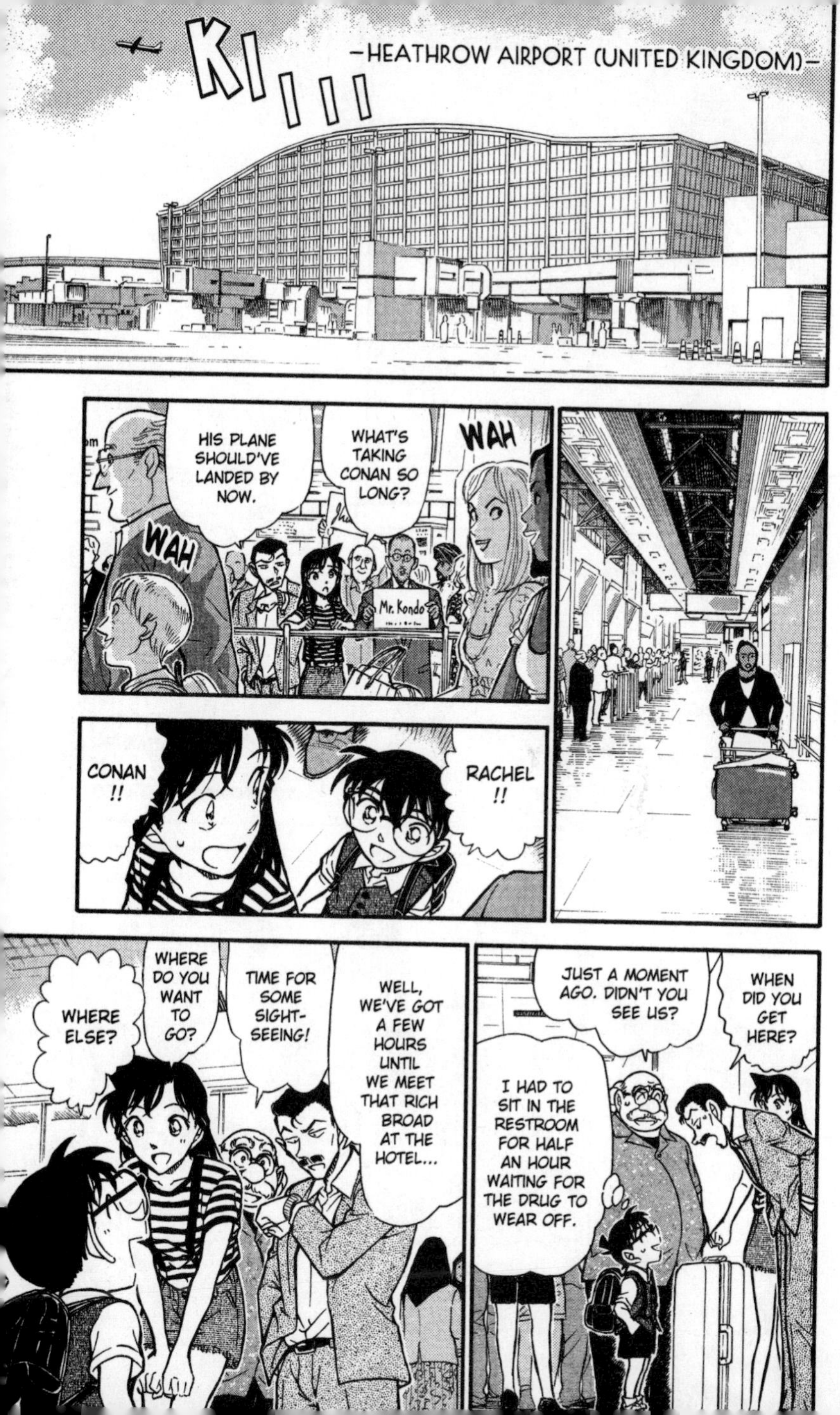
KIIII
-HEATHROW AIRPORT (UNITED KINGDOM)-
WAH
WHAT'S TAKING CONAN SO LONG?
HIS PLANE SHOULD'VE LANDED BY NOW.
WAH
Mr. Kondo
RACHEL!!
CONAN!!
WHEN DID YOU GET HERE?
JUST A MOMENT AGO. DIDN'T YOU SEE US?
I HAD TO SIT IN THE RESTROOM FOR HALF AN HOUR WAITING FOR THE DRUG TO WEAR OFF.
WELL, WE'VE GOT A FEW HOURS UNTIL WE MEET THAT RICH BROAD AT THE HOTEL...
TIME FOR SOME SIGHT-SEEING!
WHERE DO YOU WANT TO GO?
WHERE ELSE?

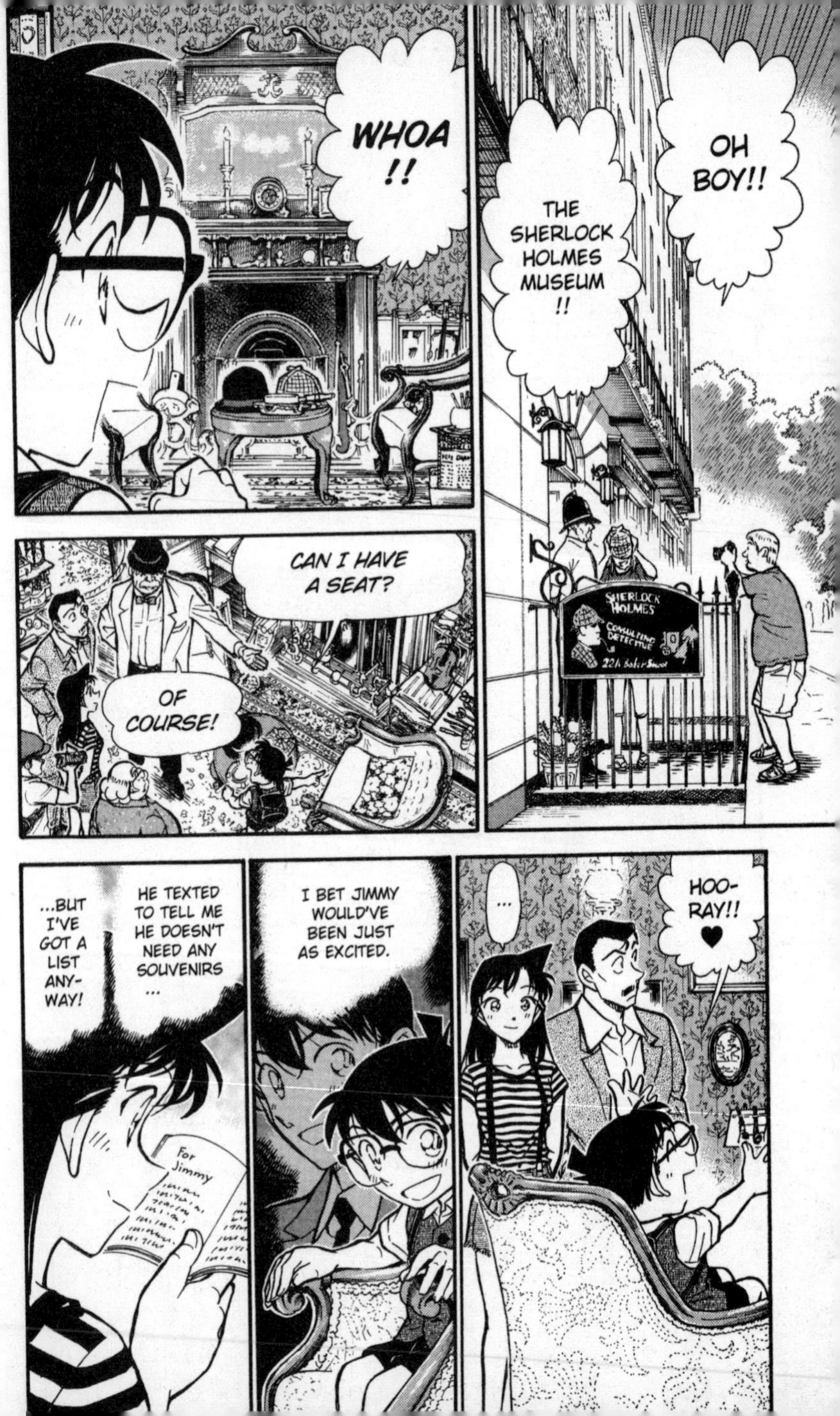
OH BOY!!
THE SHERLOCK HOLMES MUSEUM !!
SHERLOCK HOLMES
CONSULTING DETECTIVE
221b Baker Street
WHOA !!
CAN I HAVE A SEAT?
OF COURSE!
...
HOO-RAY!! ♥
I BET JIMMY WOULD'VE BEEN JUST AS EXCITED.
HE TEXTED TO TELL ME HE DOESN'T NEED ANY SOUVENIRS ...
...BUT I'VE GOT A LIST ANY-WAY!
For Jimmy

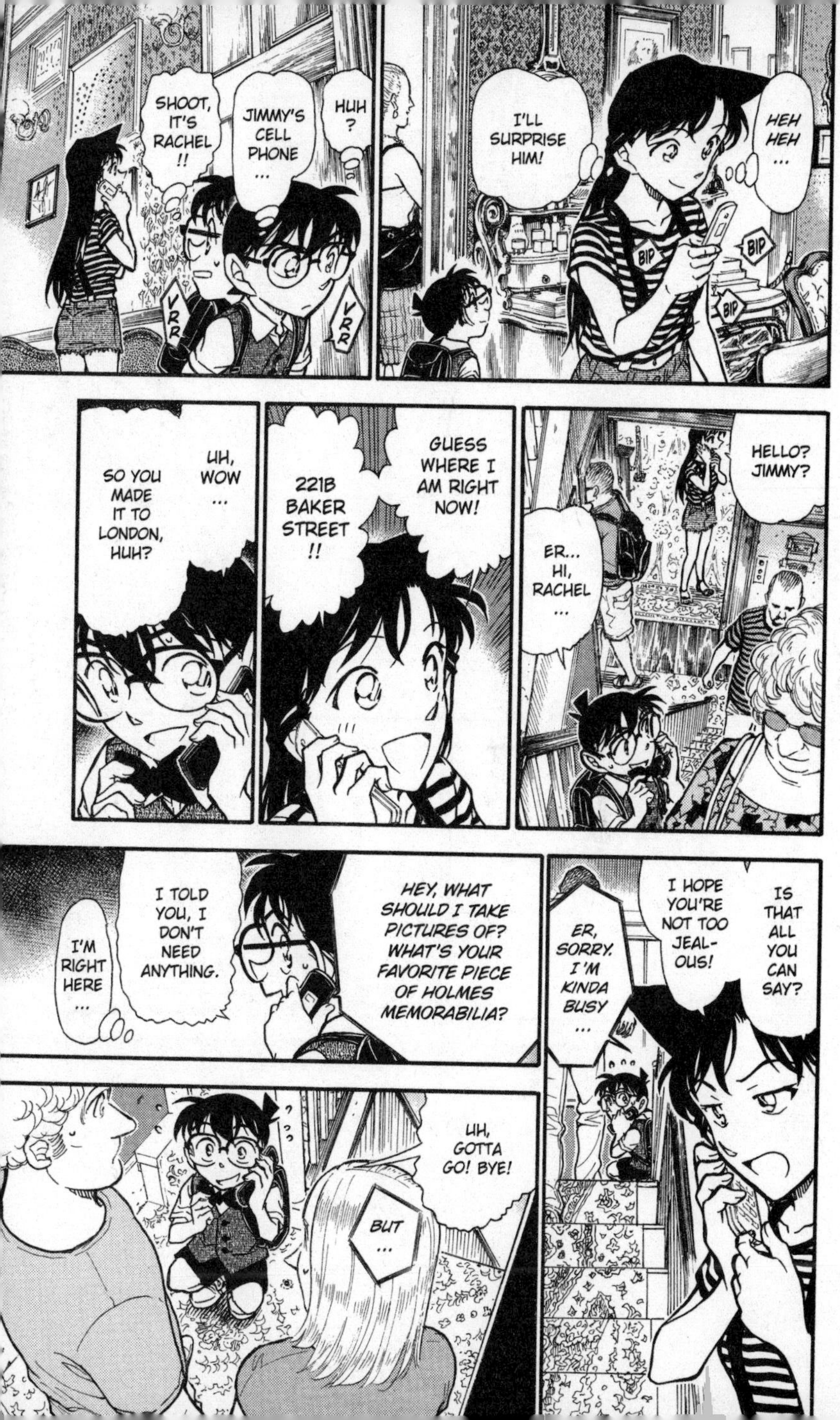
HEH HEH ...
I'LL SURPRISE HIM!
BIP
BIP
BIP
HUH?
JIMMY'S CELL PHONE ...
SHOOT, IT'S RACHEL!!
VRR
VRR
HELLO? JIMMY?
ER... HI, RACHEL ...
GUESS WHERE I AM RIGHT NOW!
221B BAKER STREET!!
UH, WOW ...
SO YOU MADE IT TO LONDON, HUH?
IS THAT ALL YOU CAN SAY?
I HOPE YOU'RE NOT TOO JEAL-OUS!
ER, SORRY. I'M KINDA BUSY ...
HEY, WHAT SHOULD I TAKE PICTURES OF? WHAT'S YOUR FAVORITE PIECE OF HOLMES MEMORABILIA?
I TOLD YOU, I DON'T NEED ANYTHING.
I'M RIGHT HERE ...
UH, GOTTA GO! BYE!
BUT ...

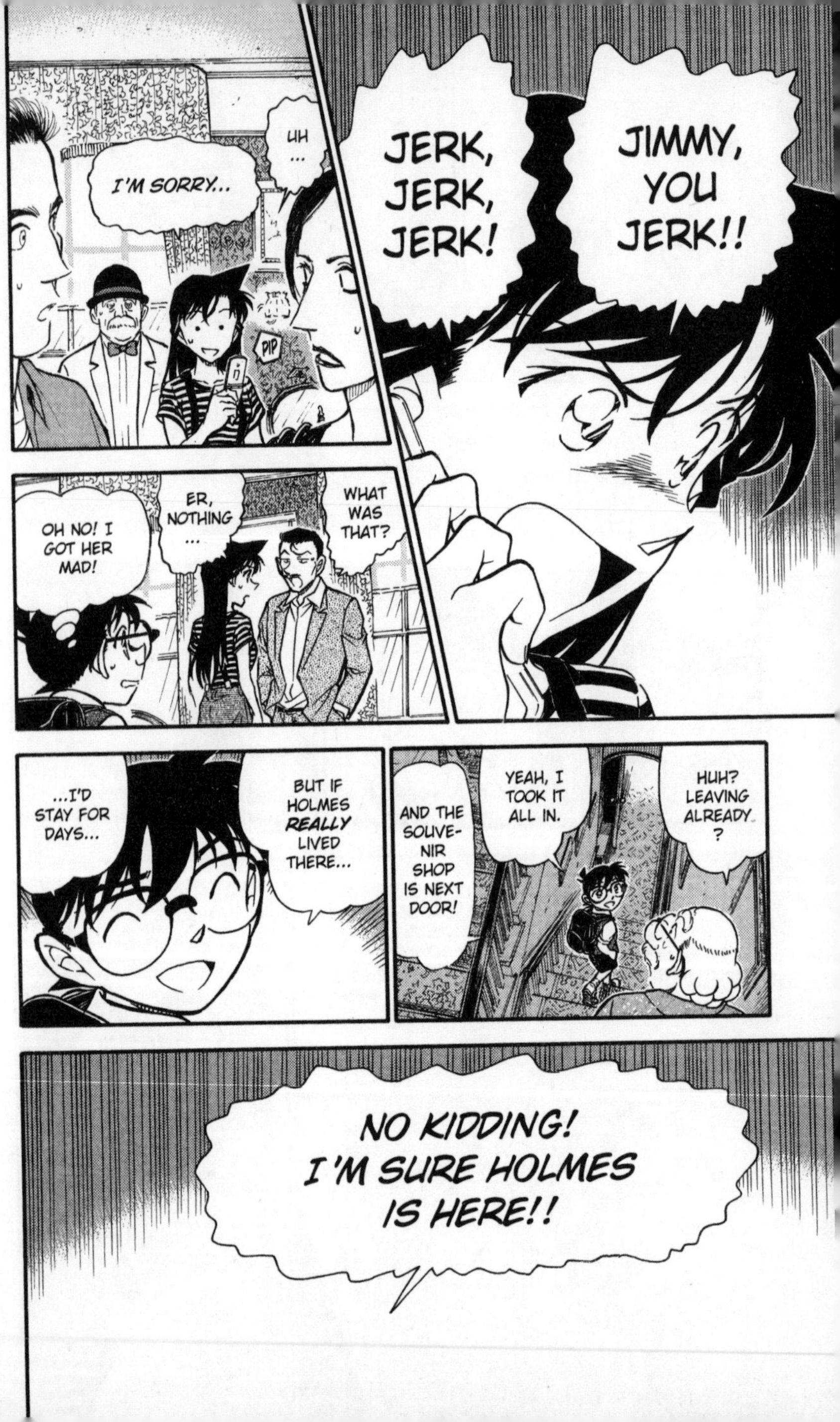

JIMMY, YOU JERK!!
JERK, JERK, JERK!
UH ...
I'M SORRY...
PIP
WHAT WAS THAT?
ER, NOTHING ...
OH NO! I GOT HER MAD!
HUH? LEAVING ALREADY ?
YEAH, I TOOK IT ALL IN.
AND THE SOUVE-NIR SHOP IS NEXT DOOR!
BUT IF HOLMES *REALLY* LIVED THERE...
...I'D STAY FOR DAYS...
NO KIDDING! I'M SURE HOLMES IS HERE!!

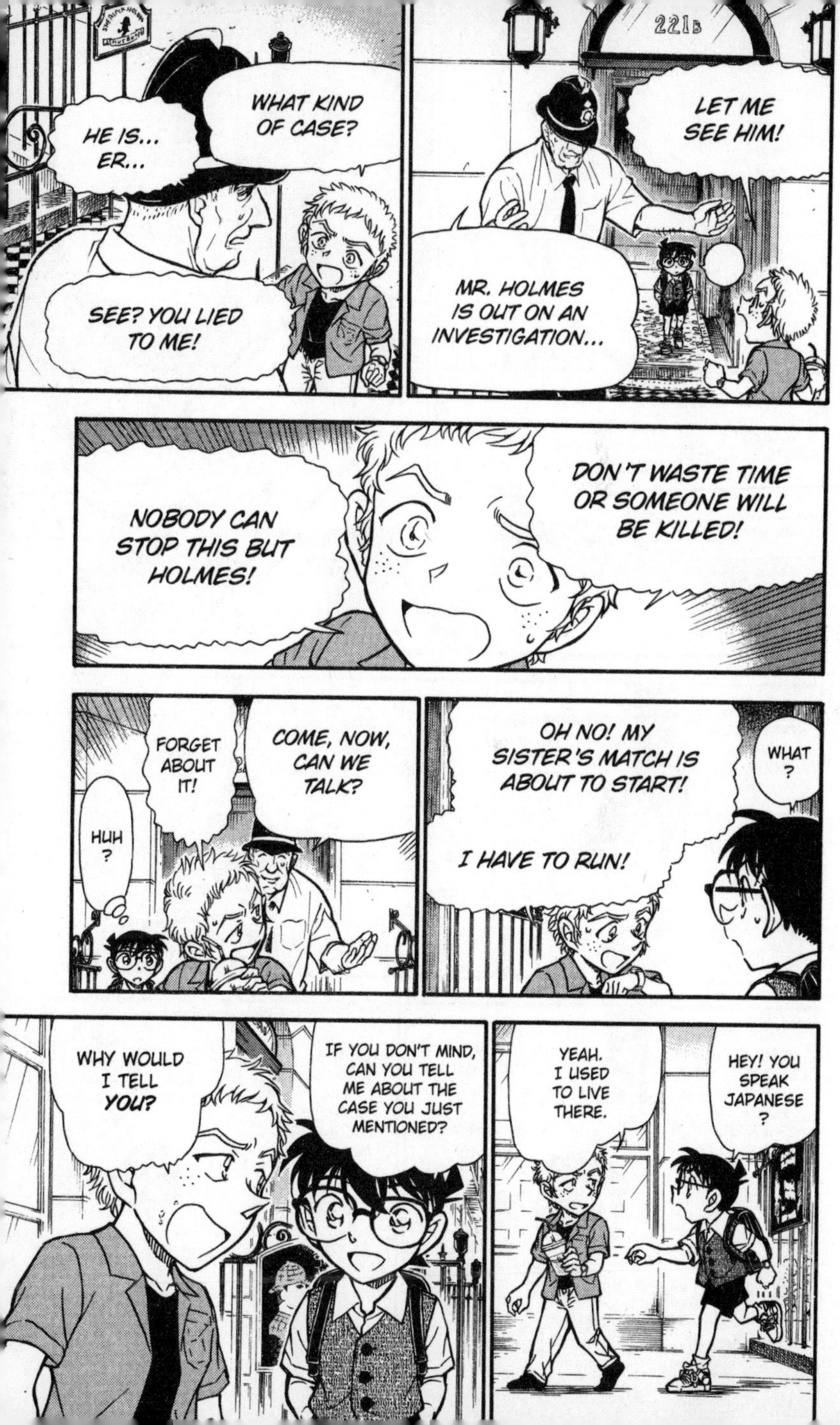
221B
LET ME SEE HIM!
MR. HOLMES IS OUT ON AN INVESTIGATION...
WHAT KIND OF CASE?
HE IS... ER...
SEE? YOU LIED TO ME!
DON'T WASTE TIME OR SOMEONE WILL BE KILLED!
NOBODY CAN STOP THIS BUT HOLMES!
WHAT?
OH NO! MY SISTER'S MATCH IS ABOUT TO START!
I HAVE TO RUN!
COME, NOW, CAN WE TALK?
FORGET ABOUT IT!
HUH?
HEY! YOU SPEAK JAPANESE?
YEAH. I USED TO LIVE THERE.
IF YOU DON'T MIND, CAN YOU TELL ME ABOUT THE CASE YOU JUST MENTIONED?
WHY WOULD I TELL YOU?

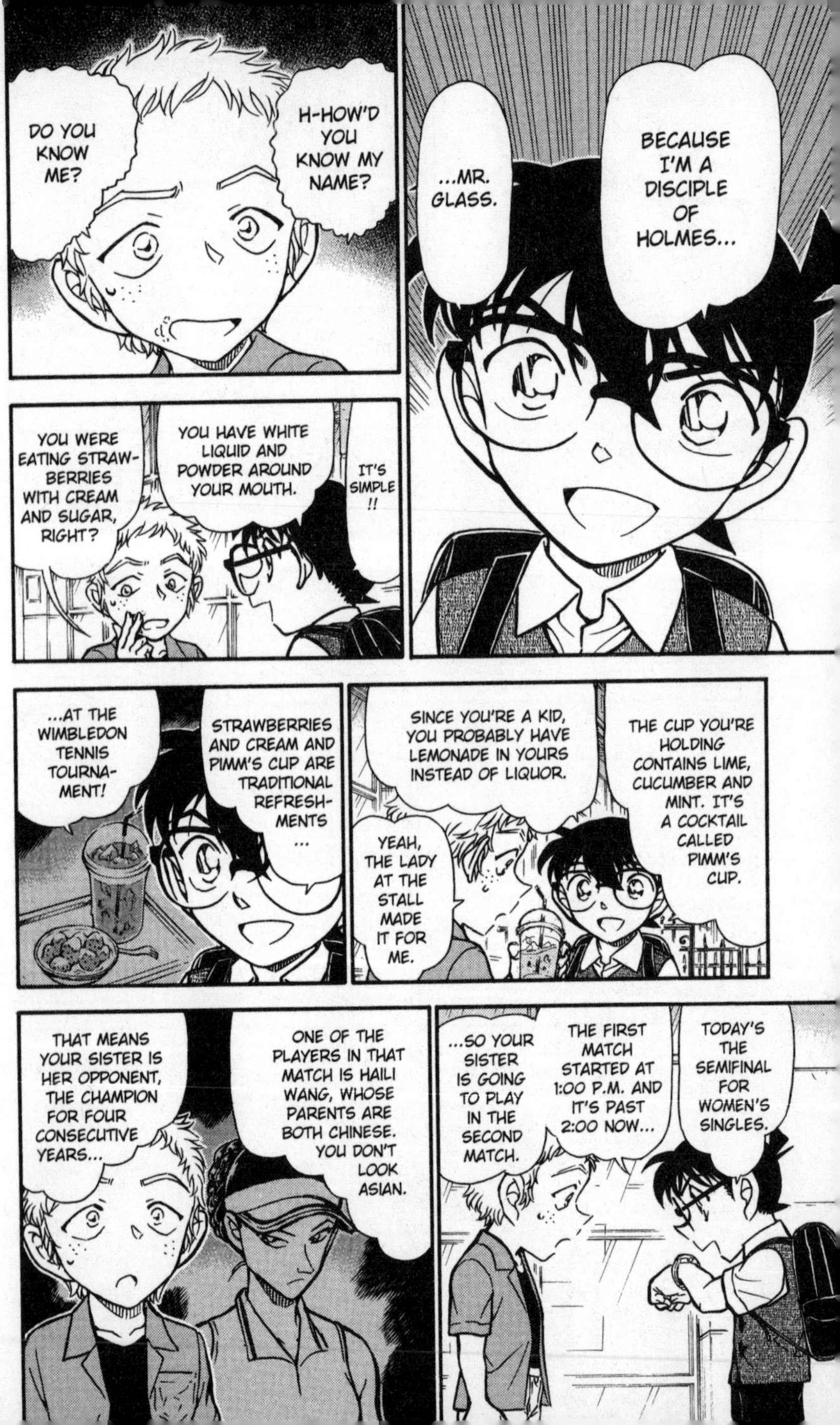
BECAUSE I'M A DISCIPLE OF HOLMES...
...MR. GLASS.
H-HOW'D YOU KNOW MY NAME?
DO YOU KNOW ME?
IT'S SIMPLE!!
YOU HAVE WHITE LIQUID AND POWDER AROUND YOUR MOUTH.
YOU WERE EATING STRAW-BERRIES WITH CREAM AND SUGAR, RIGHT?
THE CUP YOU'RE HOLDING CONTAINS LIME, CUCUMBER AND MINT. IT'S A COCKTAIL CALLED PIMM'S CUP.
SINCE YOU'RE A KID, YOU PROBABLY HAVE LEMONADE IN YOURS INSTEAD OF LIQUOR.
YEAH, THE LADY AT THE STALL MADE IT FOR ME.
STRAWBERRIES AND CREAM AND PIMM'S CUP ARE TRADITIONAL REFRESH-MENTS ...
...AT THE WIMBLEDON TENNIS TOURNA-MENT!
TODAY'S THE SEMIFINAL FOR WOMEN'S SINGLES.
THE FIRST MATCH STARTED AT 1:00 P.M. AND IT'S PAST 2:00 NOW...
...SO YOUR SISTER IS GOING TO PLAY IN THE SECOND MATCH.
ONE OF THE PLAYERS IN THAT MATCH IS HAILI WANG, WHOSE PARENTS ARE BOTH CHINESE. YOU DON'T LOOK ASIAN.
THAT MEANS YOUR SISTER IS HER OPPONENT, THE CHAMPION FOR FOUR CONSECUTIVE YEARS...

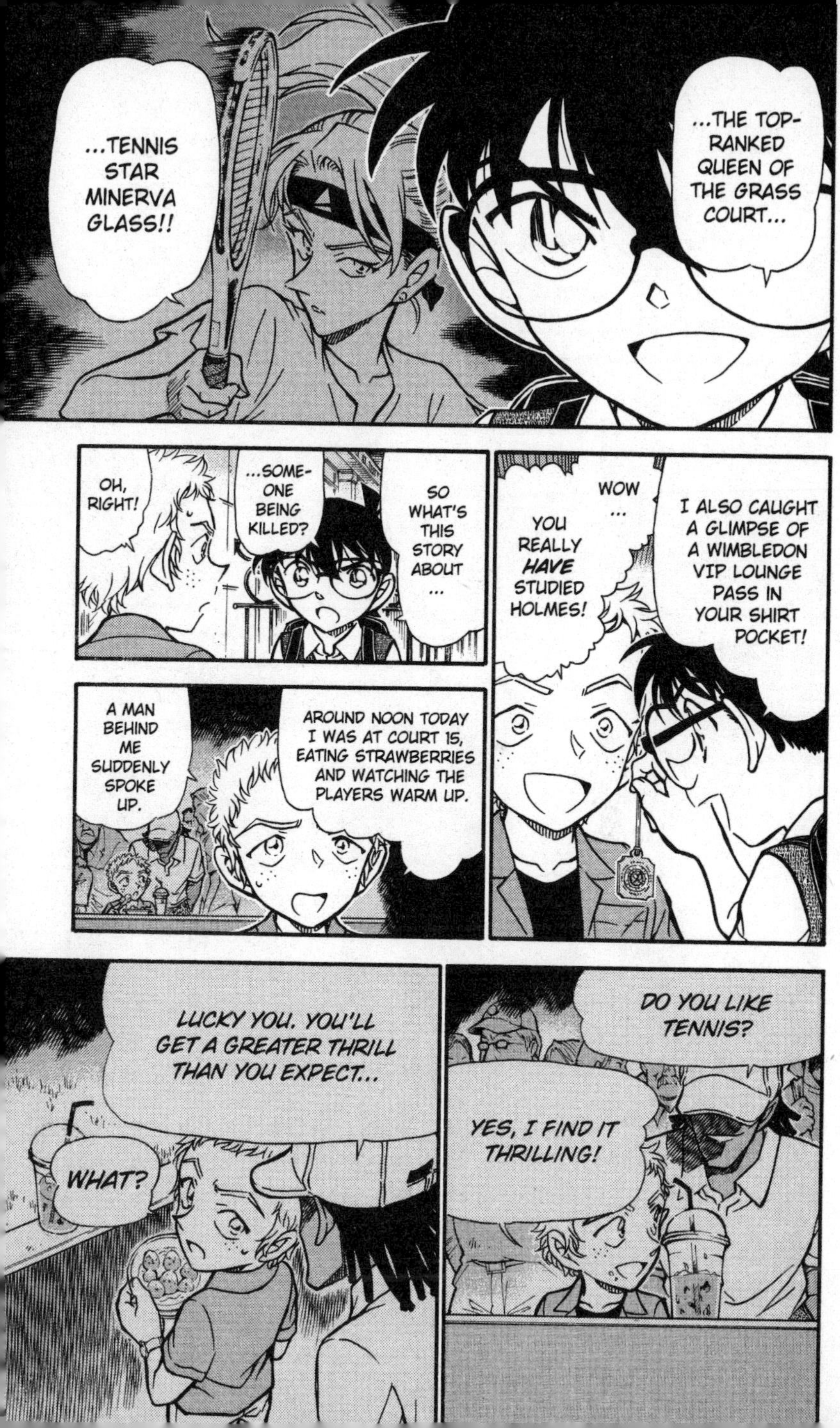
...THE TOP-RANKED QUEEN OF THE GRASS COURT...
...TENNIS STAR MINERVA GLASS!!
I ALSO CAUGHT A GLIMPSE OF A WIMBLEDON VIP LOUNGE PASS IN YOUR SHIRT POCKET!
WOW ...
YOU REALLY *HAVE* STUDIED HOLMES!
SO WHAT'S THIS STORY ABOUT ...
...SOME-ONE BEING KILLED?
OH, RIGHT!
AROUND NOON TODAY I WAS AT COURT 15, EATING STRAWBERRIES AND WATCHING THE PLAYERS WARM UP.
A MAN BEHIND ME SUDDENLY SPOKE UP.
DO YOU LIKE TENNIS?
YES, I FIND IT THRILLING!
LUCKY YOU. YOU'LL GET A GREATER THRILL THAN YOU EXPECT...
WHAT?

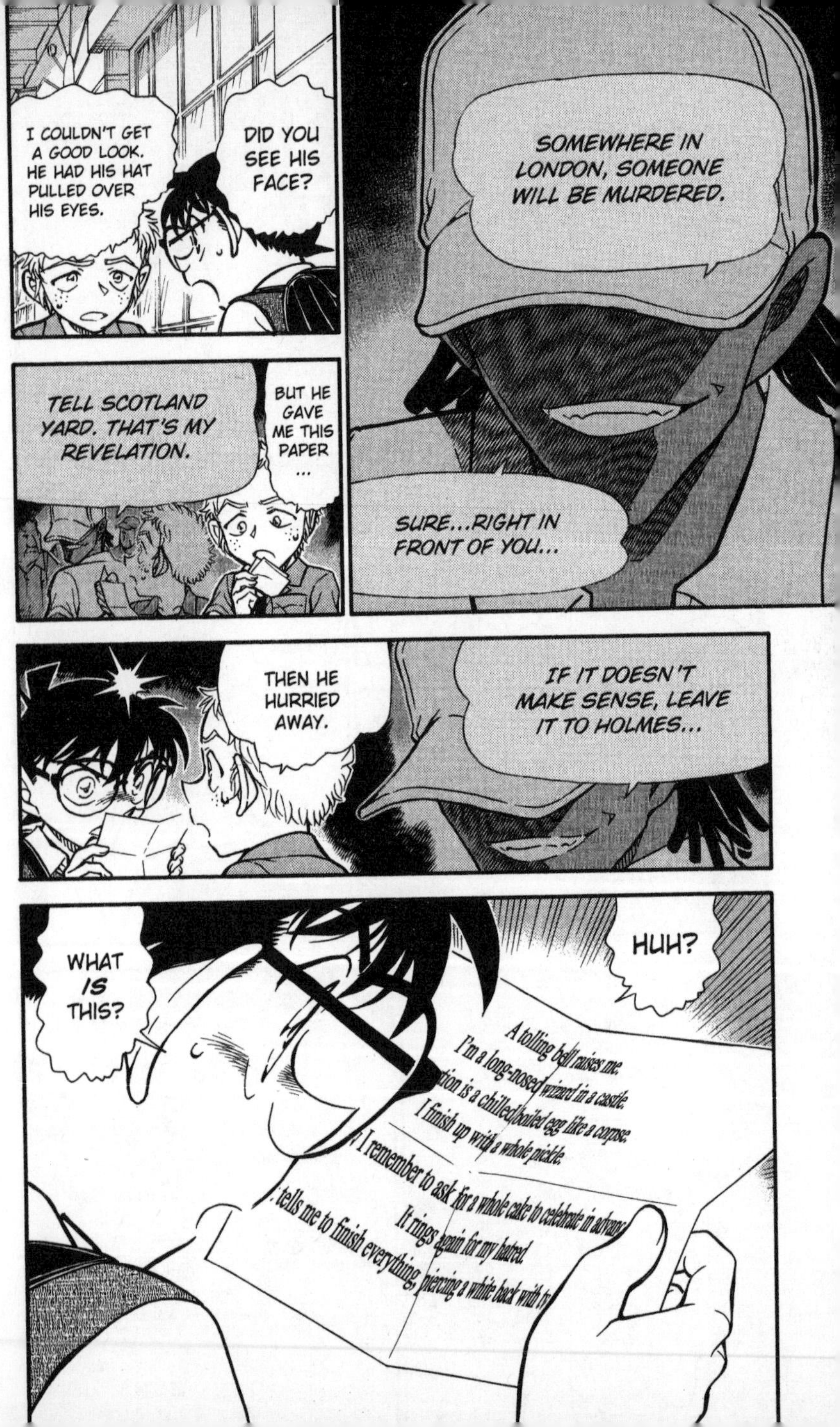
SOMEWHERE IN LONDON, SOMEONE WILL BE MURDERED.
SURE...RIGHT IN FRONT OF YOU...
DID YOU SEE HIS FACE?
I COULDN'T GET A GOOD LOOK. HE HAD HIS HAT PULLED OVER HIS EYES.
TELL SCOTLAND YARD. THAT'S MY REVELATION.
BUT HE GAVE ME THIS PAPER ...
IF IT DOESN'T MAKE SENSE, LEAVE IT TO HOLMES...
THEN HE HURRIED AWAY.
HUH?
WHAT IS THIS?
A tolling bell raises me.
I'm a long-nosed wizard in a castle.
tion is a chilled boiled egg like a corpse.
I finish up with a whole pickle.
I remember to ask for a whole cake to celebrate in advan
It rings again for my hatred.
tells me to finish everything, piercing a white back with t

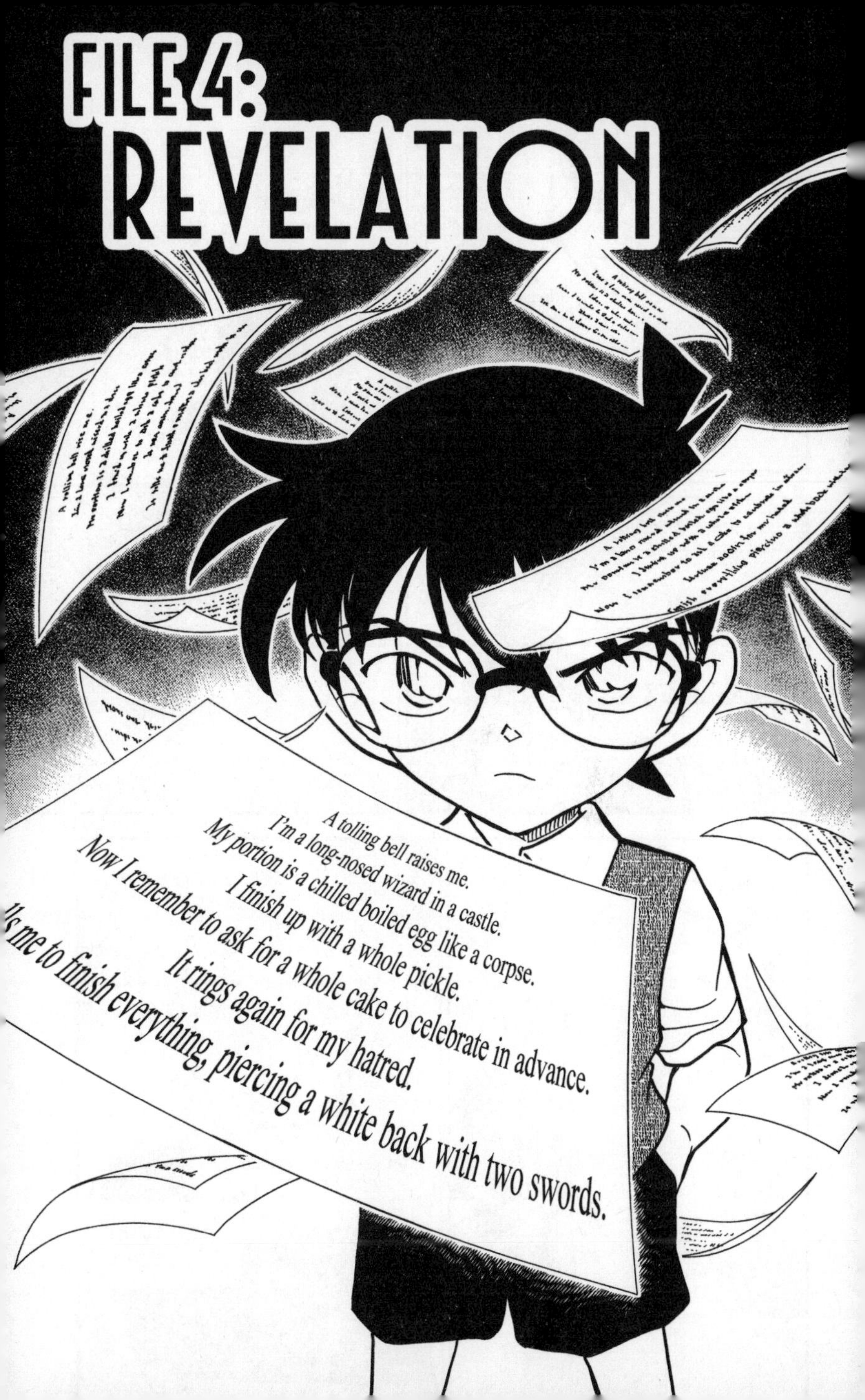
FILE 4:
REVELATION
A tolling bell raises me.
I'm a long-nosed wizard in a castle.
My portion is a chilled boiled egg like a corpse.
I finish up with a whole pickle.
Now I remember to ask for a whole cake to celebrate in advance.
It rings again for my hatred.
lls me to finish everything, piercing a white back with two swords.

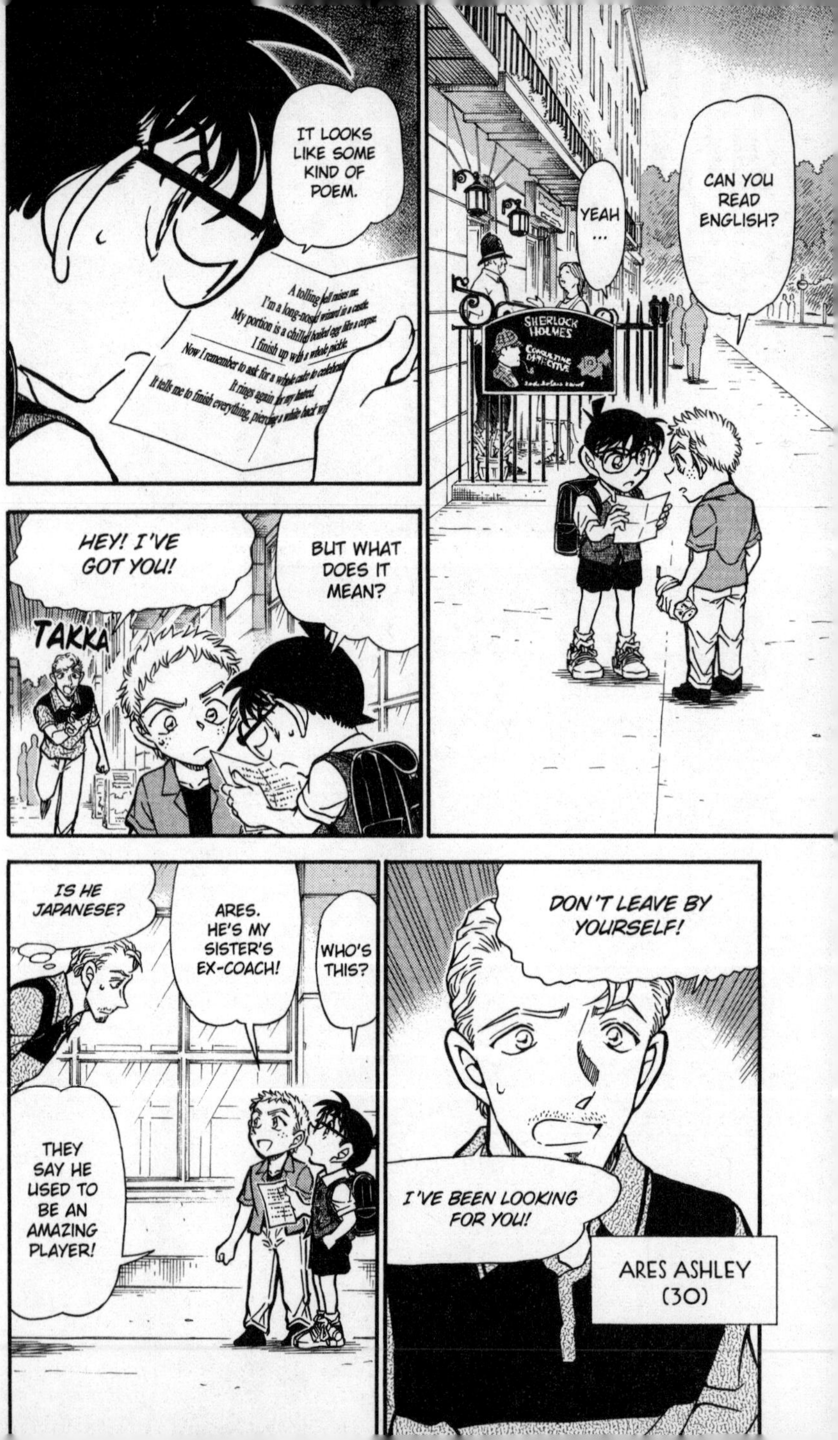
CAN YOU READ ENGLISH?
YEAH ...
SHERLOCK HOLMES
CONSULTING DETECTIVE
IT LOOKS LIKE SOME KIND OF POEM.
A tolling
I'm a long-nosed wizard in a castle.
My portion is a chilled boiled egg like a corpse.
I finish up with a whole pickle.
Now I remember to ask for a whole cafe to
It rings again for my hatred.
It tells me to finish everything, piercing a white back
BUT WHAT DOES IT MEAN?
HEY! I'VE GOT YOU!
TAKKA
DON'T LEAVE BY YOURSELF!
I'VE BEEN LOOKING FOR YOU!
ARES ASHLEY (30)
WHO'S THIS?
ARES. HE'S MY SISTER'S EX-COACH!
IS HE JAPANESE?
THEY SAY HE USED TO BE AN AMAZING PLAYER!

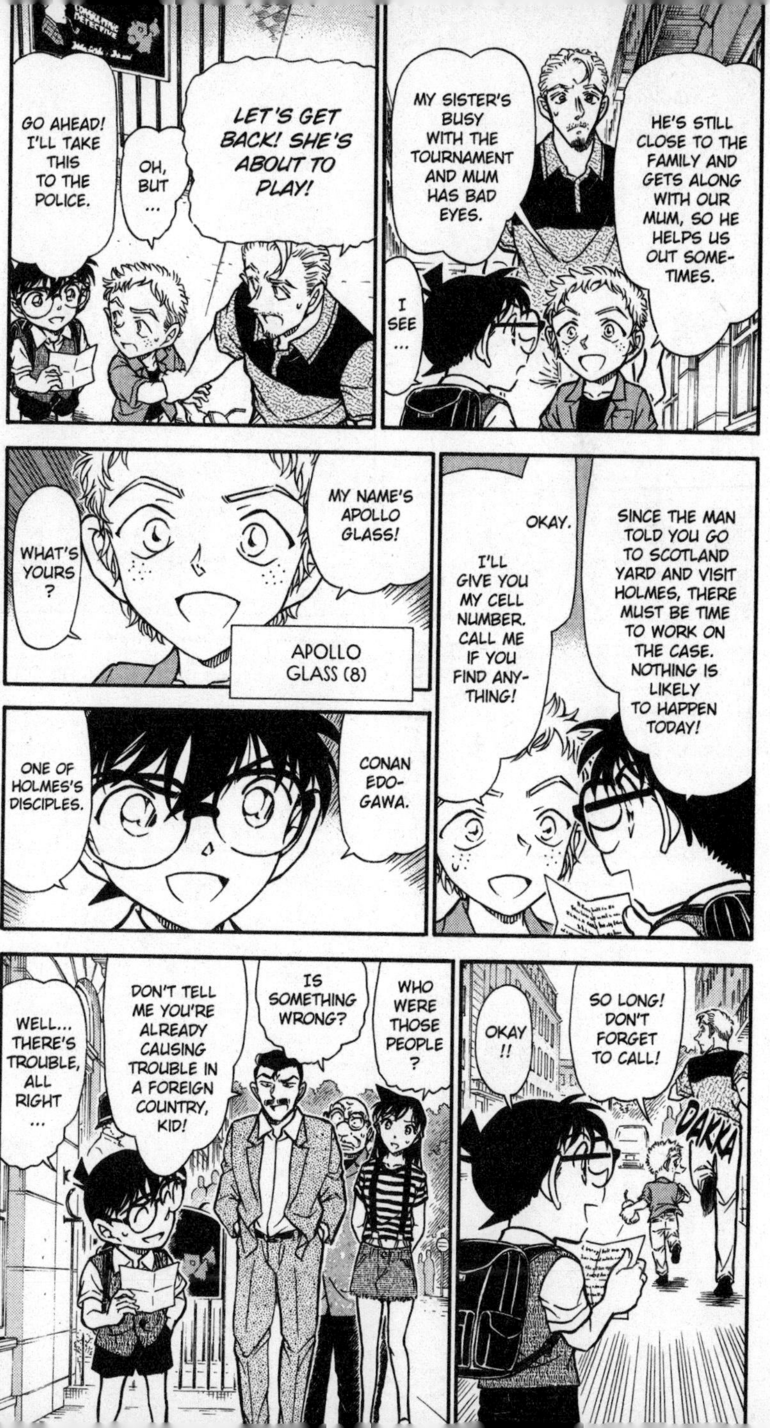
HE'S STILL CLOSE TO THE FAMILY AND GETS ALONG WITH OUR MUM, SO HE HELPS US OUT SOMETIMES.
MY SISTER'S BUSY WITH THE TOURNAMENT AND MUM HAS BAD EYES.
I SEE ...
LET'S GET BACK! SHE'S ABOUT TO PLAY!
OH, BUT ...
GO AHEAD! I'LL TAKE THIS TO THE POLICE.
SINCE THE MAN TOLD YOU GO TO SCOTLAND YARD AND VISIT HOLMES, THERE MUST BE TIME TO WORK ON THE CASE. NOTHING IS LIKELY TO HAPPEN TODAY!
OKAY.
I'LL GIVE YOU MY CELL NUMBER. CALL ME IF YOU FIND ANYTHING!
MY NAME'S APOLLO GLASS!
WHAT'S YOURS ?
APOLLO GLASS (8)
CONAN EDOGAWA.
ONE OF HOLMES'S DISCIPLES.
SO LONG! DON'T FORGET TO CALL!
OKAY !!
DAKKA
WHO WERE THOSE PEOPLE ?
IS SOMETHING WRONG?
DON'T TELL ME YOU'RE ALREADY CAUSING TROUBLE IN A FOREIGN COUNTRY, KID!
WELL... THERE'S TROUBLE, ALL RIGHT ...

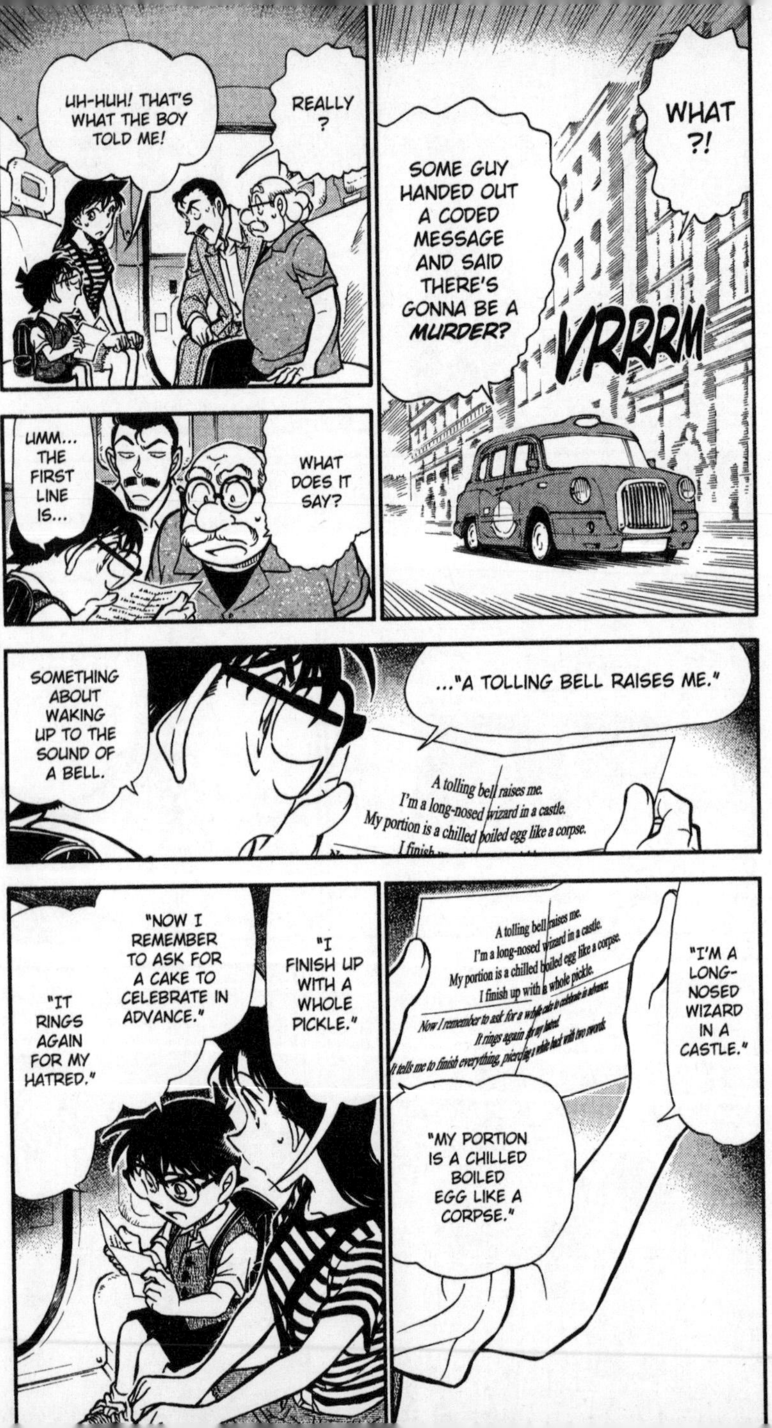
WHAT ?!
SOME GUY HANDED OUT A CODED MESSAGE AND SAID THERE'S GONNA BE A *MURDER?*
VRRRM
REALLY ?
UH-HUH! THAT'S WHAT THE BOY TOLD ME!
WHAT DOES IT SAY?
UMM... THE FIRST LINE IS...
..."A TOLLING BELL RAISES ME."
A tolling bell raises me.
I'm a long-nosed wizard in a castle.
My portion is a chilled boiled egg like a corpse.
SOMETHING ABOUT WAKING UP TO THE SOUND OF A BELL.
"I'M A LONG-NOSED WIZARD IN A CASTLE."
A tolling bell raises me.
I'm a long-nosed wizard in a castle.
My portion is a chilled boiled egg like a corpse.
I finish up with a whole pickle.
Now I remember to ask for a whole cake to celebrate in advance.
It rings again for my hatred.
It tells me to finish everything, piercing a white back with two swords.
"MY PORTION IS A CHILLED BOILED EGG LIKE A CORPSE."
"I FINISH UP WITH A WHOLE PICKLE."
"NOW I REMEMBER TO ASK FOR A CAKE TO CELEBRATE IN ADVANCE."
"IT RINGS AGAIN FOR MY HATRED."

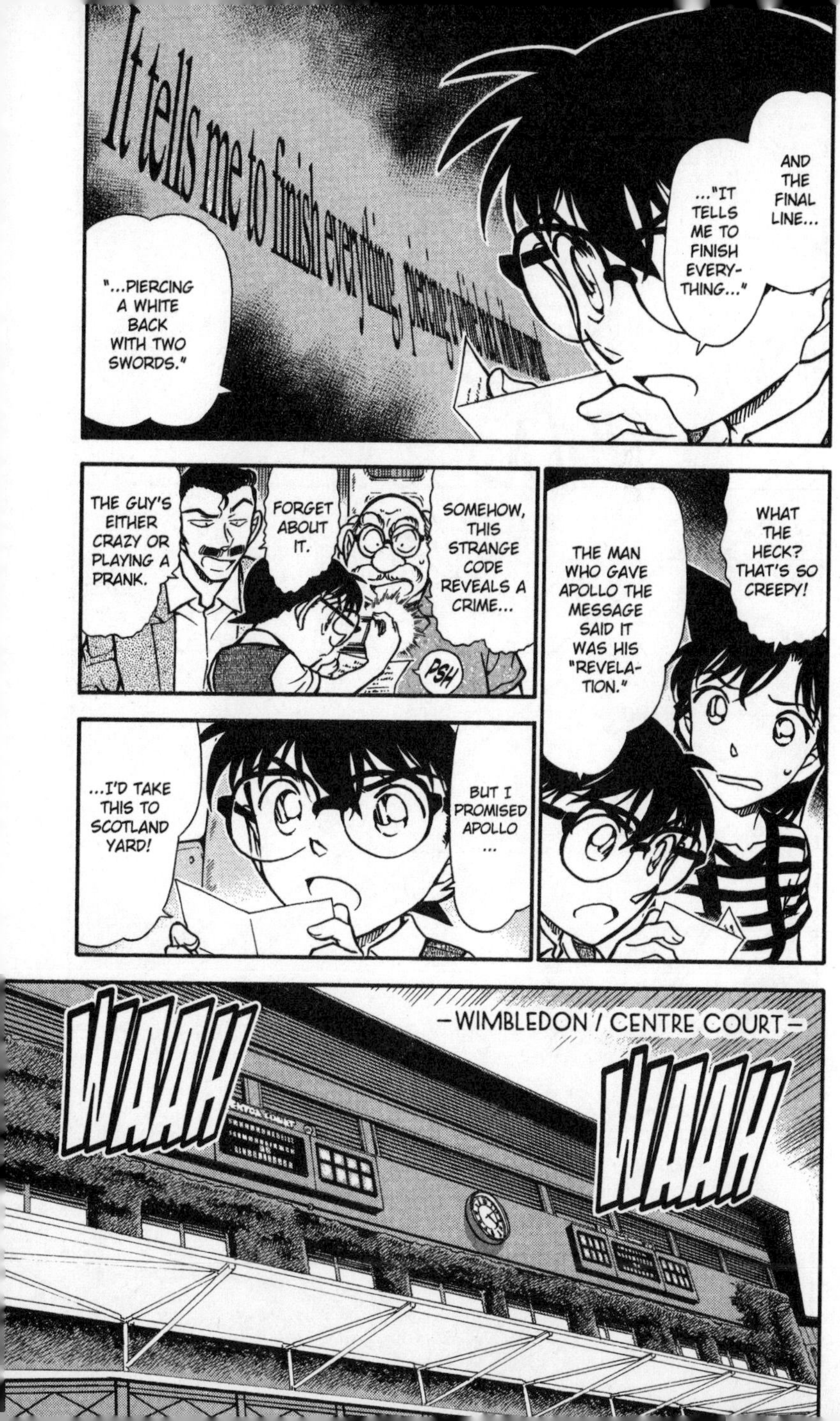
AND THE FINAL LINE...
..."IT TELLS ME TO FINISH EVERYTHING..."
It tells me to finish everything,
"...PIERCING A WHITE BACK WITH TWO SWORDS."
WHAT THE HECK? THAT'S SO CREEPY!
THE MAN WHO GAVE APOLLO THE MESSAGE SAID IT WAS HIS "REVELATION."
SOMEHOW, THIS STRANGE CODE REVEALS A CRIME...
FORGET ABOUT IT.
PSH
THE GUY'S EITHER CRAZY OR PLAYING A PRANK.
BUT I PROMISED APOLLO ...
...I'D TAKE THIS TO SCOTLAND YARD!
WAAAH
-WIMBLEDON / CENTRE COURT-
WAAAH

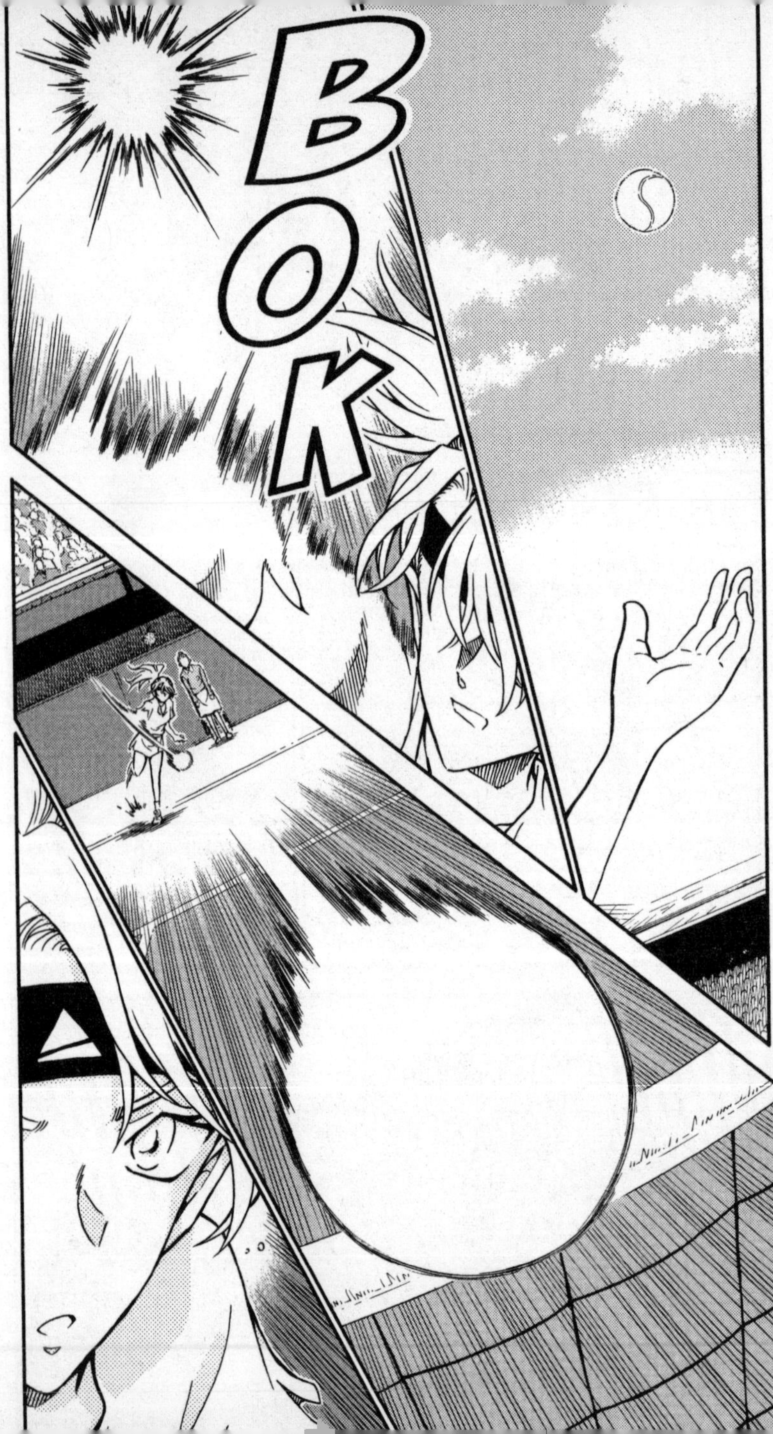
BOK

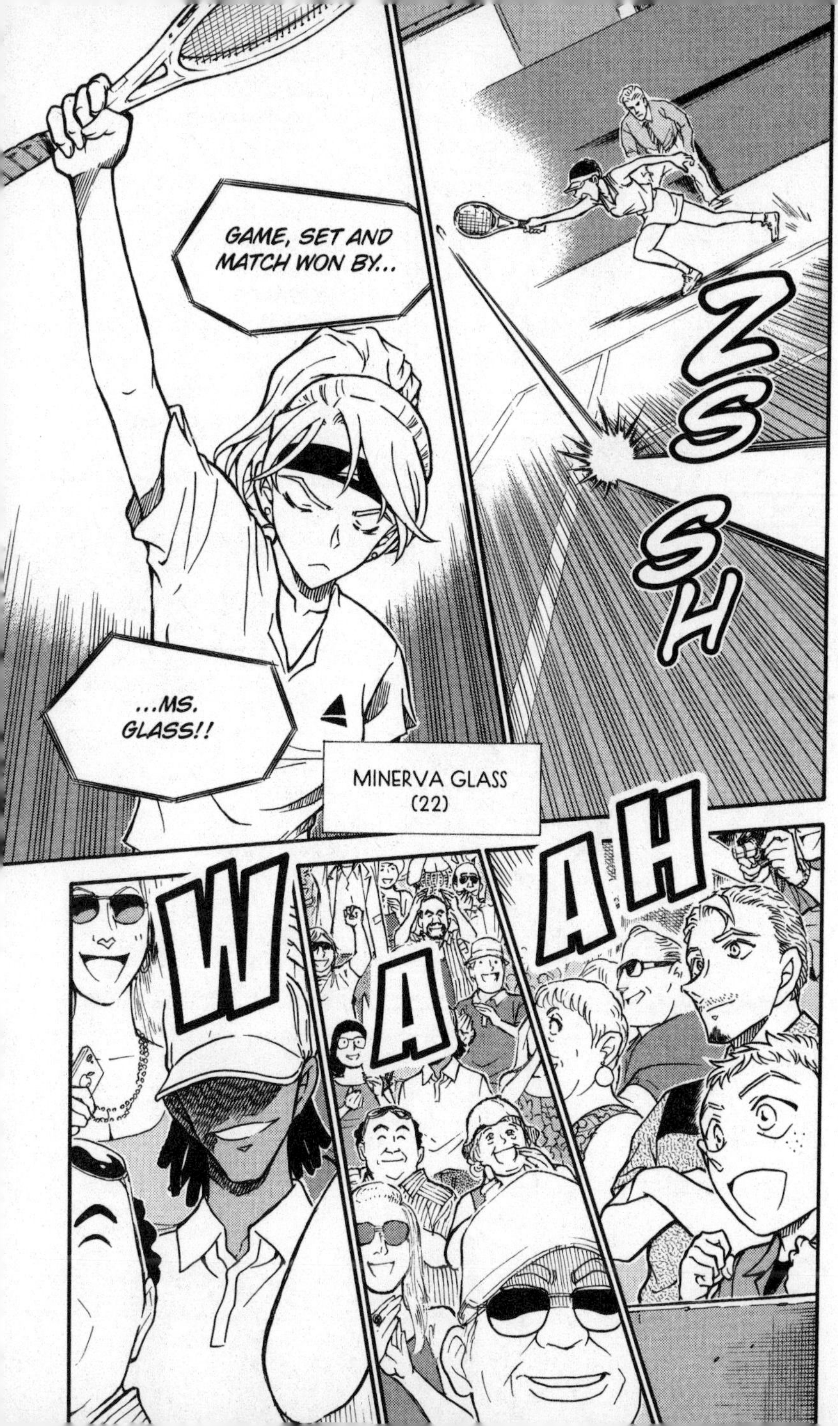
ZSSH
GAME, SET AND MATCH WON BY...
...MS. GLASS!!
MINERVA GLASS (22)
WAAH

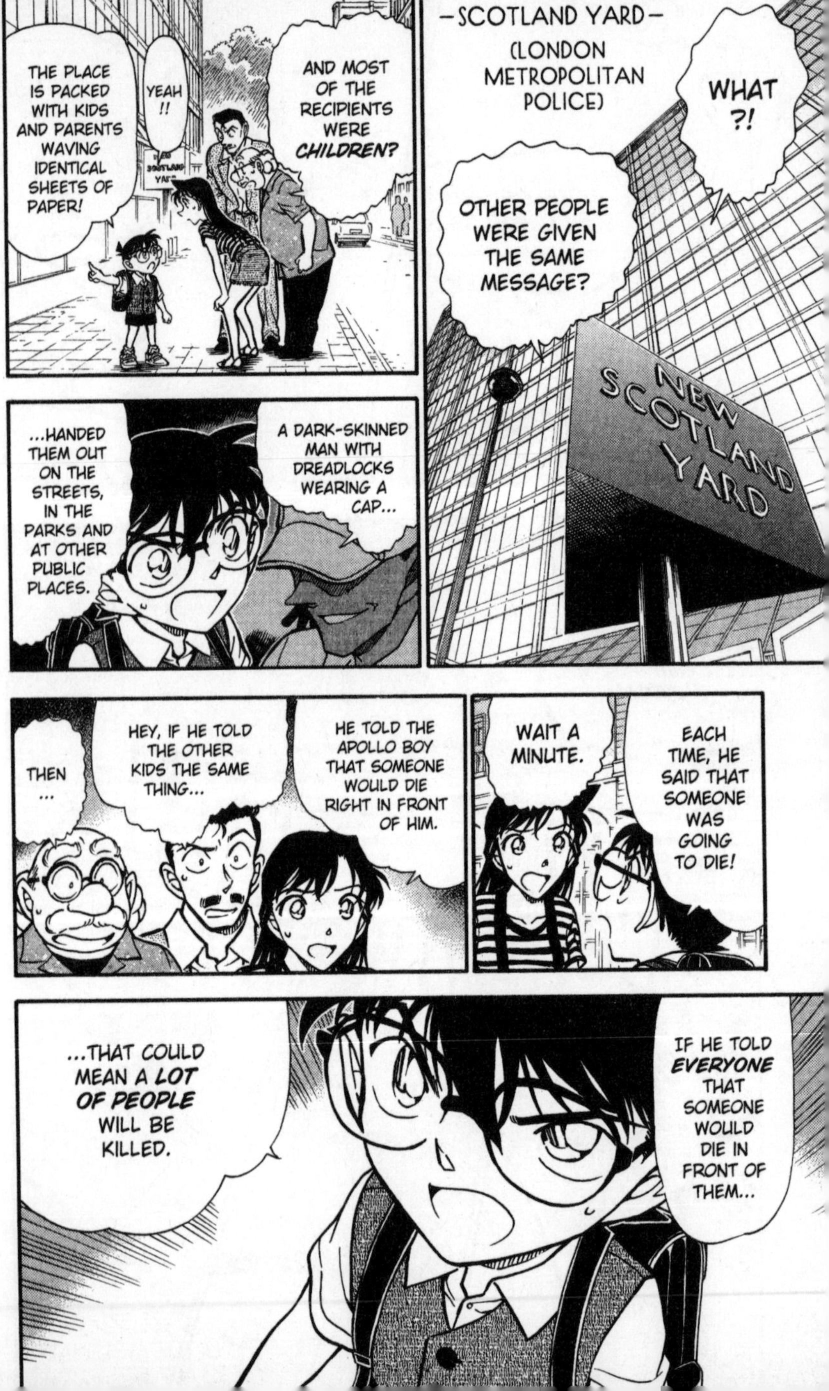

-SCOTLAND YARD-
(LONDON METROPOLITAN POLICE)
WHAT ?!
OTHER PEOPLE WERE GIVEN THE SAME MESSAGE?
NEW SCOTLAND YARD
AND MOST OF THE RECIPIENTS WERE *CHILDREN?*
YEAH !!
THE PLACE IS PACKED WITH KIDS AND PARENTS WAVING IDENTICAL SHEETS OF PAPER!
A DARK-SKINNED MAN WITH DREADLOCKS WEARING A CAP...
...HANDED THEM OUT ON THE STREETS, IN THE PARKS AND AT OTHER PUBLIC PLACES.
EACH TIME, HE SAID THAT SOMEONE WAS GOING TO DIE!
WAIT A MINUTE.
HE TOLD THE APOLLO BOY THAT SOMEONE WOULD DIE RIGHT IN FRONT OF HIM.
HEY, IF HE TOLD THE OTHER KIDS THE SAME THING...
THEN ...
IF HE TOLD *EVERYONE* THAT SOMEONE WOULD DIE IN FRONT OF THEM...
...THAT COULD MEAN A *LOT OF PEOPLE* WILL BE KILLED.

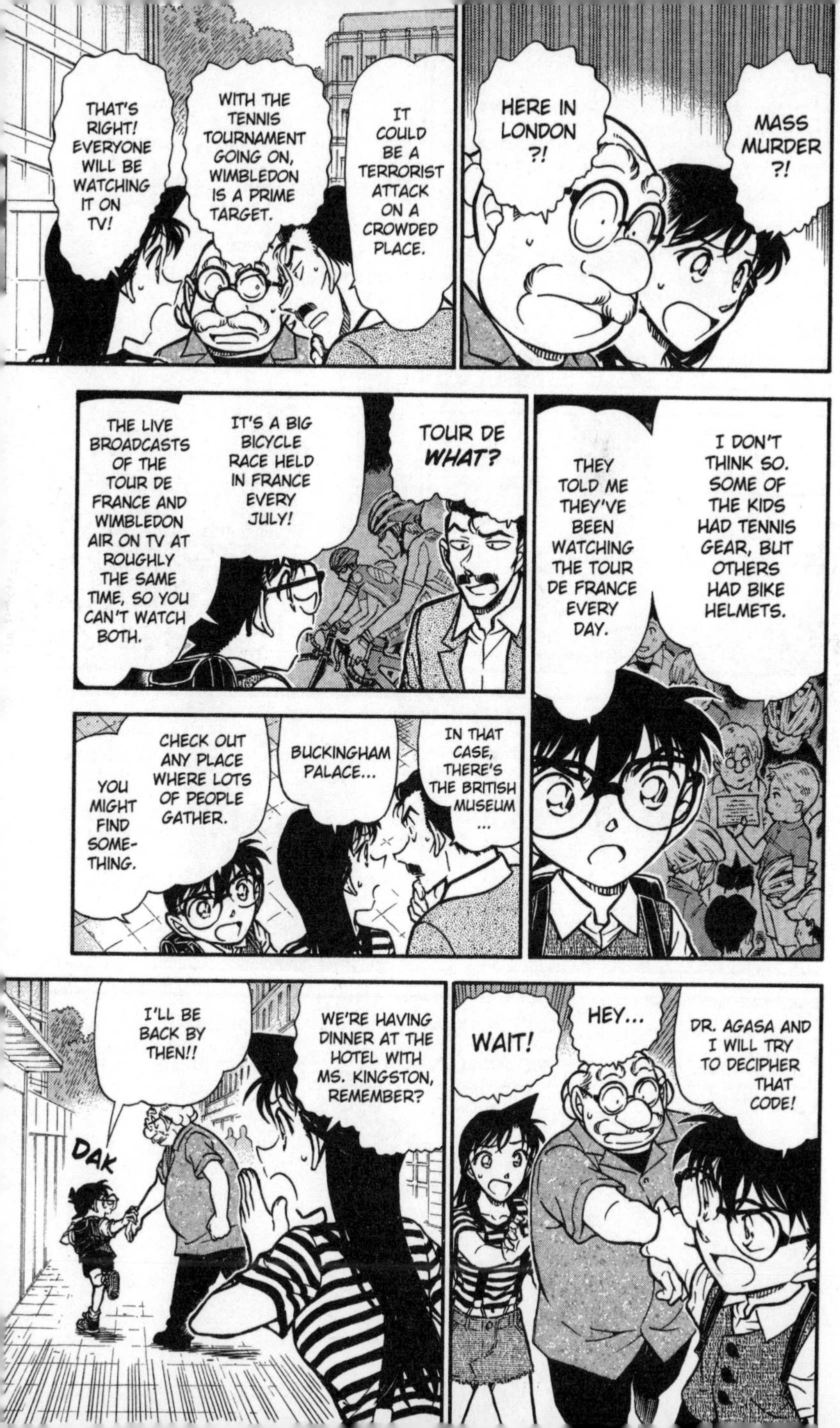
MASS MURDER ?!
HERE IN LONDON ?!
IT COULD BE A TERRORIST ATTACK ON A CROWDED PLACE.
WITH THE TENNIS TOURNAMENT GOING ON, WIMBLEDON IS A PRIME TARGET.
THAT'S RIGHT! EVERYONE WILL BE WATCHING IT ON TV!
I DON'T THINK SO. SOME OF THE KIDS HAD TENNIS GEAR, BUT OTHERS HAD BIKE HELMETS.
THEY TOLD ME THEY'VE BEEN WATCHING THE TOUR DE FRANCE EVERY DAY.
TOUR DE *WHAT?*
IT'S A BIG BICYCLE RACE HELD IN FRANCE EVERY JULY!
THE LIVE BROADCASTS OF THE TOUR DE FRANCE AND WIMBLEDON AIR ON TV AT ROUGHLY THE SAME TIME, SO YOU CAN'T WATCH BOTH.
IN THAT CASE, THERE'S THE BRITISH MUSEUM ...
BUCKINGHAM PALACE...
CHECK OUT ANY PLACE WHERE LOTS OF PEOPLE GATHER.
YOU MIGHT FIND SOME-THING.
DR. AGASA AND I WILL TRY TO DECIPHER THAT CODE!
HEY...
WAIT!
WE'RE HAVING DINNER AT THE HOTEL WITH MS. KINGSTON, REMEMBER?
I'LL BE BACK BY THEN!!
DAK

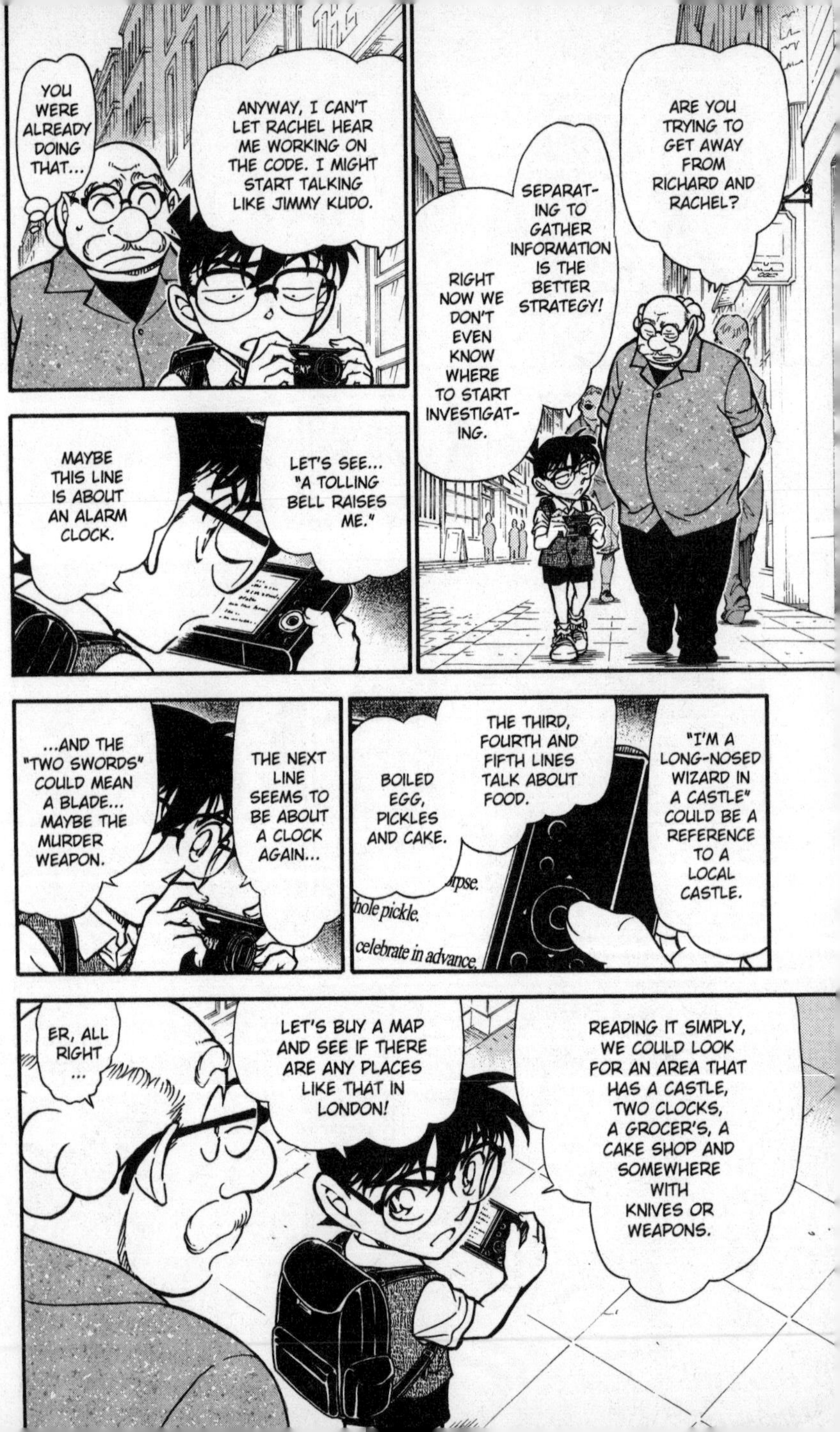
ARE YOU TRYING TO GET AWAY FROM RICHARD AND RACHEL?
SEPARATING TO GATHER INFORMATION IS THE BETTER STRATEGY!
RIGHT NOW WE DON'T EVEN KNOW WHERE TO START INVESTIGATING.
ANYWAY, I CAN'T LET RACHEL HEAR ME WORKING ON THE CODE. I MIGHT START TALKING LIKE JIMMY KUDO.
YOU WERE ALREADY DOING THAT...
LET'S SEE... "A TOLLING BELL RAISES ME."
MAYBE THIS LINE IS ABOUT AN ALARM CLOCK.
"I'M A LONG-NOSED WIZARD IN A CASTLE" COULD BE A REFERENCE TO A LOCAL CASTLE.
THE THIRD, FOURTH AND FIFTH LINES TALK ABOUT FOOD.
BOILED EGG, PICKLES AND CAKE.
orpse.
hole pickle.
celebrate in advance.
THE NEXT LINE SEEMS TO BE ABOUT A CLOCK AGAIN...
...AND THE "TWO SWORDS" COULD MEAN A BLADE... MAYBE THE MURDER WEAPON.
READING IT SIMPLY, WE COULD LOOK FOR AN AREA THAT HAS A CASTLE, TWO CLOCKS, A GROCER'S, A CAKE SHOP AND SOMEWHERE WITH KNIVES OR WEAPONS.
LET'S BUY A MAP AND SEE IF THERE ARE ANY PLACES LIKE THAT IN LONDON!
ER, ALL RIGHT...

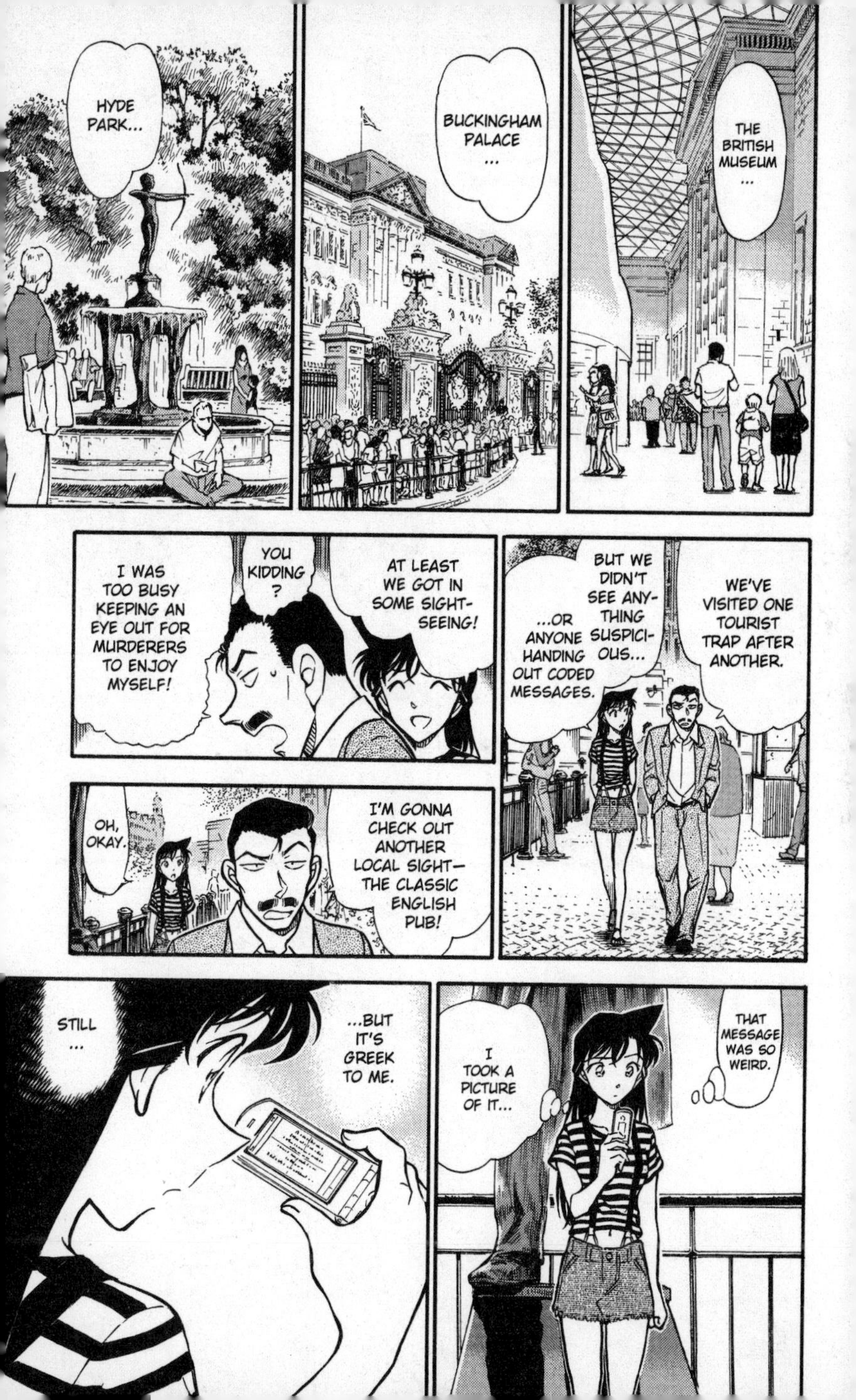
THE BRITISH MUSEUM ...
BUCKINGHAM PALACE ...
HYDE PARK...
WE'VE VISITED ONE TOURIST TRAP AFTER ANOTHER.
BUT WE DIDN'T SEE ANYTHING SUSPICIOUS...
...OR ANYONE HANDING OUT CODED MESSAGES.
AT LEAST WE GOT IN SOME SIGHT-SEEING!
YOU KIDDING?
I WAS TOO BUSY KEEPING AN EYE OUT FOR MURDERERS TO ENJOY MYSELF!
I'M GONNA CHECK OUT ANOTHER LOCAL SIGHT— THE CLASSIC ENGLISH PUB!
OH, OKAY.
THAT MESSAGE WAS SO WEIRD.
I TOOK A PICTURE OF IT...
...BUT IT'S GREEK TO ME.
STILL ...

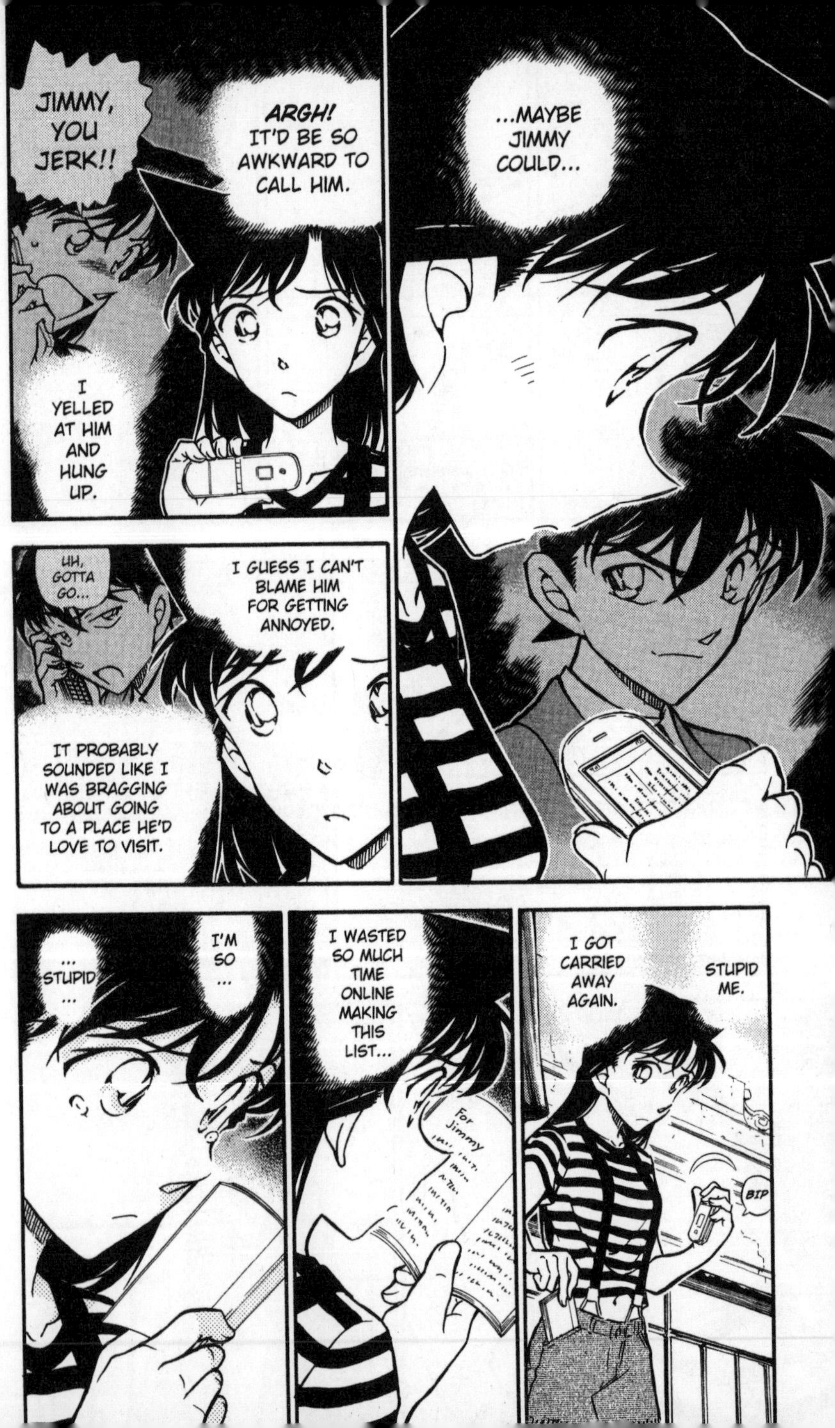
...MAYBE JIMMY COULD...
ARGH! IT'D BE SO AWKWARD TO CALL HIM.
JIMMY, YOU JERK!!
I YELLED AT HIM AND HUNG UP.
I GUESS I CAN'T BLAME HIM FOR GETTING ANNOYED.
UH, GOTTA GO...
IT PROBABLY SOUNDED LIKE I WAS BRAGGING ABOUT GOING TO A PLACE HE'D LOVE TO VISIT.
STUPID ME.
I GOT CARRIED AWAY AGAIN.
BIP
I WASTED SO MUCH TIME ONLINE MAKING THIS LIST...
For Jimmy
I'M SO ...
... STUPID ...

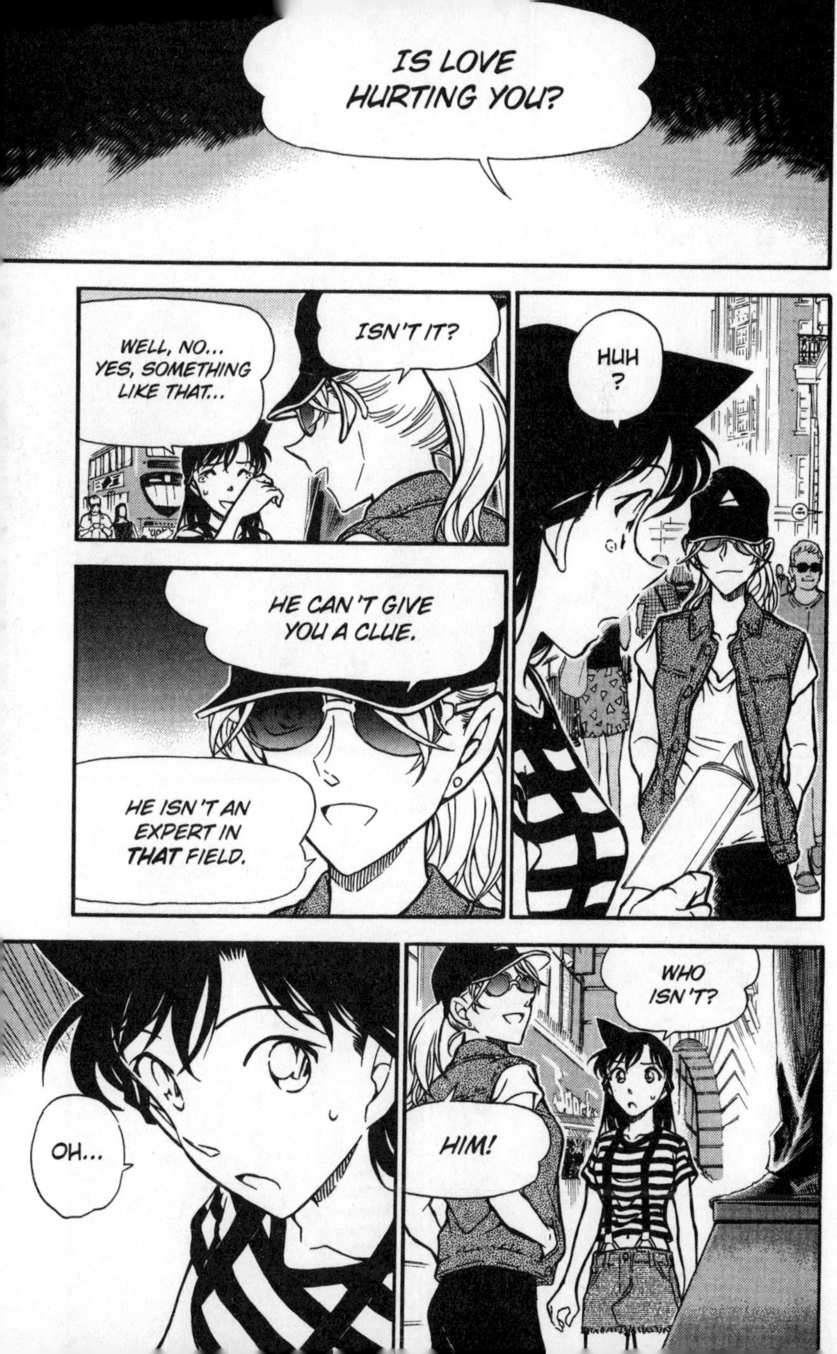
IS LOVE HURTING YOU?
HUH ?
ISN'T IT?
WELL, NO... YES, SOMETHING LIKE THAT...
HE CAN'T GIVE YOU A CLUE.
HE ISN'T AN EXPERT IN THAT FIELD.
WHO ISN'T?
HIM!
OH...

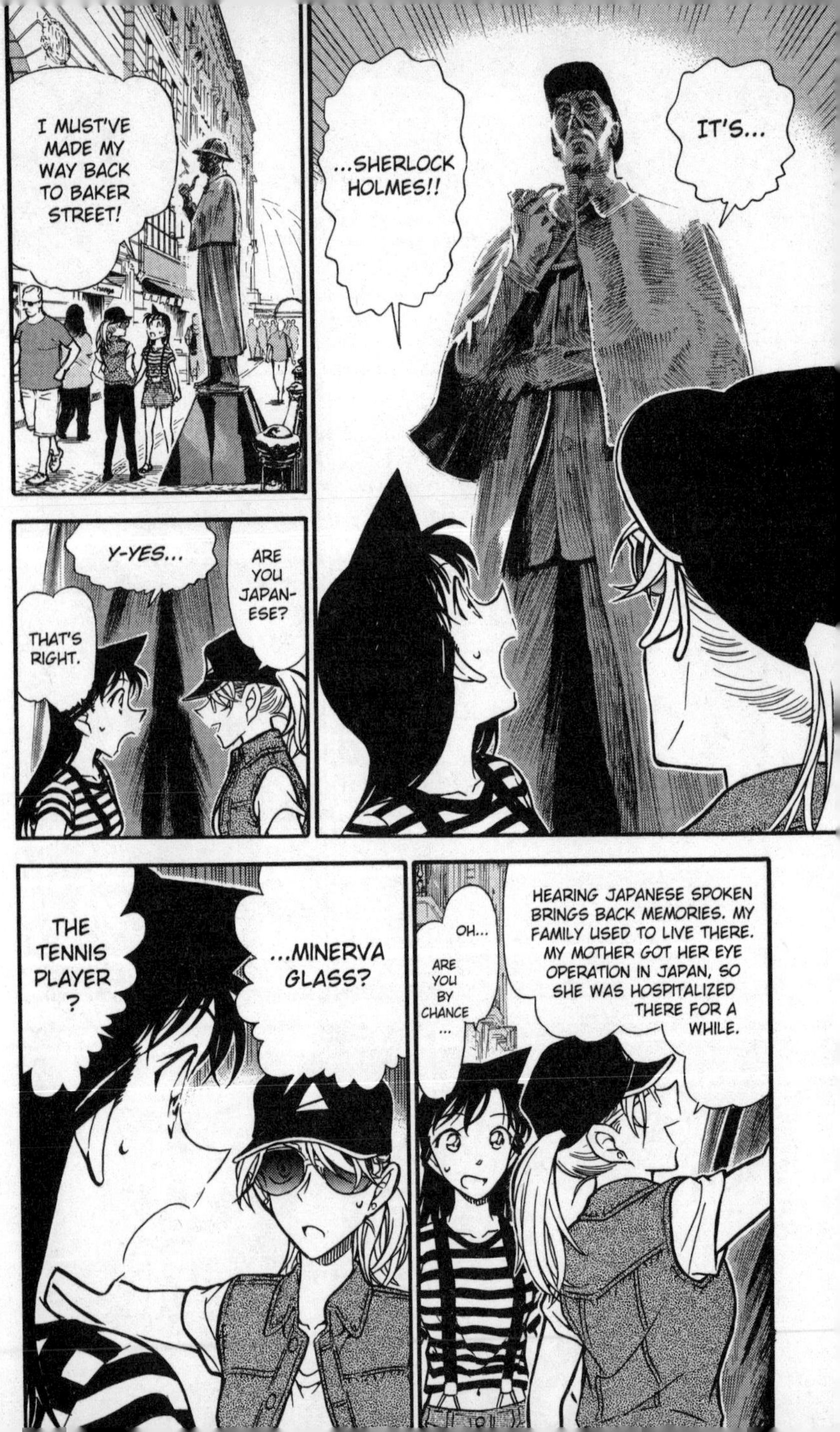
IT'S...
...SHERLOCK HOLMES!!
I MUST'VE MADE MY WAY BACK TO BAKER STREET!
ARE YOU JAPANESE?
Y-YES...
THAT'S RIGHT.
HEARING JAPANESE SPOKEN BRINGS BACK MEMORIES. MY FAMILY USED TO LIVE THERE. MY MOTHER GOT HER EYE OPERATION IN JAPAN, SO SHE WAS HOSPITALIZED THERE FOR A WHILE.
OH...
ARE YOU BY CHANCE ...
...MINERVA GLASS?
THE TENNIS PLAYER ?

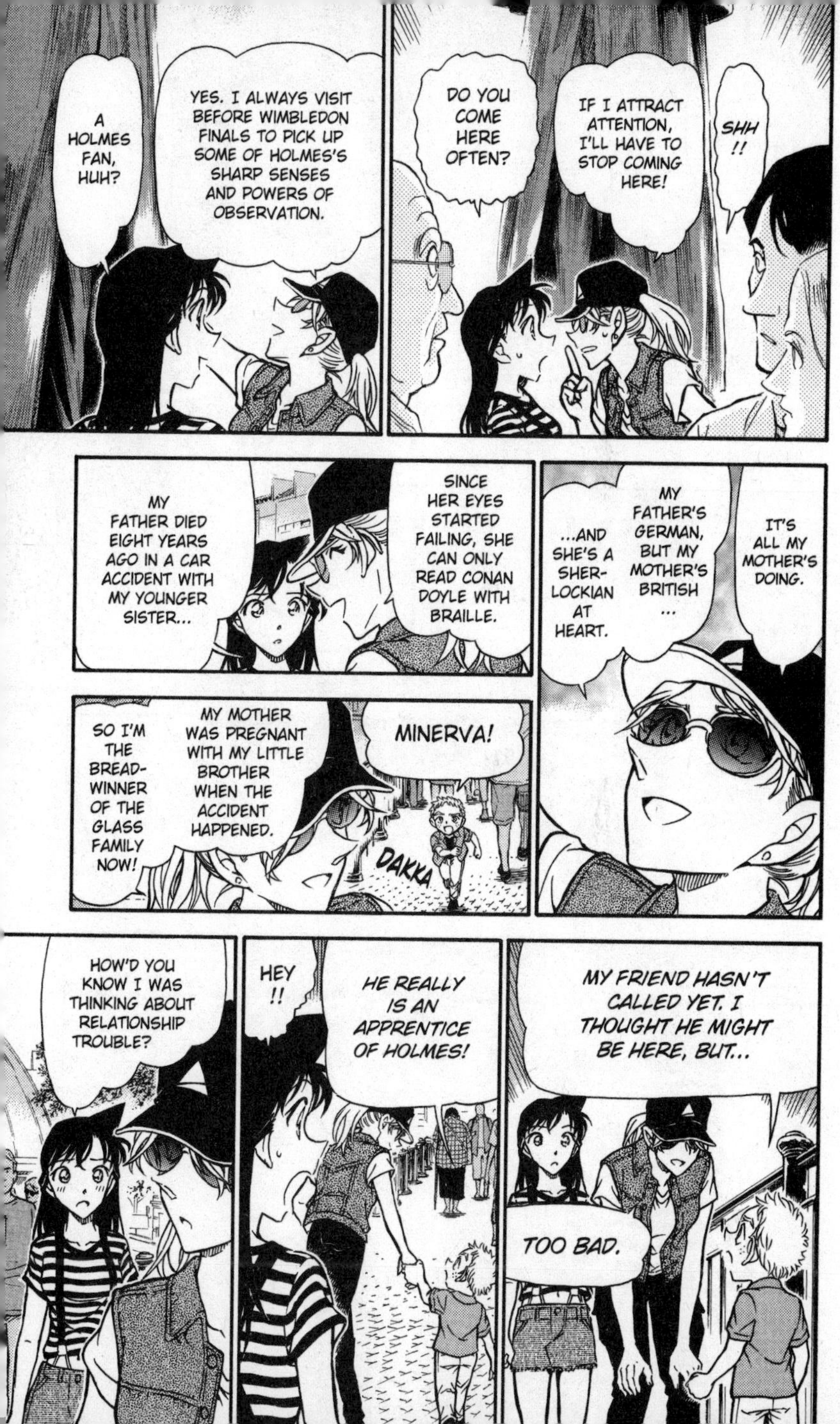
SHH !!
IF I ATTRACT ATTENTION, I'LL HAVE TO STOP COMING HERE!
DO YOU COME HERE OFTEN?
YES. I ALWAYS VISIT BEFORE WIMBLEDON FINALS TO PICK UP SOME OF HOLMES'S SHARP SENSES AND POWERS OF OBSERVATION.
A HOLMES FAN, HUH?
IT'S ALL MY MOTHER'S DOING.
MY FATHER'S GERMAN, BUT MY MOTHER'S BRITISH ...
...AND SHE'S A SHER-LOCKIAN AT HEART.
SINCE HER EYES STARTED FAILING, SHE CAN ONLY READ CONAN DOYLE WITH BRAILLE.
MY FATHER DIED EIGHT YEARS AGO IN A CAR ACCIDENT WITH MY YOUNGER SISTER...
MINERVA!
MY MOTHER WAS PREGNANT WITH MY LITTLE BROTHER WHEN THE ACCIDENT HAPPENED.
SO I'M THE BREAD-WINNER OF THE GLASS FAMILY NOW!
DAKKA
MY FRIEND HASN'T CALLED YET. I THOUGHT HE MIGHT BE HERE, BUT...
TOO BAD.
HE REALLY IS AN APPRENTICE OF HOLMES!
HEY !!
HOW'D YOU KNOW I WAS THINKING ABOUT RELATIONSHIP TROUBLE?

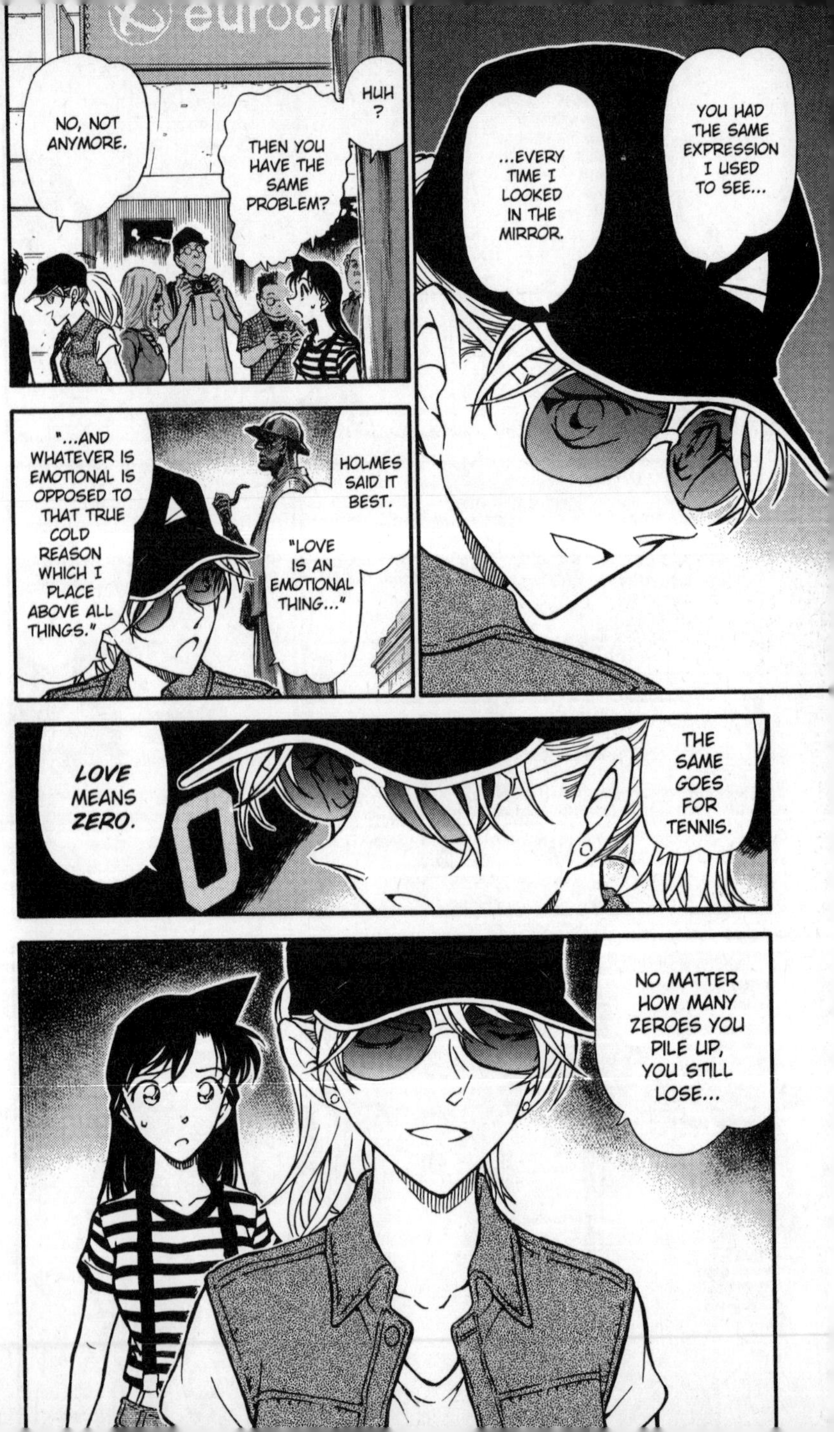
YOU HAD THE SAME EXPRESSION I USED TO SEE...
...EVERY TIME I LOOKED IN THE MIRROR.
HUH ?
THEN YOU HAVE THE SAME PROBLEM?
NO, NOT ANYMORE.
HOLMES SAID IT BEST.
"LOVE IS AN EMOTIONAL THING..."
"...AND WHATEVER IS EMOTIONAL IS OPPOSED TO THAT TRUE COLD REASON WHICH I PLACE ABOVE ALL THINGS."
THE SAME GOES FOR TENNIS.
0
LOVE MEANS *ZERO*.
NO MATTER HOW MANY ZEROES YOU PILE UP, YOU STILL LOSE...

LOVE MEANS ZERO

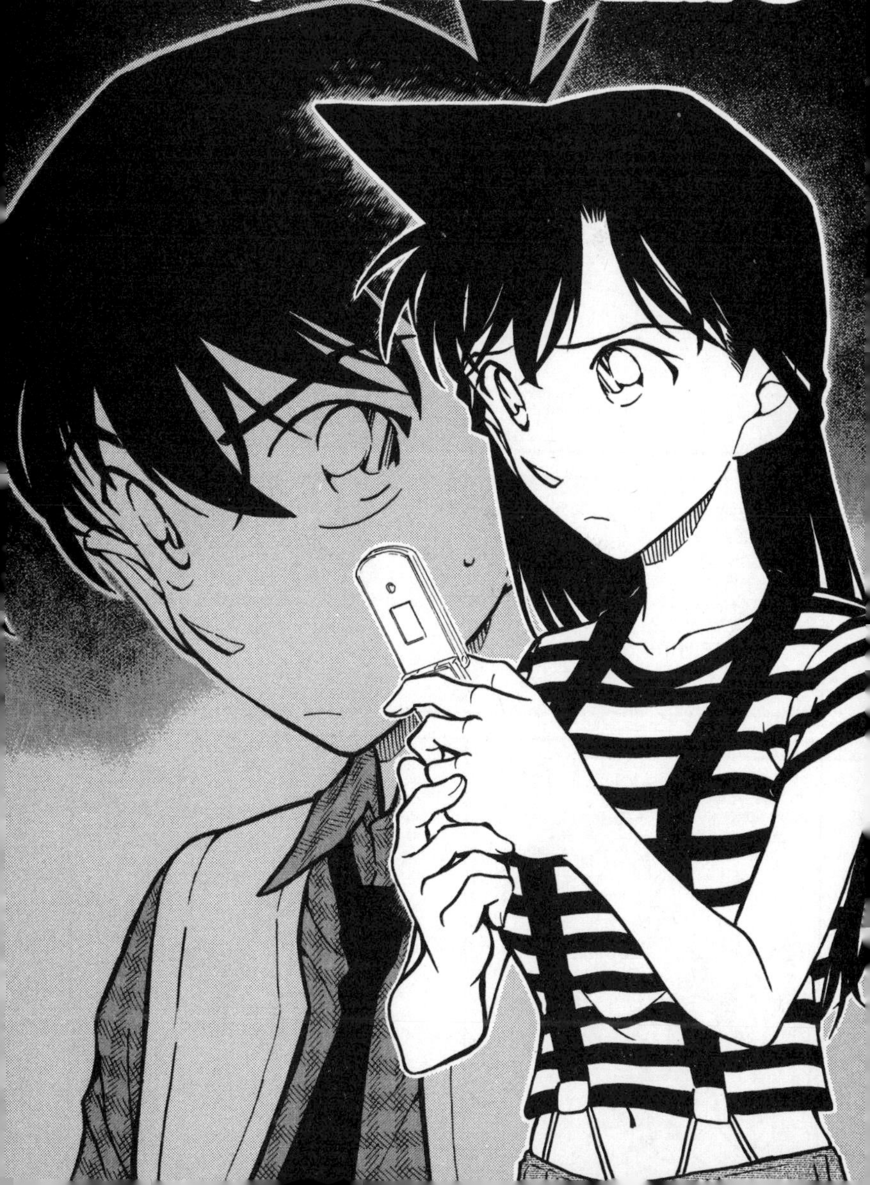

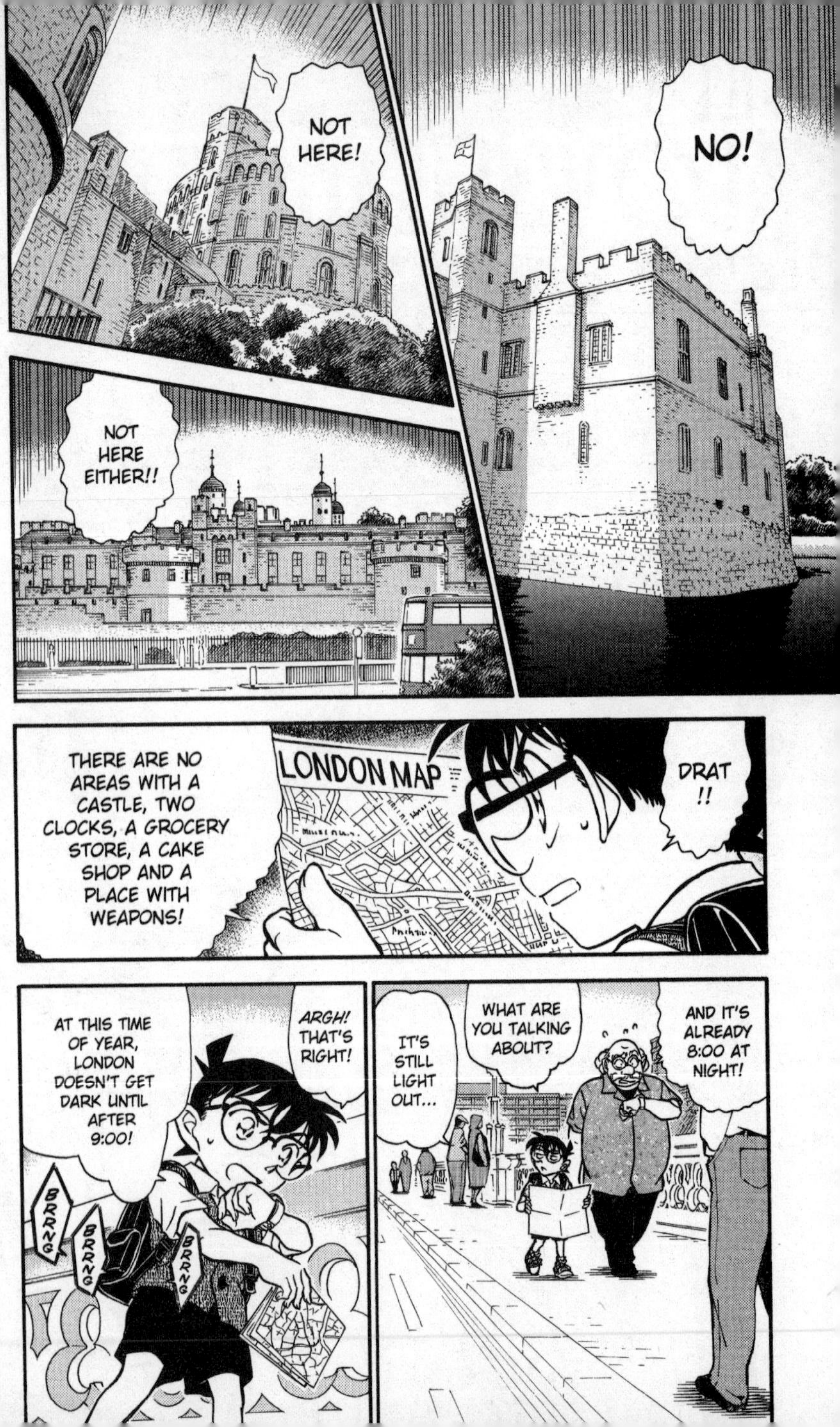
NO!
NOT HERE!
NOT HERE EITHER!!
DRAT!!
LONDON MAP
THERE ARE NO AREAS WITH A CASTLE, TWO CLOCKS, A GROCERY STORE, A CAKE SHOP AND A PLACE WITH WEAPONS!
AND IT'S ALREADY 8:00 AT NIGHT!
WHAT ARE YOU TALKING ABOUT?
IT'S STILL LIGHT OUT...
ARGH! THAT'S RIGHT!
AT THIS TIME OF YEAR, LONDON DOESN'T GET DARK UNTIL AFTER 9:00!
BRRNG
BRRNG
BRRNG

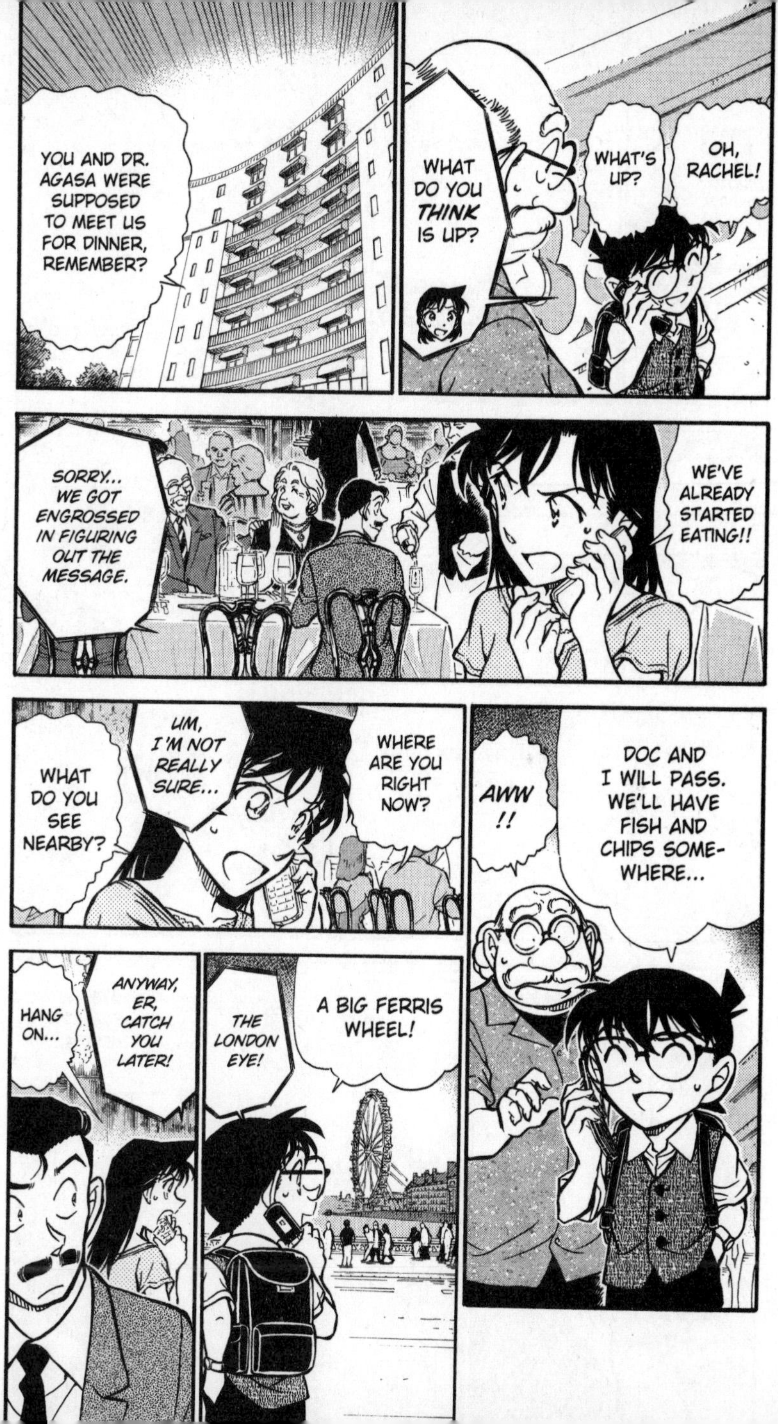
OH, RACHEL!
WHAT'S UP?
WHAT DO YOU *THINK* IS UP?
YOU AND DR. AGASA WERE SUPPOSED TO MEET US FOR DINNER, REMEMBER?
WE'VE ALREADY STARTED EATING!!
SORRY... WE GOT ENGROSSED IN FIGURING OUT THE MESSAGE.
DOC AND I WILL PASS. WE'LL HAVE FISH AND CHIPS SOME-WHERE...
AWW!!
WHERE ARE YOU RIGHT NOW?
UM, I'M NOT REALLY SURE...
WHAT DO YOU SEE NEARBY?
A BIG FERRIS WHEEL!
THE LONDON EYE!
ANYWAY, ER, CATCH YOU LATER!
HANG ON...

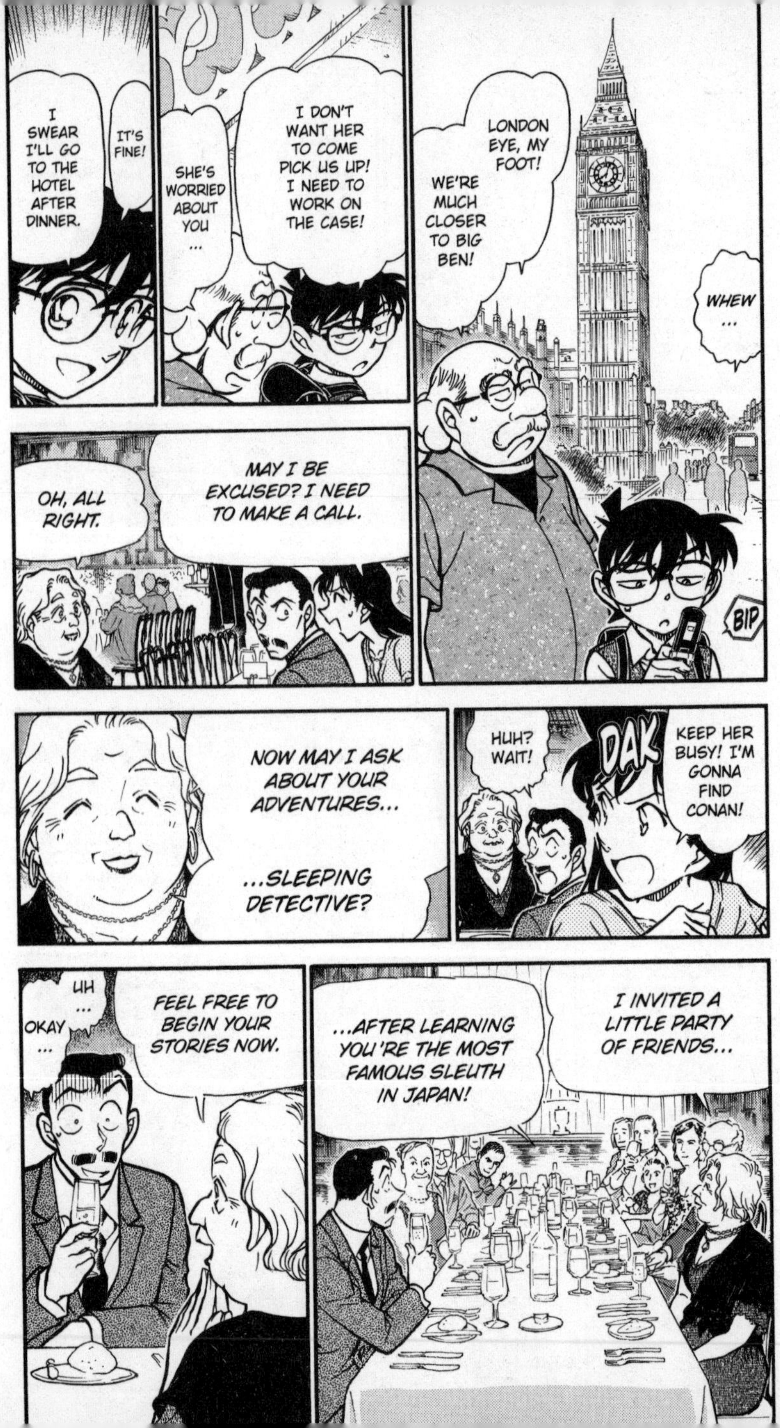
LONDON EYE, MY FOOT!
WE'RE MUCH CLOSER TO BIG BEN!
WHEW ...
BIP
I DON'T WANT HER TO COME PICK US UP! I NEED TO WORK ON THE CASE!
SHE'S WORRIED ABOUT YOU ...
IT'S FINE!
I SWEAR I'LL GO TO THE HOTEL AFTER DINNER.
MAY I BE EXCUSED? I NEED TO MAKE A CALL.
OH, ALL RIGHT.
KEEP HER BUSY! I'M GONNA FIND CONAN!
DAK
HUH? WAIT!
NOW MAY I ASK ABOUT YOUR ADVENTURES...
...SLEEPING DETECTIVE?
I INVITED A LITTLE PARTY OF FRIENDS...
...AFTER LEARNING YOU'RE THE MOST FAMOUS SLEUTH IN JAPAN!
FEEL FREE TO BEGIN YOUR STORIES NOW.
UH ...
OKAY ...

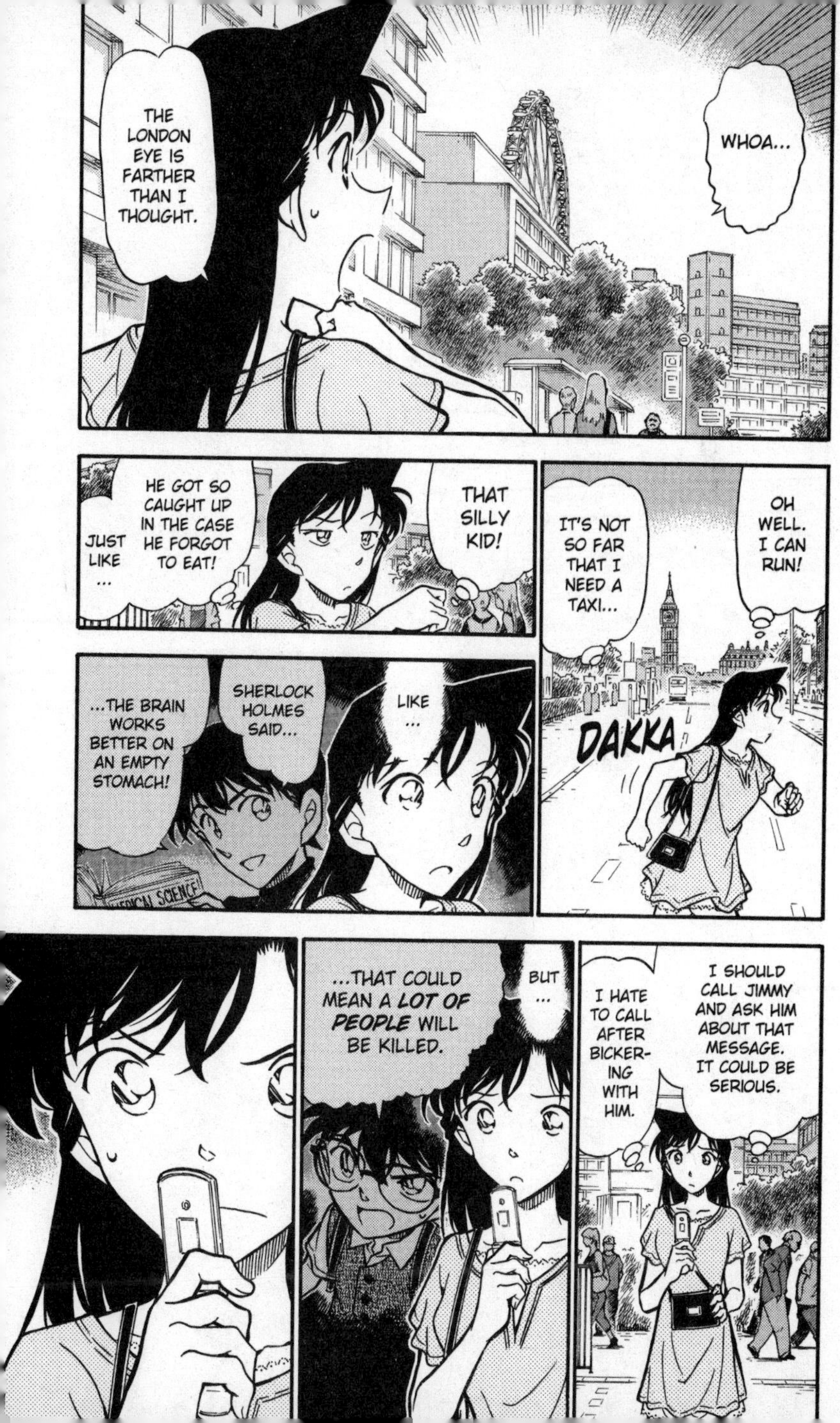
WHOA...
THE LONDON EYE IS FARTHER THAN I THOUGHT.
OH WELL. I CAN RUN!
IT'S NOT SO FAR THAT I NEED A TAXI...
DAKKA
THAT SILLY KID!
HE GOT SO CAUGHT UP IN THE CASE HE FORGOT TO EAT!
JUST LIKE ...
LIKE ...
SHERLOCK HOLMES SAID...
...THE BRAIN WORKS BETTER ON AN EMPTY STOMACH!
I SHOULD CALL JIMMY AND ASK HIM ABOUT THAT MESSAGE. IT COULD BE SERIOUS.
I HATE TO CALL AFTER BICKER-ING WITH HIM.
BUT ...
...THAT COULD MEAN A *LOT OF PEOPLE* WILL BE KILLED.

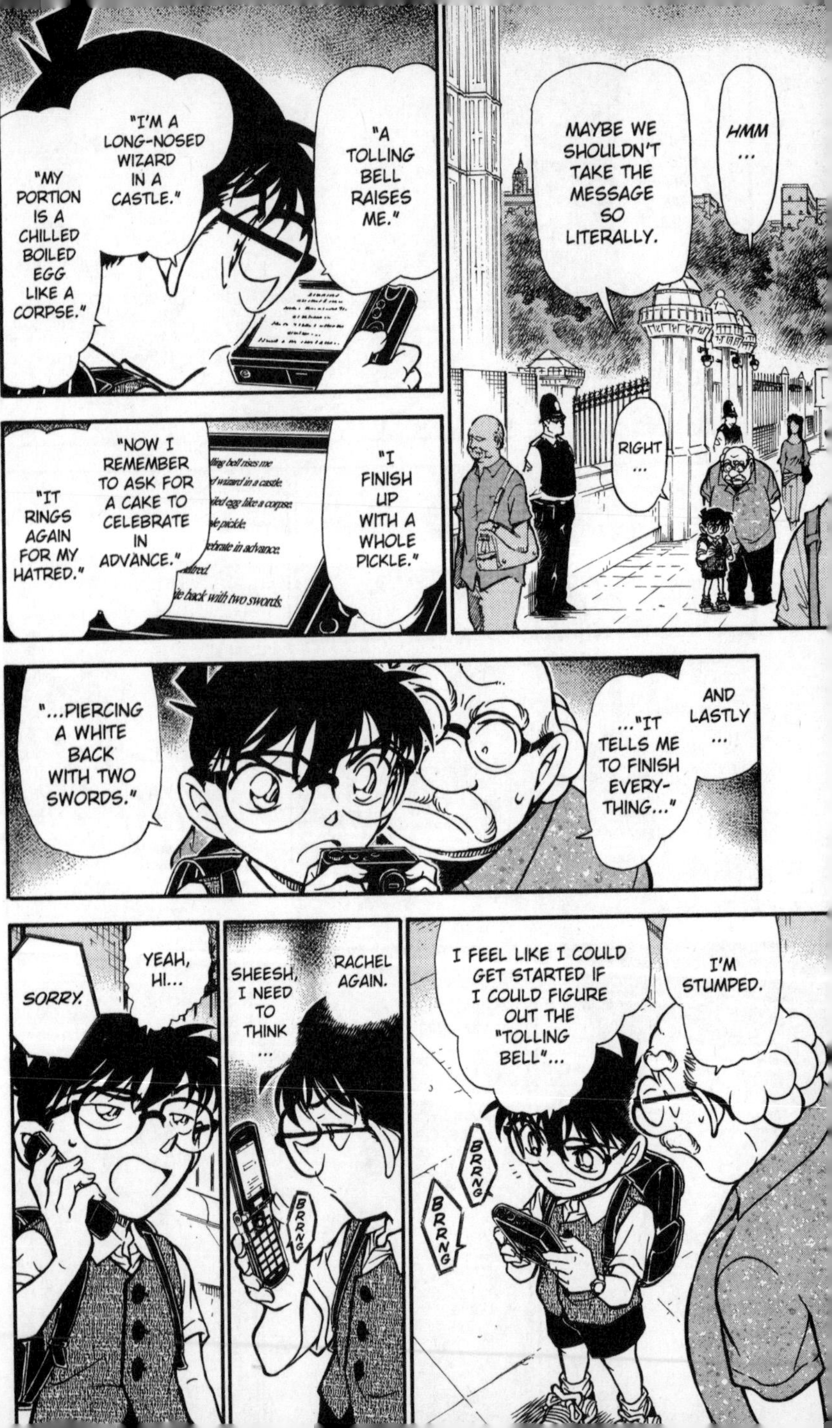
HMM ...
MAYBE WE SHOULDN'T TAKE THE MESSAGE SO LITERALLY.
RIGHT ...
"A TOLLING BELL RAISES ME."
"I'M A LONG-NOSED WIZARD IN A CASTLE."
"MY PORTION IS A CHILLED BOILED EGG LIKE A CORPSE."
"I FINISH UP WITH A WHOLE PICKLE."
"NOW I REMEMBER TO ASK FOR A CAKE TO CELEBRATE IN ADVANCE."
"IT RINGS AGAIN FOR MY HATRED."
AND LASTLY ...
..."IT TELLS ME TO FINISH EVERY-THING..."
"...PIERCING A WHITE BACK WITH TWO SWORDS."
I'M STUMPED.
I FEEL LIKE I COULD GET STARTED IF I COULD FIGURE OUT THE "TOLLING BELL"...
BRRNG
BRRNG
RACHEL AGAIN.
SHEESH, I NEED TO THINK ...
BRRNG
YEAH, HI...
SORRY.

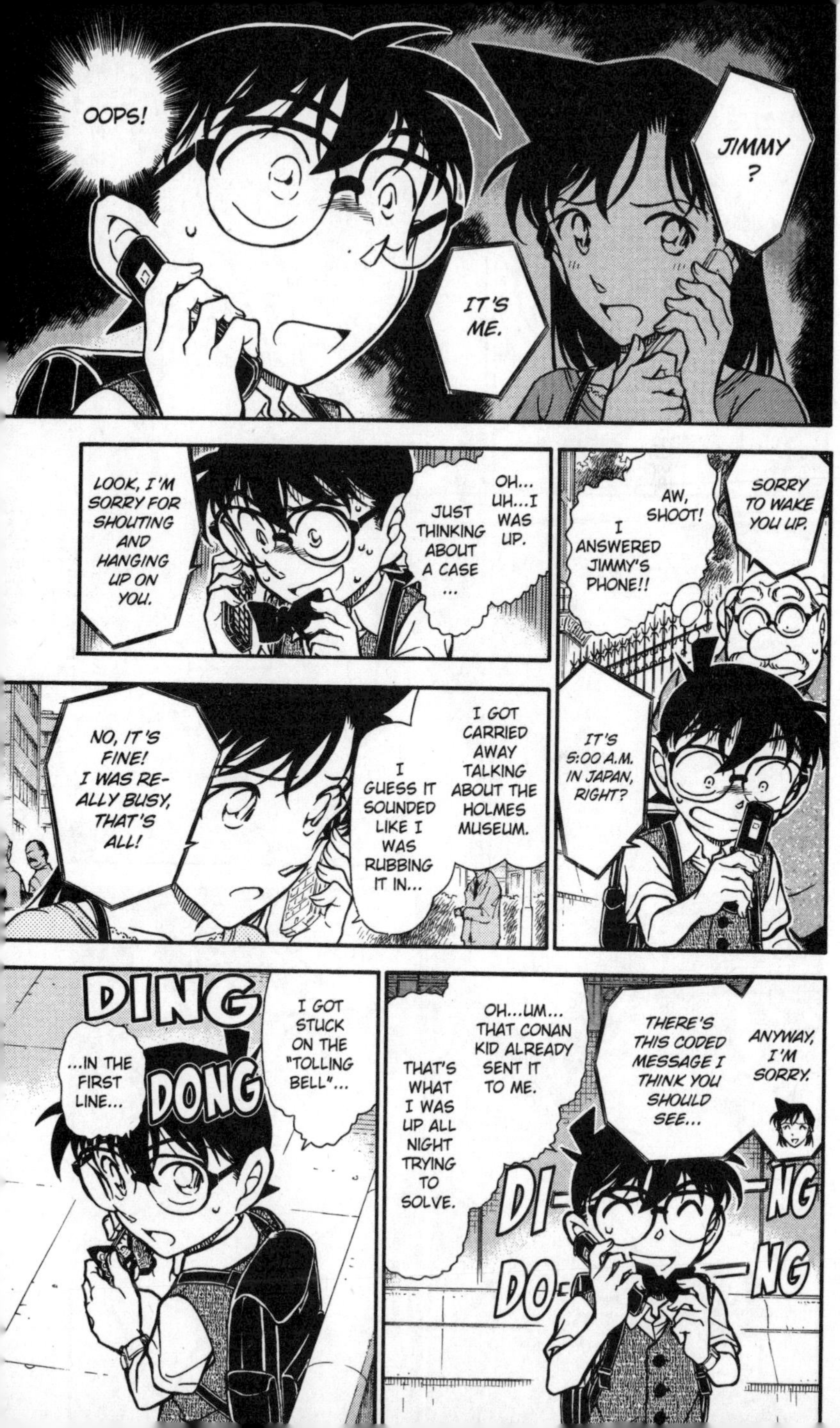
JIMMY ?
OOPS!
IT'S ME.
SORRY TO WAKE YOU UP.
AW, SHOOT! I ANSWERED JIMMY'S PHONE!!
IT'S 5:00 A.M. IN JAPAN, RIGHT?
OH... UH...I WAS UP.
JUST THINKING ABOUT A CASE ...
LOOK, I'M SORRY FOR SHOUTING AND HANGING UP ON YOU.
I GOT CARRIED AWAY TALKING ABOUT THE HOLMES MUSEUM.
I GUESS IT SOUNDED LIKE I WAS RUBBING IT IN...
NO, IT'S FINE! I WAS RE-ALLY BUSY, THAT'S ALL!
ANYWAY, I'M SORRY.
THERE'S THIS CODED MESSAGE I THINK YOU SHOULD SEE...
OH...UM... THAT CONAN KID ALREADY SENT IT TO ME.
THAT'S WHAT I WAS UP ALL NIGHT TRYING TO SOLVE.
DI-NG
DO-NG
I GOT STUCK ON THE "TOLLING BELL"...
DING
DONG
...IN THE FIRST LINE...

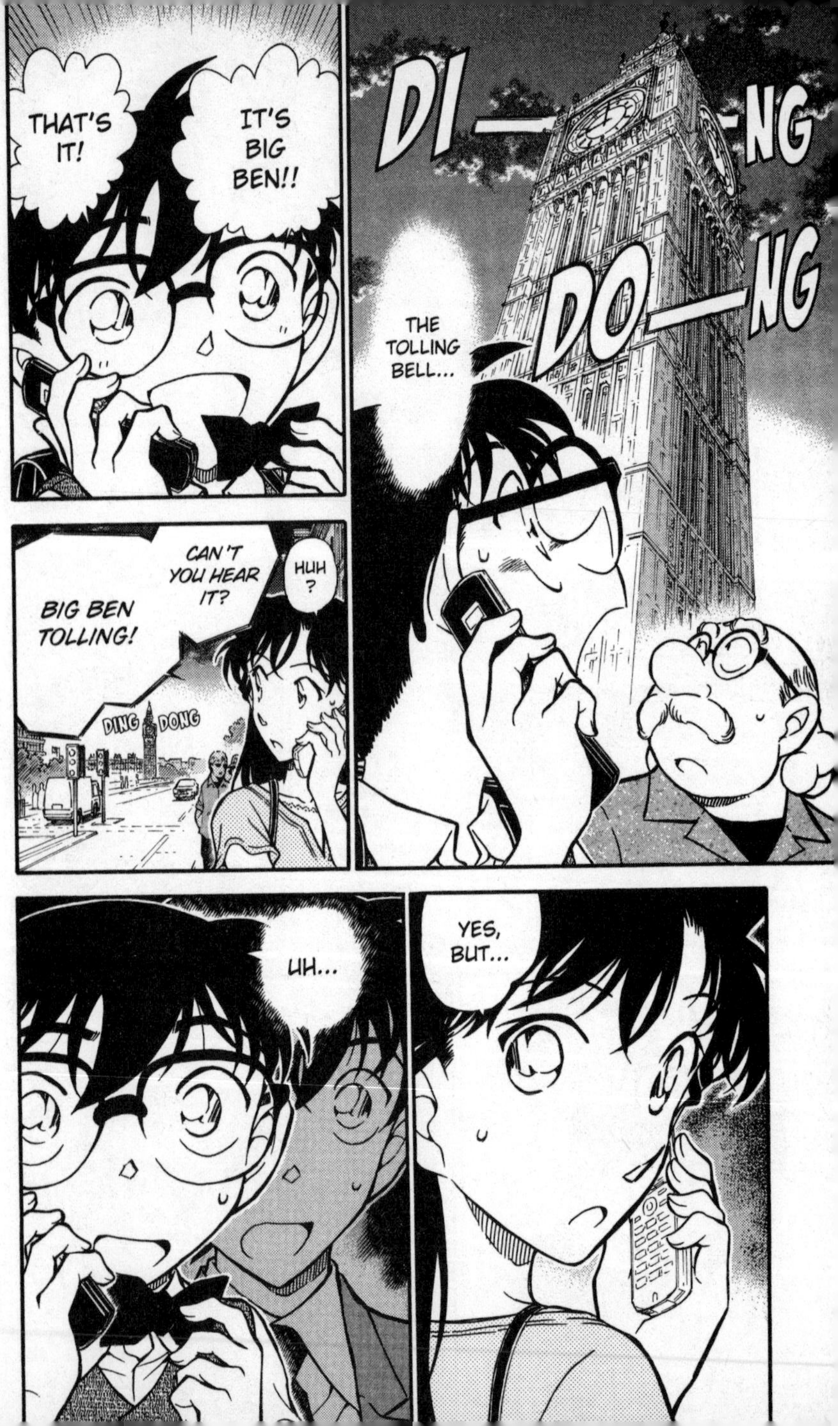
DI—NG
DO—NG
THE TOLLING BELL...
IT'S BIG BEN!!
THAT'S IT!
HUH?
CAN'T YOU HEAR IT?
BIG BEN TOLLING!
DING DONG
YES, BUT...
UH...

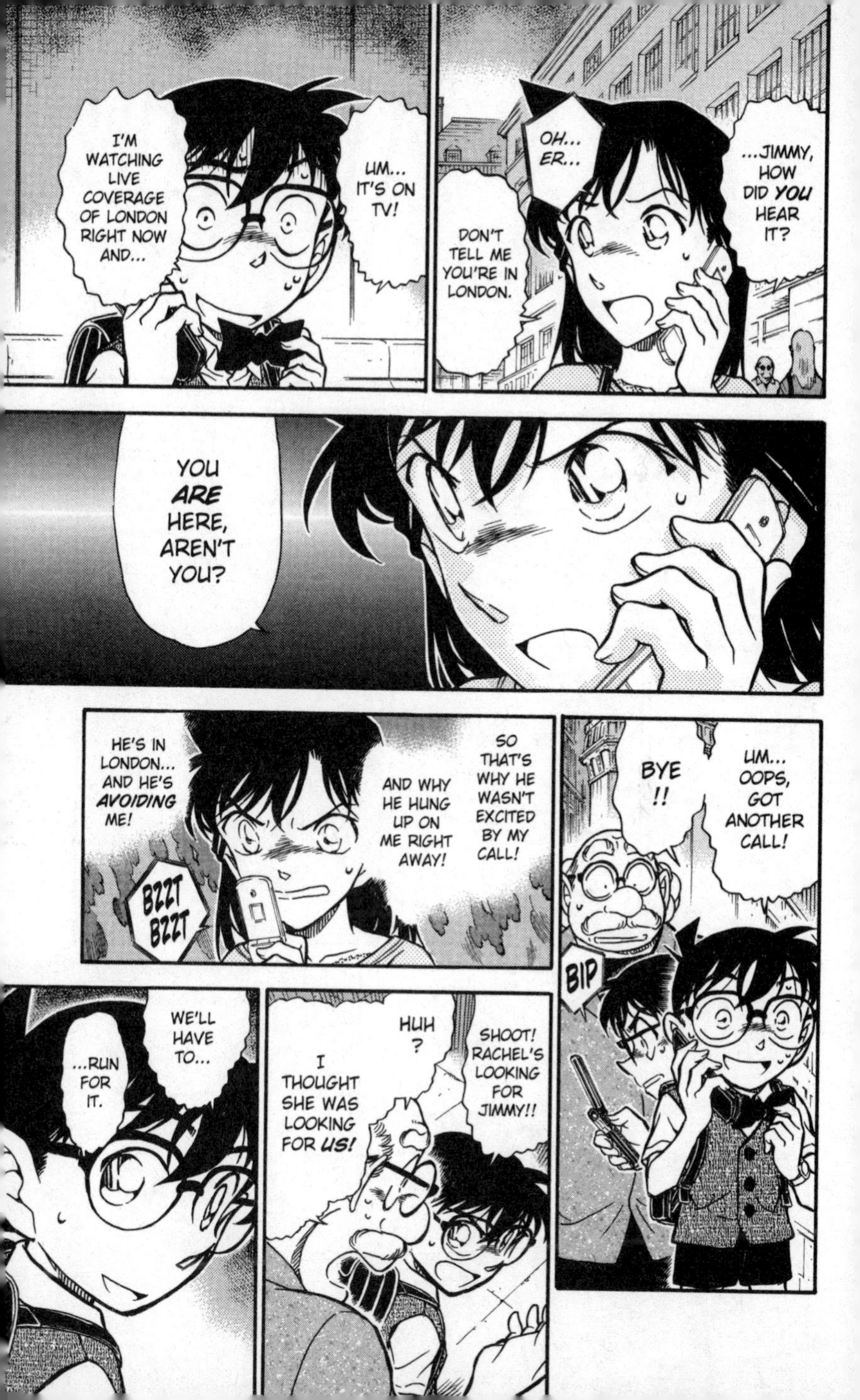
...JIMMY, HOW DID YOU HEAR IT?
OH... ER...
DON'T TELL ME YOU'RE IN LONDON.
UM... IT'S ON TV!
I'M WATCHING LIVE COVERAGE OF LONDON RIGHT NOW AND...
YOU ARE HERE, AREN'T YOU?
UM... OOPS, GOT ANOTHER CALL!
BYE !!
BIP
SO THAT'S WHY HE WASN'T EXCITED BY MY CALL!
AND WHY HE HUNG UP ON ME RIGHT AWAY!
HE'S IN LONDON... AND HE'S AVOIDING ME!
BZZT BZZT
SHOOT! RACHEL'S LOOKING FOR JIMMY!!
HUH ?
I THOUGHT SHE WAS LOOKING FOR US!
WE'LL HAVE TO...
...RUN FOR IT.

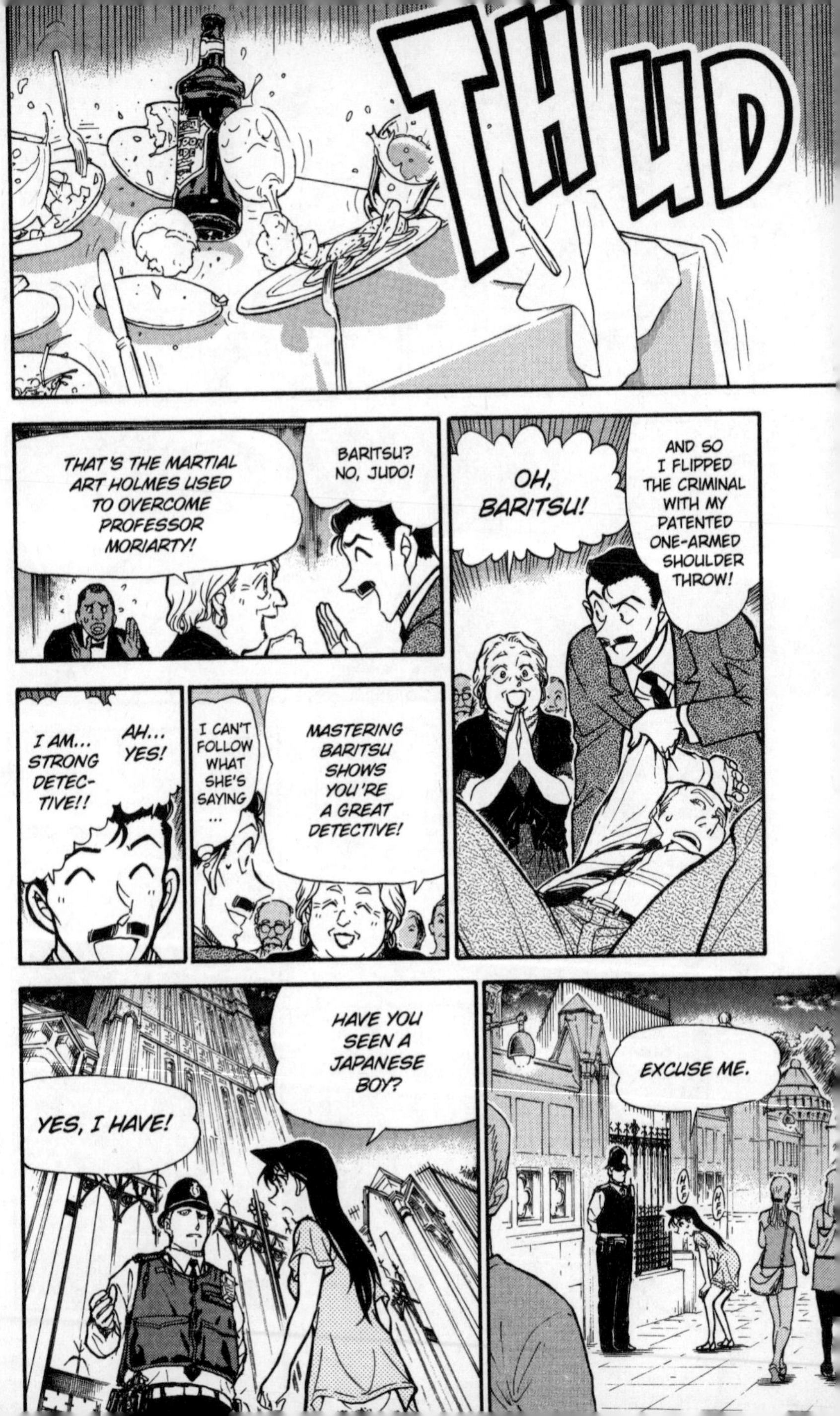
THUD
AND SO I FLIPPED THE CRIMINAL WITH MY PATENTED ONE-ARMED SHOULDER THROW!
OH, BARITSU!
BARITSU? NO, JUDO!
THAT'S THE MARTIAL ART HOLMES USED TO OVERCOME PROFESSOR MORIARTY!
MASTERING BARITSU SHOWS YOU'RE A GREAT DETECTIVE!
I CAN'T FOLLOW WHAT SHE'S SAYING ...
AH... YES!
I AM... STRONG DETEC-TIVE!!
EXCUSE ME.
HAVE YOU SEEN A JAPANESE BOY?
YES, I HAVE!

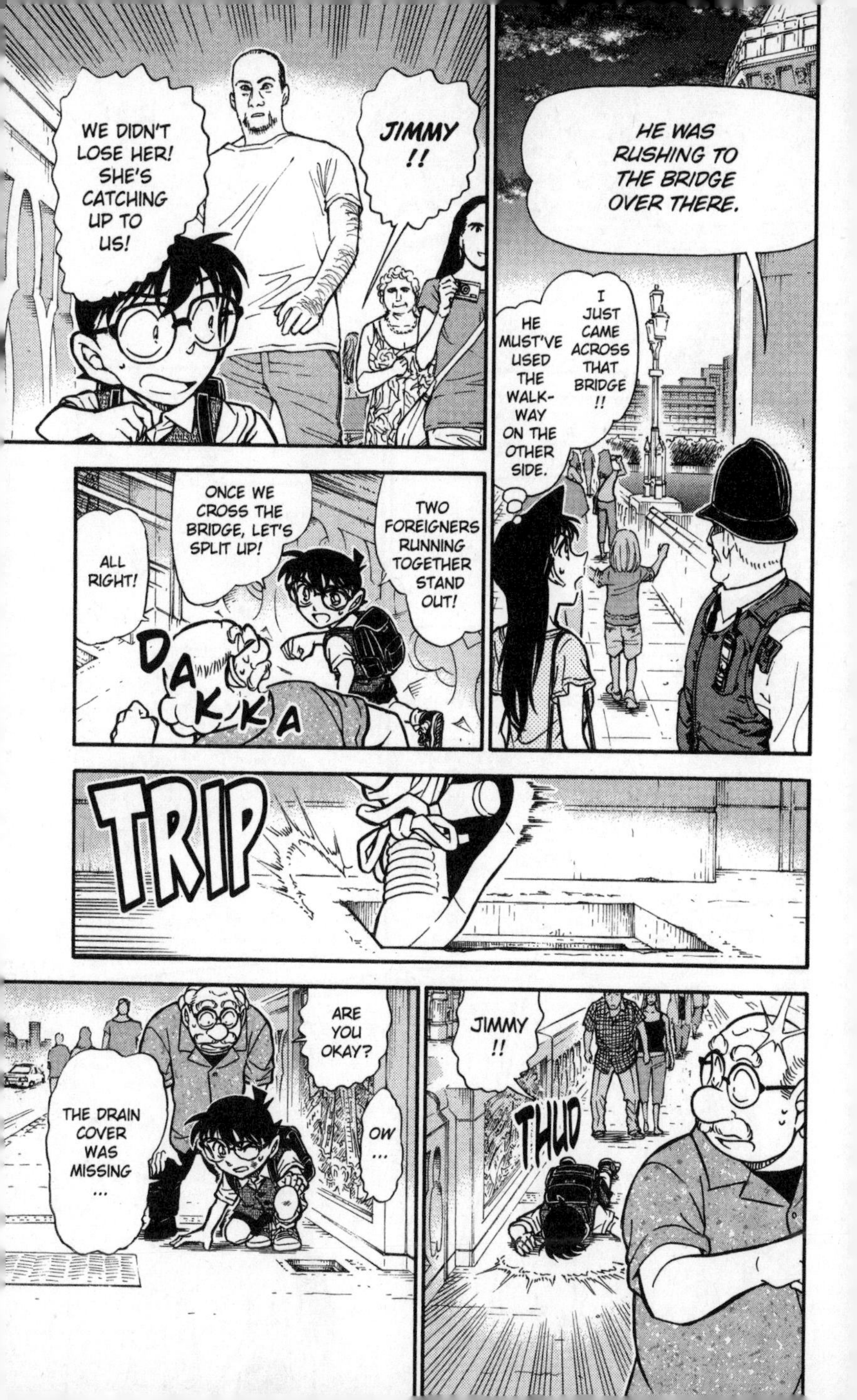
HE WAS RUSHING TO THE BRIDGE OVER THERE.
I JUST CAME ACROSS THAT BRIDGE !!
HE MUST'VE USED THE WALK-WAY ON THE OTHER SIDE.
JIMMY !!
WE DIDN'T LOSE HER! SHE'S CATCHING UP TO US!
TWO FOREIGNERS RUNNING TOGETHER STAND OUT!
ONCE WE CROSS THE BRIDGE, LET'S SPLIT UP!
ALL RIGHT!
DAKKA
TRIP
JIMMY !!
THUD
ARE YOU OKAY?
OW ...
THE DRAIN COVER WAS MISSING ...

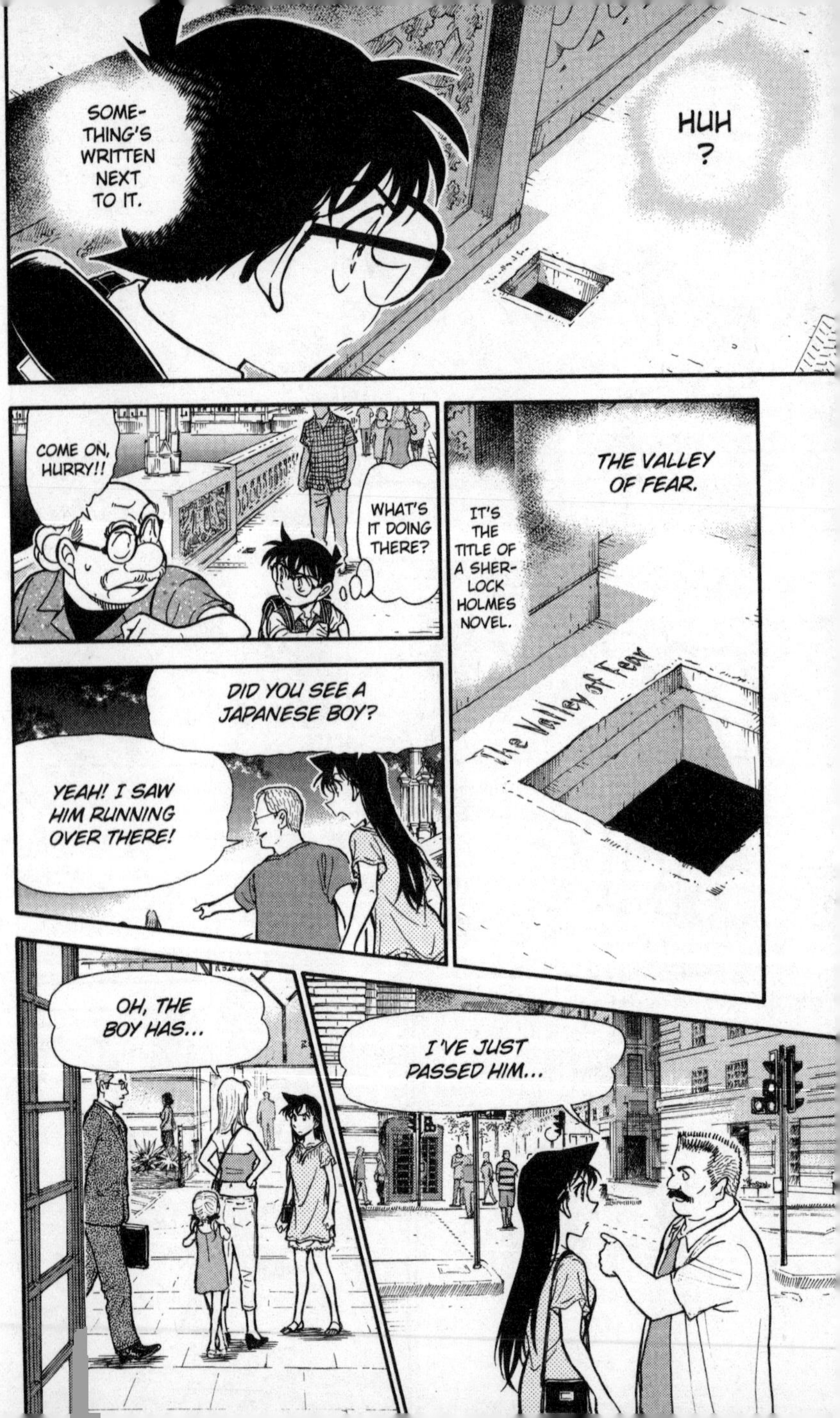
HUH?
SOMETHING'S WRITTEN NEXT TO IT.
THE VALLEY OF FEAR.
IT'S THE TITLE OF A SHERLOCK HOLMES NOVEL.
The Valley of Fear
WHAT'S IT DOING THERE?
COME ON, HURRY!!
DID YOU SEE A JAPANESE BOY?
YEAH! I SAW HIM RUNNING OVER THERE!
I'VE JUST PASSED HIM...
OH, THE BOY HAS...

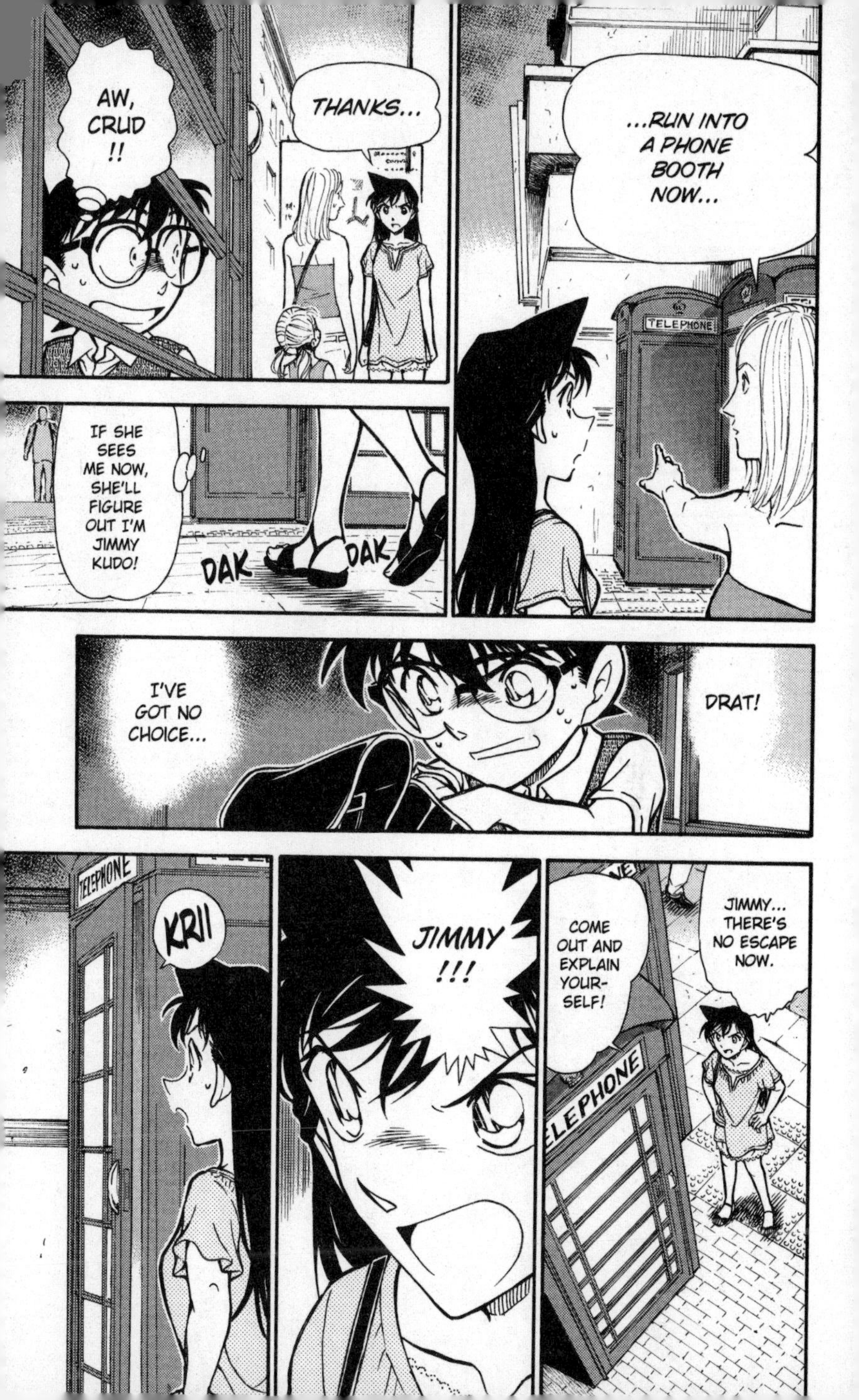
...RUN INTO A PHONE BOOTH NOW...
THANKS...
AW, CRUD !!
TELEPHONE
IF SHE SEES ME NOW, SHE'LL FIGURE OUT I'M JIMMY KUDO!
DAK
DAK
DRAT!
I'VE GOT NO CHOICE...
JIMMY... THERE'S NO ESCAPE NOW.
COME OUT AND EXPLAIN YOUR-SELF!
TELEPHONE
JIMMY !!!
TELEPHONE
KRII

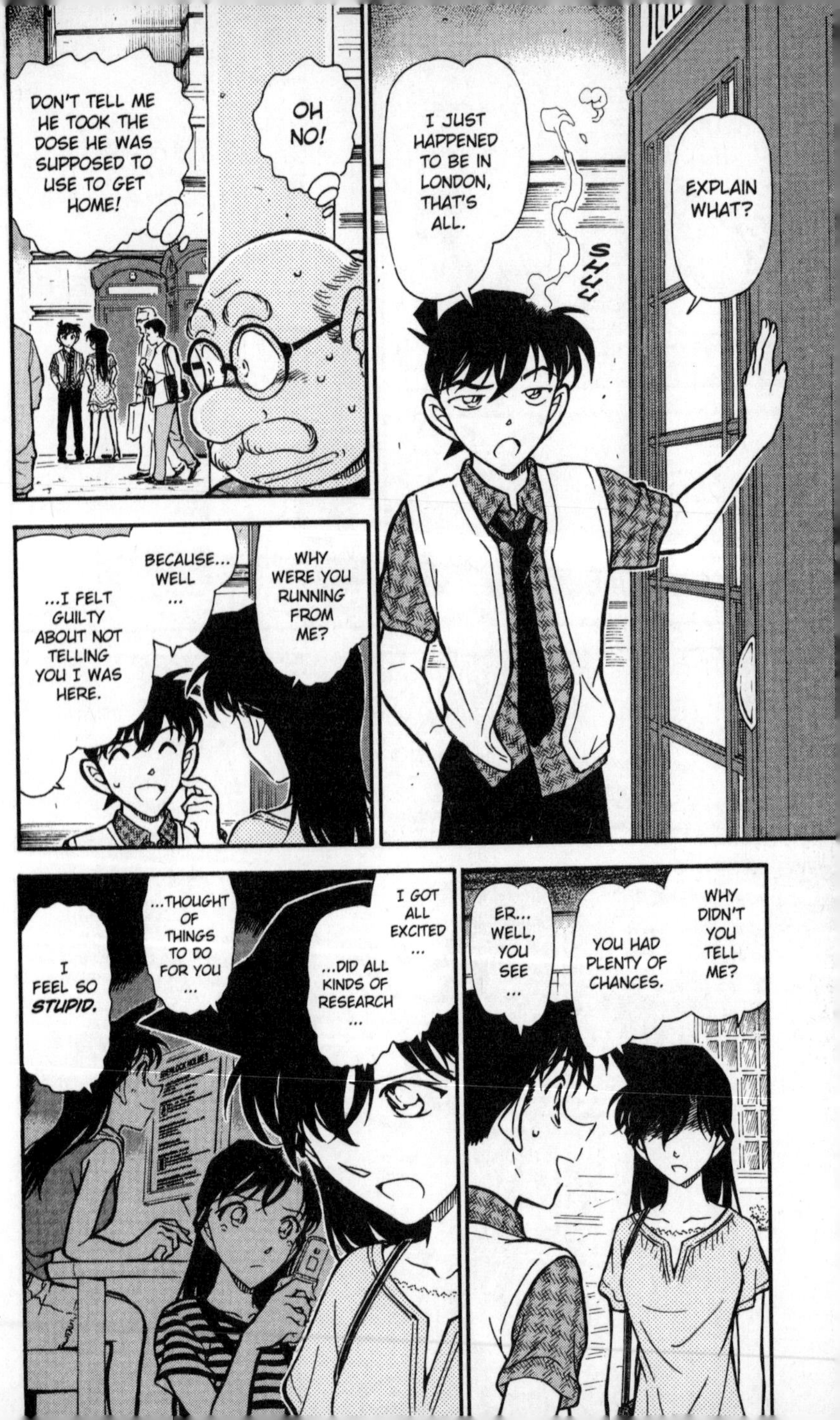
EXPLAIN WHAT?
I JUST HAPPENED TO BE IN LONDON, THAT'S ALL.
SHUU
OH NO!
DON'T TELL ME HE TOOK THE DOSE HE WAS SUPPOSED TO USE TO GET HOME!
WHY WERE YOU RUNNING FROM ME?
BECAUSE... WELL ...
...I FELT GUILTY ABOUT NOT TELLING YOU I WAS HERE.
WHY DIDN'T YOU TELL ME?
YOU HAD PLENTY OF CHANCES.
ER... WELL, YOU SEE ...
I GOT ALL EXCITED ...
...DID ALL KINDS OF RESEARCH ...
...THOUGHT OF THINGS TO DO FOR YOU ...
I FEEL SO STUPID.

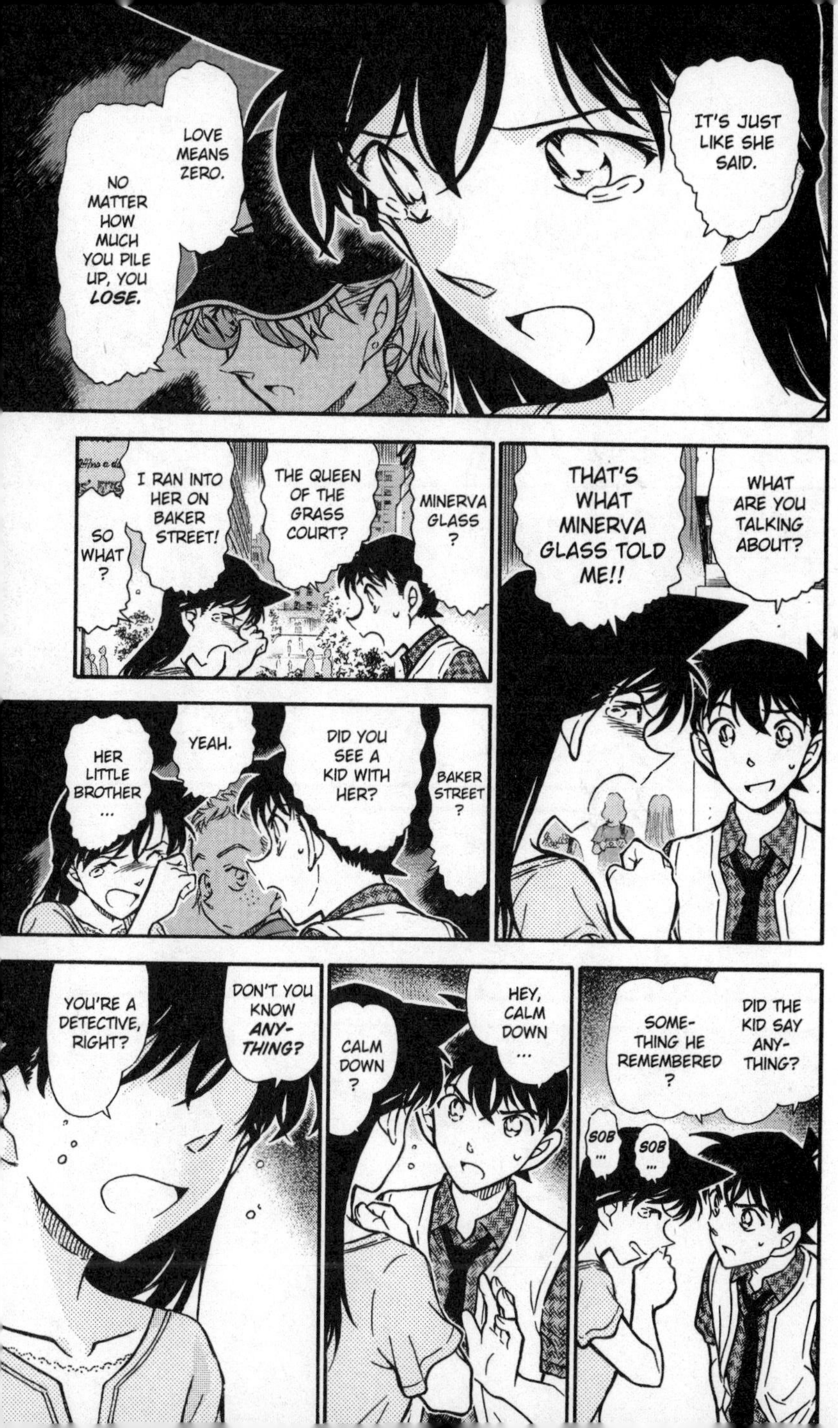
IT'S JUST LIKE SHE SAID.
LOVE MEANS ZERO.
NO MATTER HOW MUCH YOU PILE UP, YOU **LOSE.**
WHAT ARE YOU TALKING ABOUT?
THAT'S WHAT MINERVA GLASS TOLD ME!!
MINERVA GLASS?
THE QUEEN OF THE GRASS COURT?
I RAN INTO HER ON BAKER STREET!
SO WHAT?
BAKER STREET?
DID YOU SEE A KID WITH HER?
YEAH.
HER LITTLE BROTHER...
DID THE KID SAY ANY-THING?
SOME-THING HE REMEMBERED?
SOB...
SOB...
HEY, CALM DOWN...
CALM DOWN?
DON'T YOU KNOW ***ANY-THING?***
YOU'RE A DETECTIVE, RIGHT?

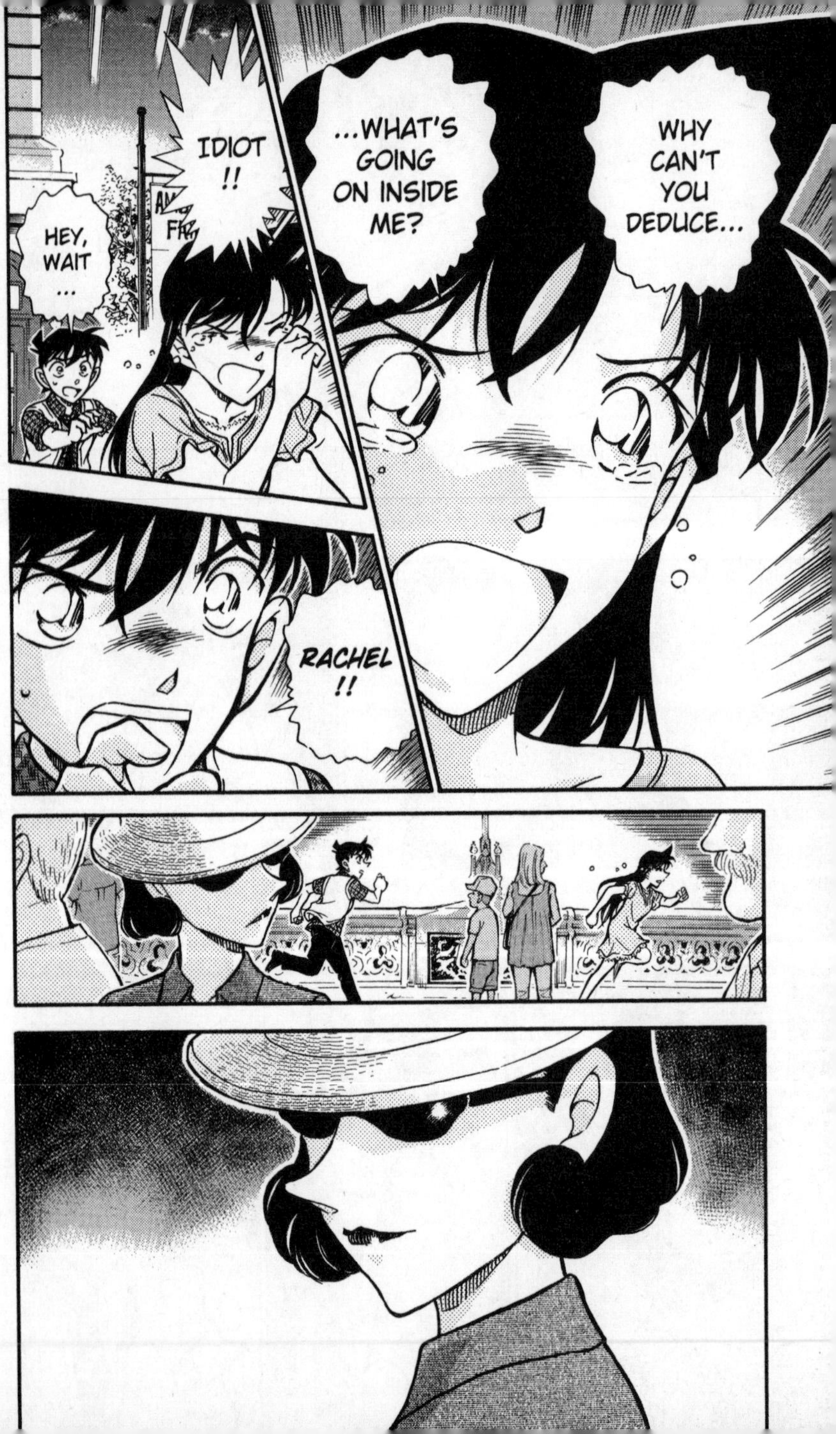
WHY CAN'T YOU DEDUCE...
...WHAT'S GOING ON INSIDE ME?
IDIOT !!
HEY, WAIT ...
RACHEL !!

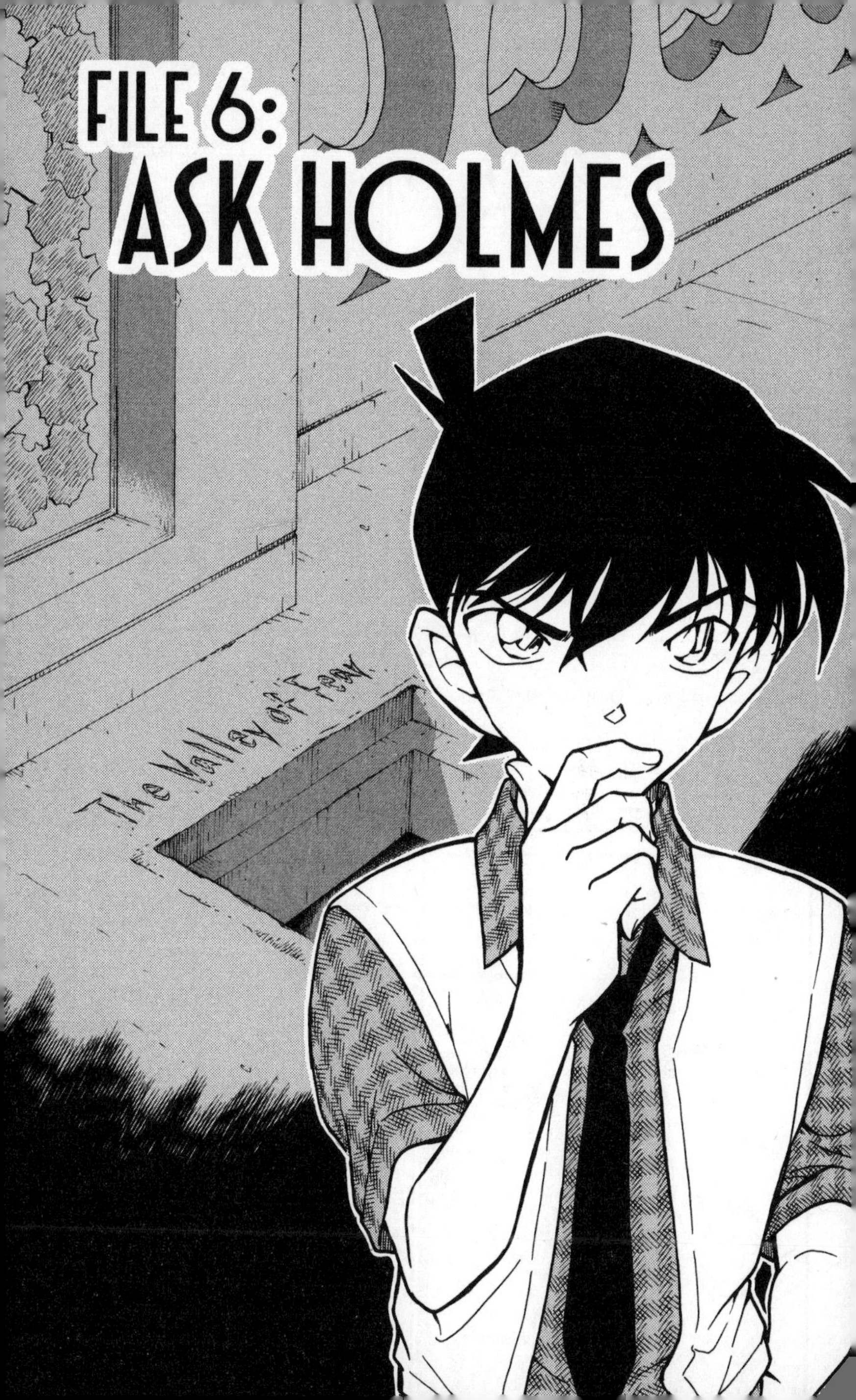
FILE 6:
ASK HOLMES
The Valley of Fear

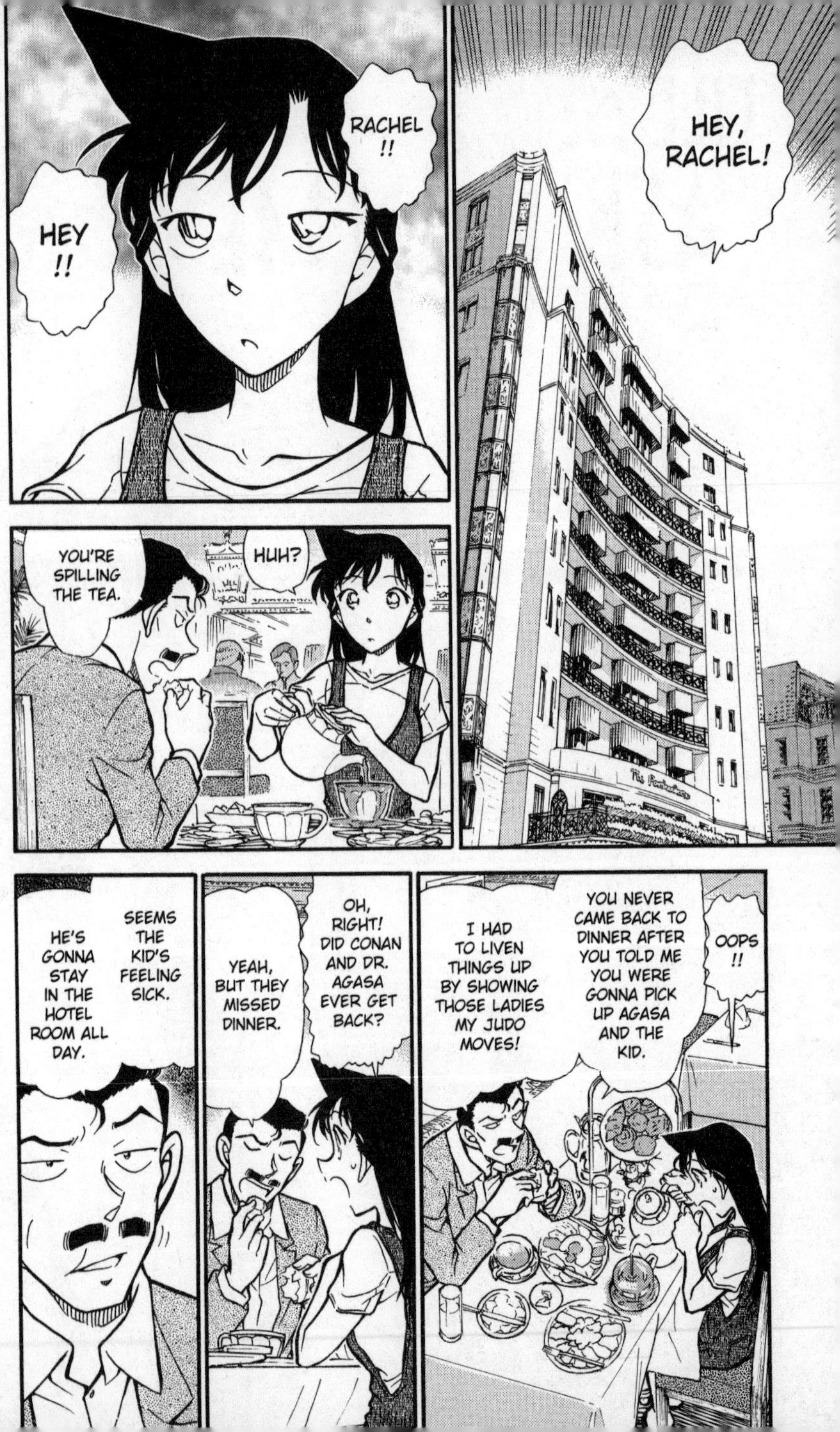
HEY, RACHEL!
RACHEL !!
HEY !!
HUH?
YOU'RE SPILLING THE TEA.
OOPS !!
YOU NEVER CAME BACK TO DINNER AFTER YOU TOLD ME YOU WERE GONNA PICK UP AGASA AND THE KID.
I HAD TO LIVEN THINGS UP BY SHOWING THOSE LADIES MY JUDO MOVES!
OH, RIGHT! DID CONAN AND DR. AGASA EVER GET BACK?
YEAH, BUT THEY MISSED DINNER.
SEEMS THE KID'S FEELING SICK.
HE'S GONNA STAY IN THE HOTEL ROOM ALL DAY.

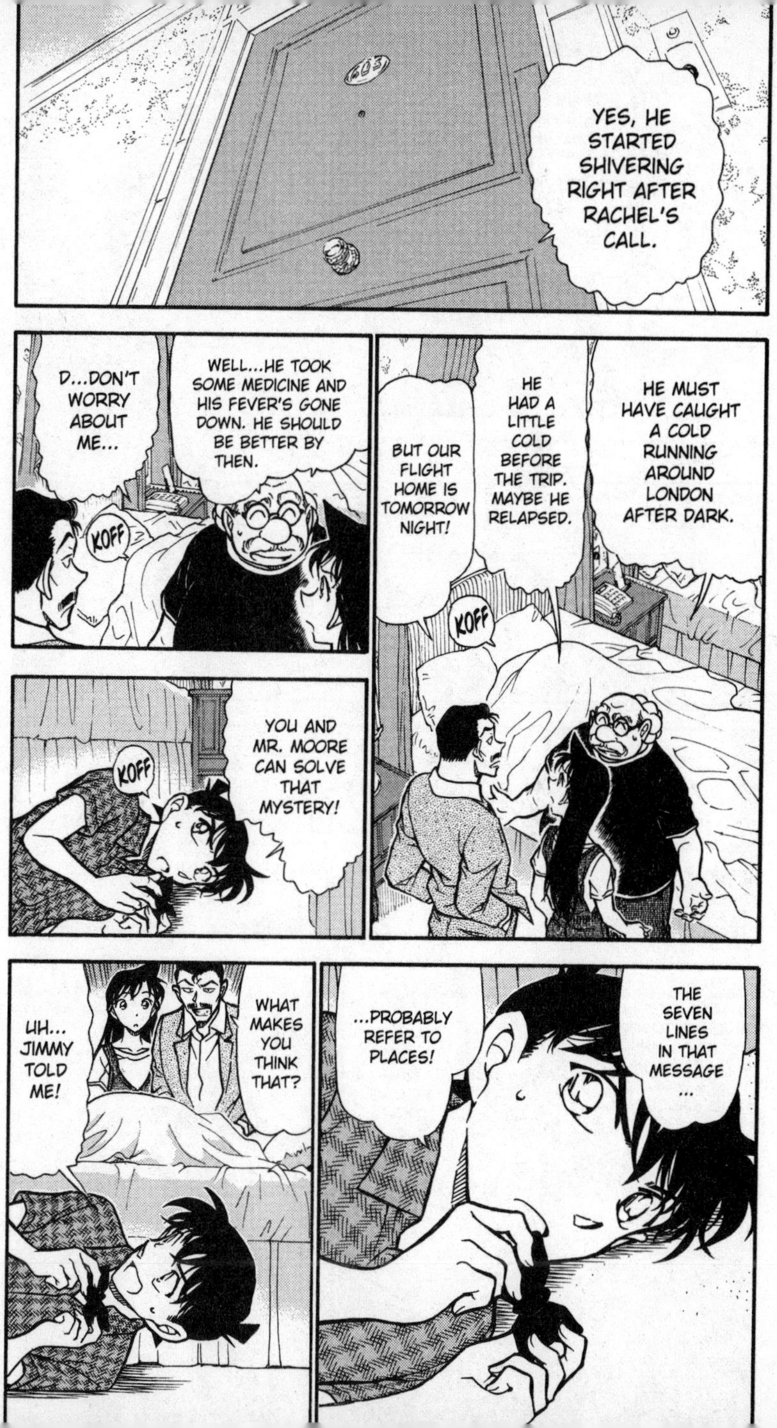
YES, HE STARTED SHIVERING RIGHT AFTER RACHEL'S CALL.
HE MUST HAVE CAUGHT A COLD RUNNING AROUND LONDON AFTER DARK.
HE HAD A LITTLE COLD BEFORE THE TRIP. MAYBE HE RELAPSED.
BUT OUR FLIGHT HOME IS TOMORROW NIGHT!
KOFF
WELL...HE TOOK SOME MEDICINE AND HIS FEVER'S GONE DOWN. HE SHOULD BE BETTER BY THEN.
D...DON'T WORRY ABOUT ME...
KOFF
YOU AND MR. MOORE CAN SOLVE THAT MYSTERY!
KOFF
THE SEVEN LINES IN THAT MESSAGE ...
...PROBABLY REFER TO PLACES!
WHAT MAKES YOU THINK THAT?
UH... JIMMY TOLD ME!

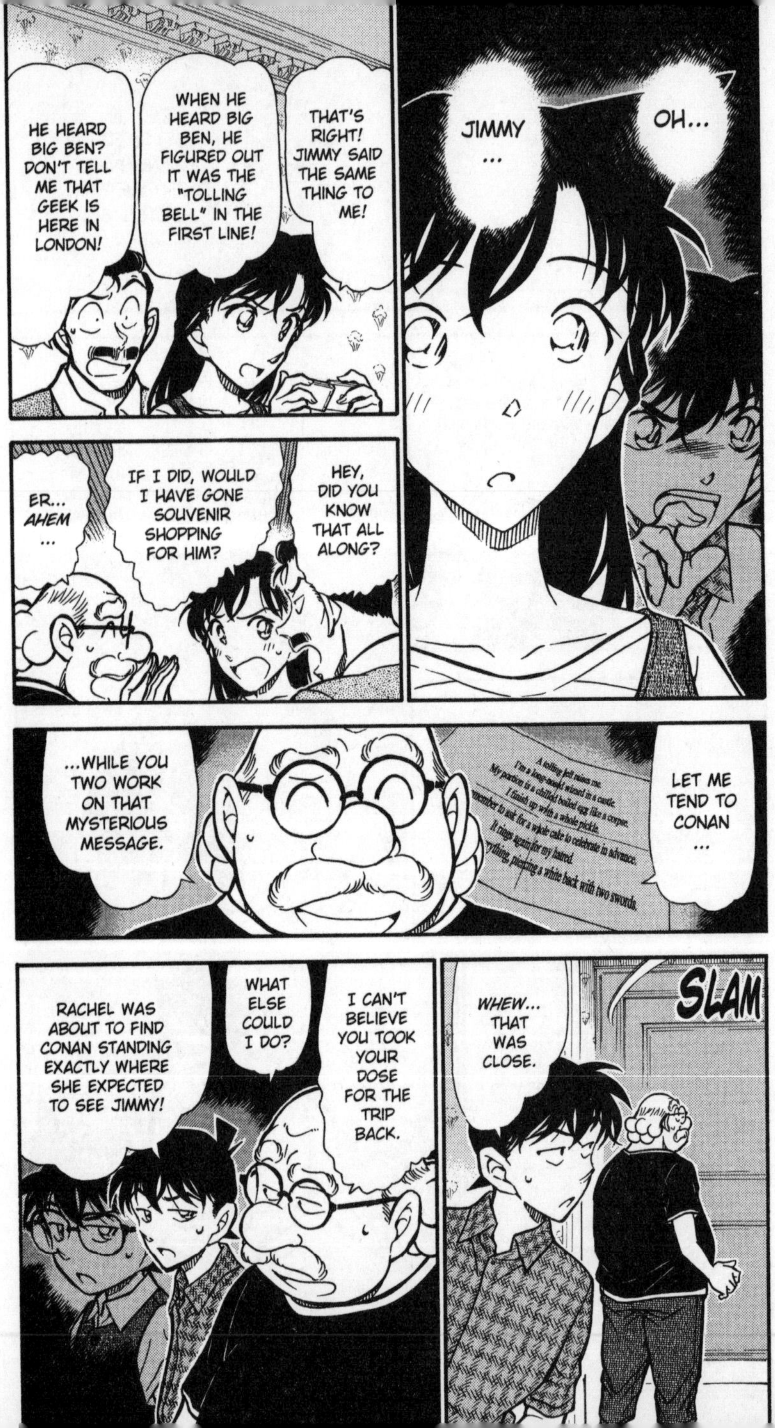
OH...
JIMMY ...
THAT'S RIGHT! JIMMY SAID THE SAME THING TO ME!
WHEN HE HEARD BIG BEN, HE FIGURED OUT IT WAS THE "TOLLING BELL" IN THE FIRST LINE!
HE HEARD BIG BEN? DON'T TELL ME THAT GEEK IS HERE IN LONDON!
HEY, DID YOU KNOW THAT ALL ALONG?
IF I DID, WOULD I HAVE GONE SOUVENIR SHOPPING FOR HIM?
ER... AHEM ...
LET ME TEND TO CONAN ...
A tolling bell raises me.
I'm a long-nosed wizard in a castle.
My portion is a chilled boiled egg like a corpse.
I finish up with a whole pickle.
member to ask for a whole cake to celebrate in advance.
It rings again for my hatred.
rything, piercing a white back with two swords.
...WHILE YOU TWO WORK ON THAT MYSTERIOUS MESSAGE.
SLAM
WHEW... THAT WAS CLOSE.
I CAN'T BELIEVE YOU TOOK YOUR DOSE FOR THE TRIP BACK.
WHAT ELSE COULD I DO?
RACHEL WAS ABOUT TO FIND CONAN STANDING EXACTLY WHERE SHE EXPECTED TO SEE JIMMY!

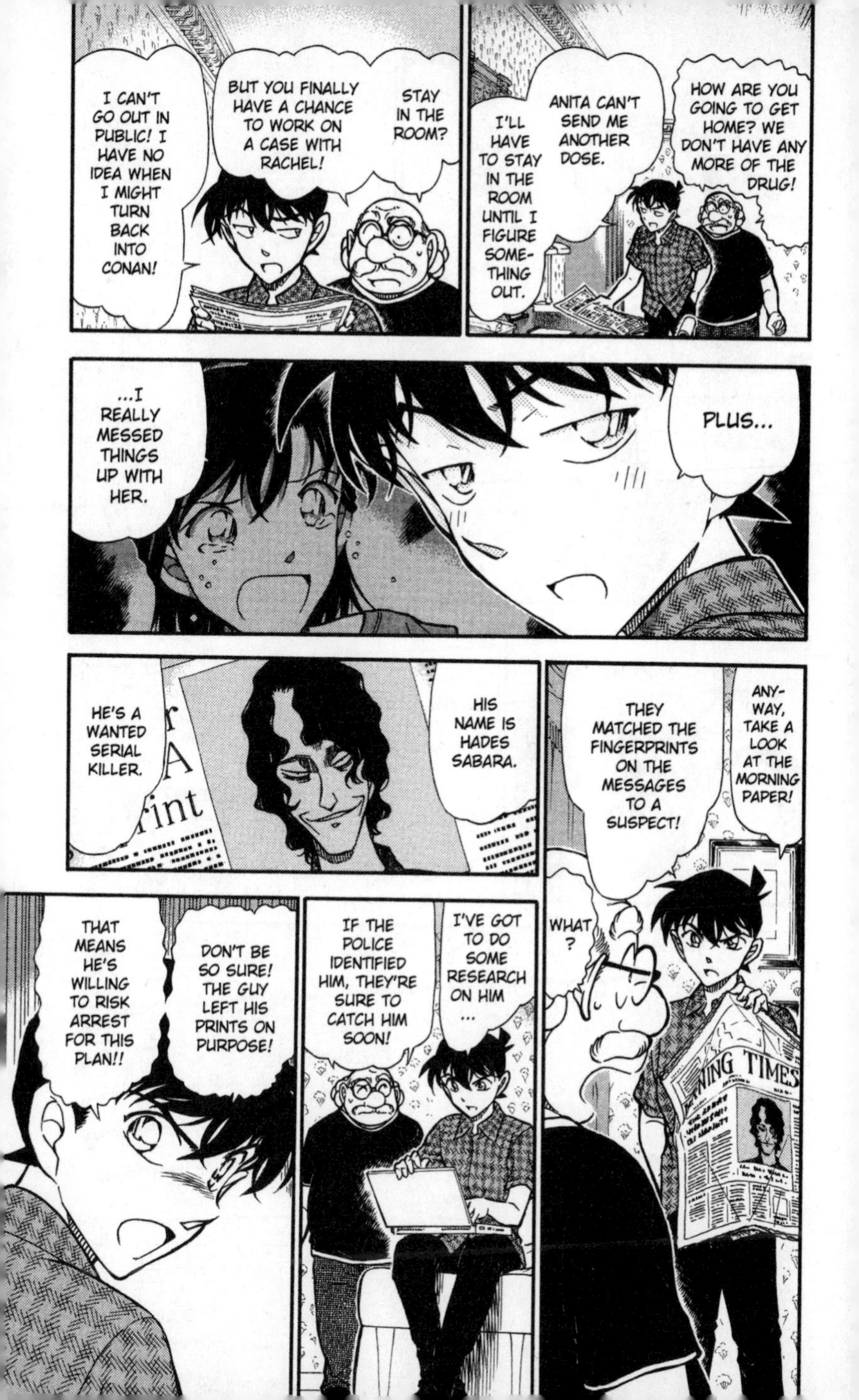
HOW ARE YOU GOING TO GET HOME? WE DON'T HAVE ANY MORE OF THE DRUG!
ANITA CAN'T SEND ME ANOTHER DOSE.
I'LL HAVE TO STAY IN THE ROOM UNTIL I FIGURE SOME-THING OUT.
STAY IN THE ROOM?
BUT YOU FINALLY HAVE A CHANCE TO WORK ON A CASE WITH RACHEL!
I CAN'T GO OUT IN PUBLIC! I HAVE NO IDEA WHEN I MIGHT TURN BACK INTO CONAN!
PLUS...
...I REALLY MESSED THINGS UP WITH HER.
ANY-WAY, TAKE A LOOK AT THE MORNING PAPER!
THEY MATCHED THE FINGERPRINTS ON THE MESSAGES TO A SUSPECT!
WHAT?
NING TIMES
HIS NAME IS HADES SABARA.
HE'S A WANTED SERIAL KILLER.
I'VE GOT TO DO SOME RESEARCH ON HIM ...
IF THE POLICE IDENTIFIED HIM, THEY'RE SURE TO CATCH HIM SOON!
DON'T BE SO SURE! THE GUY LEFT HIS PRINTS ON PURPOSE!
THAT MEANS HE'S WILLING TO RISK ARREST FOR THIS PLAN!!

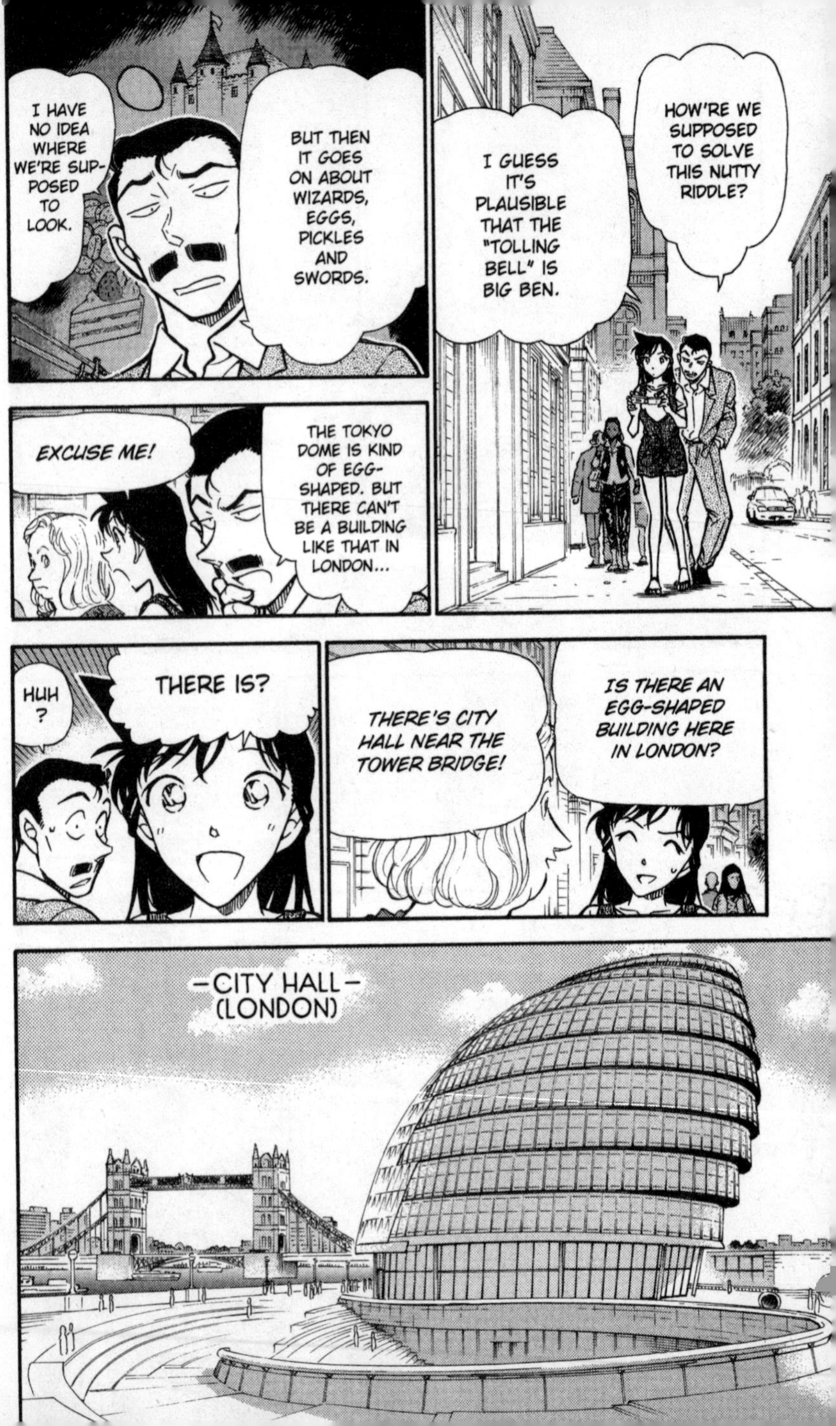
HOW'RE WE SUPPOSED TO SOLVE THIS NUTTY RIDDLE?
I GUESS IT'S PLAUSIBLE THAT THE "TOLLING BELL" IS BIG BEN.
BUT THEN IT GOES ON ABOUT WIZARDS, EGGS, PICKLES AND SWORDS.
I HAVE NO IDEA WHERE WE'RE SUPPOSED TO LOOK.
THE TOKYO DOME IS KIND OF EGG-SHAPED. BUT THERE CAN'T BE A BUILDING LIKE THAT IN LONDON...
EXCUSE ME!
IS THERE AN EGG-SHAPED BUILDING HERE IN LONDON?
THERE'S CITY HALL NEAR THE TOWER BRIDGE!
THERE IS?
HUH ?
—CITY HALL— (LONDON)

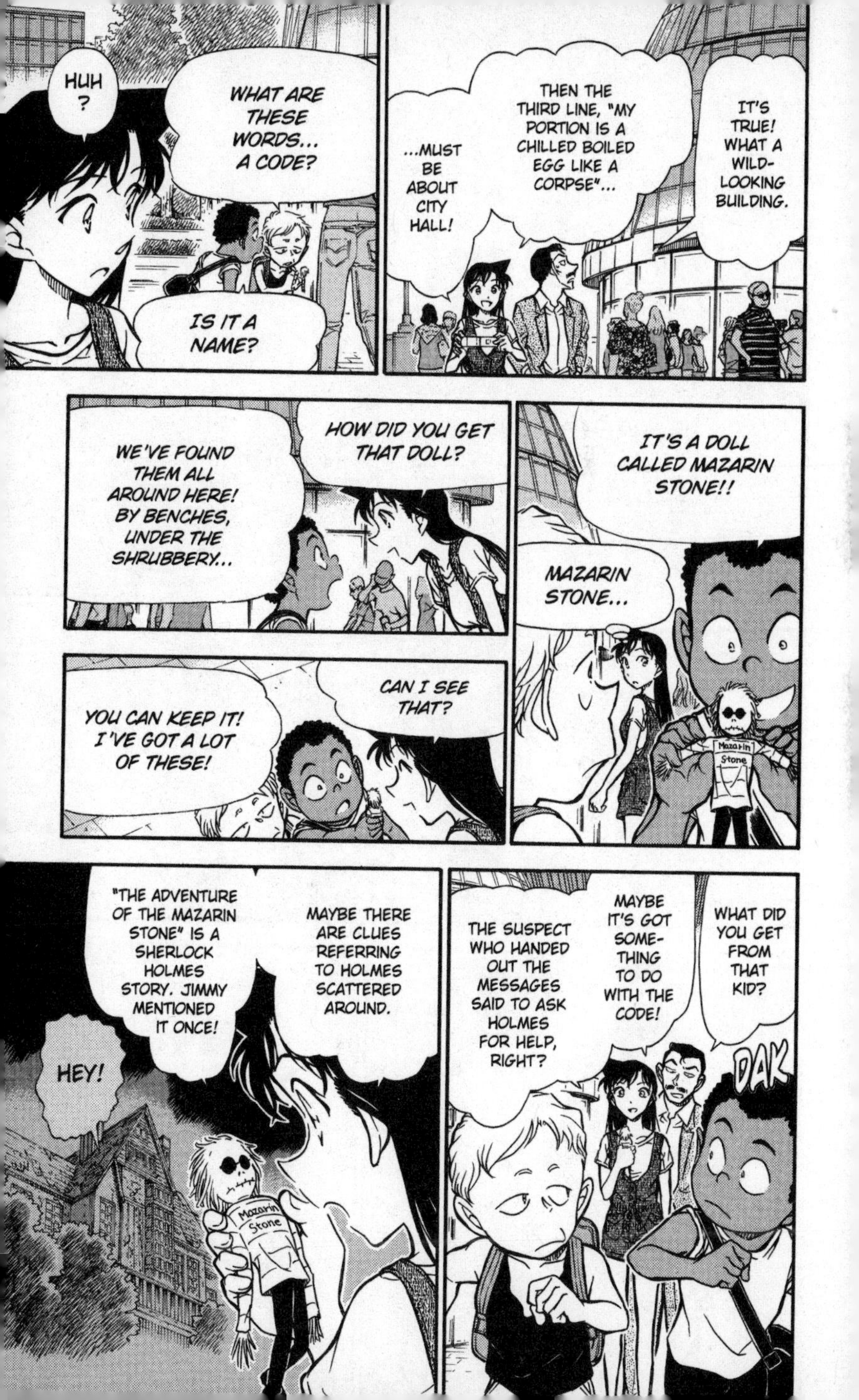
IT'S TRUE! WHAT A WILD-LOOKING BUILDING.
THEN THE THIRD LINE, "MY PORTION IS A CHILLED BOILED EGG LIKE A CORPSE"...
...MUST BE ABOUT CITY HALL!
WHAT ARE THESE WORDS... A CODE?
HUH?
IS IT A NAME?
IT'S A DOLL CALLED MAZARIN STONE!!
MAZARIN STONE...
Mazarin Stone
HOW DID YOU GET THAT DOLL?
WE'VE FOUND THEM ALL AROUND HERE! BY BENCHES, UNDER THE SHRUBBERY...
CAN I SEE THAT?
YOU CAN KEEP IT! I'VE GOT A LOT OF THESE!
WHAT DID YOU GET FROM THAT KID?
DAK
MAYBE IT'S GOT SOMETHING TO DO WITH THE CODE!
THE SUSPECT WHO HANDED OUT THE MESSAGES SAID TO ASK HOLMES FOR HELP, RIGHT?
MAYBE THERE ARE CLUES REFERRING TO HOLMES SCATTERED AROUND.
"THE ADVENTURE OF THE MAZARIN STONE" IS A SHERLOCK HOLMES STORY. JIMMY MENTIONED IT ONCE!
HEY!
Mazarin Stone

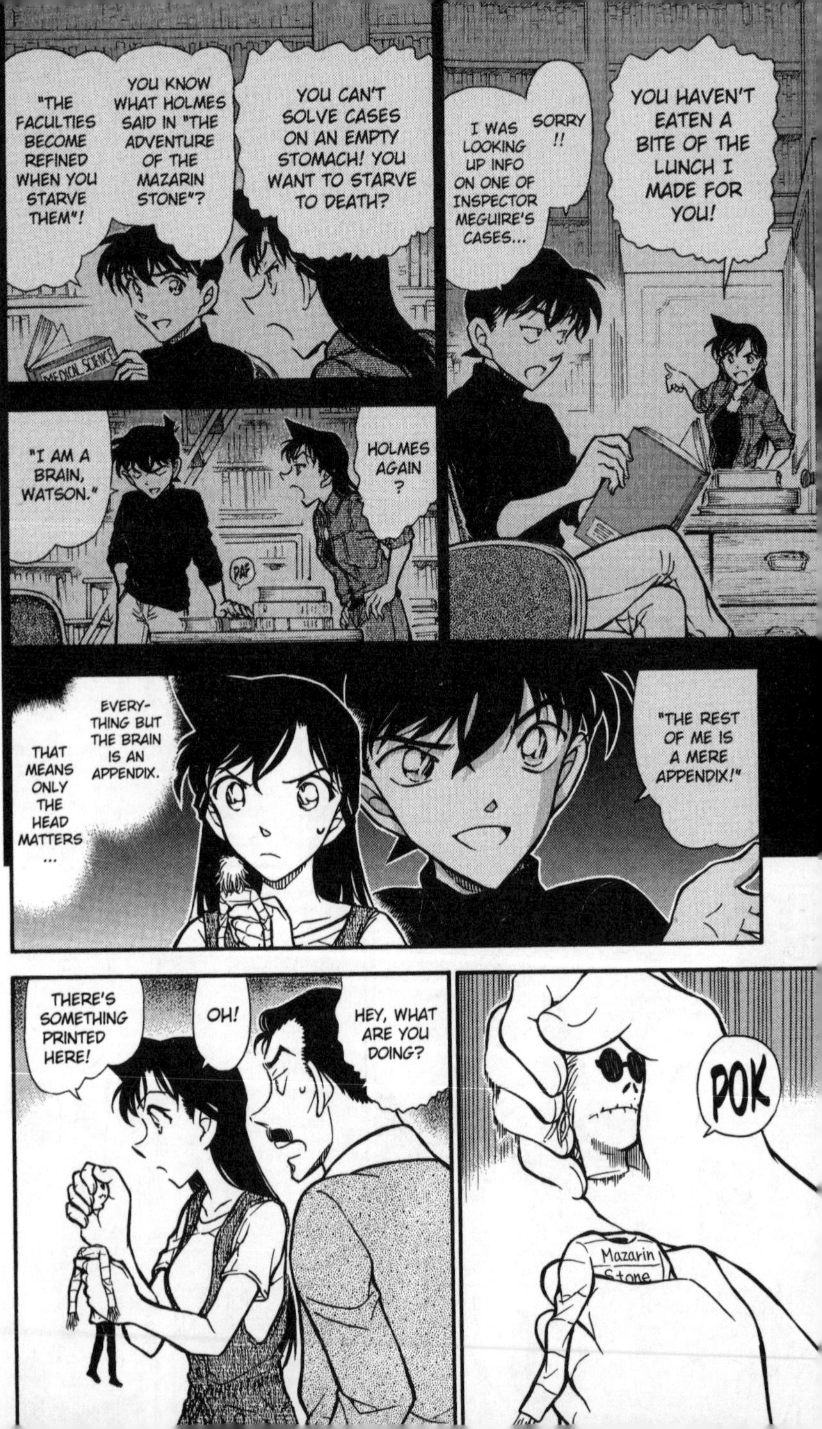
YOU HAVEN'T EATEN A BITE OF THE LUNCH I MADE FOR YOU!
SORRY!!
I WAS LOOKING UP INFO ON ONE OF INSPECTOR MEGUIRE'S CASES...
YOU CAN'T SOLVE CASES ON AN EMPTY STOMACH! YOU WANT TO STARVE TO DEATH?
YOU KNOW WHAT HOLMES SAID IN "THE ADVENTURE OF THE MAZARIN STONE"?
"THE FACULTIES BECOME REFINED WHEN YOU STARVE THEM"!
MEDICAL SCIENCE
HOLMES AGAIN?
PAF
"I AM A BRAIN, WATSON."
"THE REST OF ME IS A MERE APPENDIX!"
EVERYTHING BUT THE BRAIN IS AN APPENDIX.
THAT MEANS ONLY THE HEAD MATTERS...
POK
Mazarin Stone
HEY, WHAT ARE YOU DOING?
OH!
THERE'S SOMETHING PRINTED HERE!

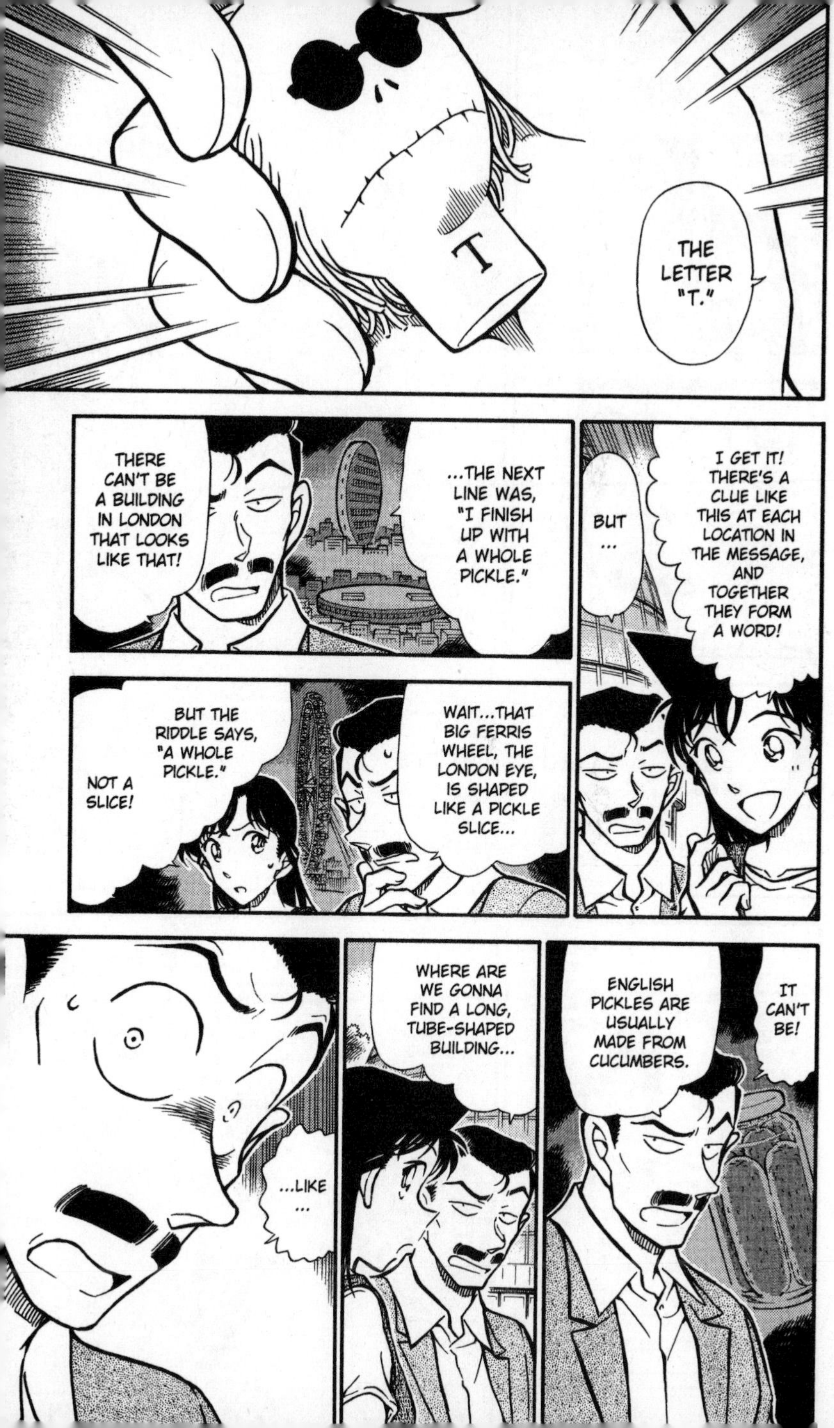
THE LETTER "T."
I GET IT! THERE'S A CLUE LIKE THIS AT EACH LOCATION IN THE MESSAGE, AND TOGETHER THEY FORM A WORD!
BUT ...
...THE NEXT LINE WAS, "I FINISH UP WITH A WHOLE PICKLE."
THERE CAN'T BE A BUILDING IN LONDON THAT LOOKS LIKE THAT!
WAIT...THAT BIG FERRIS WHEEL, THE LONDON EYE, IS SHAPED LIKE A PICKLE SLICE...
BUT THE RIDDLE SAYS, "A WHOLE PICKLE."
NOT A SLICE!
IT CAN'T BE!
ENGLISH PICKLES ARE USUALLY MADE FROM CUCUMBERS.
WHERE ARE WE GONNA FIND A LONG, TUBE-SHAPED BUILDING...
...LIKE ...

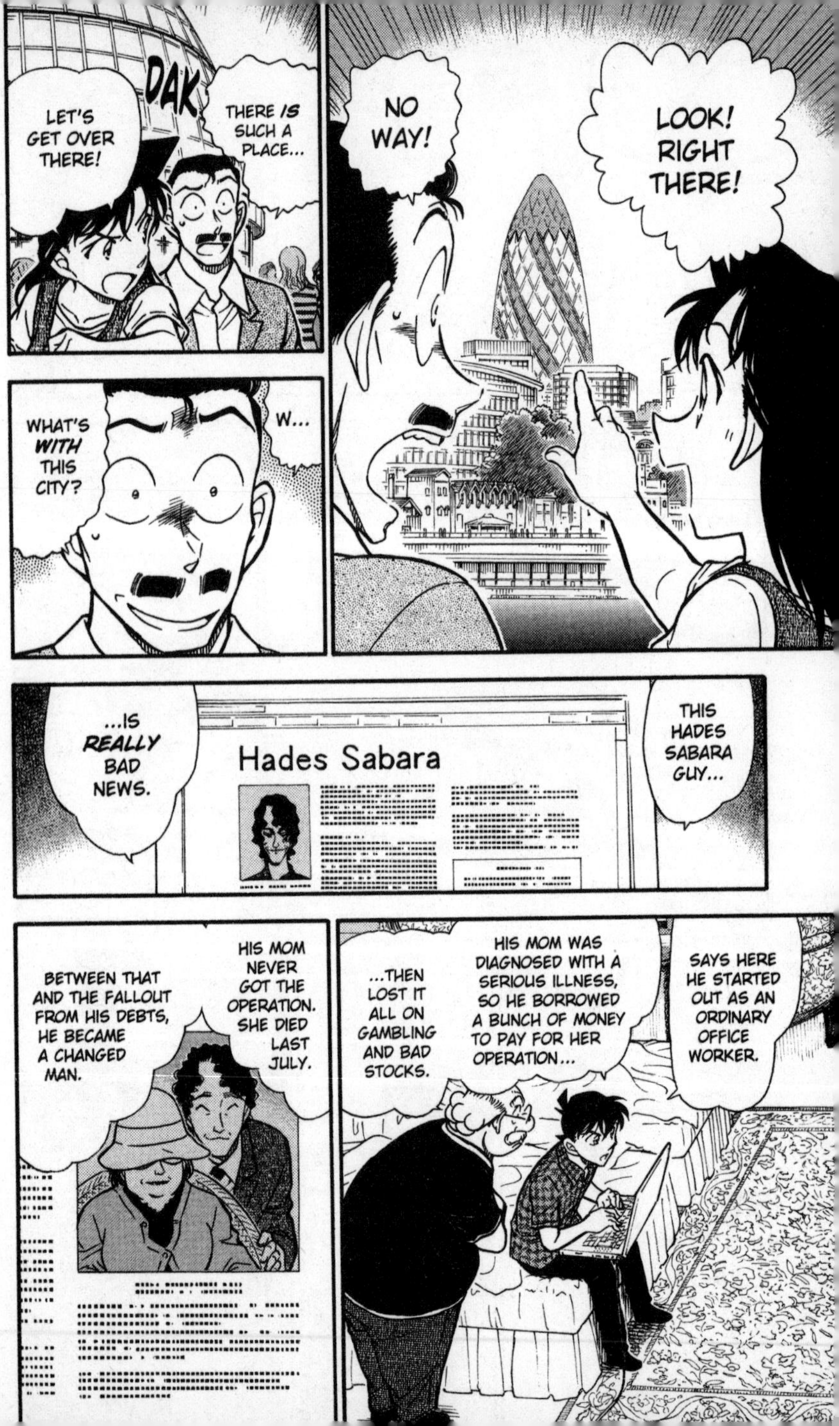
LOOK! RIGHT THERE!
NO WAY!
THERE *IS* SUCH A PLACE...
DAK
LET'S GET OVER THERE!
W...
WHAT'S *WITH* THIS CITY?
THIS HADES SABARA GUY...
Hades Sabara
...IS *REALLY* BAD NEWS.
SAYS HERE HE STARTED OUT AS AN ORDINARY OFFICE WORKER.
HIS MOM WAS DIAGNOSED WITH A SERIOUS ILLNESS, SO HE BORROWED A BUNCH OF MONEY TO PAY FOR HER OPERATION...
...THEN LOST IT ALL ON GAMBLING AND BAD STOCKS.
HIS MOM NEVER GOT THE OPERATION. SHE DIED LAST JULY.
BETWEEN THAT AND THE FALLOUT FROM HIS DEBTS, HE BECAME A CHANGED MAN.

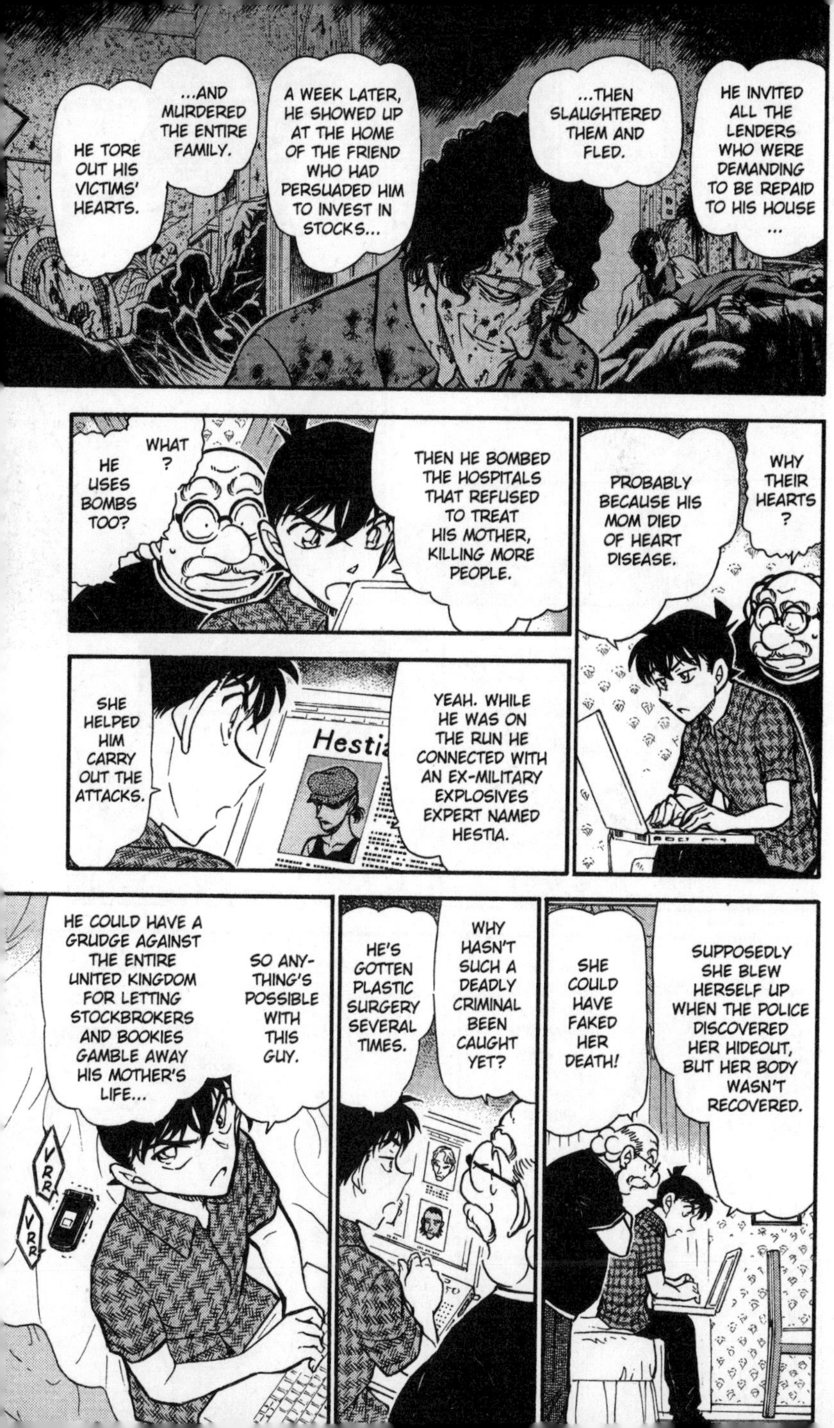
HE INVITED ALL THE LENDERS WHO WERE DEMANDING TO BE REPAID TO HIS HOUSE ...
...THEN SLAUGHTERED THEM AND FLED.
A WEEK LATER, HE SHOWED UP AT THE HOME OF THE FRIEND WHO HAD PERSUADED HIM TO INVEST IN STOCKS...
...AND MURDERED THE ENTIRE FAMILY.
HE TORE OUT HIS VICTIMS' HEARTS.
WHY THEIR HEARTS?
PROBABLY BECAUSE HIS MOM DIED OF HEART DISEASE.
THEN HE BOMBED THE HOSPITALS THAT REFUSED TO TREAT HIS MOTHER, KILLING MORE PEOPLE.
WHAT?
HE USES BOMBS TOO?
YEAH. WHILE HE WAS ON THE RUN HE CONNECTED WITH AN EX-MILITARY EXPLOSIVES EXPERT NAMED HESTIA.
Hestia
SHE HELPED HIM CARRY OUT THE ATTACKS.
SUPPOSEDLY SHE BLEW HERSELF UP WHEN THE POLICE DISCOVERED HER HIDEOUT, BUT HER BODY WASN'T RECOVERED.
SHE COULD HAVE FAKED HER DEATH!
WHY HASN'T SUCH A DEADLY CRIMINAL BEEN CAUGHT YET?
HE'S GOTTEN PLASTIC SURGERY SEVERAL TIMES.
SO ANY-THING'S POSSIBLE WITH THIS GUY.
HE COULD HAVE A GRUDGE AGAINST THE ENTIRE UNITED KINGDOM FOR LETTING STOCKBROKERS AND BOOKIES GAMBLE AWAY HIS MOTHER'S LIFE...
VRR
VRR

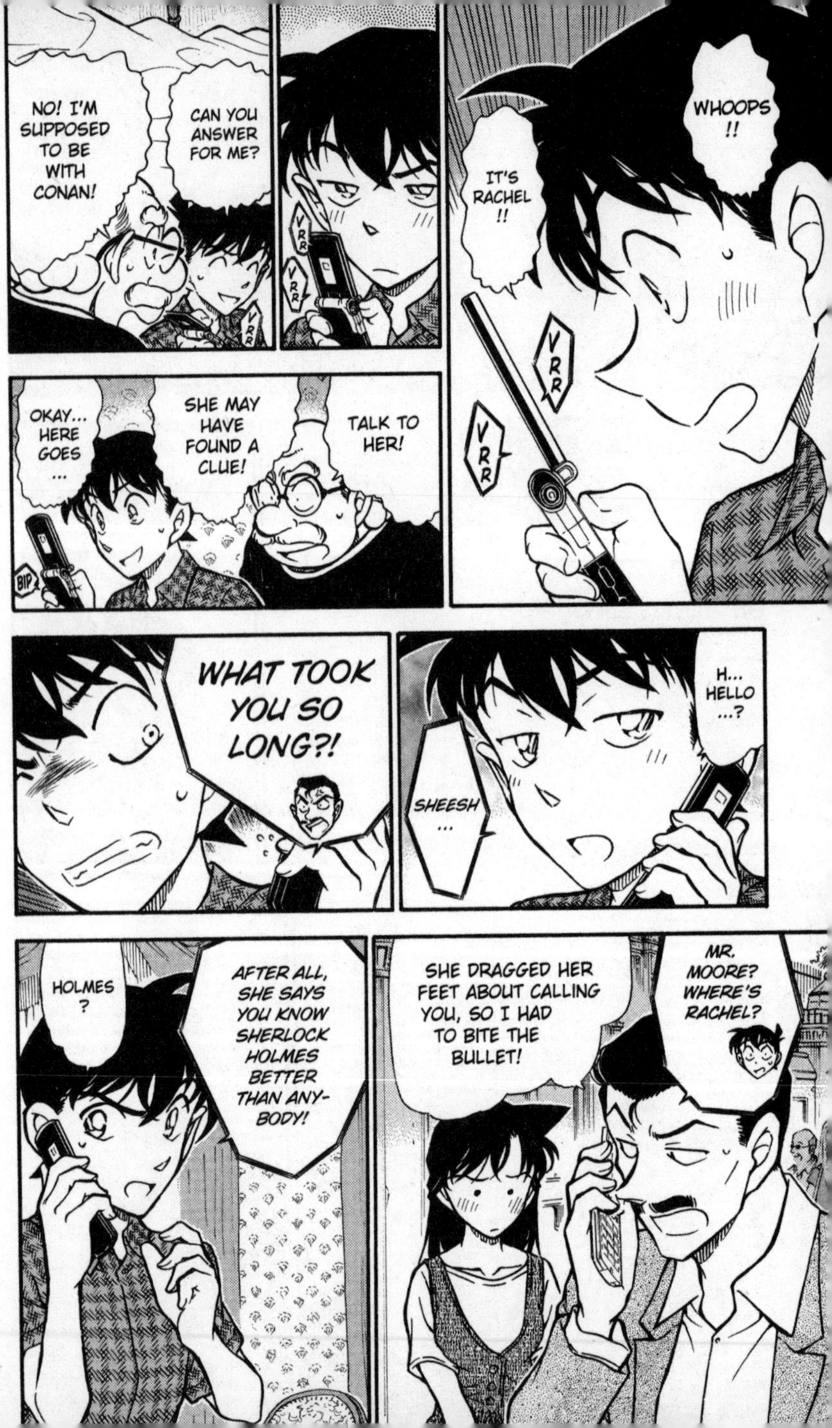
WHOOPS!!
IT'S RACHEL!!
VRR
VRR
VRR
VRR
CAN YOU ANSWER FOR ME?
NO! I'M SUPPOSED TO BE WITH CONAN!
VRR
TALK TO HER!
SHE MAY HAVE FOUND A CLUE!
OKAY... HERE GOES...
BIP
H... HELLO...?
SHEESH...
WHAT TOOK YOU SO LONG?!
MR. MOORE? WHERE'S RACHEL?
SHE DRAGGED HER FEET ABOUT CALLING YOU, SO I HAD TO BITE THE BULLET!
AFTER ALL, SHE SAYS YOU KNOW SHERLOCK HOLMES BETTER THAN ANYBODY!
HOLMES?

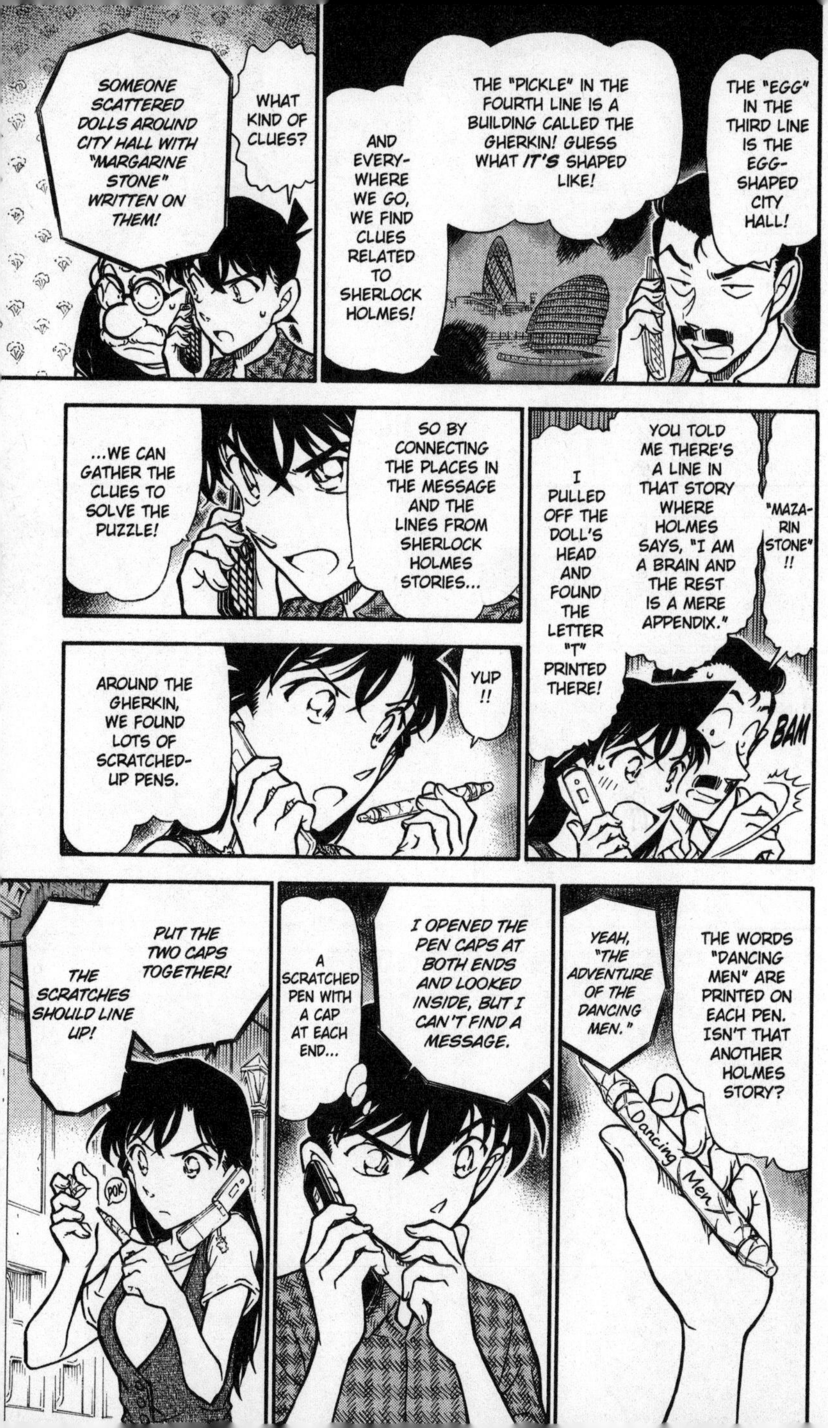
THE "EGG" IN THE THIRD LINE IS THE EGG-SHAPED CITY HALL!
THE "PICKLE" IN THE FOURTH LINE IS A BUILDING CALLED THE GHERKIN! GUESS WHAT *IT'S* SHAPED LIKE!
AND EVERY-WHERE WE GO, WE FIND CLUES RELATED TO SHERLOCK HOLMES!
WHAT KIND OF CLUES?
SOMEONE SCATTERED DOLLS AROUND CITY HALL WITH "MARGARINE STONE" WRITTEN ON THEM!
"MAZA-RIN STONE" !!
YOU TOLD ME THERE'S A LINE IN THAT STORY WHERE HOLMES SAYS, "I AM A BRAIN AND THE REST IS A MERE APPENDIX."
I PULLED OFF THE DOLL'S HEAD AND FOUND THE LETTER "T" PRINTED THERE!
BAM
SO BY CONNECTING THE PLACES IN THE MESSAGE AND THE LINES FROM SHERLOCK HOLMES STORIES...
...WE CAN GATHER THE CLUES TO SOLVE THE PUZZLE!
YUP !!
AROUND THE GHERKIN, WE FOUND LOTS OF SCRATCHED-UP PENS.
THE WORDS "DANCING MEN" ARE PRINTED ON EACH PEN. ISN'T THAT ANOTHER HOLMES STORY?
YEAH, "THE ADVENTURE OF THE DANCING MEN."
Dancing Men
I OPENED THE PEN CAPS AT BOTH ENDS AND LOOKED INSIDE, BUT I CAN'T FIND A MESSAGE.
A SCRATCHED PEN WITH A CAP AT EACH END...
PUT THE TWO CAPS TOGETHER!
THE SCRATCHES SHOULD LINE UP!
POK

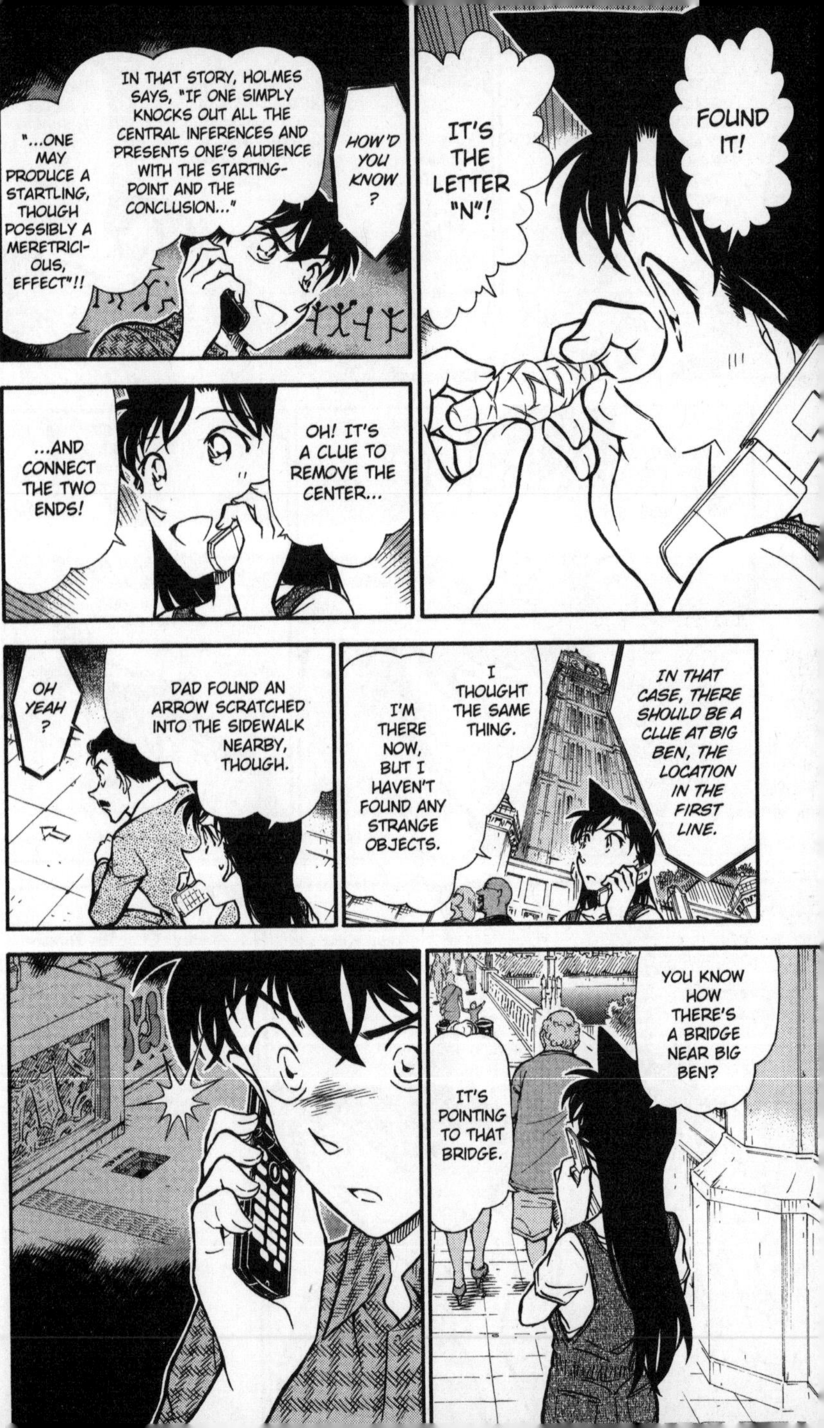
FOUND IT!
IT'S THE LETTER "N"!
HOW'D YOU KNOW?
IN THAT STORY, HOLMES SAYS, "IF ONE SIMPLY KNOCKS OUT ALL THE CENTRAL INFERENCES AND PRESENTS ONE'S AUDIENCE WITH THE STARTING-POINT AND THE CONCLUSION..."
"...ONE MAY PRODUCE A STARTLING, THOUGH POSSIBLY A MERETRICI-OUS, EFFECT"!!
OH! IT'S A CLUE TO REMOVE THE CENTER...
...AND CONNECT THE TWO ENDS!
IN THAT CASE, THERE SHOULD BE A CLUE AT BIG BEN, THE LOCATION IN THE FIRST LINE.
I THOUGHT THE SAME THING.
I'M THERE NOW, BUT I HAVEN'T FOUND ANY STRANGE OBJECTS.
DAD FOUND AN ARROW SCRATCHED INTO THE SIDEWALK NEARBY, THOUGH.
OH YEAH?
YOU KNOW HOW THERE'S A BRIDGE NEAR BIG BEN?
IT'S POINTING TO THAT BRIDGE.

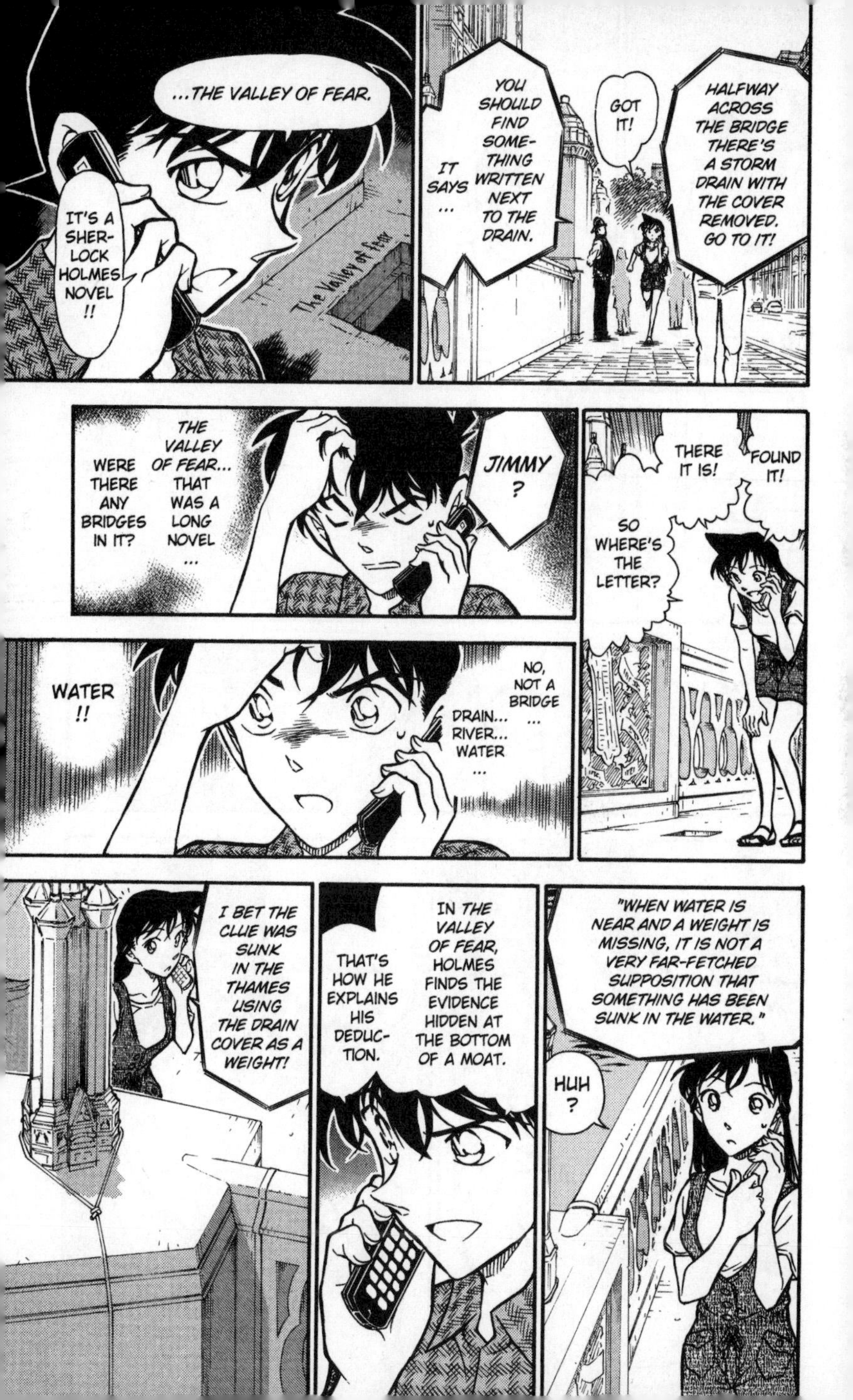
HALFWAY ACROSS THE BRIDGE THERE'S A STORM DRAIN WITH THE COVER REMOVED. GO TO IT!
GOT IT!
YOU SHOULD FIND SOMETHING WRITTEN NEXT TO THE DRAIN.
IT SAYS ...
...THE VALLEY OF FEAR.
The Valley of Fear
IT'S A SHERLOCK HOLMES NOVEL !!
FOUND IT!
THERE IT IS!
SO WHERE'S THE LETTER?
JIMMY ?
THE VALLEY OF FEAR... THAT WAS A LONG NOVEL ...
WERE THERE ANY BRIDGES IN IT?
NO, NOT A BRIDGE ...
DRAIN... RIVER... WATER ...
WATER !!
"WHEN WATER IS NEAR AND A WEIGHT IS MISSING, IT IS NOT A VERY FAR-FETCHED SUPPOSITION THAT SOMETHING HAS BEEN SUNK IN THE WATER."
HUH ?
IN THE VALLEY OF FEAR, HOLMES FINDS THE EVIDENCE HIDDEN AT THE BOTTOM OF A MOAT.
THAT'S HOW HE EXPLAINS HIS DEDUCTION.
I BET THE CLUE WAS SUNK IN THE THAMES USING THE DRAIN COVER AS A WEIGHT!

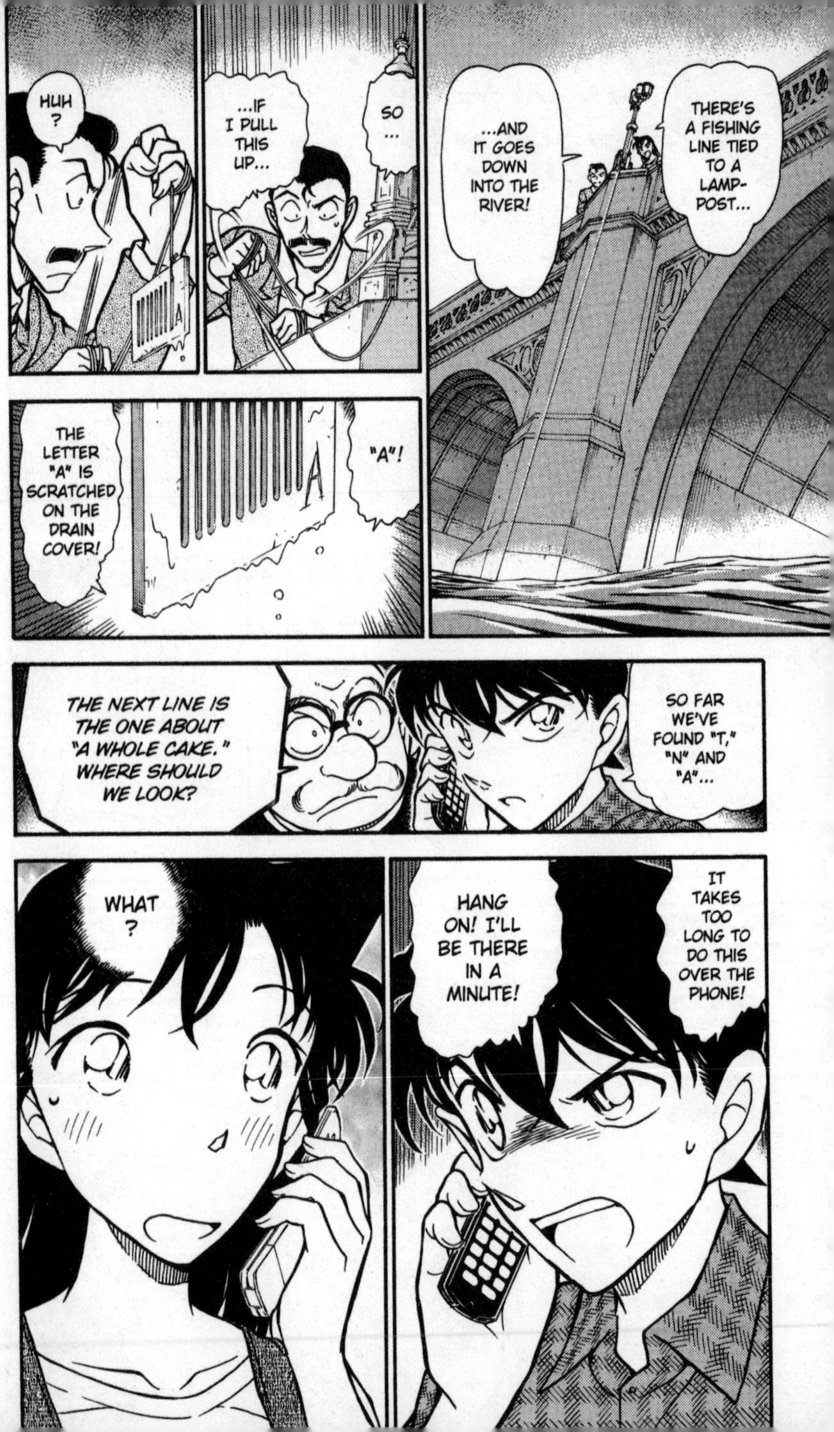
THERE'S A FISHING LINE TIED TO A LAMP-POST...
...AND IT GOES DOWN INTO THE RIVER!
SO...
...IF I PULL THIS UP...
HUH?
"A"!
THE LETTER "A" IS SCRATCHED ON THE DRAIN COVER!
SO FAR WE'VE FOUND "T," "N" AND "A"...
THE NEXT LINE IS THE ONE ABOUT "A WHOLE CAKE." WHERE SHOULD WE LOOK?
IT TAKES TOO LONG TO DO THIS OVER THE PHONE!
HANG ON! I'LL BE THERE IN A MINUTE!
WHAT?

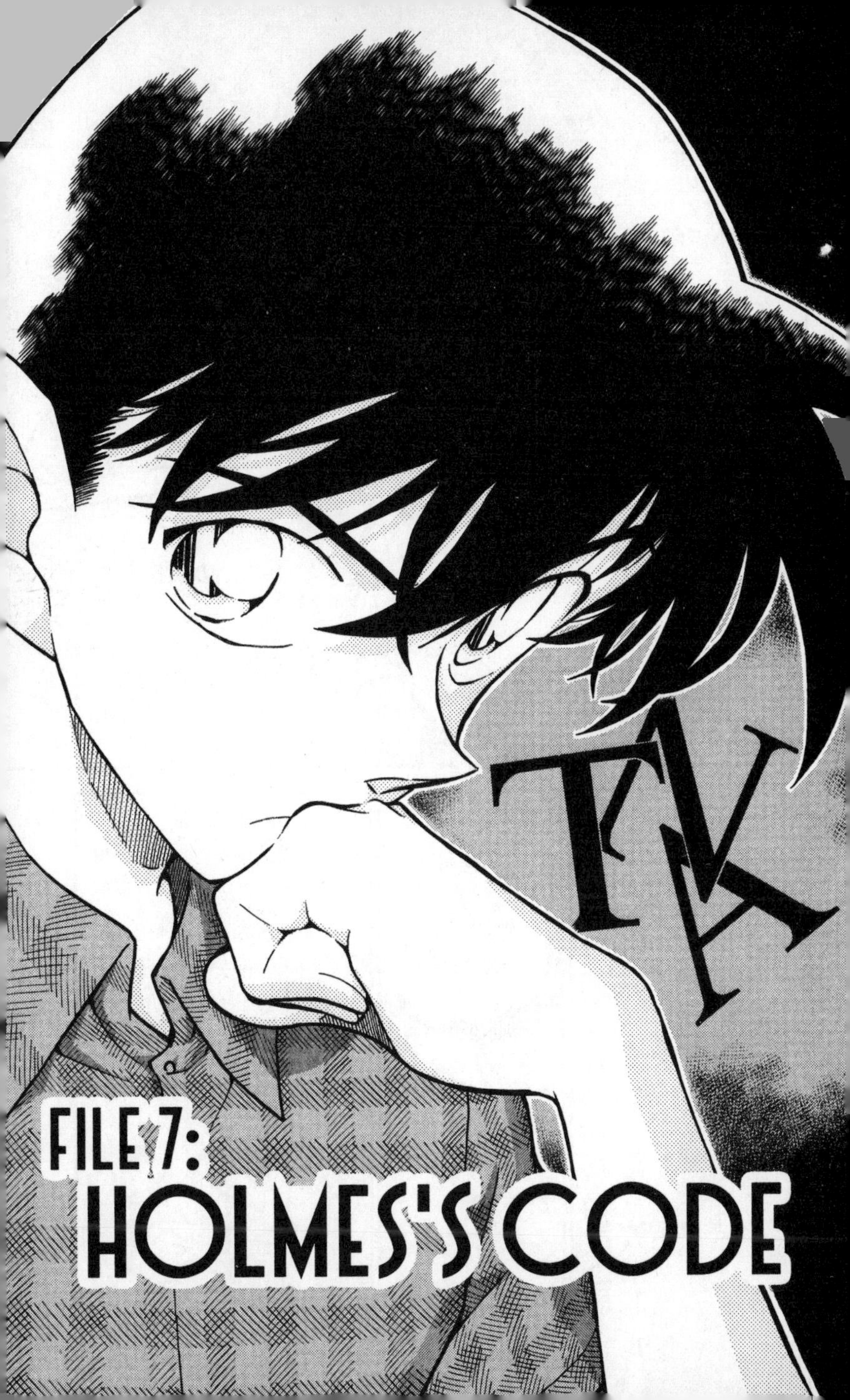
TN
FILE 7:
HOLMES'S CODE

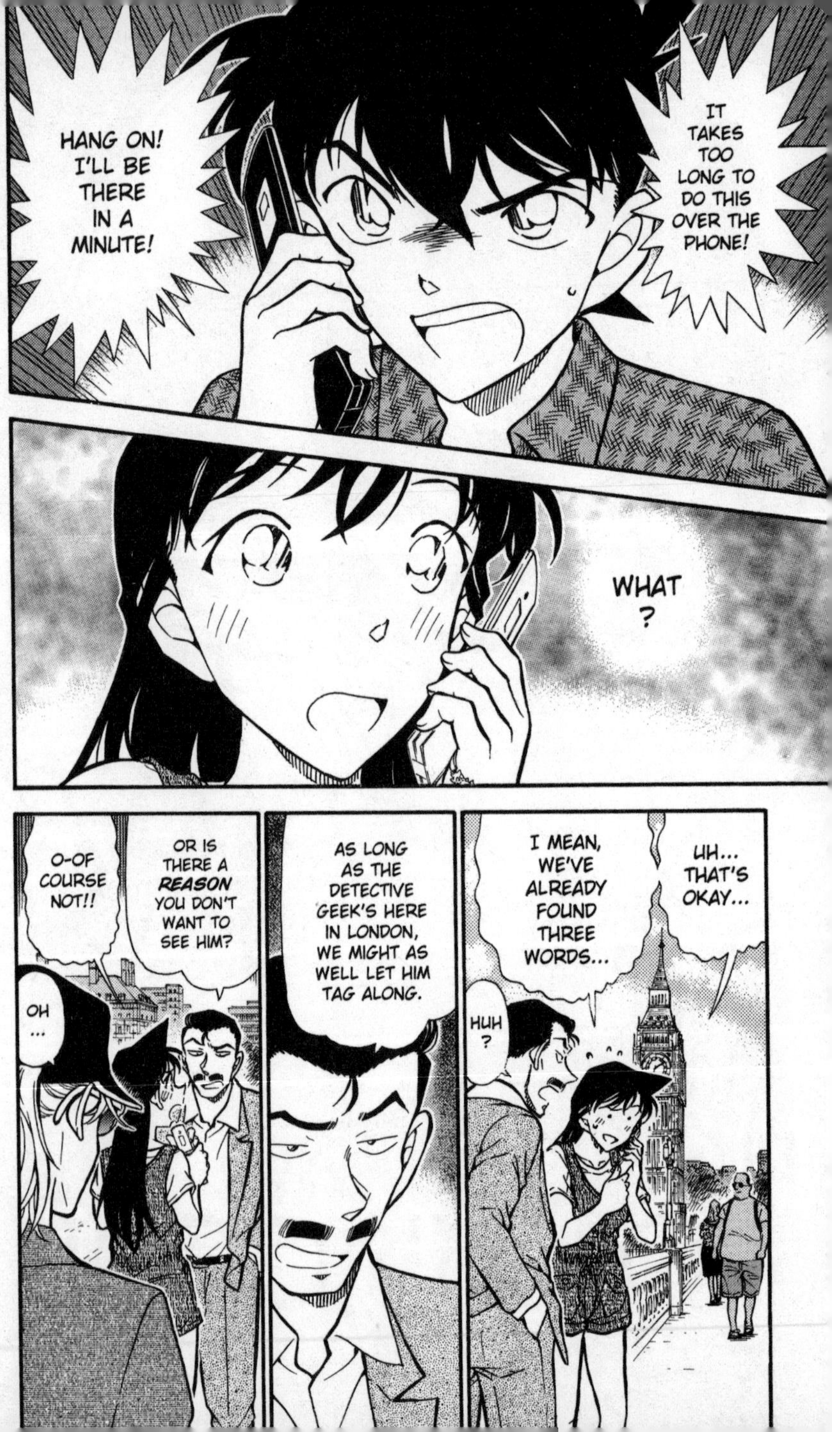
IT TAKES TOO LONG TO DO THIS OVER THE PHONE!
HANG ON! I'LL BE THERE IN A MINUTE!
WHAT?
UH... THAT'S OKAY...
I MEAN, WE'VE ALREADY FOUND THREE WORDS...
HUH?
AS LONG AS THE DETECTIVE GEEK'S HERE IN LONDON, WE MIGHT AS WELL LET HIM TAG ALONG.
OR IS THERE A *REASON* YOU DON'T WANT TO SEE HIM?
O-OF COURSE NOT!!
OH ...

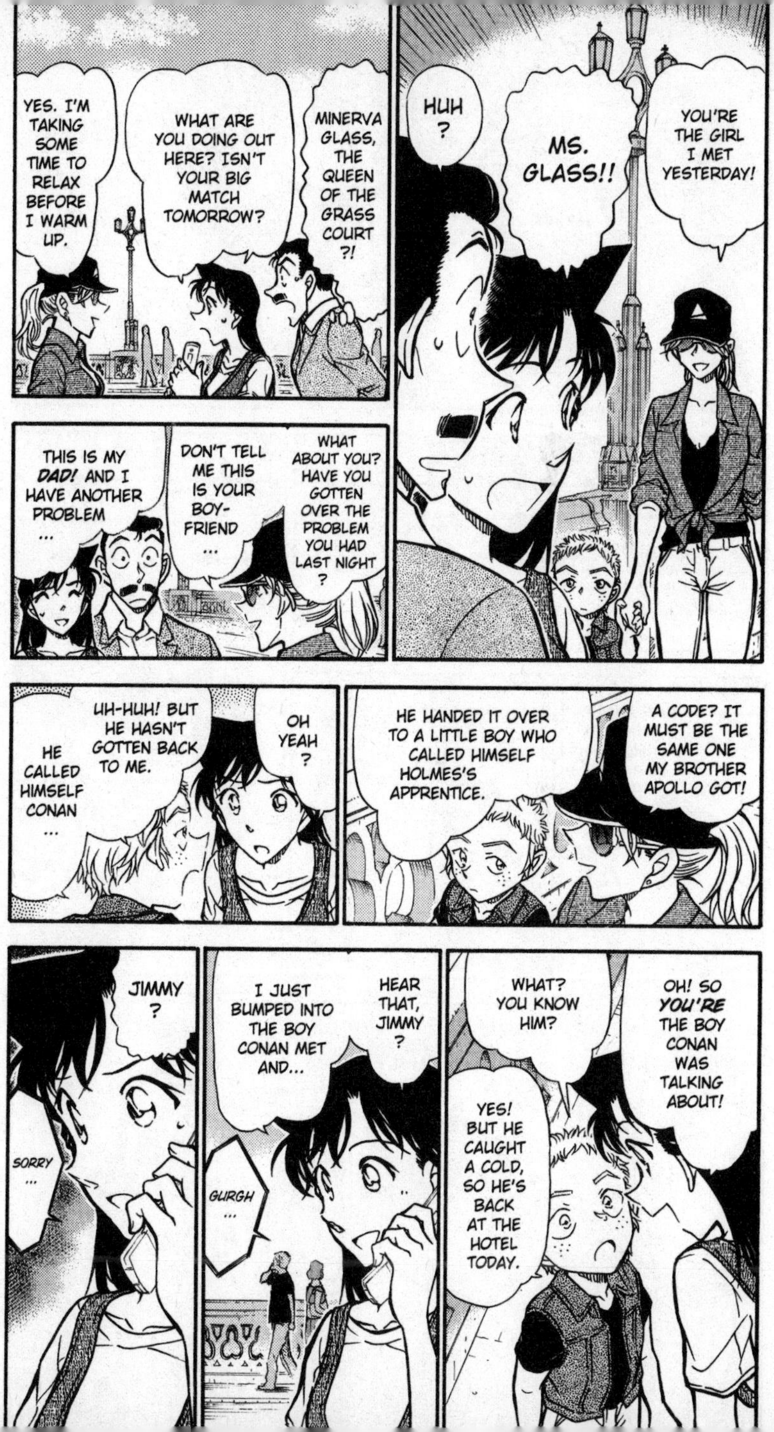
YOU'RE THE GIRL I MET YESTERDAY!
MS. GLASS!!
HUH ?
MINERVA GLASS, THE QUEEN OF THE GRASS COURT ?!
WHAT ARE YOU DOING OUT HERE? ISN'T YOUR BIG MATCH TOMORROW?
YES. I'M TAKING SOME TIME TO RELAX BEFORE I WARM UP.
WHAT ABOUT YOU? HAVE YOU GOTTEN OVER THE PROBLEM YOU HAD LAST NIGHT ?
DON'T TELL ME THIS IS YOUR BOY-FRIEND ...
THIS IS MY DAD! AND I HAVE ANOTHER PROBLEM ...
A CODE? IT MUST BE THE SAME ONE MY BROTHER APOLLO GOT!
HE HANDED IT OVER TO A LITTLE BOY WHO CALLED HIMSELF HOLMES'S APPRENTICE.
OH YEAH ?
UH-HUH! BUT HE HASN'T GOTTEN BACK TO ME.
HE CALLED HIMSELF CONAN ...
OH! SO YOU'RE THE BOY CONAN WAS TALKING ABOUT!
WHAT? YOU KNOW HIM?
YES! BUT HE CAUGHT A COLD, SO HE'S BACK AT THE HOTEL TODAY.
HEAR THAT, JIMMY ?
I JUST BUMPED INTO THE BOY CONAN MET AND...
GURGH ...
JIMMY ?
SORRY ...

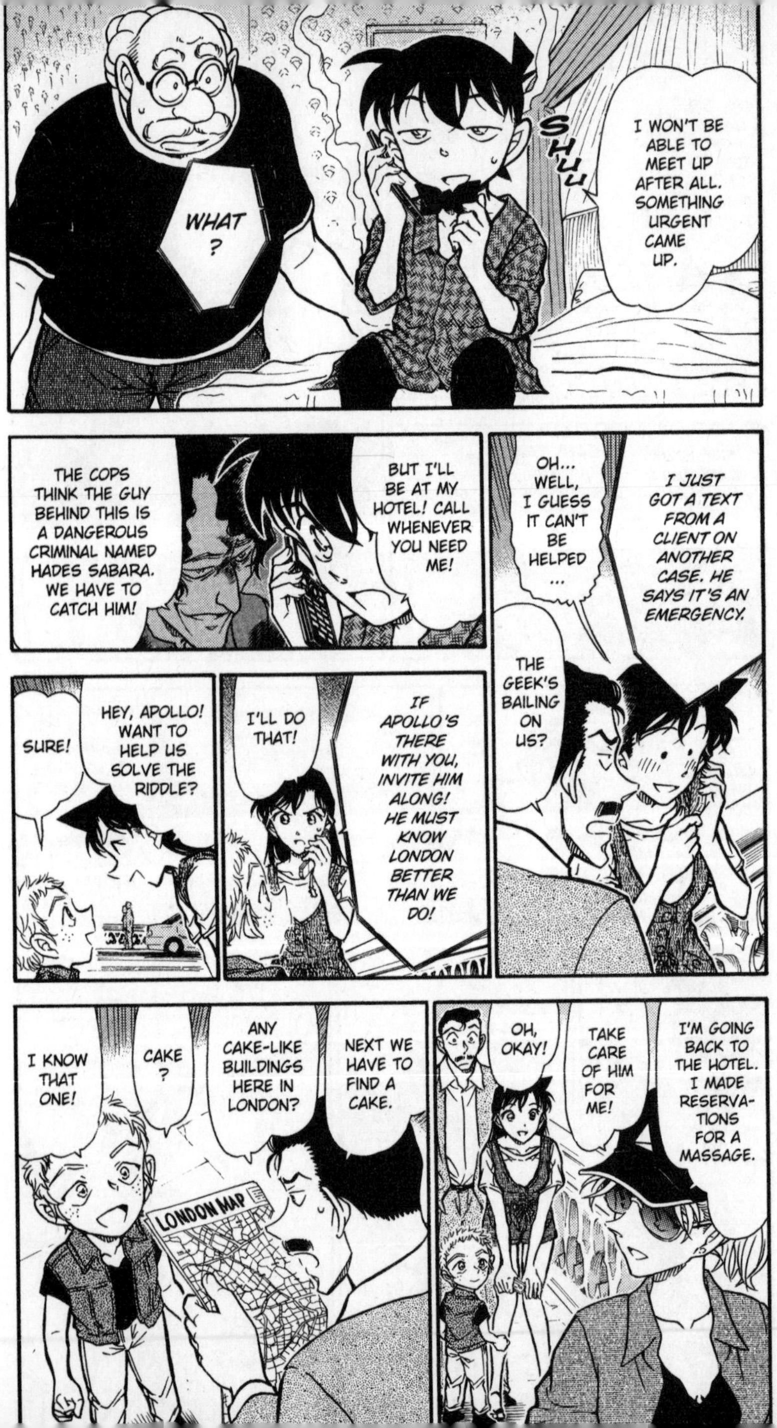
I WON'T BE ABLE TO MEET UP AFTER ALL. SOMETHING URGENT CAME UP.
SHUU
WHAT?
I JUST GOT A TEXT FROM A CLIENT ON ANOTHER CASE. HE SAYS IT'S AN EMERGENCY.
OH... WELL, I GUESS IT CAN'T BE HELPED...
THE GEEK'S BAILING ON US?
BUT I'LL BE AT MY HOTEL! CALL WHENEVER YOU NEED ME!
THE COPS THINK THE GUY BEHIND THIS IS A DANGEROUS CRIMINAL NAMED HADES SABARA. WE HAVE TO CATCH HIM!
IF APOLLO'S THERE WITH YOU, INVITE HIM ALONG! HE MUST KNOW LONDON BETTER THAN WE DO!
I'LL DO THAT!
HEY, APOLLO! WANT TO HELP US SOLVE THE RIDDLE?
SURE!
I'M GOING BACK TO THE HOTEL. I MADE RESERVATIONS FOR A MASSAGE.
TAKE CARE OF HIM FOR ME!
OH, OKAY!
NEXT WE HAVE TO FIND A CAKE.
ANY CAKE-LIKE BUILDINGS HERE IN LONDON?
CAKE?
I KNOW THAT ONE!
LONDON MAP

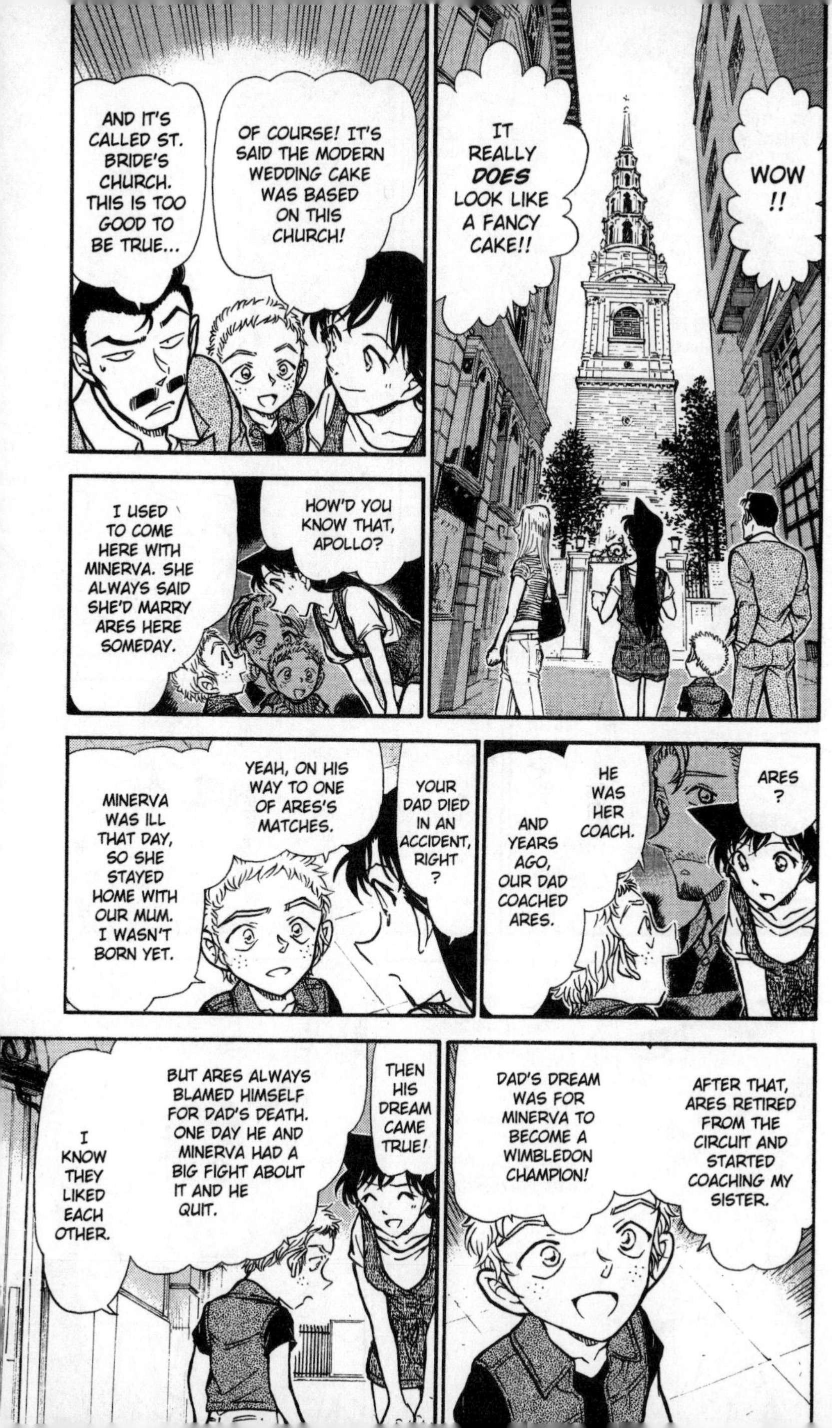
WOW!!
IT REALLY DOES LOOK LIKE A FANCY CAKE!!
OF COURSE! IT'S SAID THE MODERN WEDDING CAKE WAS BASED ON THIS CHURCH!
AND IT'S CALLED ST. BRIDE'S CHURCH. THIS IS TOO GOOD TO BE TRUE...
HOW'D YOU KNOW THAT, APOLLO?
I USED TO COME HERE WITH MINERVA. SHE ALWAYS SAID SHE'D MARRY ARES HERE SOMEDAY.
ARES?
HE WAS HER COACH.
AND YEARS AGO, OUR DAD COACHED ARES.
YOUR DAD DIED IN AN ACCIDENT, RIGHT?
YEAH, ON HIS WAY TO ONE OF ARES'S MATCHES.
MINERVA WAS ILL THAT DAY, SO SHE STAYED HOME WITH OUR MUM. I WASN'T BORN YET.
AFTER THAT, ARES RETIRED FROM THE CIRCUIT AND STARTED COACHING MY SISTER.
DAD'S DREAM WAS FOR MINERVA TO BECOME A WIMBLEDON CHAMPION!
THEN HIS DREAM CAME TRUE!
BUT ARES ALWAYS BLAMED HIMSELF FOR DAD'S DEATH. ONE DAY HE AND MINERVA HAD A BIG FIGHT ABOUT IT AND HE QUIT.
I KNOW THEY LIKED EACH OTHER.

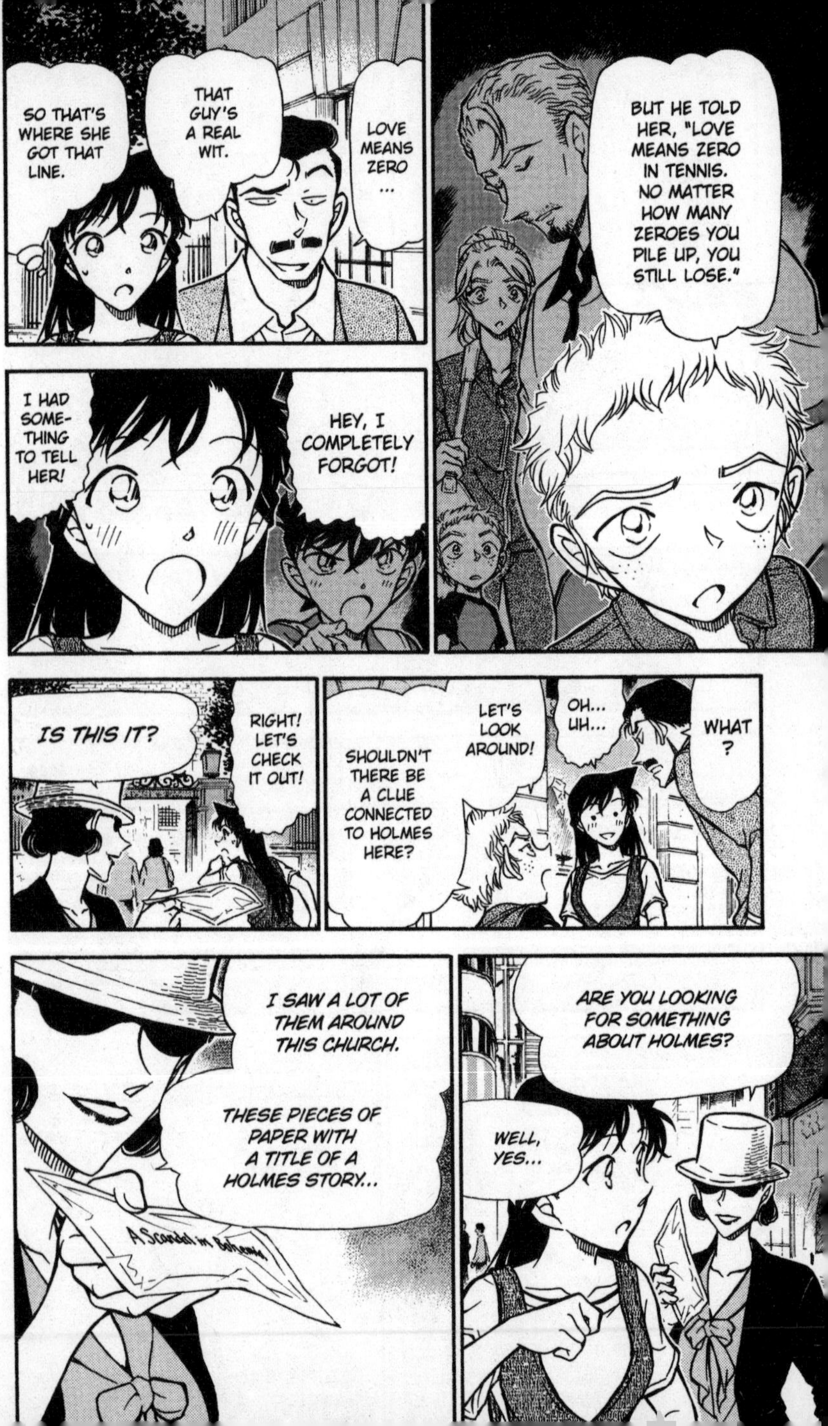
BUT HE TOLD HER, "LOVE MEANS ZERO IN TENNIS. NO MATTER HOW MANY ZEROES YOU PILE UP, YOU STILL LOSE."
LOVE MEANS ZERO ...
THAT GUY'S A REAL WIT.
SO THAT'S WHERE SHE GOT THAT LINE.
HEY, I COMPLETELY FORGOT!
I HAD SOME-THING TO TELL HER!
WHAT?
OH... UH...
LET'S LOOK AROUND!
SHOULDN'T THERE BE A CLUE CONNECTED TO HOLMES HERE?
RIGHT! LET'S CHECK IT OUT!
IS THIS IT?
ARE YOU LOOKING FOR SOMETHING ABOUT HOLMES?
WELL, YES...
I SAW A LOT OF THEM AROUND THIS CHURCH.
THESE PIECES OF PAPER WITH A TITLE OF A HOLMES STORY...
A Scandal in Bohemia

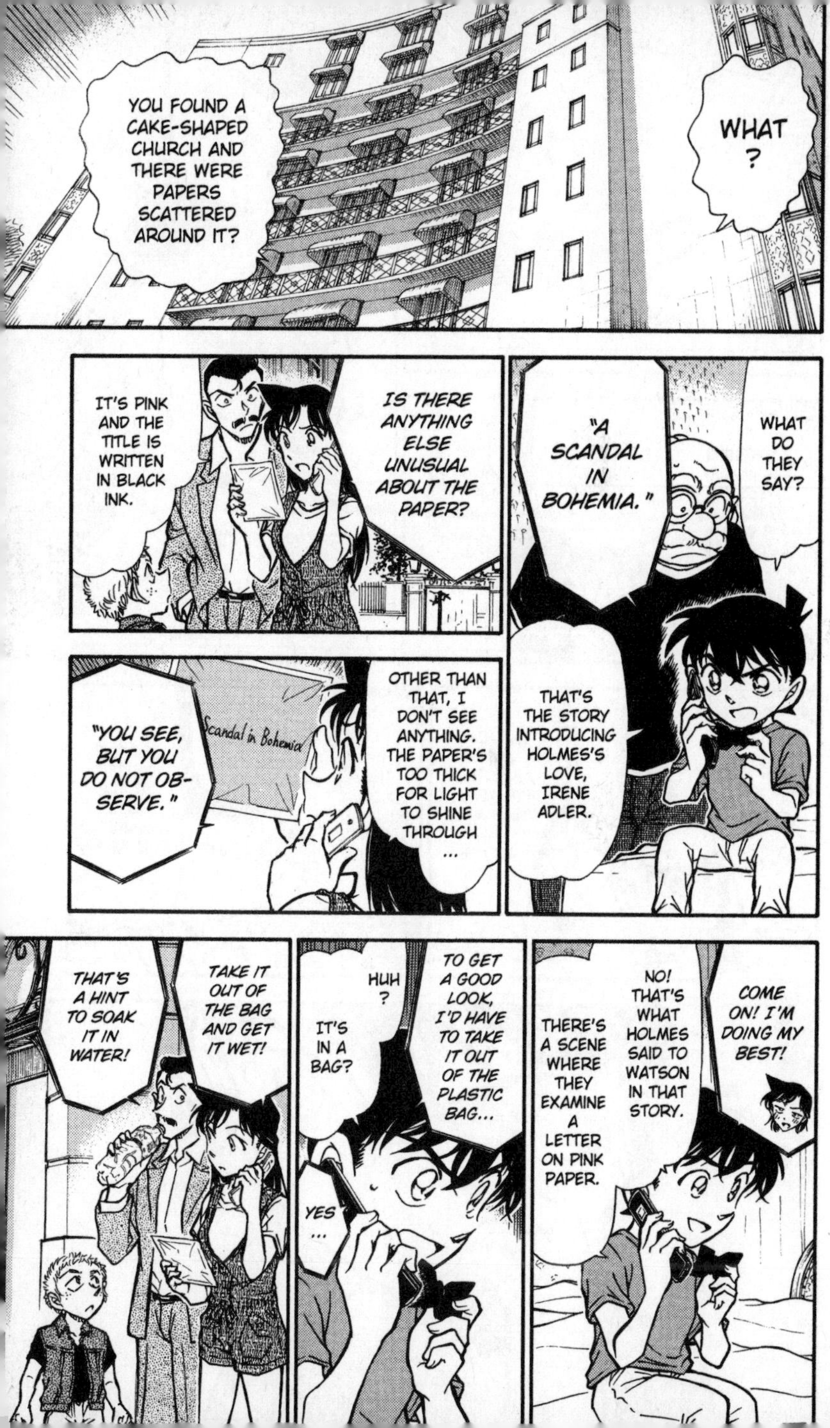
WHAT ?
YOU FOUND A CAKE-SHAPED CHURCH AND THERE WERE PAPERS SCATTERED AROUND IT?
WHAT DO THEY SAY?
"A SCANDAL IN BOHEMIA."
THAT'S THE STORY INTRODUCING HOLMES'S LOVE, IRENE ADLER.
IS THERE ANYTHING ELSE UNUSUAL ABOUT THE PAPER?
IT'S PINK AND THE TITLE IS WRITTEN IN BLACK INK.
OTHER THAN THAT, I DON'T SEE ANYTHING. THE PAPER'S TOO THICK FOR LIGHT TO SHINE THROUGH ...
Scandal in Bohemia
"YOU SEE, BUT YOU DO NOT OB-SERVE."
COME ON! I'M DOING MY BEST!
NO! THAT'S WHAT HOLMES SAID TO WATSON IN THAT STORY.
THERE'S A SCENE WHERE THEY EXAMINE A LETTER ON PINK PAPER.
TO GET A GOOD LOOK, I'D HAVE TO TAKE IT OUT OF THE PLASTIC BAG...
HUH ?
IT'S IN A BAG?
YES ...
TAKE IT OUT OF THE BAG AND GET IT WET!
THAT'S A HINT TO SOAK IT IN WATER!

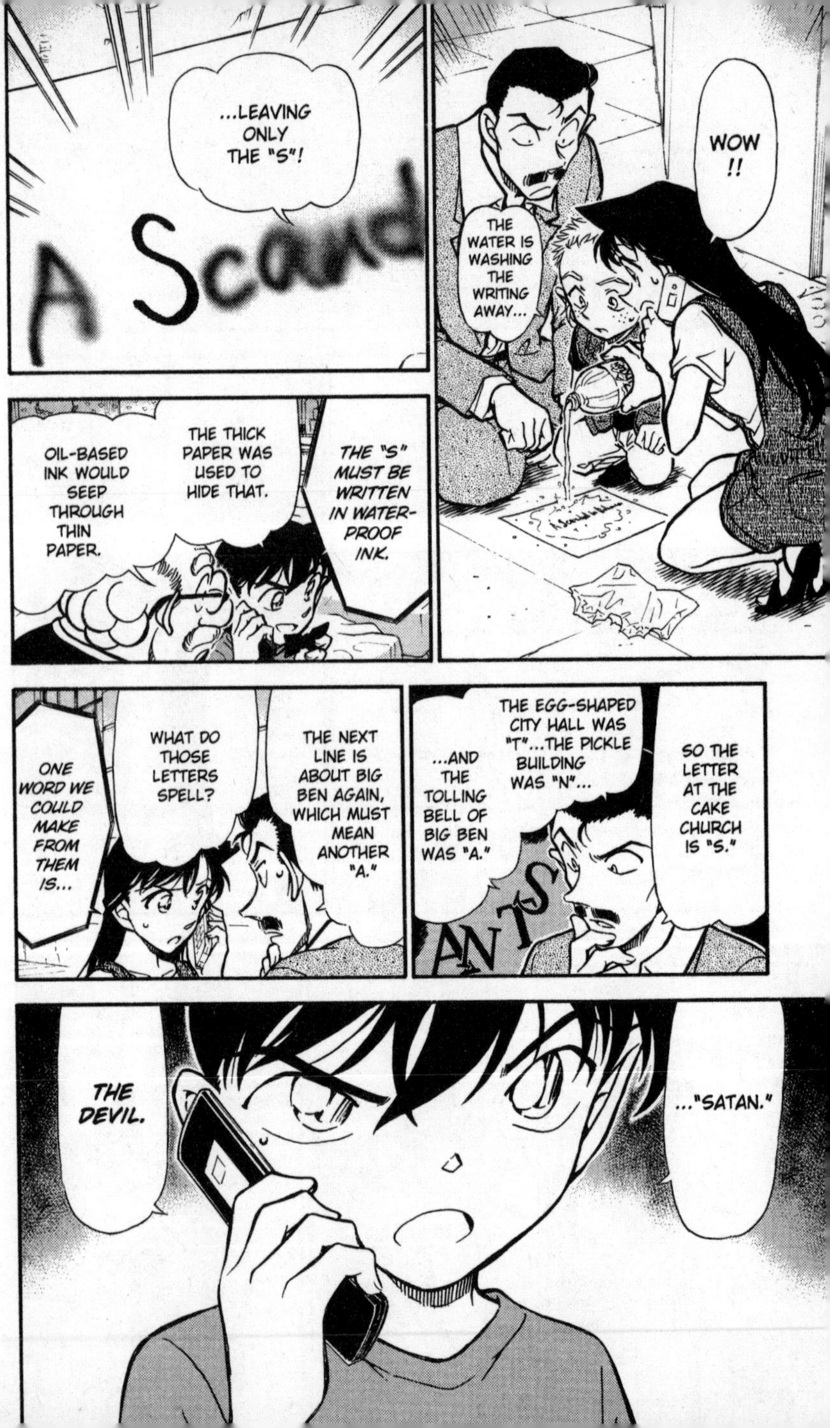
WOW !!
THE WATER IS WASHING THE WRITING AWAY...
...LEAVING ONLY THE "S"!
A Scand
THE "S" MUST BE WRITTEN IN WATER-PROOF INK.
THE THICK PAPER WAS USED TO HIDE THAT.
OIL-BASED INK WOULD SEEP THROUGH THIN PAPER.
SO THE LETTER AT THE CAKE CHURCH IS "S."
THE EGG-SHAPED CITY HALL WAS "T"...THE PICKLE BUILDING WAS "N"...
...AND THE TOLLING BELL OF BIG BEN WAS "A."
ANTS
THE NEXT LINE IS ABOUT BIG BEN AGAIN, WHICH MUST MEAN ANOTHER "A."
WHAT DO THOSE LETTERS SPELL?
ONE WORD WE COULD MAKE FROM THEM IS...
..."SATAN."
THE DEVIL.

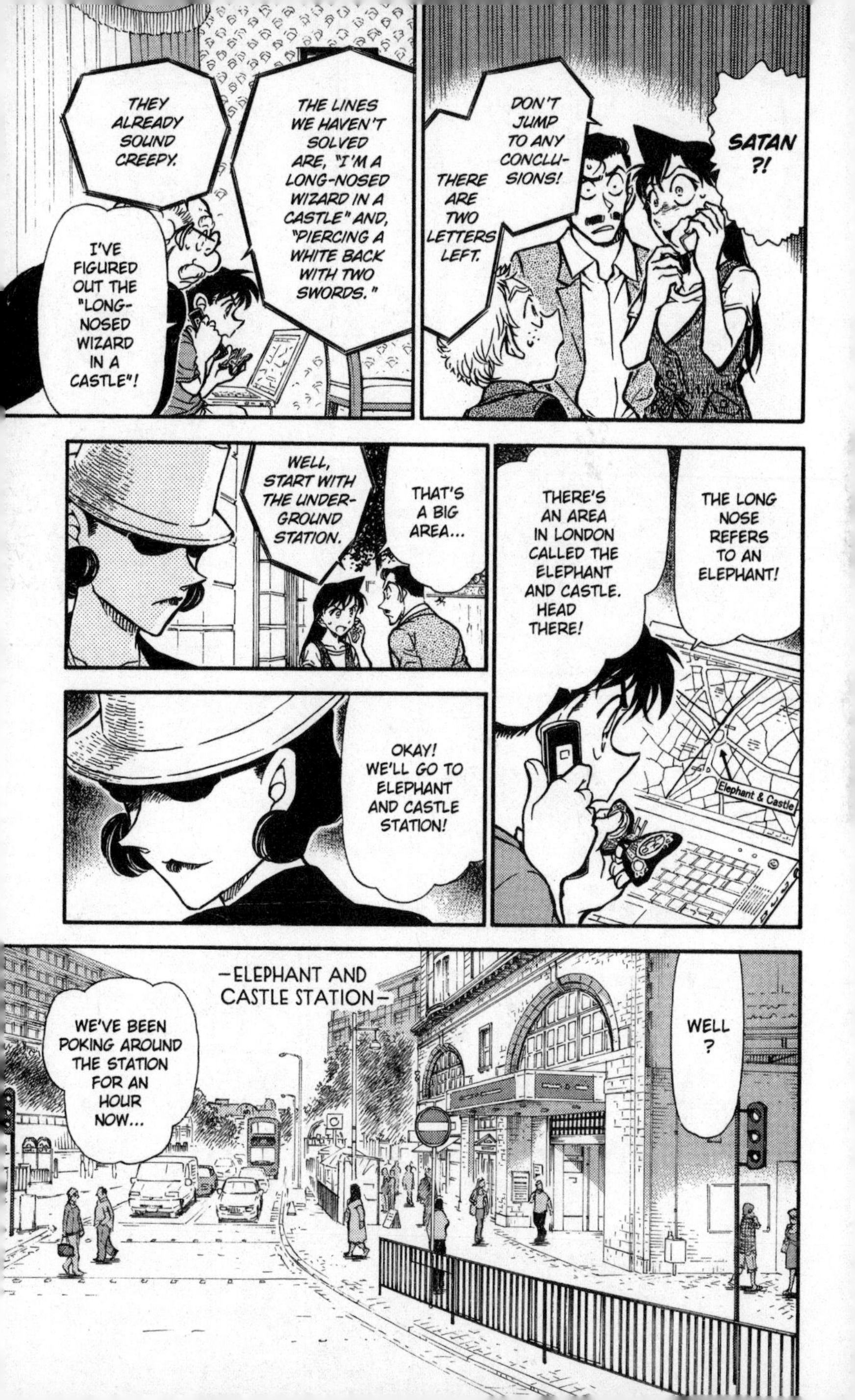
SATAN ?!
DON'T JUMP TO ANY CONCLUSIONS!
THERE ARE TWO LETTERS LEFT.
THE LINES WE HAVEN'T SOLVED ARE, "I'M A LONG-NOSED WIZARD IN A CASTLE" AND, "PIERCING A WHITE BACK WITH TWO SWORDS."
THEY ALREADY SOUND CREEPY.
I'VE FIGURED OUT THE "LONG-NOSED WIZARD IN A CASTLE"!
THE LONG NOSE REFERS TO AN ELEPHANT!
THERE'S AN AREA IN LONDON CALLED THE ELEPHANT AND CASTLE. HEAD THERE!
Elephant & Castle
THAT'S A BIG AREA...
WELL, START WITH THE UNDERGROUND STATION.
OKAY! WE'LL GO TO ELEPHANT AND CASTLE STATION!
WELL ?
—ELEPHANT AND CASTLE STATION—
WE'VE BEEN POKING AROUND THE STATION FOR AN HOUR NOW...

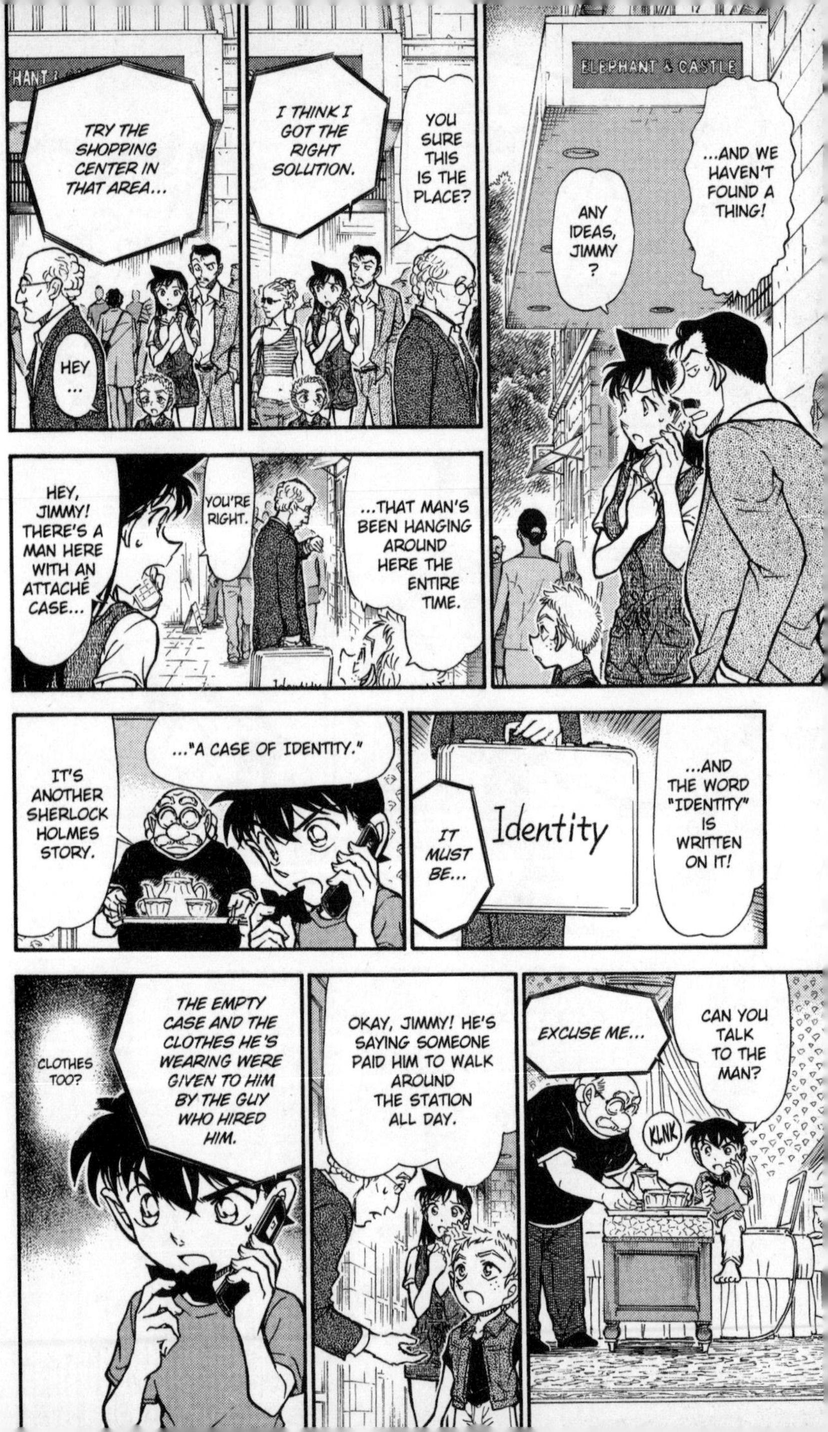
ELEPHANT & CASTLE
...AND WE HAVEN'T FOUND A THING!
ANY IDEAS, JIMMY?
YOU SURE THIS IS THE PLACE?
I THINK I GOT THE RIGHT SOLUTION.
TRY THE SHOPPING CENTER IN THAT AREA...
HEY ...
...THAT MAN'S BEEN HANGING AROUND HERE THE ENTIRE TIME.
YOU'RE RIGHT.
HEY, JIMMY! THERE'S A MAN HERE WITH AN ATTACHÉ CASE...
...AND THE WORD "IDENTITY" IS WRITTEN ON IT!
Identity
IT MUST BE...
..."A CASE OF IDENTITY."
IT'S ANOTHER SHERLOCK HOLMES STORY.
CAN YOU TALK TO THE MAN?
EXCUSE ME...
KLNK
OKAY, JIMMY! HE'S SAYING SOMEONE PAID HIM TO WALK AROUND THE STATION ALL DAY.
THE EMPTY CASE AND THE CLOTHES HE'S WEARING WERE GIVEN TO HIM BY THE GUY WHO HIRED HIM.
CLOTHES TOO?

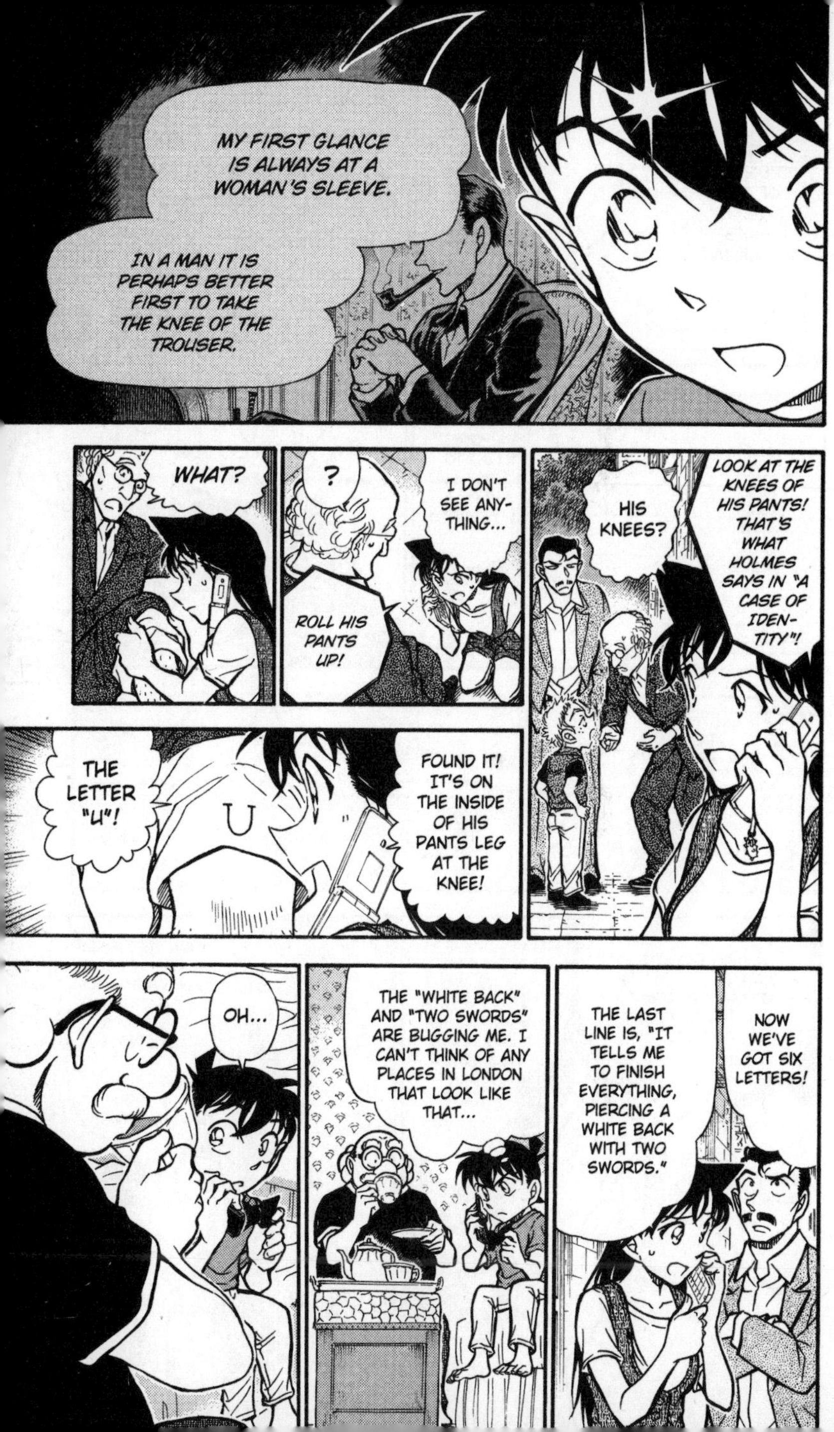
MY FIRST GLANCE IS ALWAYS AT A WOMAN'S SLEEVE.
IN A MAN IT IS PERHAPS BETTER FIRST TO TAKE THE KNEE OF THE TROUSER.
LOOK AT THE KNEES OF HIS PANTS! THAT'S WHAT HOLMES SAYS IN "A CASE OF IDENTITY"!
HIS KNEES?
I DON'T SEE ANYTHING...
?
ROLL HIS PANTS UP!
WHAT?
FOUND IT! IT'S ON THE INSIDE OF HIS PANTS LEG AT THE KNEE!
U
THE LETTER "U"!
NOW WE'VE GOT SIX LETTERS!
THE LAST LINE IS, "IT TELLS ME TO FINISH EVERYTHING, PIERCING A WHITE BACK WITH TWO SWORDS."
THE "WHITE BACK" AND "TWO SWORDS" ARE BUGGING ME. I CAN'T THINK OF ANY PLACES IN LONDON THAT LOOK LIKE THAT...
OH...

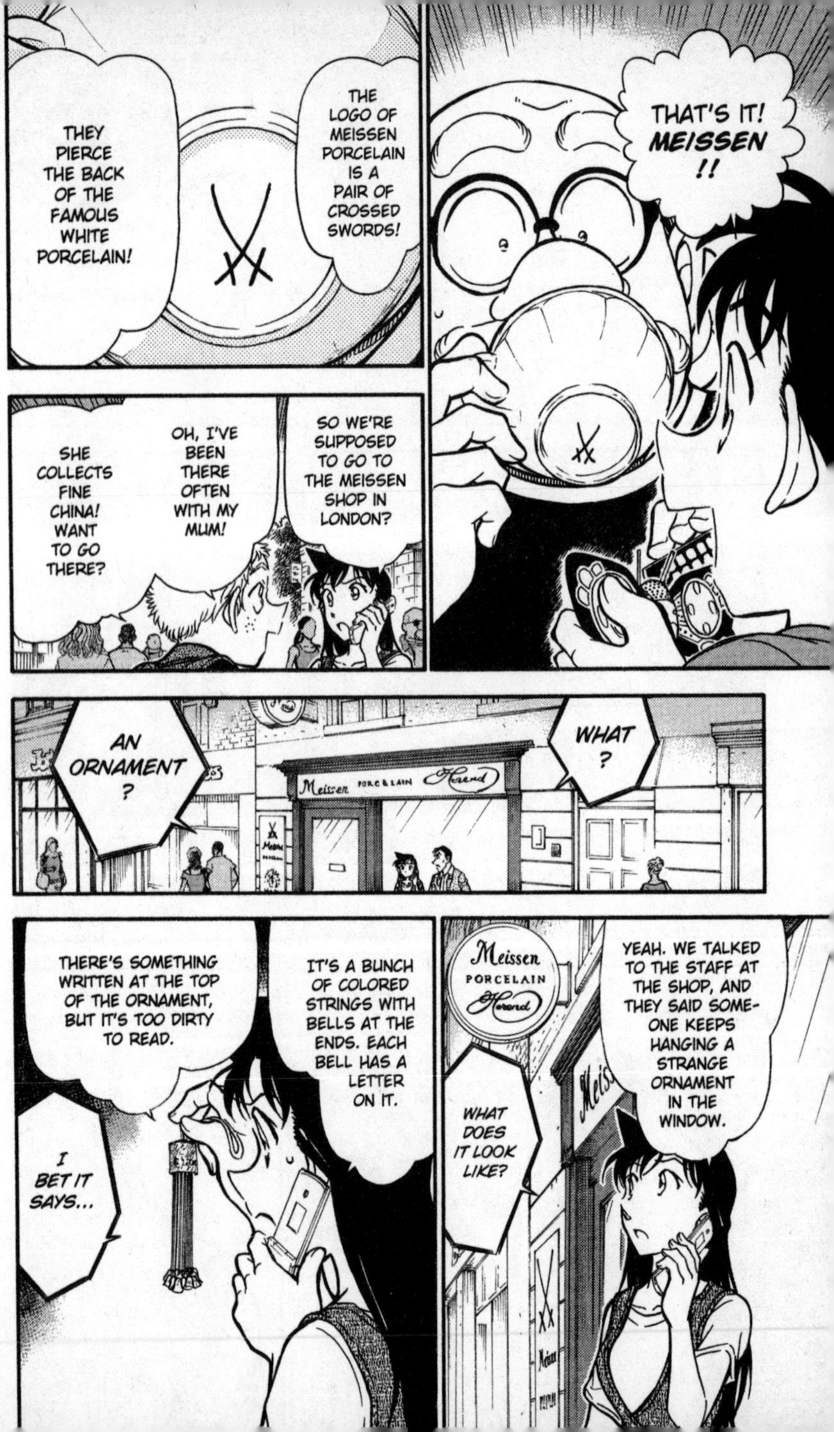
THAT'S IT! MEISSEN!!
THE LOGO OF MEISSEN PORCELAIN IS A PAIR OF CROSSED SWORDS!
THEY PIERCE THE BACK OF THE FAMOUS WHITE PORCELAIN!
SO WE'RE SUPPOSED TO GO TO THE MEISSEN SHOP IN LONDON?
OH, I'VE BEEN THERE OFTEN WITH MY MUM!
SHE COLLECTS FINE CHINA! WANT TO GO THERE?
WHAT?
AN ORNAMENT?
Meissen PORCELAIN Herend
YEAH. WE TALKED TO THE STAFF AT THE SHOP, AND THEY SAID SOME-ONE KEEPS HANGING A STRANGE ORNAMENT IN THE WINDOW.
WHAT DOES IT LOOK LIKE?
IT'S A BUNCH OF COLORED STRINGS WITH BELLS AT THE ENDS. EACH BELL HAS A LETTER ON IT.
THERE'S SOMETHING WRITTEN AT THE TOP OF THE ORNAMENT, BUT IT'S TOO DIRTY TO READ.
I BET IT SAYS...

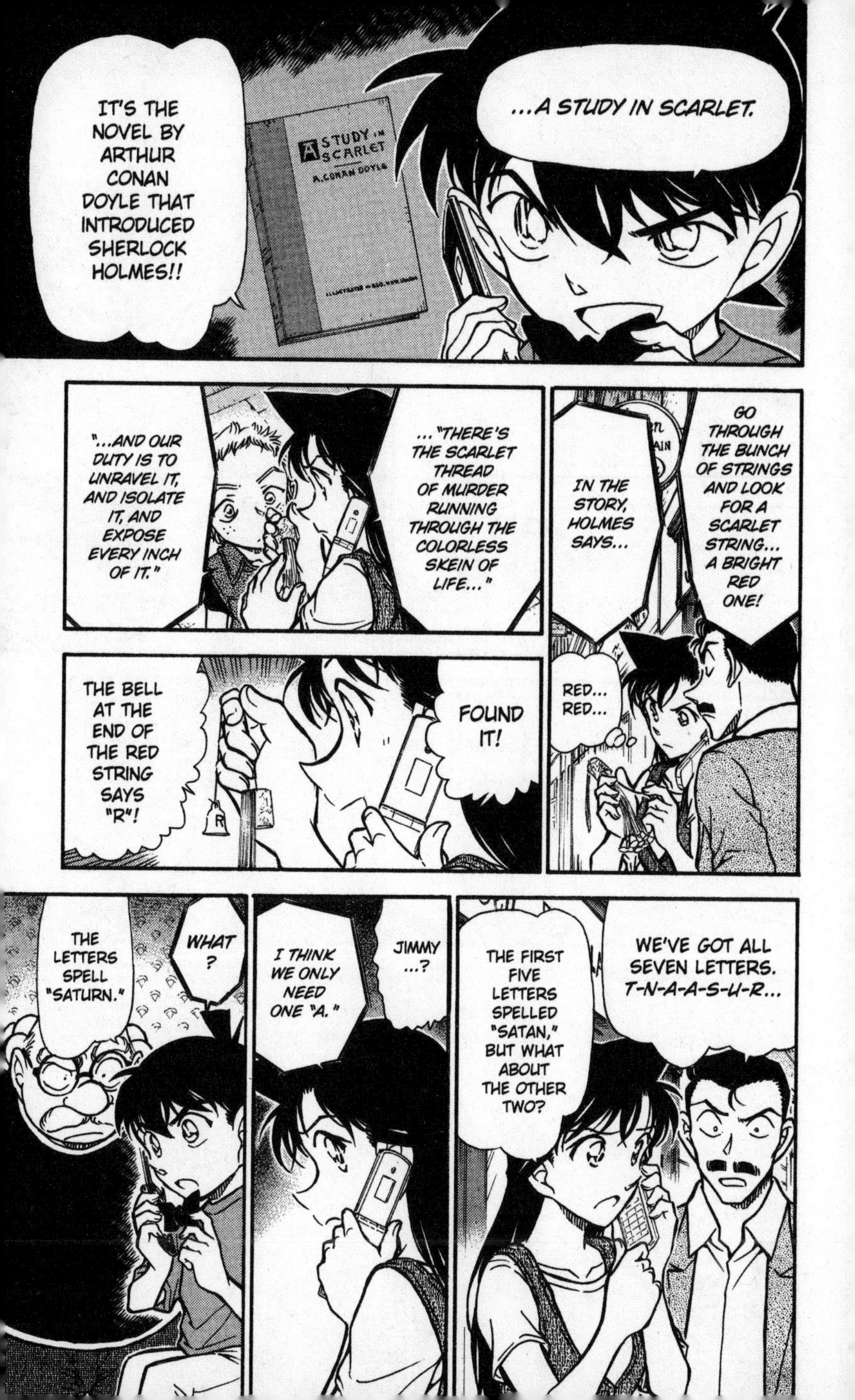
...A STUDY IN SCARLET.
IT'S THE NOVEL BY ARTHUR CONAN DOYLE THAT INTRODUCED SHERLOCK HOLMES!!
A STUDY IN SCARLET
A. CONAN DOYLE
IN THE STORY, HOLMES SAYS...
..."THERE'S THE SCARLET THREAD OF MURDER RUNNING THROUGH THE COLORLESS SKEIN OF LIFE..."
"...AND OUR DUTY IS TO UNRAVEL IT, AND ISOLATE IT, AND EXPOSE EVERY INCH OF IT."
GO THROUGH THE BUNCH OF STRINGS AND LOOK FOR A SCARLET STRING... A BRIGHT RED ONE!
RED... RED...
FOUND IT!
THE BELL AT THE END OF THE RED STRING SAYS "R"!
WE'VE GOT ALL SEVEN LETTERS. T-N-A-A-S-U-R...
THE FIRST FIVE LETTERS SPELLED "SATAN," BUT WHAT ABOUT THE OTHER TWO?
JIMMY ...?
I THINK WE ONLY NEED ONE "A."
WHAT?
THE LETTERS SPELL "SATURN."

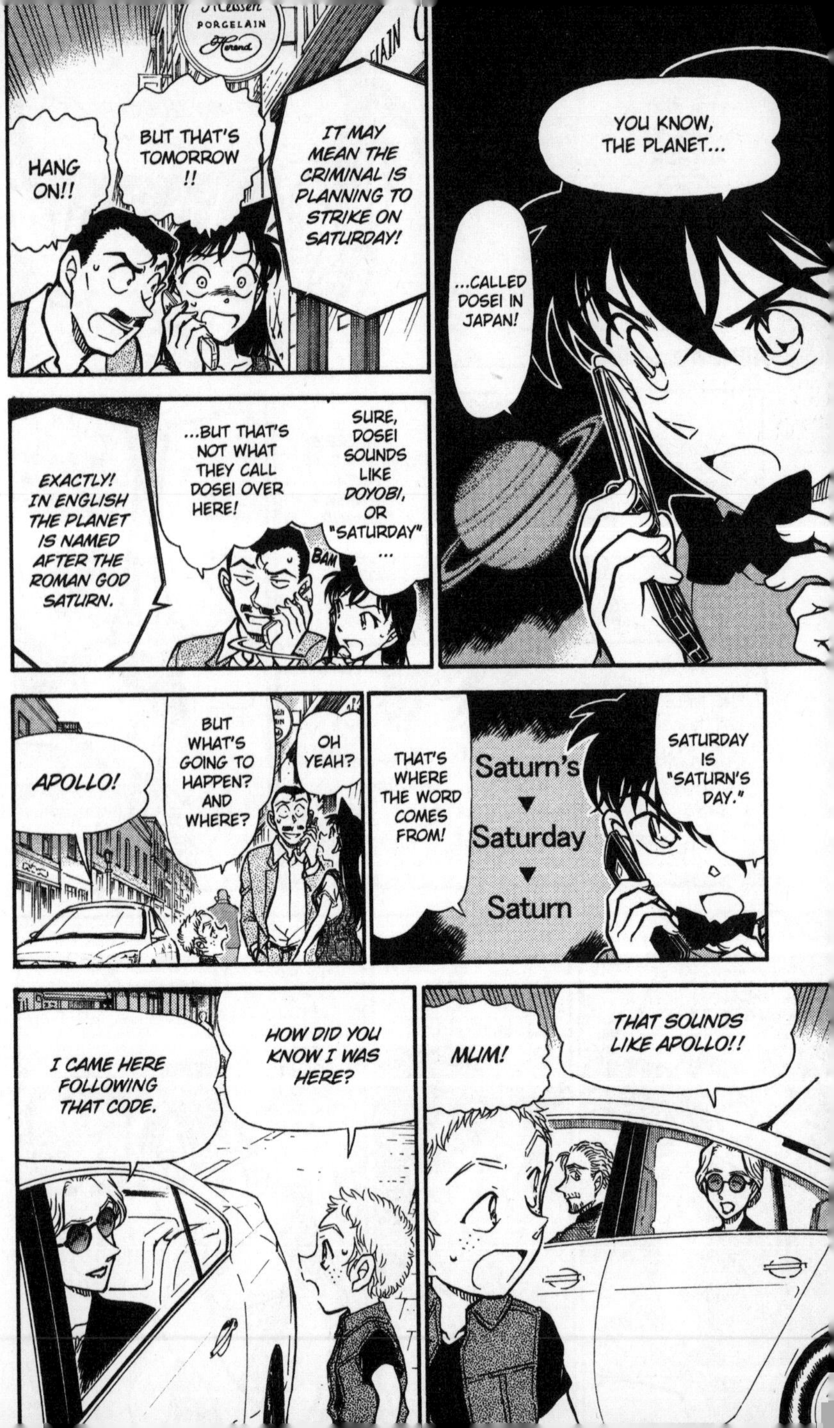
YOU KNOW, THE PLANET...
...CALLED DOSEI IN JAPAN!
PORCELAIN
Herend
IT MAY MEAN THE CRIMINAL IS PLANNING TO STRIKE ON SATURDAY!
BUT THAT'S TOMORROW !!
HANG ON!!
SURE, DOSEI SOUNDS LIKE DOYOBI, OR "SATURDAY" ...
BAM
...BUT THAT'S NOT WHAT THEY CALL DOSEI OVER HERE!
EXACTLY! IN ENGLISH THE PLANET IS NAMED AFTER THE ROMAN GOD SATURN.
SATURDAY IS "SATURN'S DAY."
Saturn's ▼ Saturday ▼ Saturn
THAT'S WHERE THE WORD COMES FROM!
OH YEAH?
BUT WHAT'S GOING TO HAPPEN? AND WHERE?
APOLLO!
THAT SOUNDS LIKE APOLLO!!
MUM!
HOW DID YOU KNOW I WAS HERE?
I CAME HERE FOLLOWING THAT CODE.

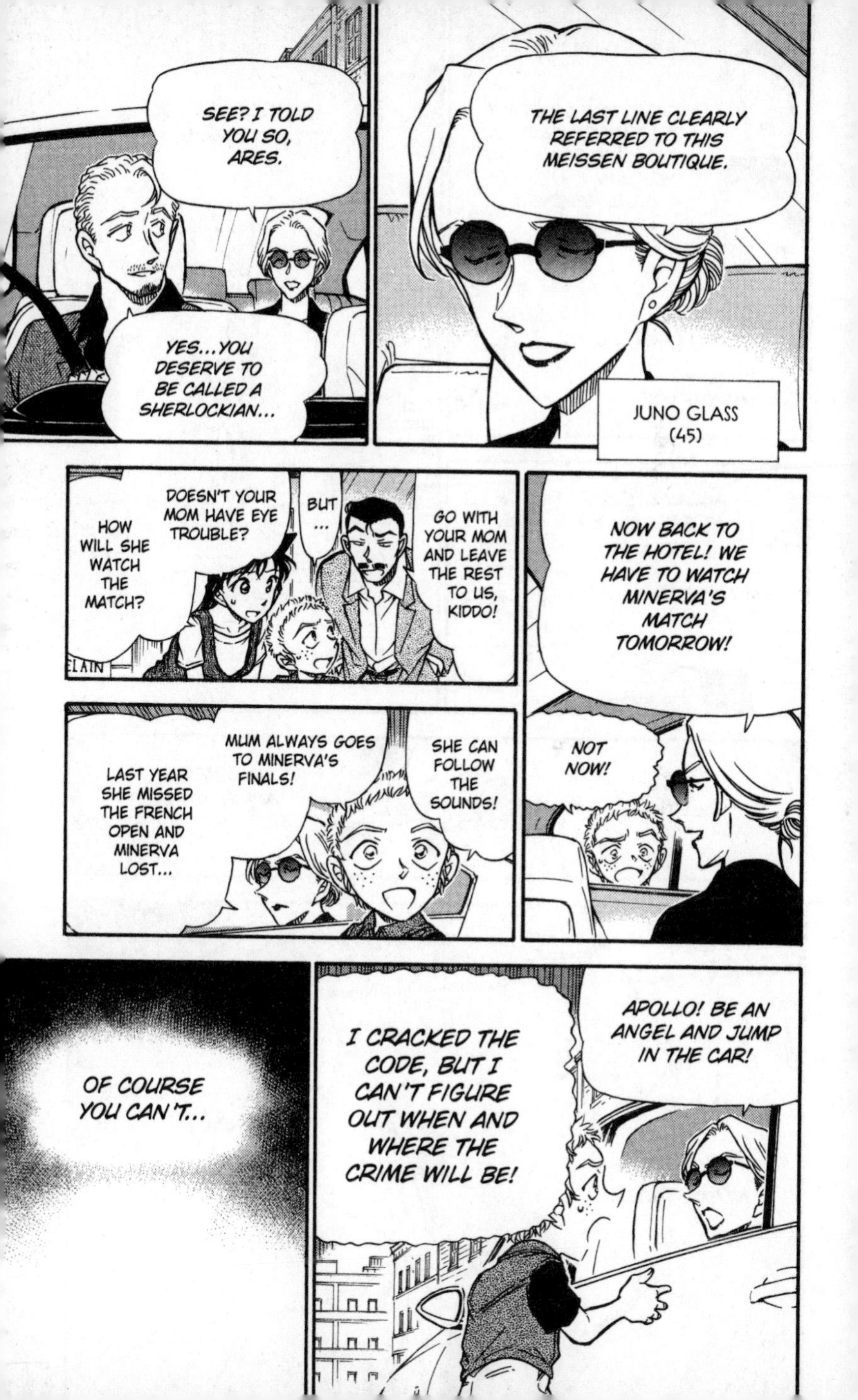
THE LAST LINE CLEARLY REFERRED TO THIS MEISSEN BOUTIQUE.
JUNO GLASS (45)
SEE? I TOLD YOU SO, ARES.
YES...YOU DESERVE TO BE CALLED A SHERLOCKIAN...
NOW BACK TO THE HOTEL! WE HAVE TO WATCH MINERVA'S MATCH TOMORROW!
GO WITH YOUR MOM AND LEAVE THE REST TO US, KIDDO!
BUT ...
DOESN'T YOUR MOM HAVE EYE TROUBLE?
HOW WILL SHE WATCH THE MATCH?
NOT NOW!
SHE CAN FOLLOW THE SOUNDS!
MUM ALWAYS GOES TO MINERVA'S FINALS!
LAST YEAR SHE MISSED THE FRENCH OPEN AND MINERVA LOST...
APOLLO! BE AN ANGEL AND JUMP IN THE CAR!
I CRACKED THE CODE, BUT I CAN'T FIGURE OUT WHEN AND WHERE THE CRIME WILL BE!
OF COURSE YOU CAN'T...

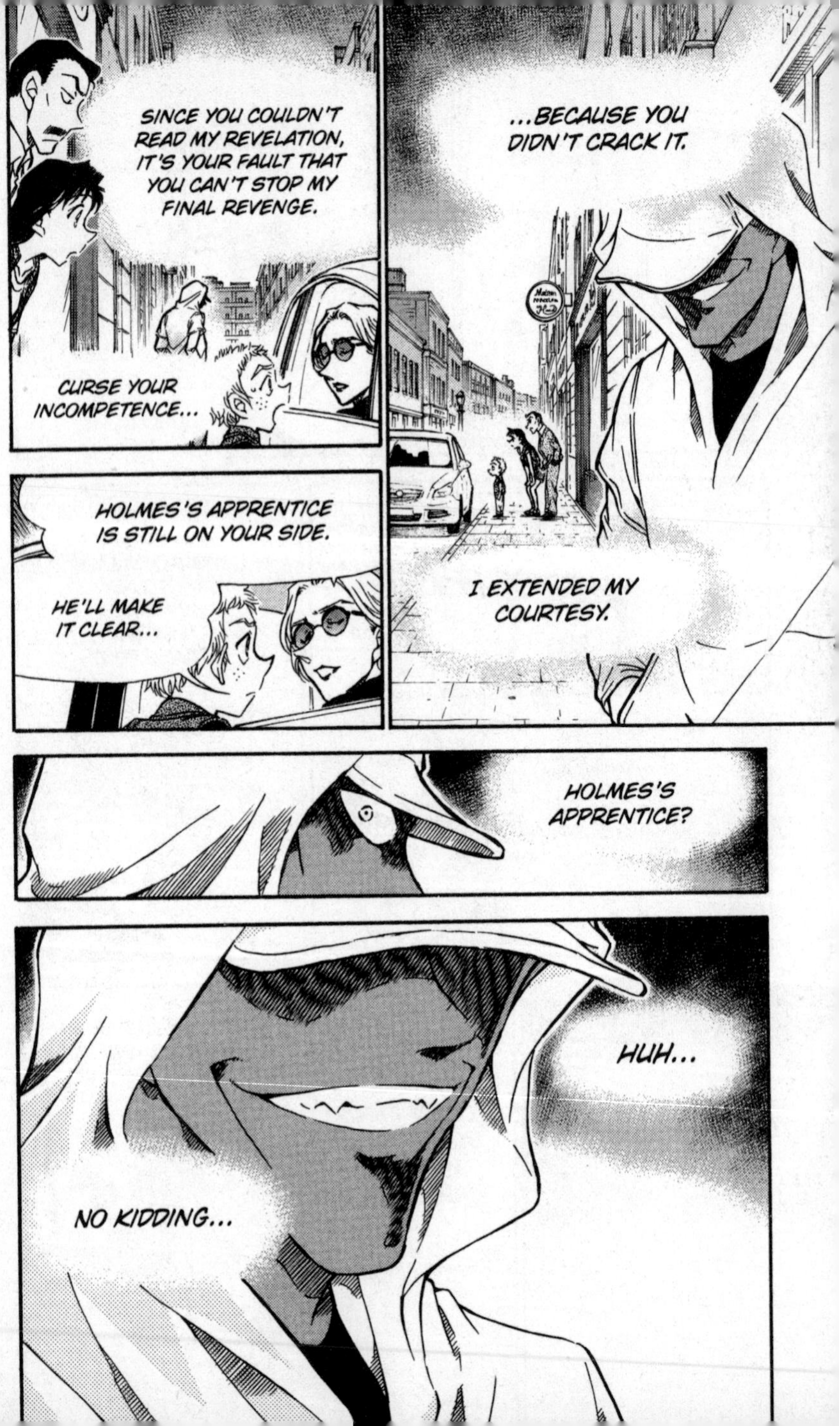
...BECAUSE YOU DIDN'T CRACK IT.
I EXTENDED MY COURTESY.
SINCE YOU COULDN'T READ MY REVELATION, IT'S YOUR FAULT THAT YOU CAN'T STOP MY FINAL REVENGE.
CURSE YOUR INCOMPETENCE...
HOLMES'S APPRENTICE IS STILL ON YOUR SIDE.
HE'LL MAKE IT CLEAR...
HOLMES'S APPRENTICE?
HUH...
NO KIDDING...

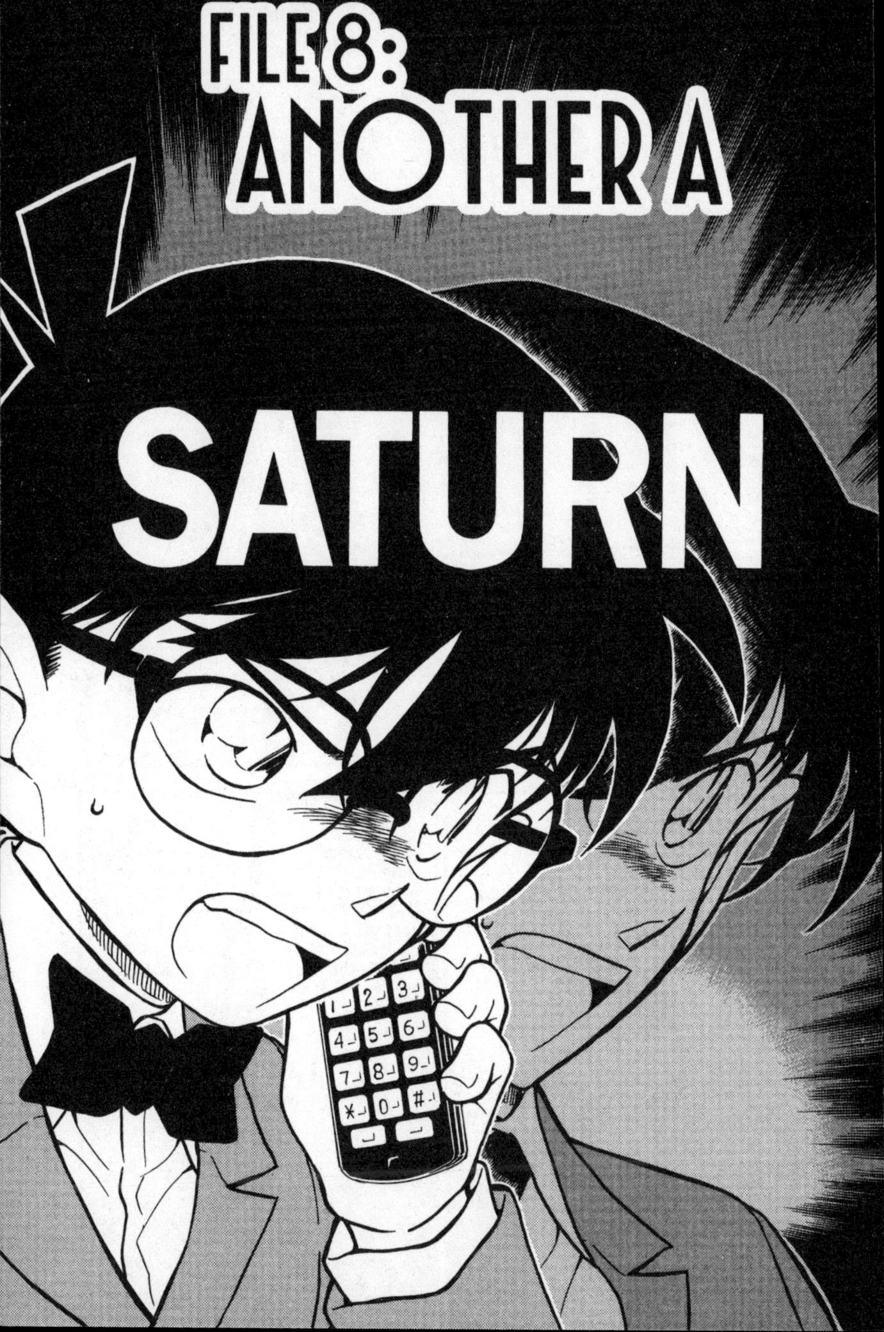
FILE 8:
ANOTHER A
SATURN

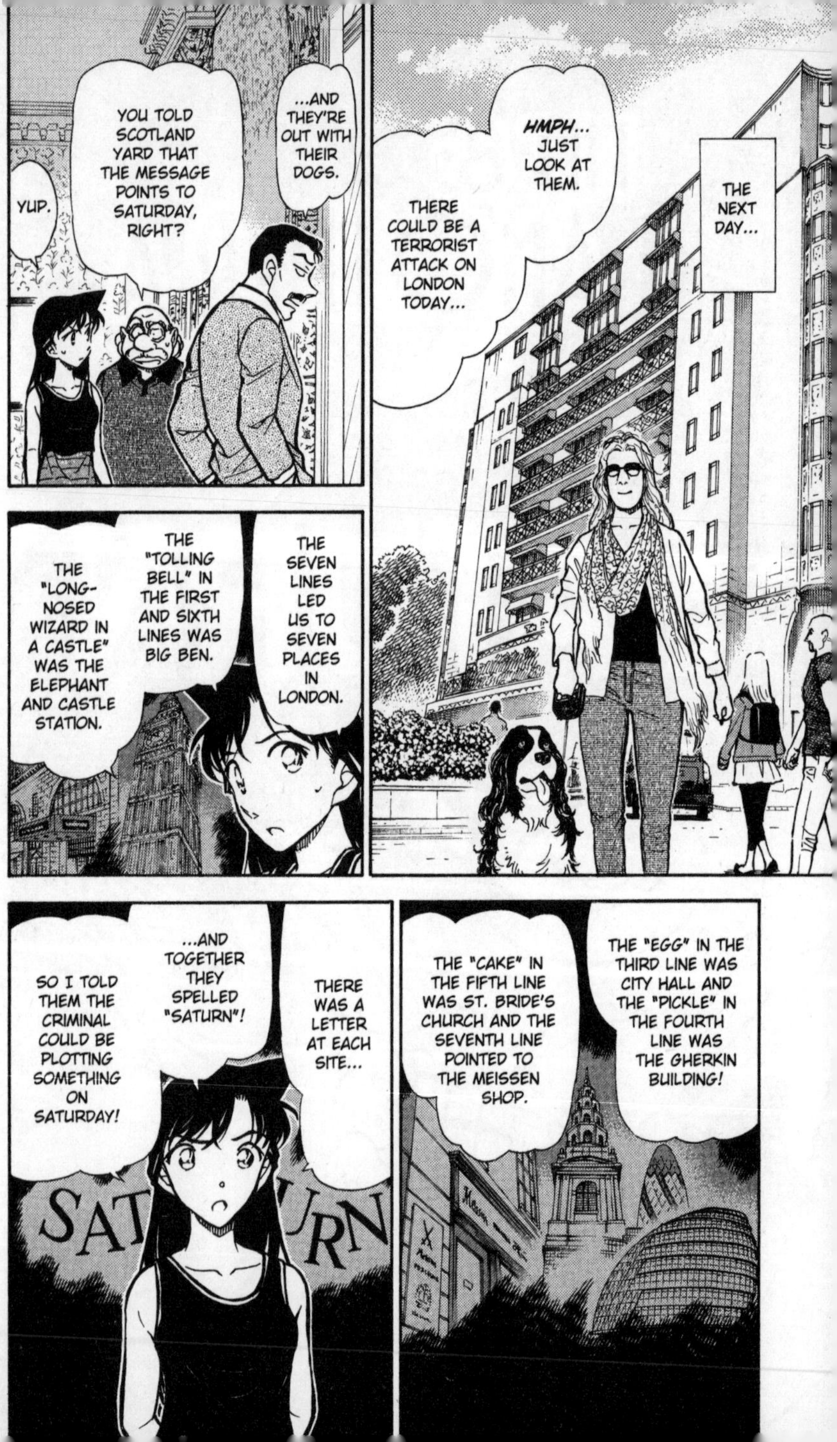
THE NEXT DAY...
HMPH... JUST LOOK AT THEM.
THERE COULD BE A TERRORIST ATTACK ON LONDON TODAY...
...AND THEY'RE OUT WITH THEIR DOGS.
YOU TOLD SCOTLAND YARD THAT THE MESSAGE POINTS TO SATURDAY, RIGHT?
YUP.
THE SEVEN LINES LED US TO SEVEN PLACES IN LONDON.
THE "TOLLING BELL" IN THE FIRST AND SIXTH LINES WAS BIG BEN.
THE "LONG-NOSED WIZARD IN A CASTLE" WAS THE ELEPHANT AND CASTLE STATION.
THE "EGG" IN THE THIRD LINE WAS CITY HALL AND THE "PICKLE" IN THE FOURTH LINE WAS THE GHERKIN BUILDING!
THE "CAKE" IN THE FIFTH LINE WAS ST. BRIDE'S CHURCH AND THE SEVENTH LINE POINTED TO THE MEISSEN SHOP.
THERE WAS A LETTER AT EACH SITE...
...AND TOGETHER THEY SPELLED "SATURN"!
SO I TOLD THEM THE CRIMINAL COULD BE PLOTTING SOMETHING ON SATURDAY!

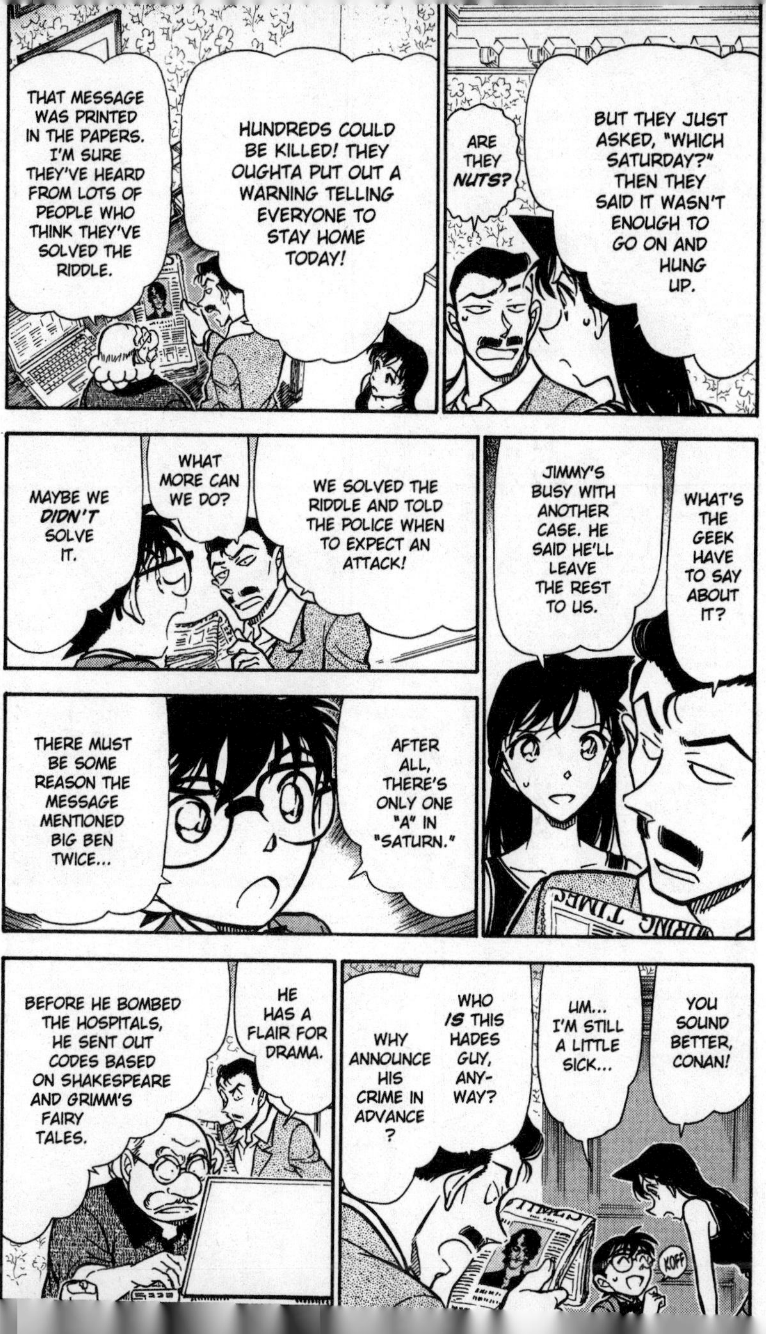
BUT THEY JUST ASKED, "WHICH SATURDAY?" THEN THEY SAID IT WASN'T ENOUGH TO GO ON AND HUNG UP.
ARE THEY *NUTS?*
HUNDREDS COULD BE KILLED! THEY OUGHTA PUT OUT A WARNING TELLING EVERYONE TO STAY HOME TODAY!
THAT MESSAGE WAS PRINTED IN THE PAPERS. I'M SURE THEY'VE HEARD FROM LOTS OF PEOPLE WHO THINK THEY'VE SOLVED THE RIDDLE.
WHAT'S THE GEEK HAVE TO SAY ABOUT IT?
JIMMY'S BUSY WITH ANOTHER CASE. HE SAID HE'LL LEAVE THE REST TO US.
WE SOLVED THE RIDDLE AND TOLD THE POLICE WHEN TO EXPECT AN ATTACK!
WHAT MORE CAN WE DO?
MAYBE WE *DIDN'T* SOLVE IT.
AFTER ALL, THERE'S ONLY ONE "A" IN "SATURN."
THERE MUST BE SOME REASON THE MESSAGE MENTIONED BIG BEN TWICE...
YOU SOUND BETTER, CONAN!
UM... I'M STILL A LITTLE SICK...
KOFF
WHO *IS* THIS HADES GUY, ANYWAY?
WHY ANNOUNCE HIS CRIME IN ADVANCE?
HE HAS A FLAIR FOR DRAMA.
BEFORE HE BOMBED THE HOSPITALS, HE SENT OUT CODES BASED ON SHAKESPEARE AND GRIMM'S FAIRY TALES.

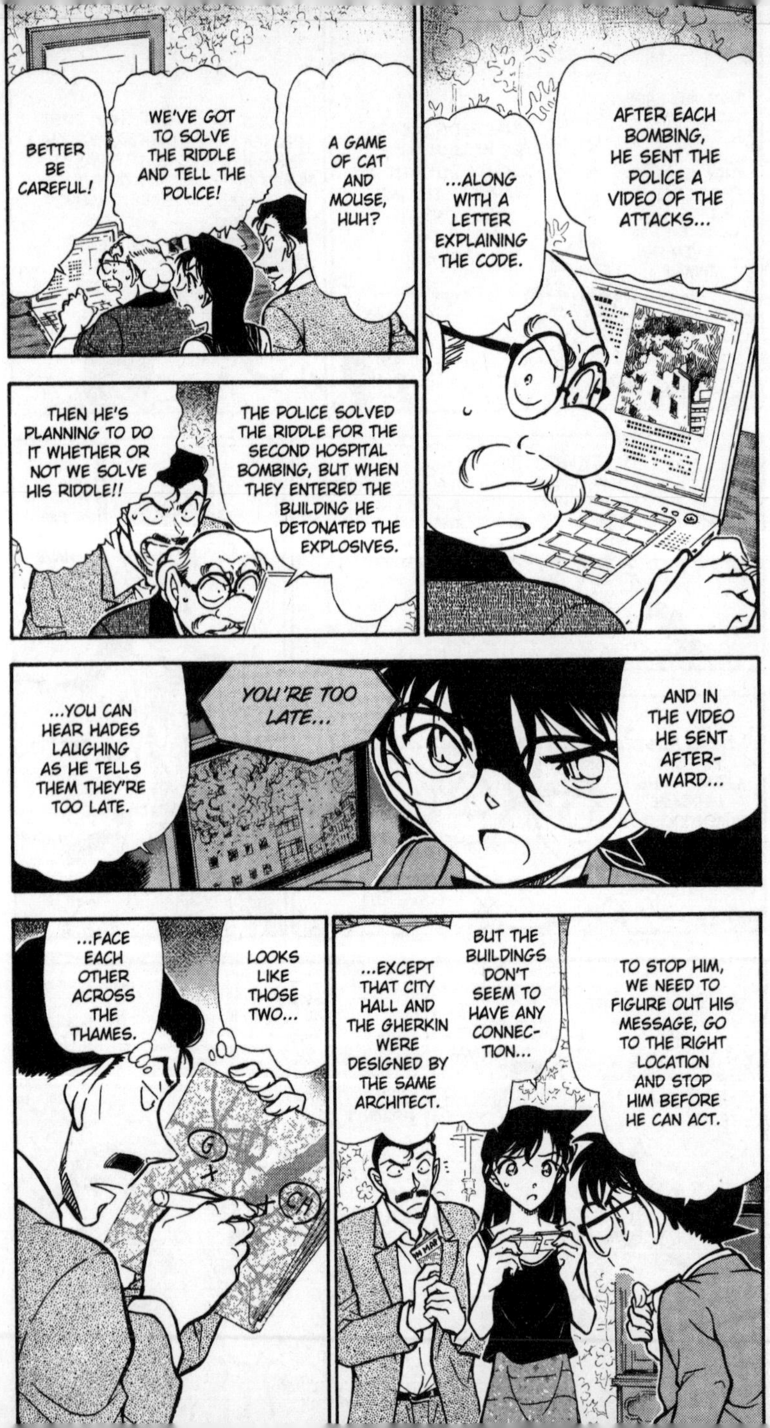
AFTER EACH BOMBING, HE SENT THE POLICE A VIDEO OF THE ATTACKS...
...ALONG WITH A LETTER EXPLAINING THE CODE.
A GAME OF CAT AND MOUSE, HUH?
WE'VE GOT TO SOLVE THE RIDDLE AND TELL THE POLICE!
BETTER BE CAREFUL!
THE POLICE SOLVED THE RIDDLE FOR THE SECOND HOSPITAL BOMBING, BUT WHEN THEY ENTERED THE BUILDING HE DETONATED THE EXPLOSIVES.
THEN HE'S PLANNING TO DO IT WHETHER OR NOT WE SOLVE HIS RIDDLE!!
AND IN THE VIDEO HE SENT AFTER-WARD...
YOU'RE TOO LATE...
...YOU CAN HEAR HADES LAUGHING AS HE TELLS THEM THEY'RE TOO LATE.
TO STOP HIM, WE NEED TO FIGURE OUT HIS MESSAGE, GO TO THE RIGHT LOCATION AND STOP HIM BEFORE HE CAN ACT.
BUT THE BUILDINGS DON'T SEEM TO HAVE ANY CONNEC-TION...
...EXCEPT THAT CITY HALL AND THE GHERKIN WERE DESIGNED BY THE SAME ARCHITECT.
LOOKS LIKE THOSE TWO...
...FACE EACH OTHER ACROSS THE THAMES.

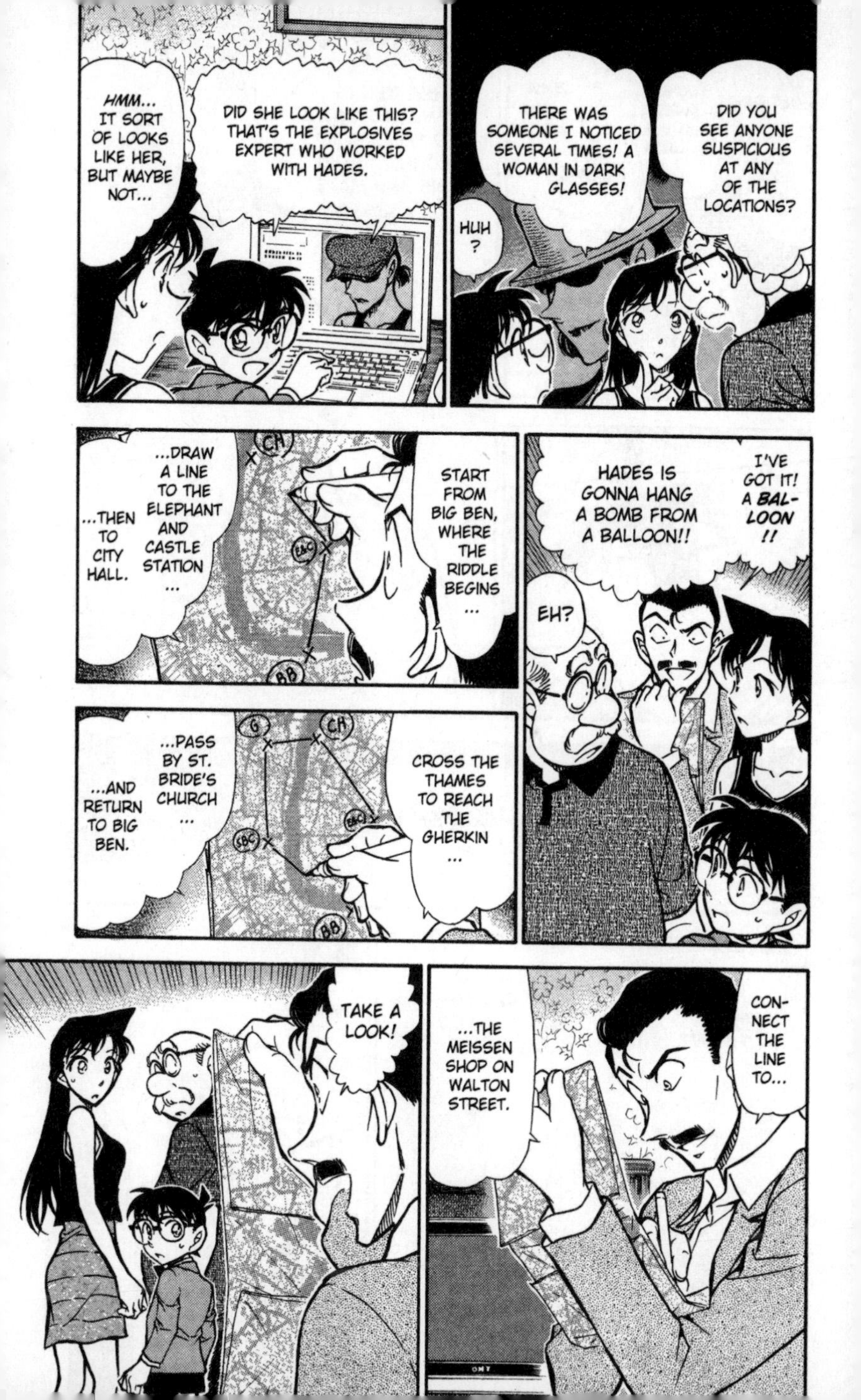
DID YOU SEE ANYONE SUSPICIOUS AT ANY OF THE LOCATIONS?
THERE WAS SOMEONE I NOTICED SEVERAL TIMES! A WOMAN IN DARK GLASSES!
HUH ?
DID SHE LOOK LIKE THIS? THAT'S THE EXPLOSIVES EXPERT WHO WORKED WITH HADES.
HMM... IT SORT OF LOOKS LIKE HER, BUT MAYBE NOT...
I'VE GOT IT! A *BALLOON* !!
HADES IS GONNA HANG A BOMB FROM A BALLOON!!
EH?
START FROM BIG BEN, WHERE THE RIDDLE BEGINS...
...DRAW A LINE TO THE ELEPHANT AND CASTLE STATION...
...THEN TO CITY HALL.
CH
E&C
BB
CROSS THE THAMES TO REACH THE GHERKIN...
...PASS BY ST. BRIDE'S CHURCH...
...AND RETURN TO BIG BEN.
G
CH
E&C
SBC
BB
CON-NECT THE LINE TO...
...THE MEISSEN SHOP ON WALTON STREET.
TAKE A LOOK!

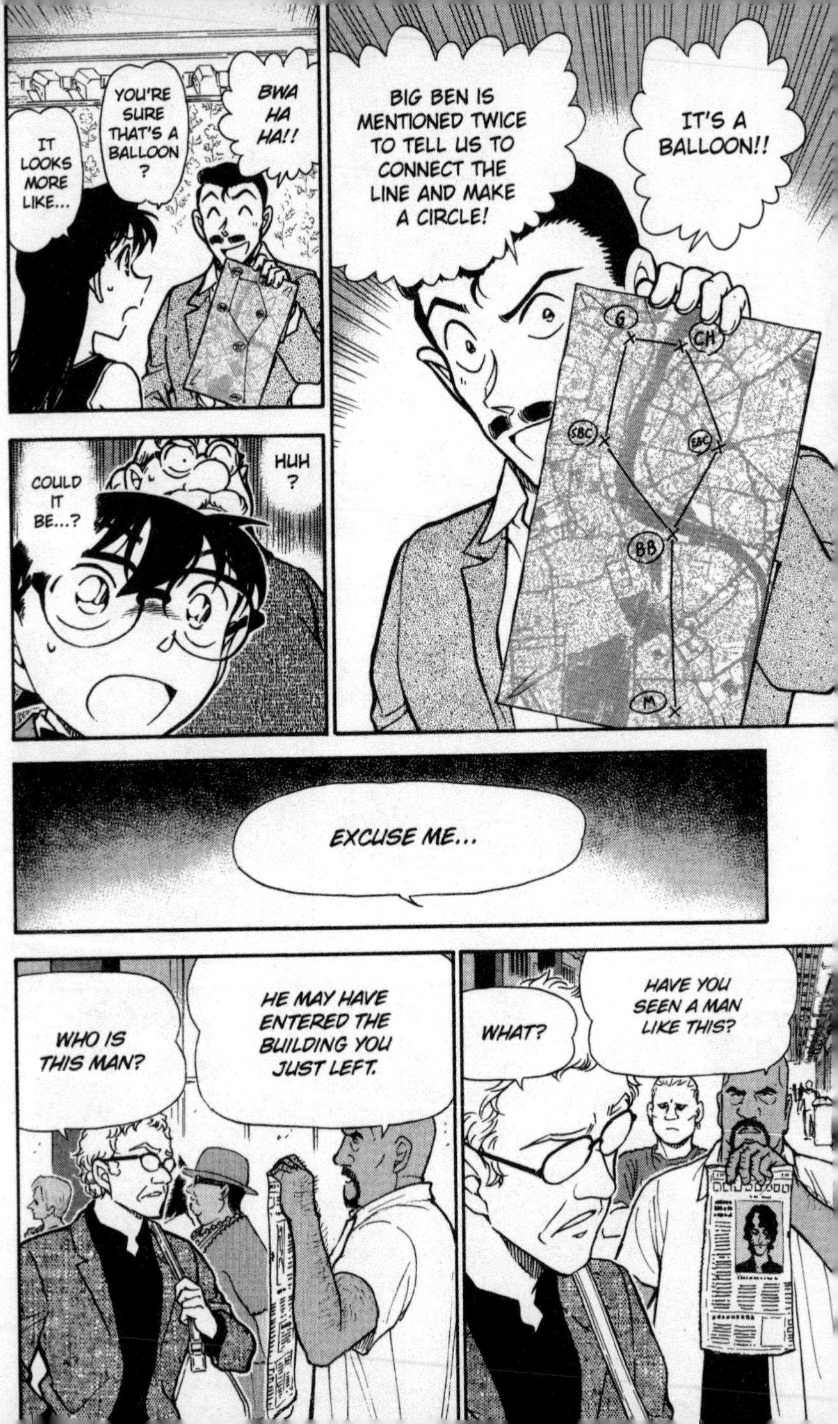
IT'S A BALLOON!!
BIG BEN IS MENTIONED TWICE TO TELL US TO CONNECT THE LINE AND MAKE A CIRCLE!
G
CH
SBC
E&C
BB
M
BWA HA HA!!
YOU'RE SURE THAT'S A BALLOON ?
IT LOOKS MORE LIKE...
HUH ?
COULD IT BE...?
EXCUSE ME...
HAVE YOU SEEN A MAN LIKE THIS?
WHAT?
HE MAY HAVE ENTERED THE BUILDING YOU JUST LEFT.
WHO IS THIS MAN?

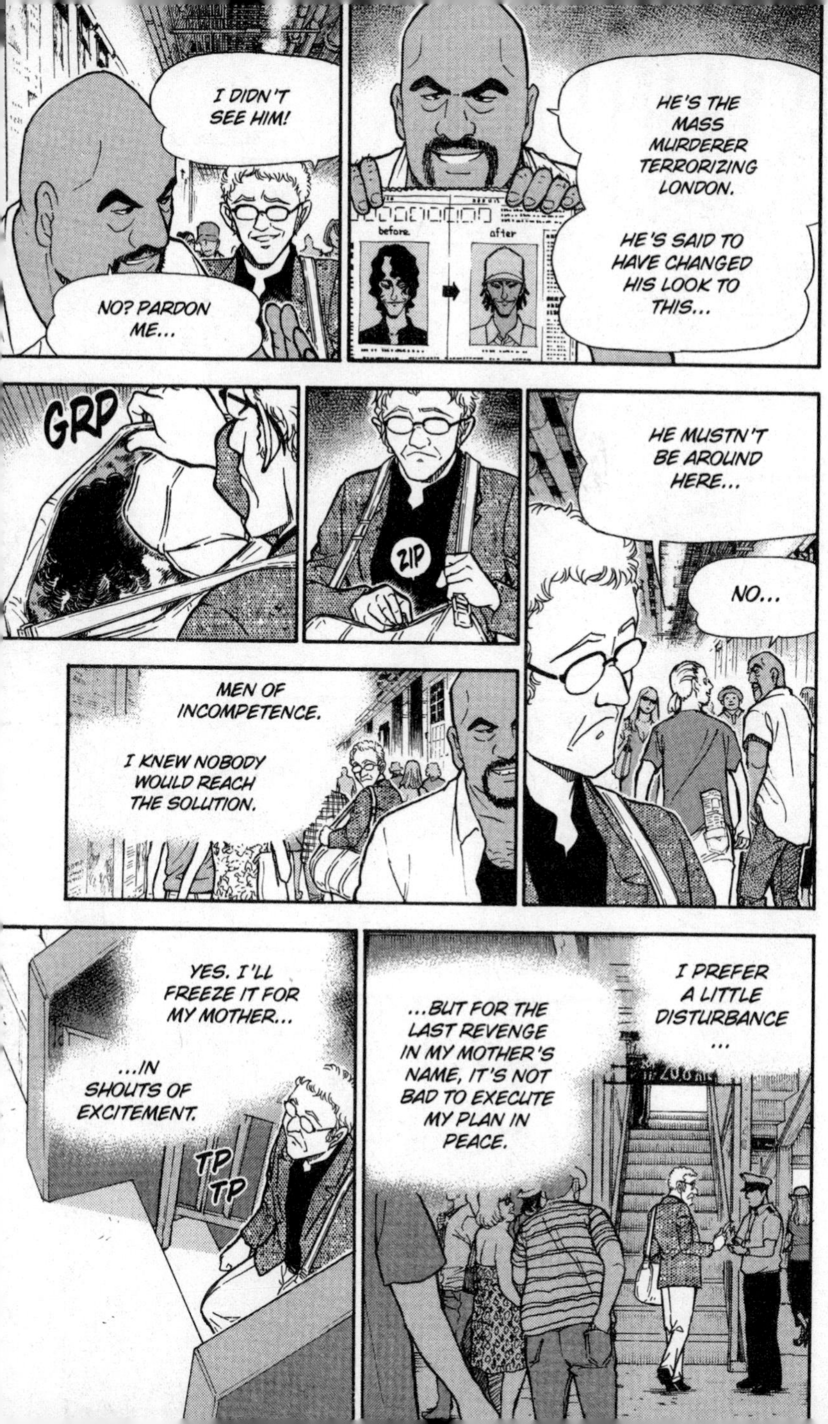
HE'S THE MASS MURDERER TERRORIZING LONDON.
HE'S SAID TO HAVE CHANGED HIS LOOK TO THIS...
before
after
I DIDN'T SEE HIM!
NO? PARDON ME...
HE MUSTN'T BE AROUND HERE...
NO...
ZIP
GRP
MEN OF INCOMPETENCE.
I KNEW NOBODY WOULD REACH THE SOLUTION.
I PREFER A LITTLE DISTURBANCE ...
...BUT FOR THE LAST REVENGE IN MY MOTHER'S NAME, IT'S NOT BAD TO EXECUTE MY PLAN IN PEACE.
YES. I'LL FREEZE IT FOR MY MOTHER...
...IN SHOUTS OF EXCITEMENT.
TP TP

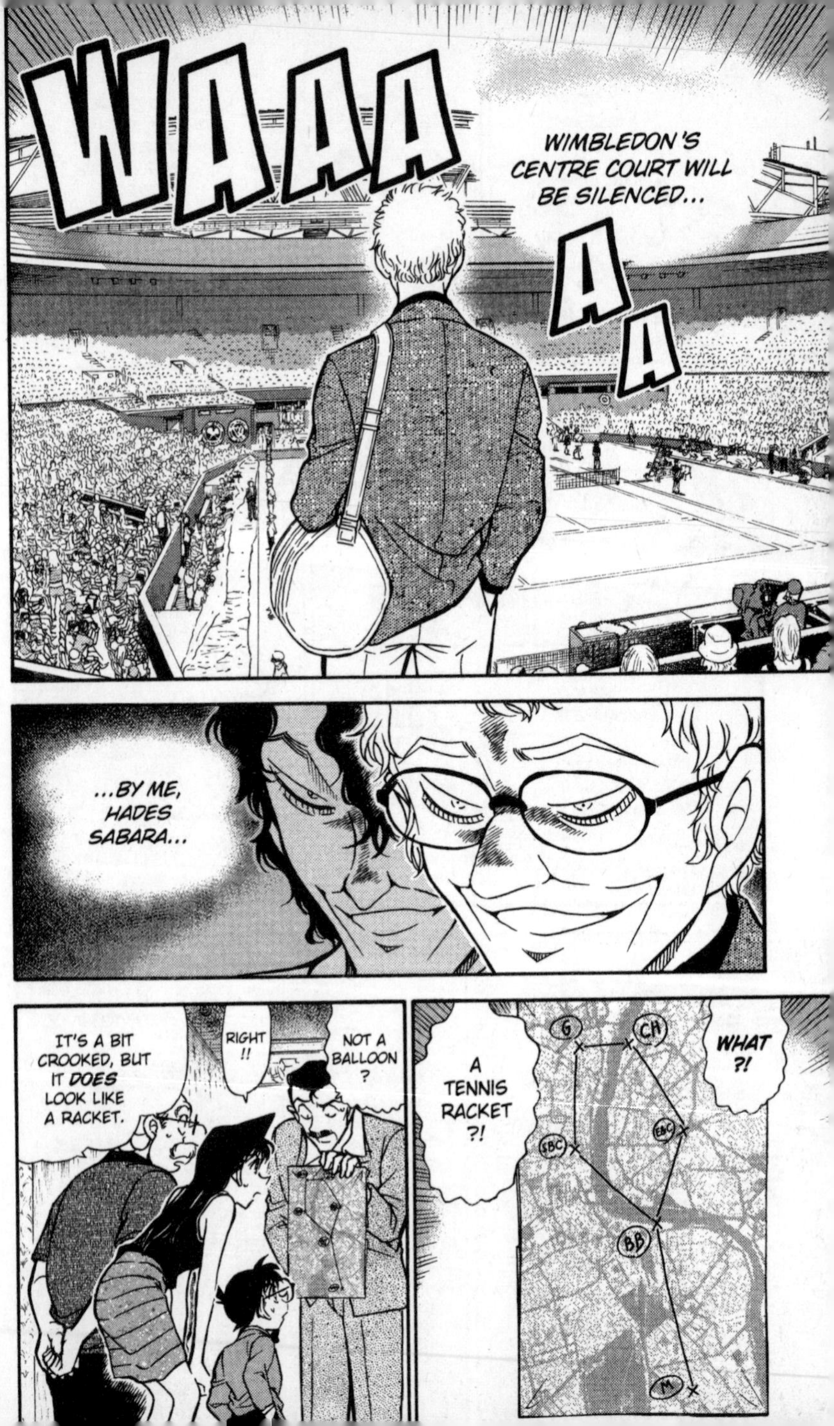
WAAAA
WIMBLEDON'S CENTRE COURT WILL BE SILENCED...
A
A
...BY ME, HADES SABARA...
WHAT?!
A TENNIS RACKET?!
G
CH
EBC
SBC
BB
M
NOT A BALLOON?
RIGHT!!
IT'S A BIT CROOKED, BUT IT DOES LOOK LIKE A RACKET.

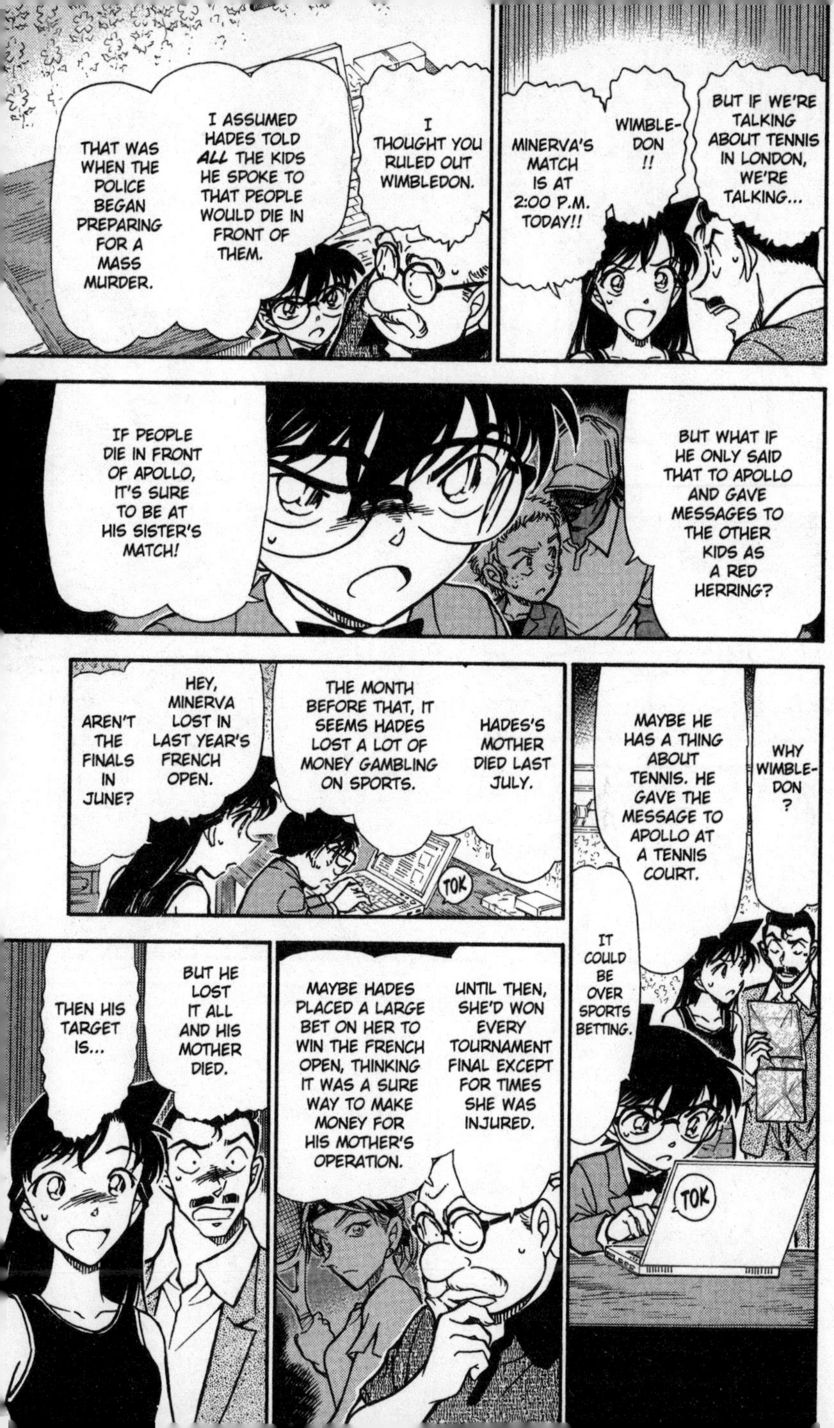
BUT IF WE'RE TALKING ABOUT TENNIS IN LONDON, WE'RE TALKING...
WIMBLE-DON!!
MINERVA'S MATCH IS AT 2:00 P.M. TODAY!!
I THOUGHT YOU RULED OUT WIMBLEDON.
I ASSUMED HADES TOLD *ALL* THE KIDS HE SPOKE TO THAT PEOPLE WOULD DIE IN FRONT OF THEM.
THAT WAS WHEN THE POLICE BEGAN PREPARING FOR A MASS MURDER.
BUT WHAT IF HE ONLY SAID THAT TO APOLLO AND GAVE MESSAGES TO THE OTHER KIDS AS A RED HERRING?
IF PEOPLE DIE IN FRONT OF APOLLO, IT'S SURE TO BE AT HIS SISTER'S MATCH!
WHY WIMBLE-DON?
MAYBE HE HAS A THING ABOUT TENNIS. HE GAVE THE MESSAGE TO APOLLO AT A TENNIS COURT.
IT COULD BE OVER SPORTS BETTING.
TOK
HADES'S MOTHER DIED LAST JULY.
THE MONTH BEFORE THAT, IT SEEMS HADES LOST A LOT OF MONEY GAMBLING ON SPORTS.
HEY, MINERVA LOST IN LAST YEAR'S FRENCH OPEN.
AREN'T THE FINALS IN JUNE?
TOK
UNTIL THEN, SHE'D WON EVERY TOURNAMENT FINAL EXCEPT FOR TIMES SHE WAS INJURED.
MAYBE HADES PLACED A LARGE BET ON HER TO WIN THE FRENCH OPEN, THINKING IT WAS A SURE WAY TO MAKE MONEY FOR HIS MOTHER'S OPERATION.
BUT HE LOST IT ALL AND HIS MOTHER DIED.
THEN HIS TARGET IS...

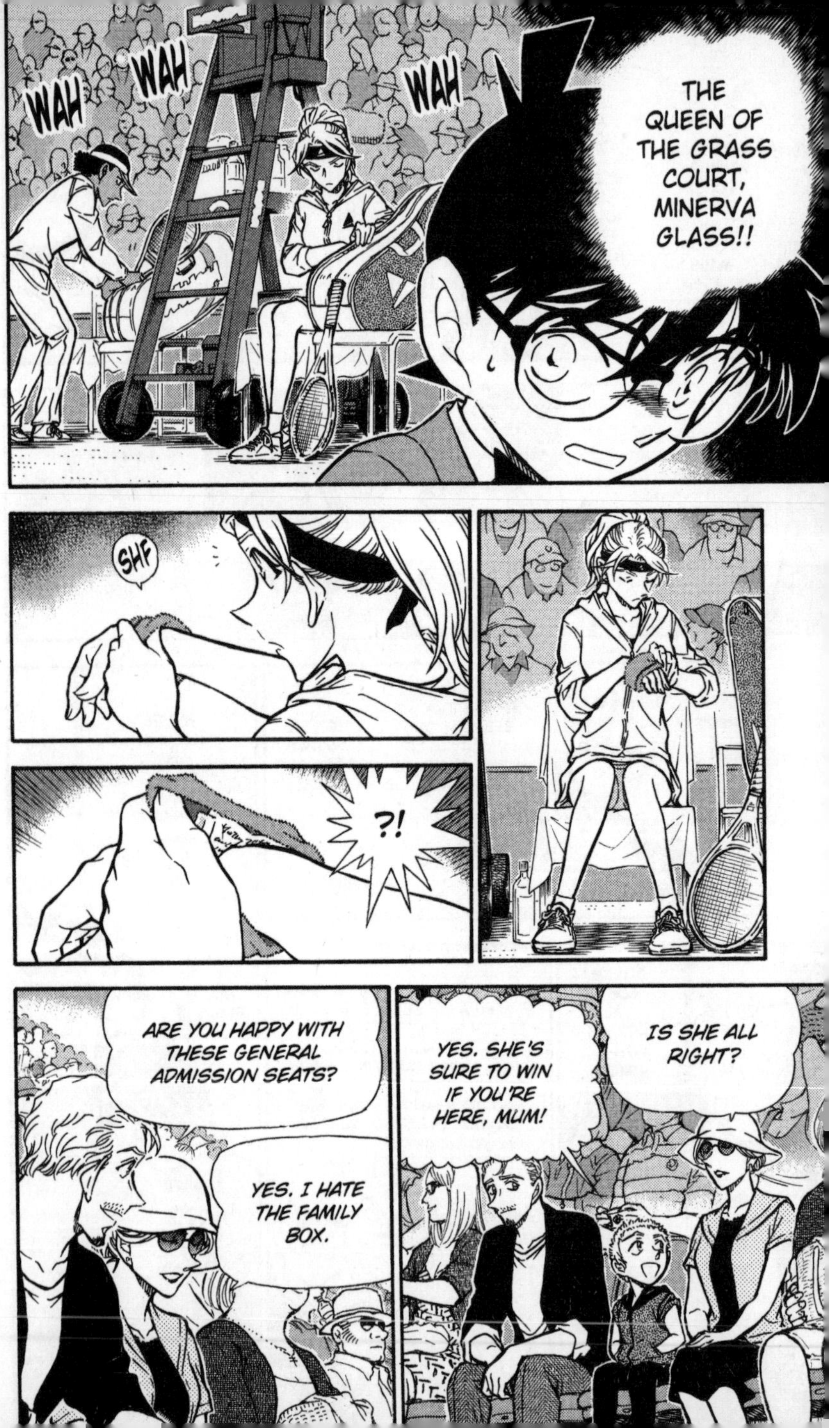
THE QUEEN OF THE GRASS COURT, MINERVA GLASS!!
WAH
WAH
WAH
SHF
?!
IS SHE ALL RIGHT?
YES. SHE'S SURE TO WIN IF YOU'RE HERE, MUM!
ARE YOU HAPPY WITH THESE GENERAL ADMISSION SEATS?
YES. I HATE THE FAMILY BOX.

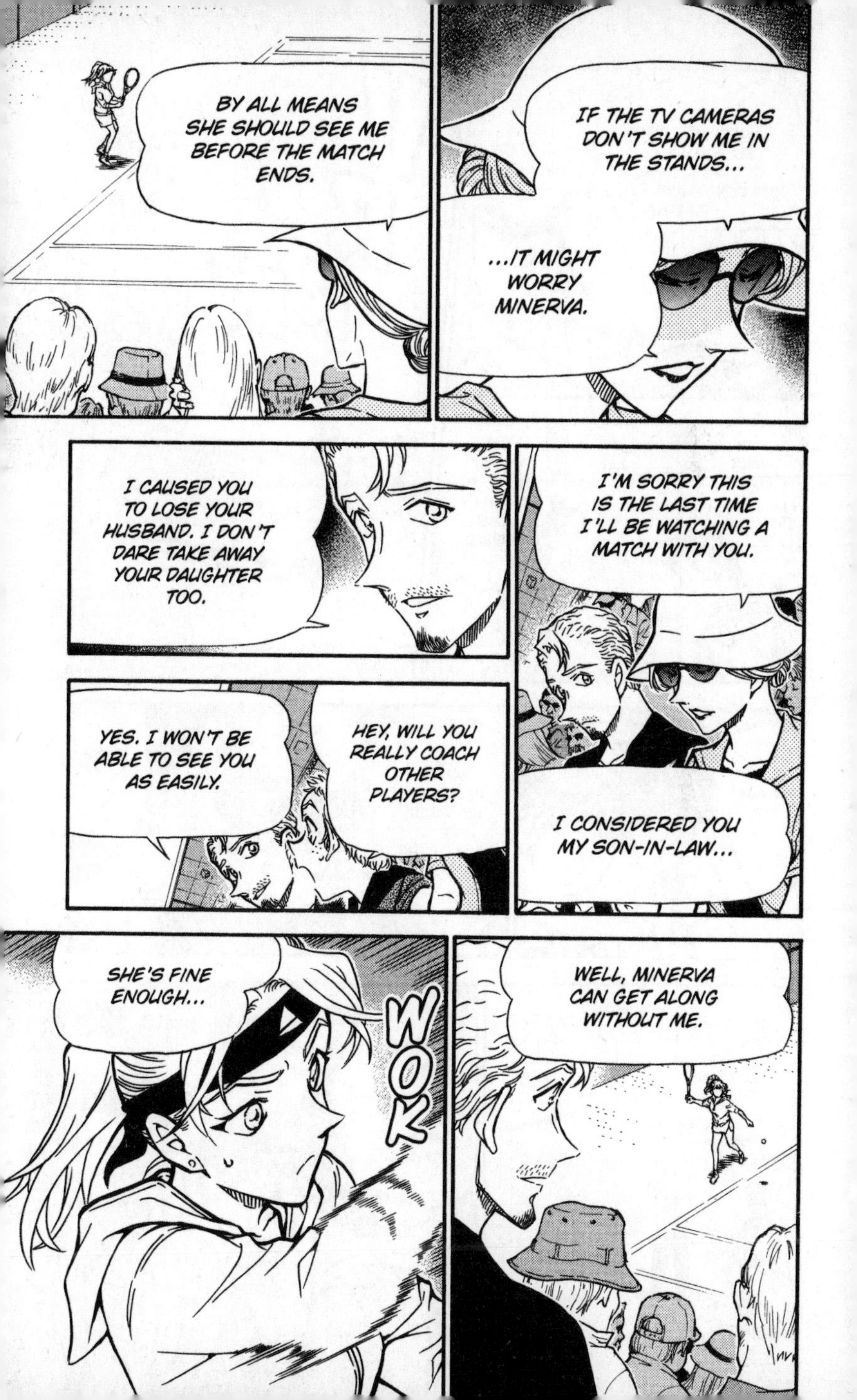
IF THE TV CAMERAS DON'T SHOW ME IN THE STANDS...
...IT MIGHT WORRY MINERVA.
BY ALL MEANS SHE SHOULD SEE ME BEFORE THE MATCH ENDS.
I'M SORRY THIS IS THE LAST TIME I'LL BE WATCHING A MATCH WITH YOU.
I CONSIDERED YOU MY SON-IN-LAW...
I CAUSED YOU TO LOSE YOUR HUSBAND. I DON'T DARE TAKE AWAY YOUR DAUGHTER TOO.
HEY, WILL YOU REALLY COACH OTHER PLAYERS?
YES. I WON'T BE ABLE TO SEE YOU AS EASILY.
WELL, MINERVA CAN GET ALONG WITHOUT ME.
SHE'S FINE ENOUGH...
WOK

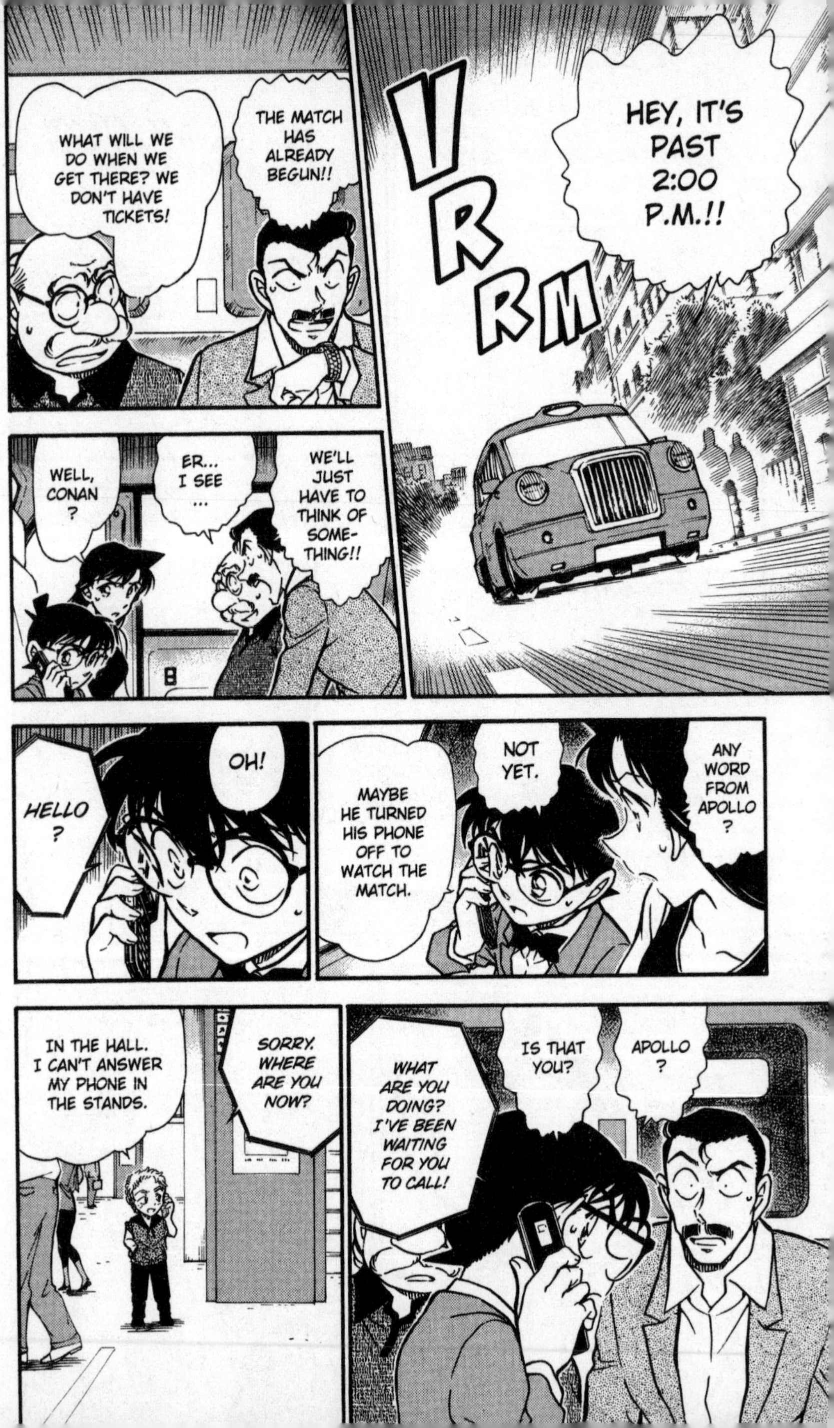
HEY, IT'S PAST 2:00 P.M.!!
VRRM
THE MATCH HAS ALREADY BEGUN!!
WHAT WILL WE DO WHEN WE GET THERE? WE DON'T HAVE TICKETS!
WE'LL JUST HAVE TO THINK OF SOME-THING!!
ER... I SEE ...
WELL, CONAN ?
ANY WORD FROM APOLLO ?
NOT YET.
MAYBE HE TURNED HIS PHONE OFF TO WATCH THE MATCH.
OH!
HELLO ?
APOLLO ?
IS THAT YOU?
WHAT ARE YOU DOING? I'VE BEEN WAITING FOR YOU TO CALL!
SORRY. WHERE ARE YOU NOW?
IN THE HALL. I CAN'T ANSWER MY PHONE IN THE STANDS.

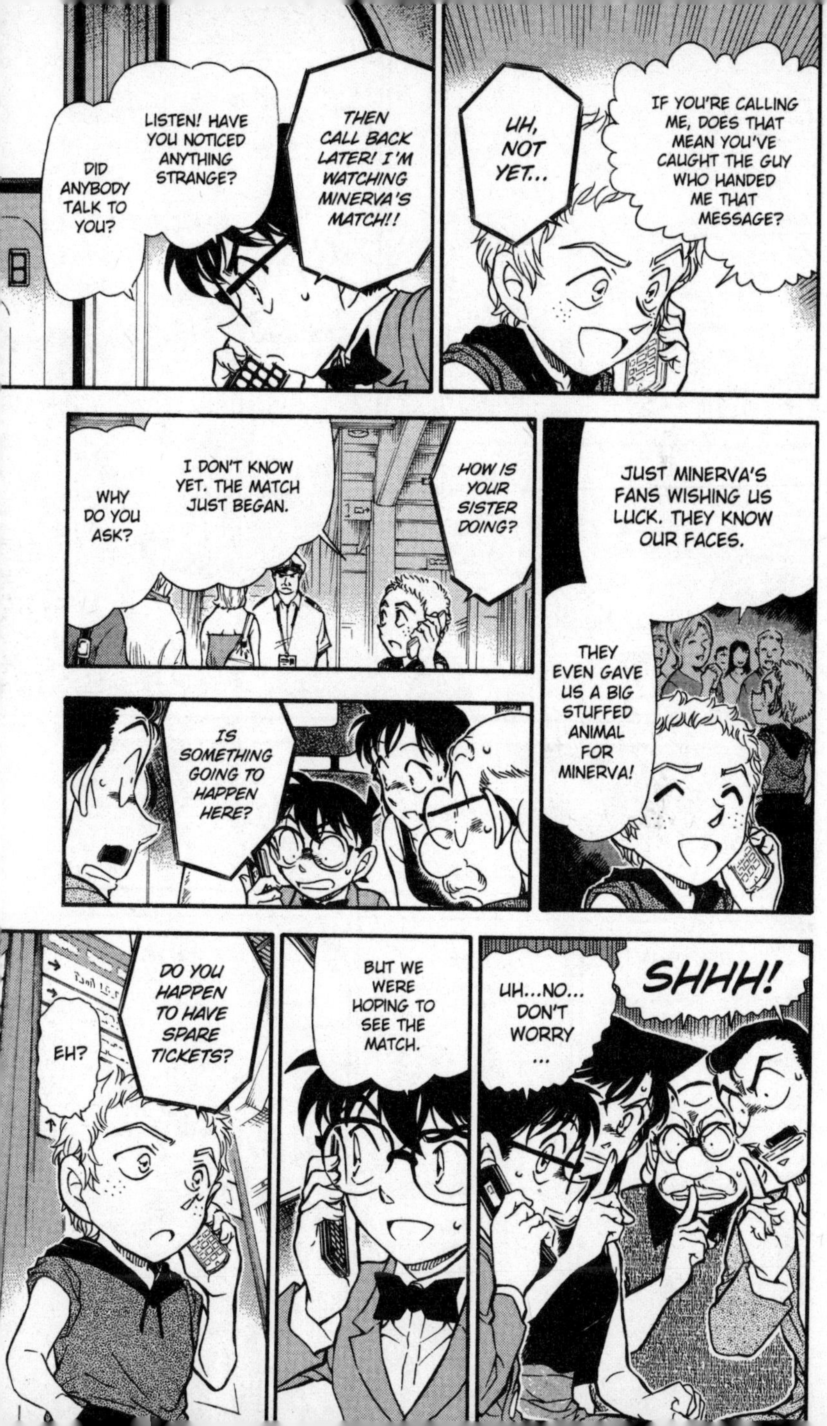
IF YOU'RE CALLING ME, DOES THAT MEAN YOU'VE CAUGHT THE GUY WHO HANDED ME THAT MESSAGE?
UH, NOT YET...
THEN CALL BACK LATER! I'M WATCHING MINERVA'S MATCH!!
LISTEN! HAVE YOU NOTICED ANYTHING STRANGE?
DID ANYBODY TALK TO YOU?
JUST MINERVA'S FANS WISHING US LUCK. THEY KNOW OUR FACES.
THEY EVEN GAVE US A BIG STUFFED ANIMAL FOR MINERVA!
HOW IS YOUR SISTER DOING?
I DON'T KNOW YET. THE MATCH JUST BEGAN.
WHY DO YOU ASK?
IS SOMETHING GOING TO HAPPEN HERE?
SHHH!
UH...NO... DON'T WORRY ...
BUT WE WERE HOPING TO SEE THE MATCH.
DO YOU HAPPEN TO HAVE SPARE TICKETS?
EH?

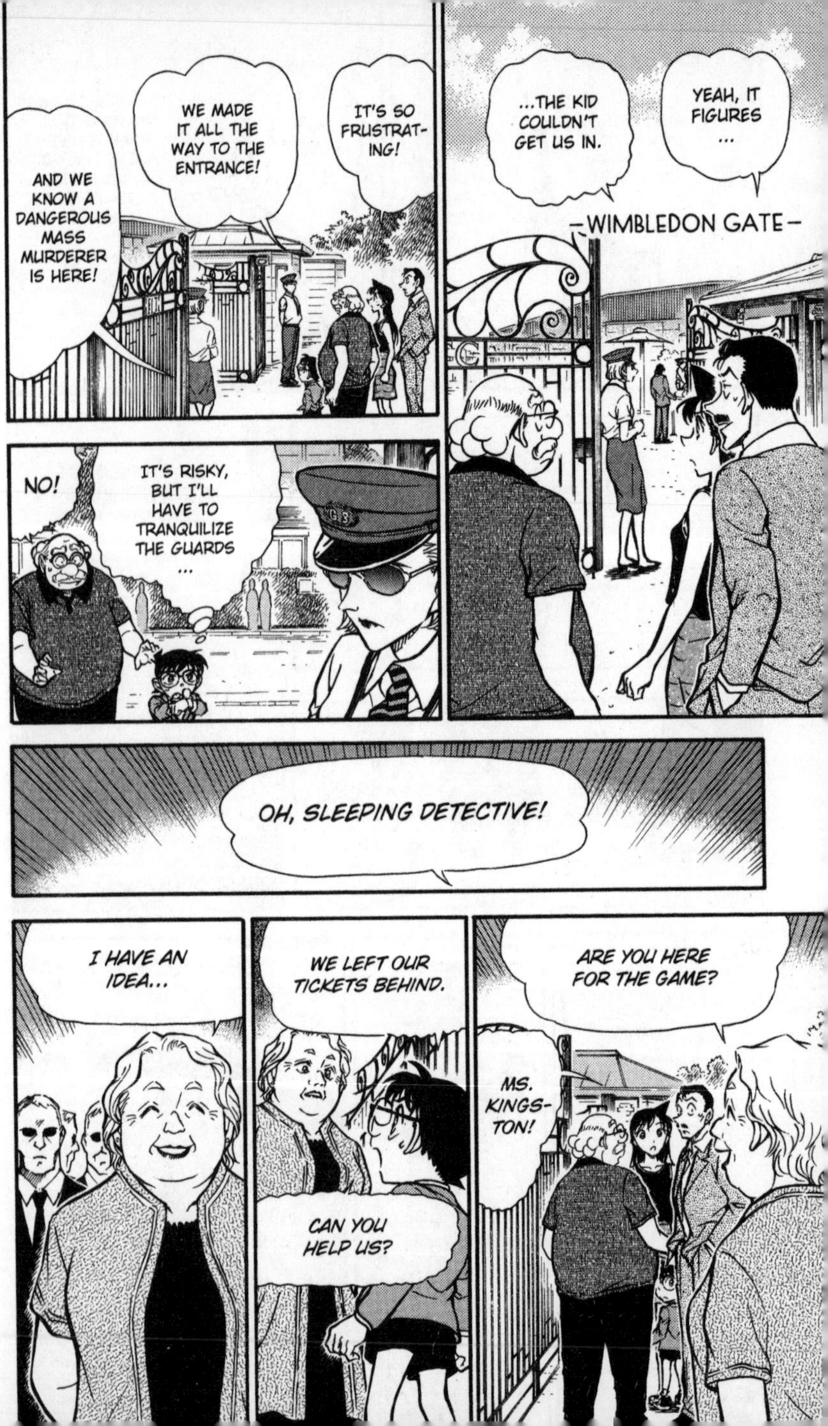
YEAH, IT FIGURES ...
...THE KID COULDN'T GET US IN.
—WIMBLEDON GATE—
IT'S SO FRUSTRATING!
WE MADE IT ALL THE WAY TO THE ENTRANCE!
AND WE KNOW A DANGEROUS MASS MURDERER IS HERE!
IT'S RISKY, BUT I'LL HAVE TO TRANQUILIZE THE GUARDS ...
NO!
OH, SLEEPING DETECTIVE!
ARE YOU HERE FOR THE GAME?
MS. KINGSTON!
WE LEFT OUR TICKETS BEHIND.
CAN YOU HELP US?
I HAVE AN IDEA...

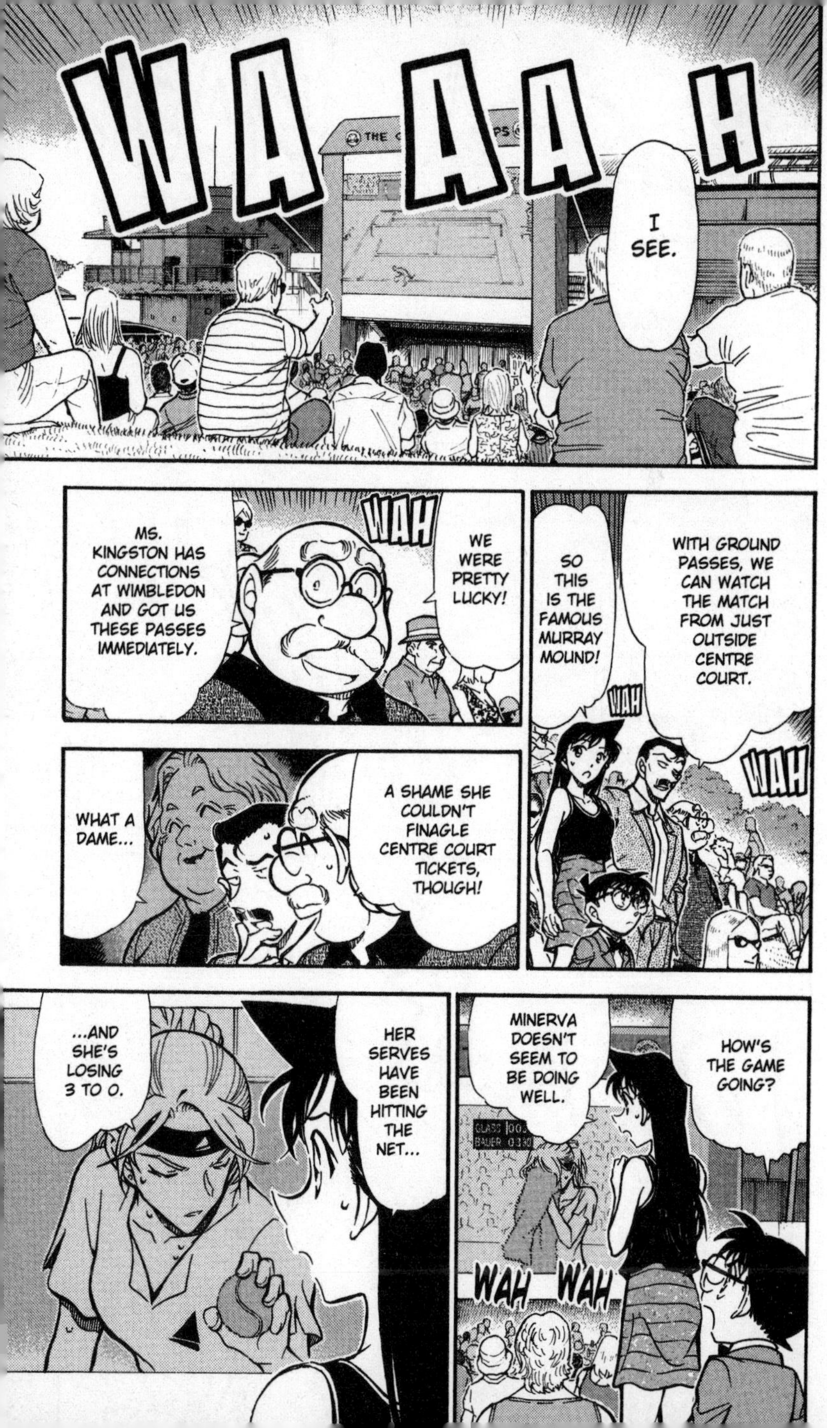
WAAAAH
I SEE.
WITH GROUND PASSES, WE CAN WATCH THE MATCH FROM JUST OUTSIDE CENTRE COURT.
SO THIS IS THE FAMOUS MURRAY MOUND!
WAH
WAH
WE WERE PRETTY LUCKY!
WAH
MS. KINGSTON HAS CONNECTIONS AT WIMBLEDON AND GOT US THESE PASSES IMMEDIATELY.
A SHAME SHE COULDN'T FINAGLE CENTRE COURT TICKETS, THOUGH!
WHAT A DAME...
HOW'S THE GAME GOING?
MINERVA DOESN'T SEEM TO BE DOING WELL.
WAH WAH
HER SERVES HAVE BEEN HITTING THE NET...
...AND SHE'S LOSING 3 TO 0.

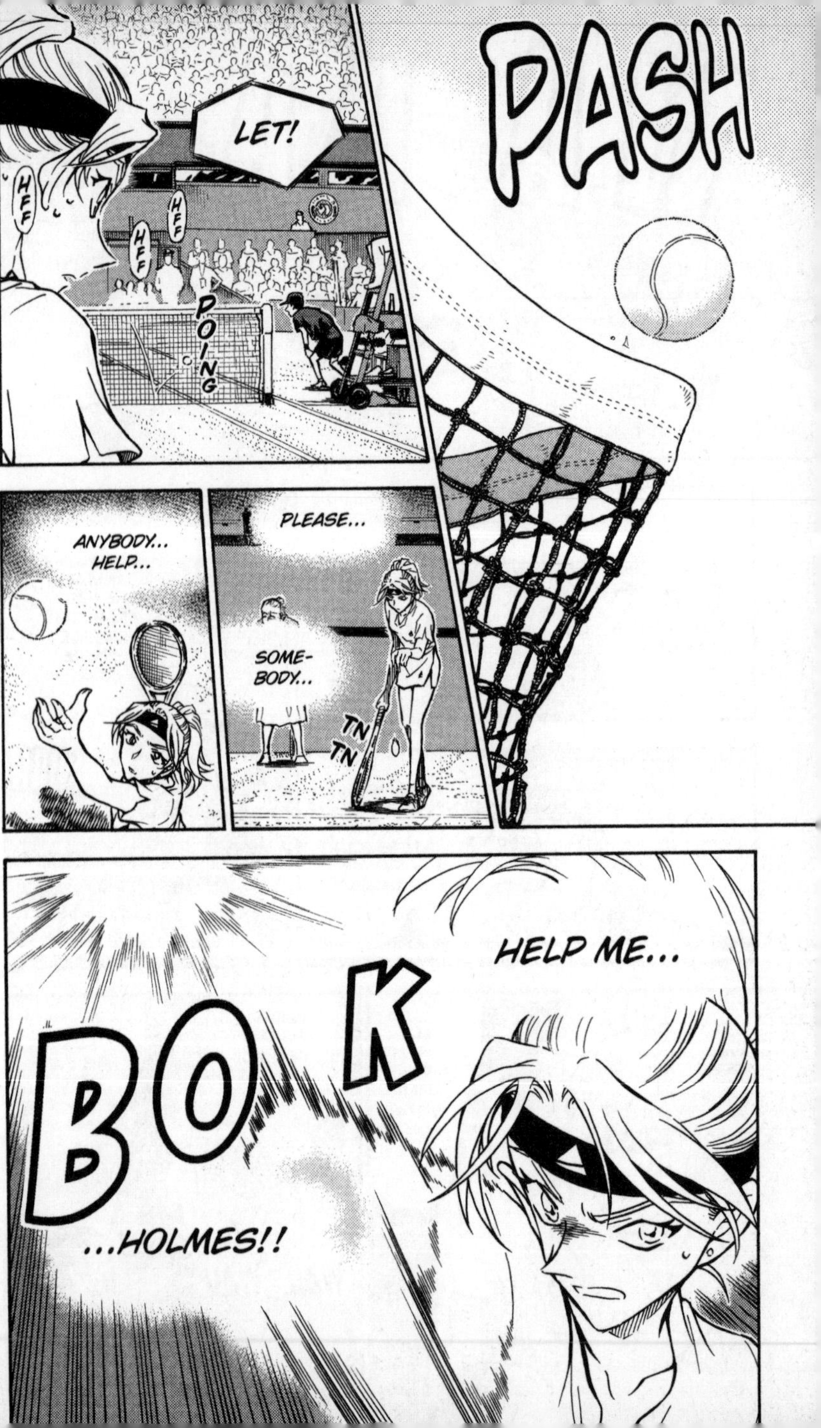
PASH
LET!
HFF
HFF
HFF
POING
PLEASE...
SOME-BODY...
TN TN
ANYBODY... HELP...
HELP ME...
BOK
...HOLMES!!

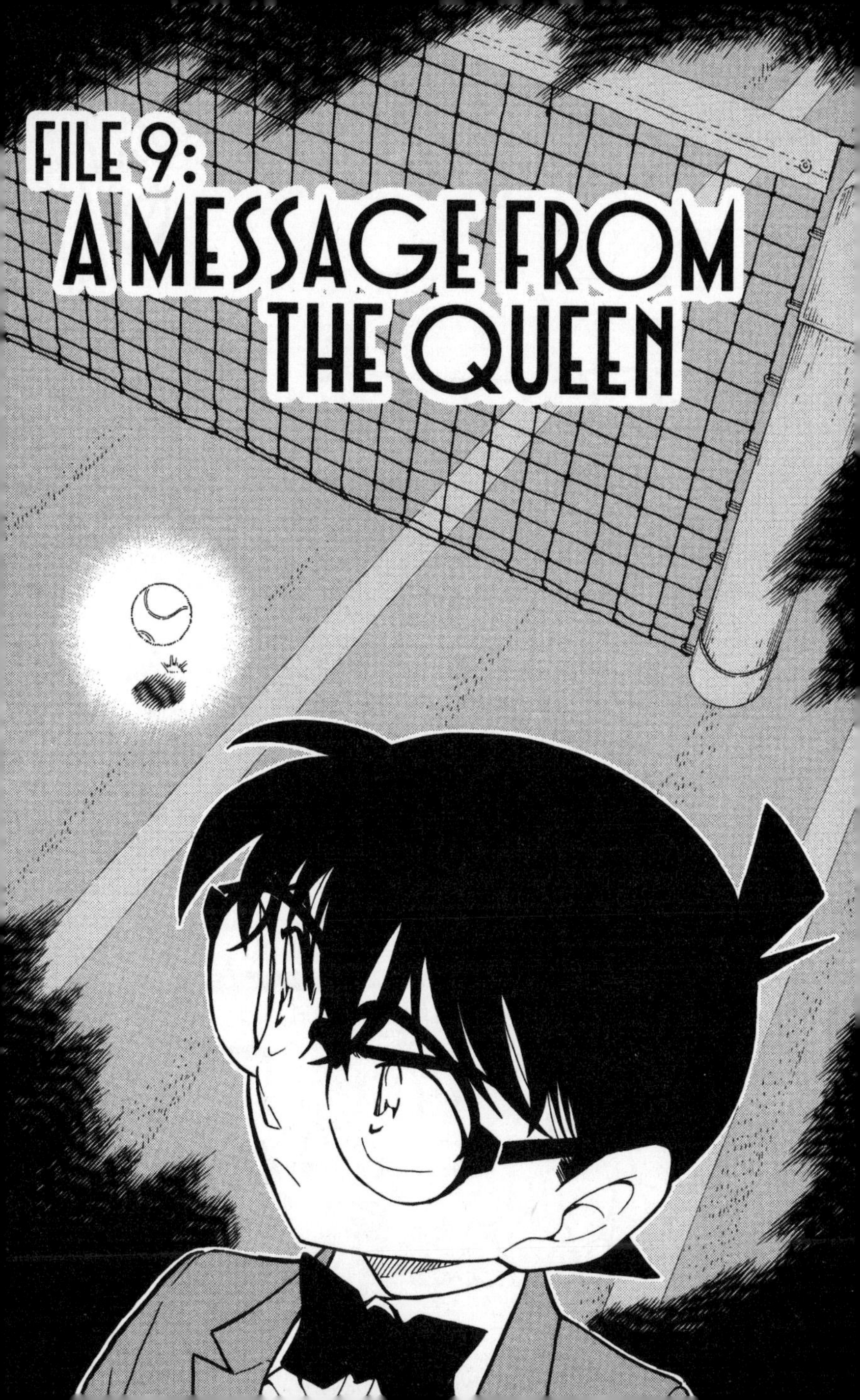
FILE 9:
A MESSAGE FROM THE QUEEN

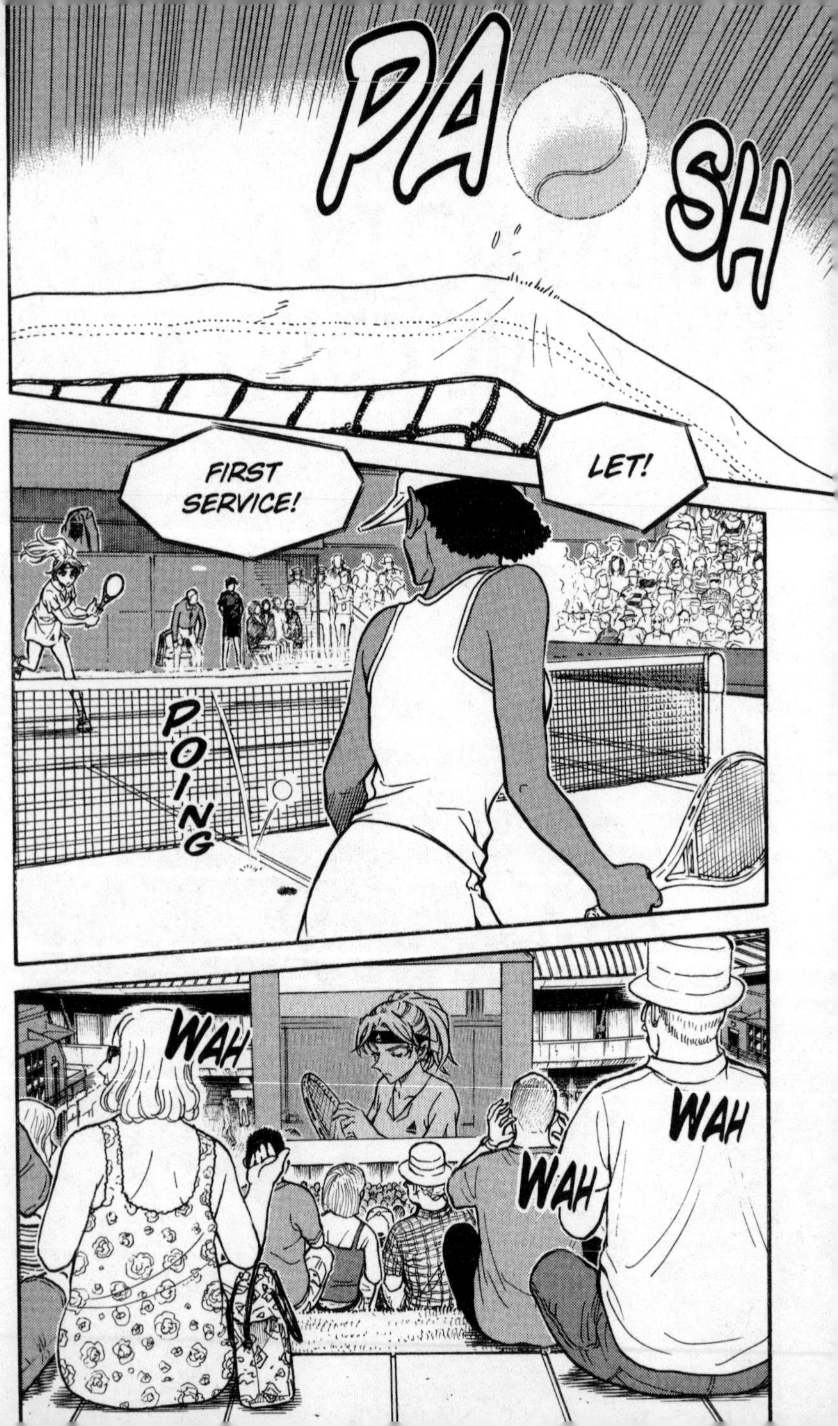
PA SH
LET!
FIRST SERVICE!
POING
WAH
WAH
WAH

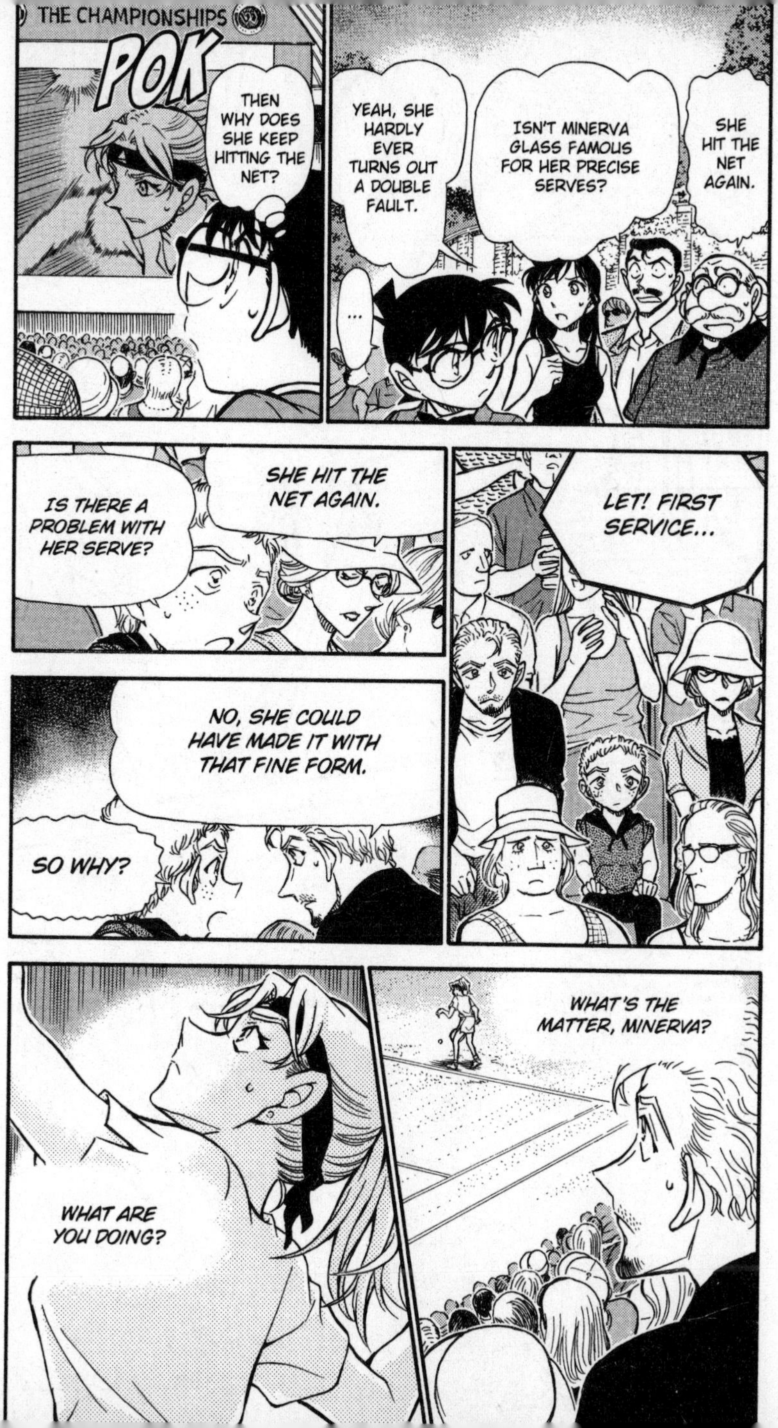
SHE HIT THE NET AGAIN.
ISN'T MINERVA GLASS FAMOUS FOR HER PRECISE SERVES?
YEAH, SHE HARDLY EVER TURNS OUT A DOUBLE FAULT.
...
THE CHAMPIONSHIPS
POK
THEN WHY DOES SHE KEEP HITTING THE NET?
LET! FIRST SERVICE...
SHE HIT THE NET AGAIN.
IS THERE A PROBLEM WITH HER SERVE?
NO, SHE COULD HAVE MADE IT WITH THAT FINE FORM.
SO WHY?
WHAT'S THE MATTER, MINERVA?
WHAT ARE YOU DOING?

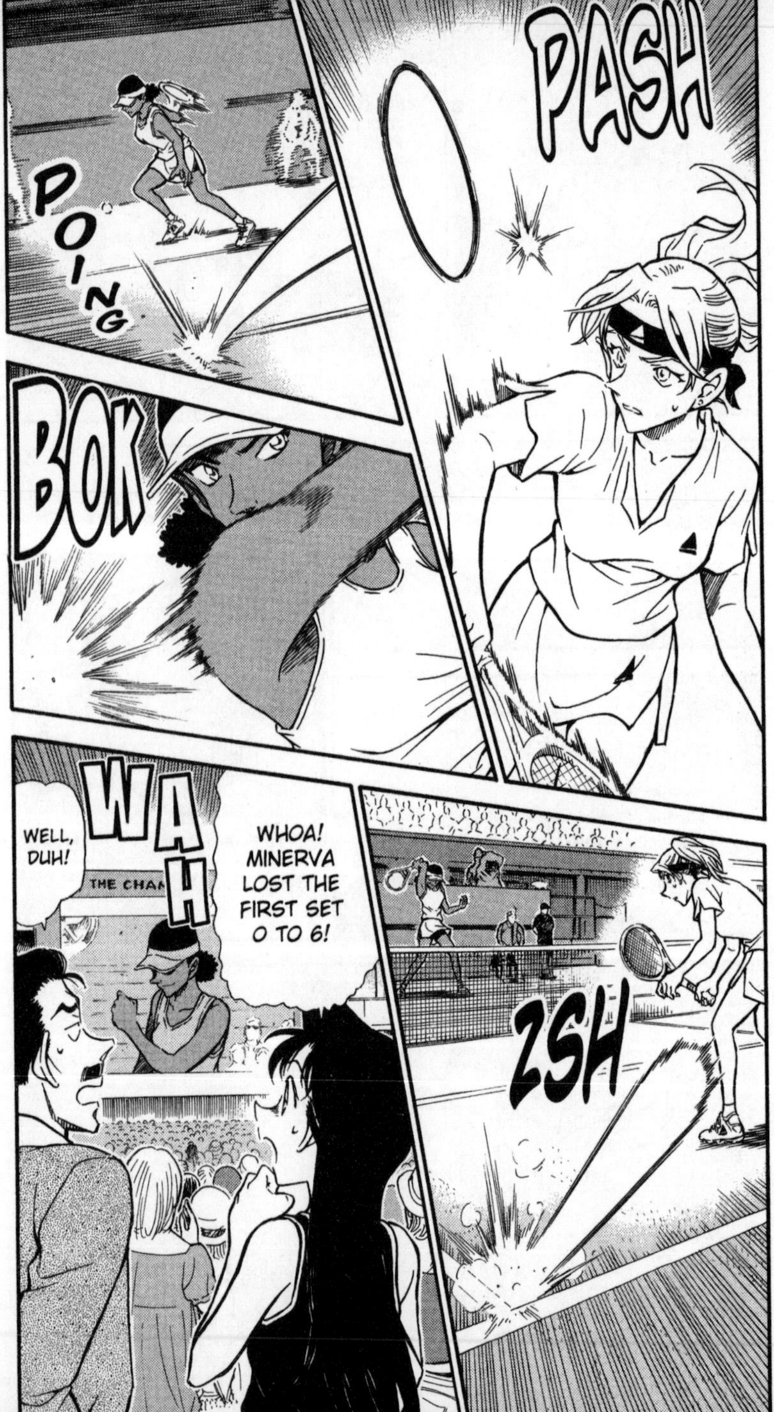
PASH
POING
BOK
ZSH
WAH
WHOA! MINERVA LOST THE FIRST SET 0 TO 6!
WELL, DUH!
THE CHAM

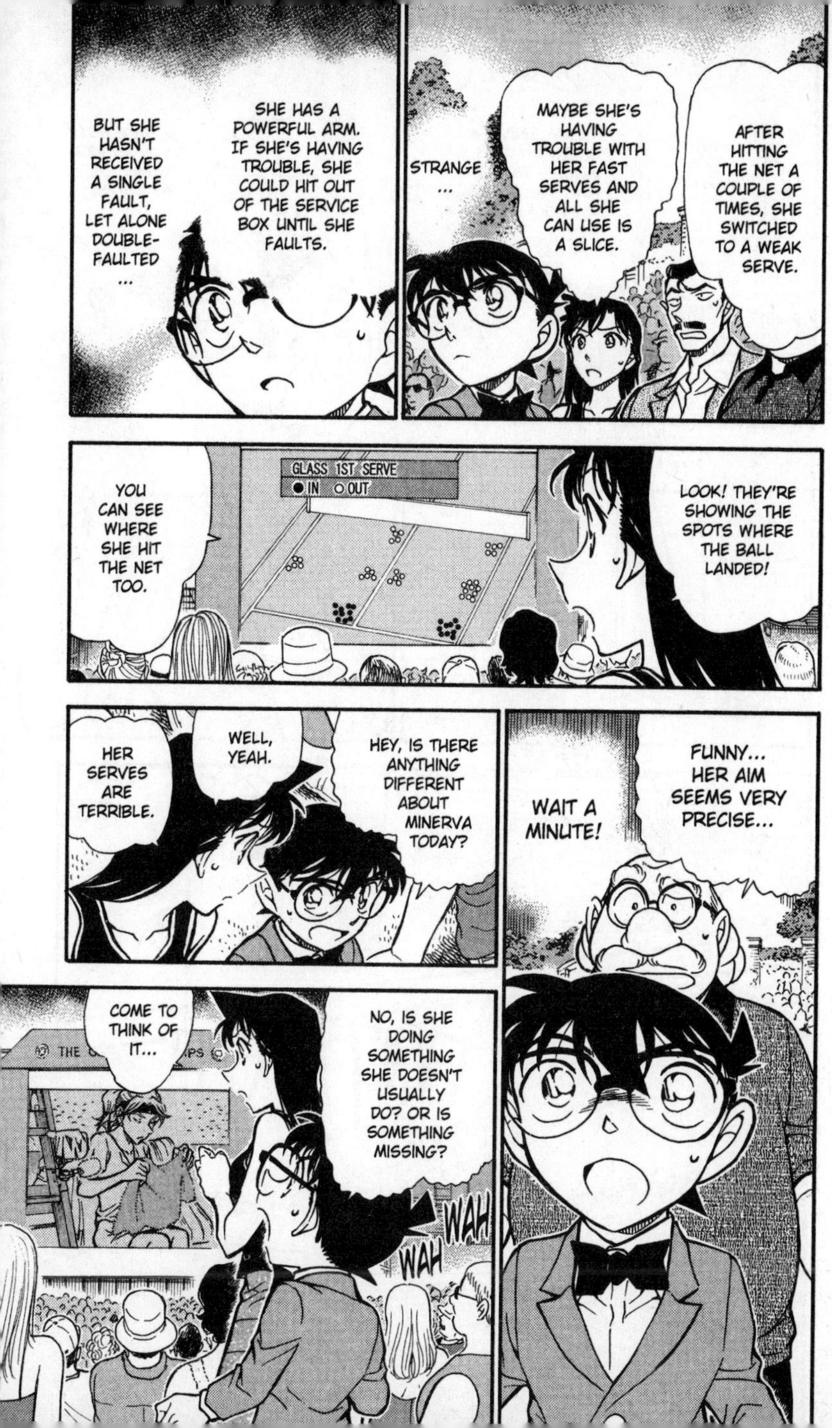
AFTER HITTING THE NET A COUPLE OF TIMES, SHE SWITCHED TO A WEAK SERVE.
MAYBE SHE'S HAVING TROUBLE WITH HER FAST SERVES AND ALL SHE CAN USE IS A SLICE.
STRANGE ...
SHE HAS A POWERFUL ARM. IF SHE'S HAVING TROUBLE, SHE COULD HIT OUT OF THE SERVICE BOX UNTIL SHE FAULTS.
BUT SHE HASN'T RECEIVED A SINGLE FAULT, LET ALONE DOUBLE-FAULTED ...
LOOK! THEY'RE SHOWING THE SPOTS WHERE THE BALL LANDED!
GLASS 1ST SERVE
IN
OUT
YOU CAN SEE WHERE SHE HIT THE NET TOO.
FUNNY... HER AIM SEEMS VERY PRECISE...
WAIT A MINUTE!
HEY, IS THERE ANYTHING DIFFERENT ABOUT MINERVA TODAY?
WELL, YEAH.
HER SERVES ARE TERRIBLE.
NO, IS SHE DOING SOMETHING SHE DOESN'T USUALLY DO? OR IS SOMETHING MISSING?
COME TO THINK OF IT...
WAH
WAH

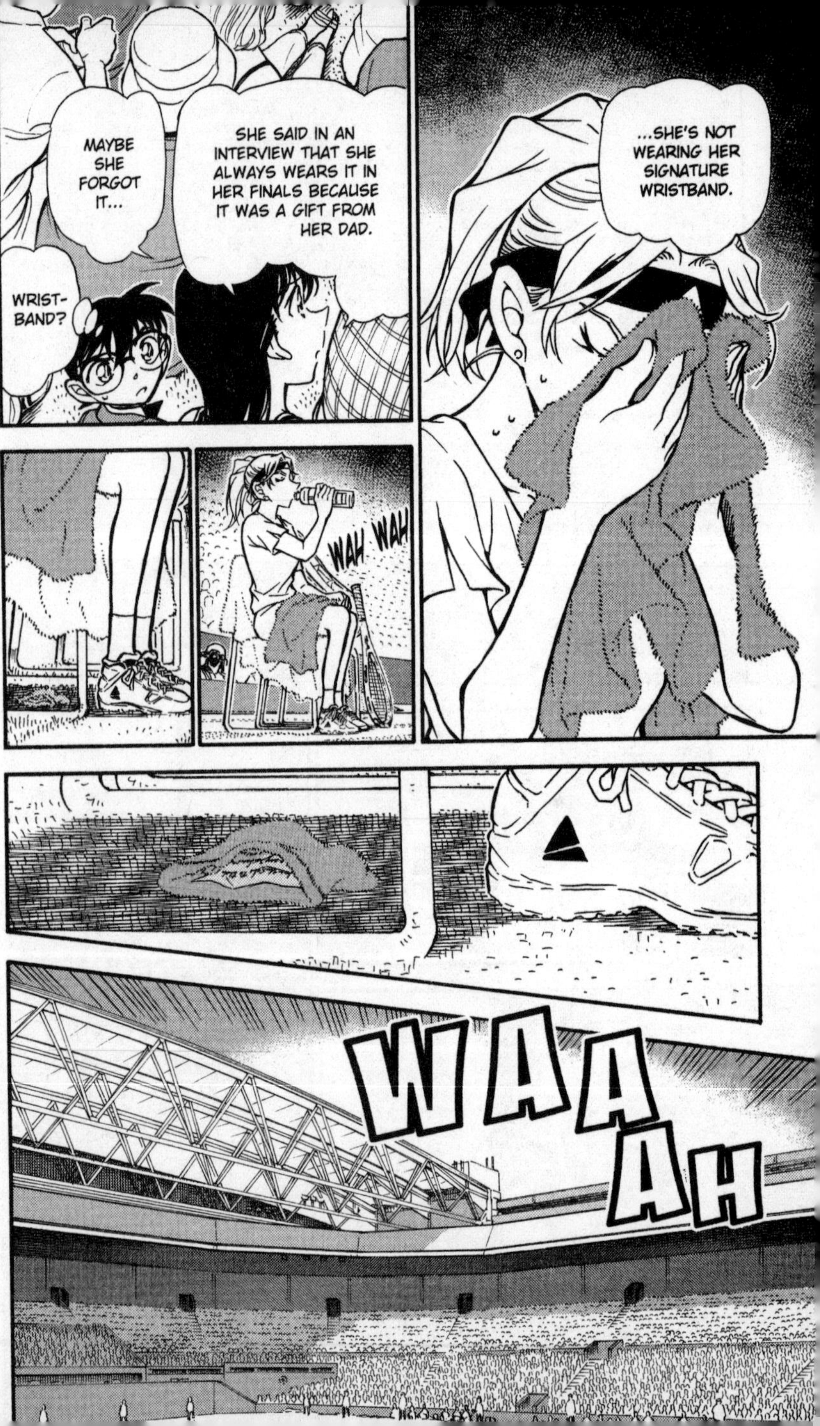
...SHE'S NOT WEARING HER SIGNATURE WRISTBAND.
SHE SAID IN AN INTERVIEW THAT SHE ALWAYS WEARS IT IN HER FINALS BECAUSE IT WAS A GIFT FROM HER DAD.
MAYBE SHE FORGOT IT...
WRIST-BAND?
WAH WAH
WAAAAH

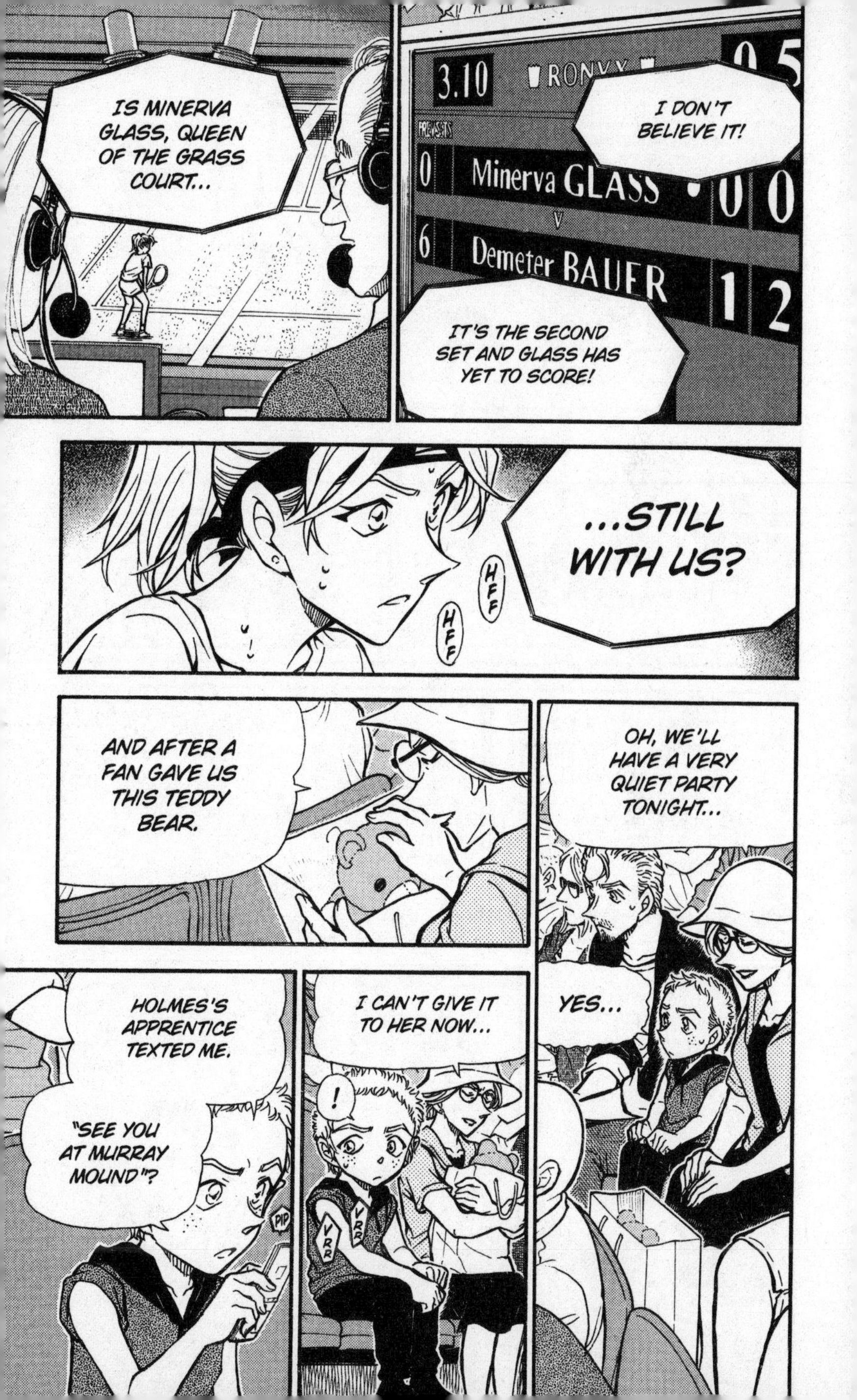
3.10
PREV SETS
0 Minerva GLASS 0 0
v
6 Demeter BAUER 1 2
I DON'T BELIEVE IT!
IT'S THE SECOND SET AND GLASS HAS YET TO SCORE!
IS MINERVA GLASS, QUEEN OF THE GRASS COURT...
HFF
HFF
...STILL WITH US?
OH, WE'LL HAVE A VERY QUIET PARTY TONIGHT...
YES...
AND AFTER A FAN GAVE US THIS TEDDY BEAR.
I CAN'T GIVE IT TO HER NOW...
!
VRR
VRR
HOLMES'S APPRENTICE TEXTED ME.
"SEE YOU AT MURRAY MOUND"?
PIP

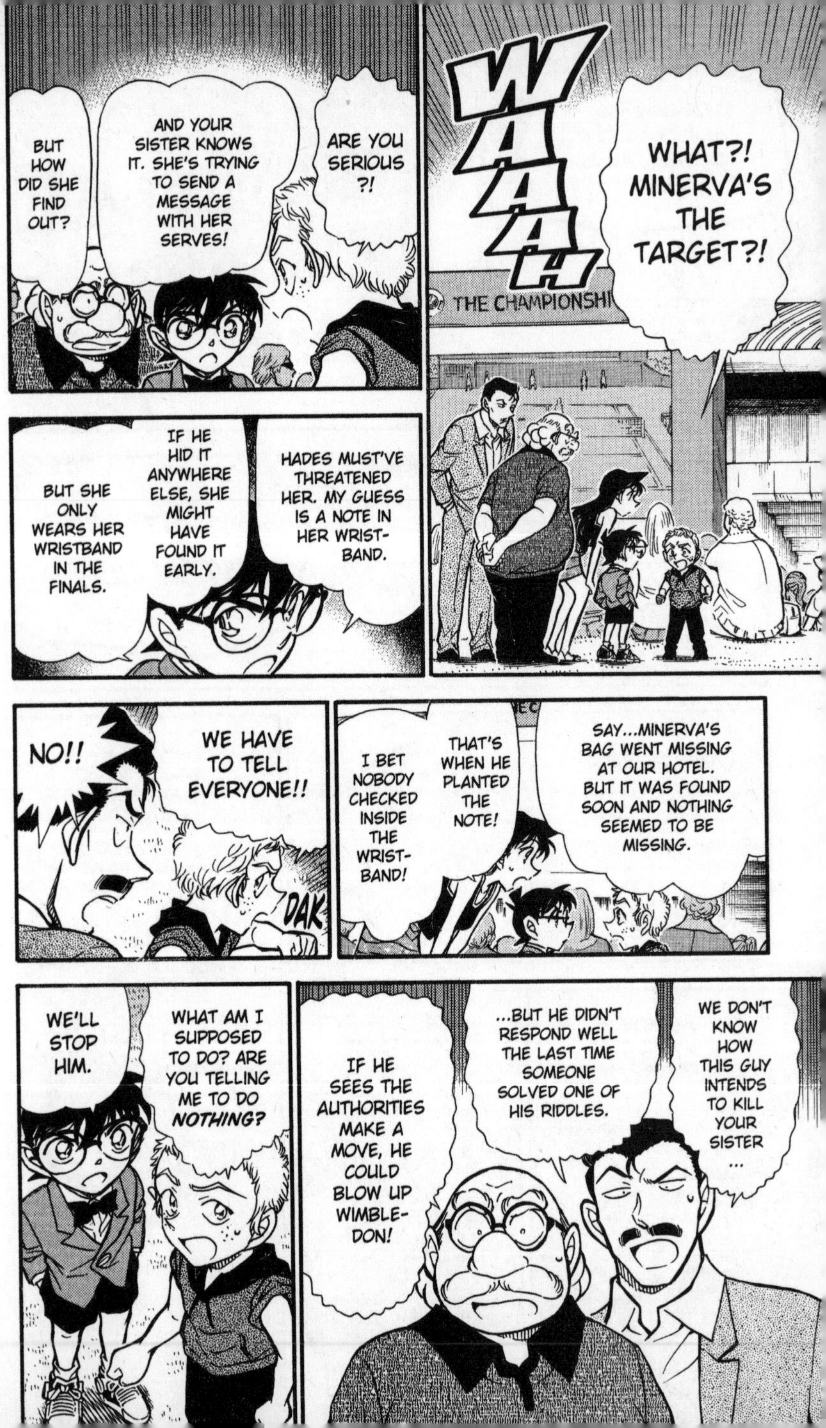
WHAT?! MINERVA'S THE TARGET?!
WAAAH
THE CHAMPIONSHI
ARE YOU SERIOUS?!
AND YOUR SISTER KNOWS IT. SHE'S TRYING TO SEND A MESSAGE WITH HER SERVES!
BUT HOW DID SHE FIND OUT?
HADES MUST'VE THREATENED HER. MY GUESS IS A NOTE IN HER WRIST-BAND.
IF HE HID IT ANYWHERE ELSE, SHE MIGHT HAVE FOUND IT EARLY.
BUT SHE ONLY WEARS HER WRISTBAND IN THE FINALS.
SAY...MINERVA'S BAG WENT MISSING AT OUR HOTEL. BUT IT WAS FOUND SOON AND NOTHING SEEMED TO BE MISSING.
THAT'S WHEN HE PLANTED THE NOTE!
I BET NOBODY CHECKED INSIDE THE WRIST-BAND!
WE HAVE TO TELL EVERYONE!!
NO!!
DAK
WE DON'T KNOW HOW THIS GUY INTENDS TO KILL YOUR SISTER ...
...BUT HE DIDN'T RESPOND WELL THE LAST TIME SOMEONE SOLVED ONE OF HIS RIDDLES.
IF HE SEES THE AUTHORITIES MAKE A MOVE, HE COULD BLOW UP WIMBLE-DON!
WHAT AM I SUPPOSED TO DO? ARE YOU TELLING ME TO DO NOTHING?
WE'LL STOP HIM.

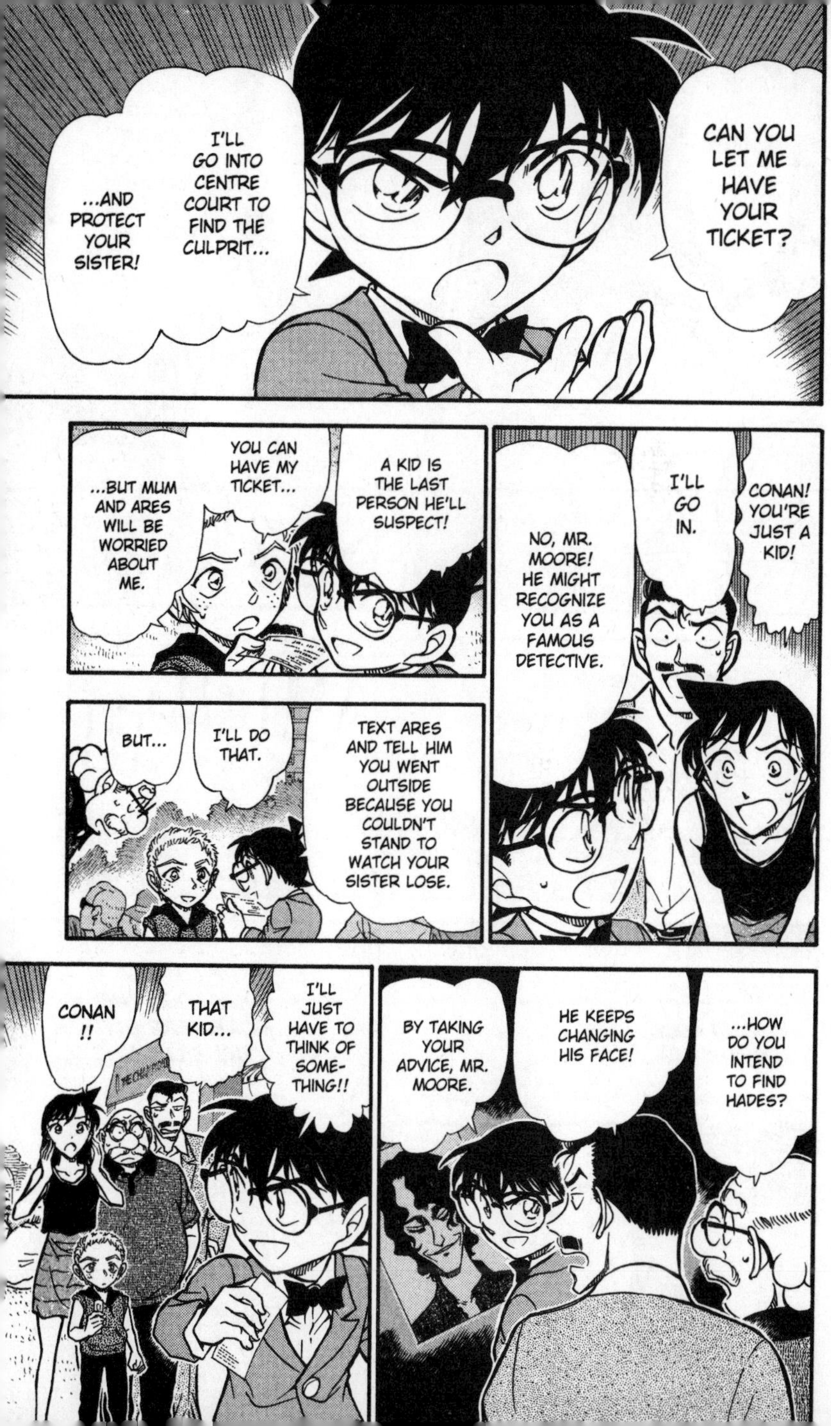
CAN YOU LET ME HAVE YOUR TICKET?
I'LL GO INTO CENTRE COURT TO FIND THE CULPRIT...
...AND PROTECT YOUR SISTER!
CONAN! YOU'RE JUST A KID!
I'LL GO IN.
NO, MR. MOORE! HE MIGHT RECOGNIZE YOU AS A FAMOUS DETECTIVE.
A KID IS THE LAST PERSON HE'LL SUSPECT!
YOU CAN HAVE MY TICKET...
...BUT MUM AND ARES WILL BE WORRIED ABOUT ME.
TEXT ARES AND TELL HIM YOU WENT OUTSIDE BECAUSE YOU COULDN'T STAND TO WATCH YOUR SISTER LOSE.
I'LL DO THAT.
BUT...
...HOW DO YOU INTEND TO FIND HADES?
HE KEEPS CHANGING HIS FACE!
BY TAKING YOUR ADVICE, MR. MOORE.
I'LL JUST HAVE TO THINK OF SOME-THING!!
THAT KID...
CONAN !!

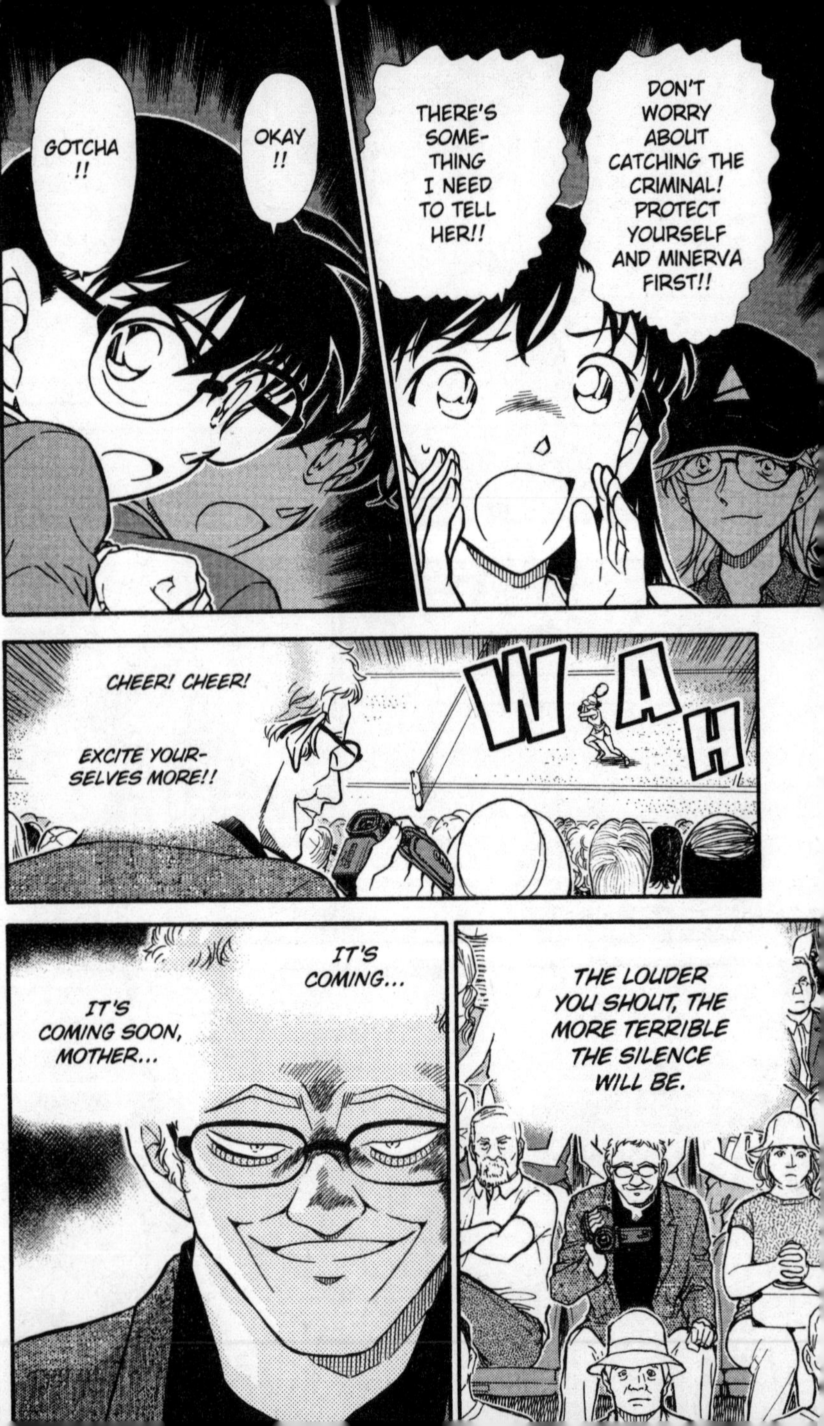
DON'T WORRY ABOUT CATCHING THE CRIMINAL! PROTECT YOURSELF AND MINERVA FIRST!!
THERE'S SOME- THING I NEED TO TELL HER!!
OKAY !!
GOTCHA !!
WAH
CHEER! CHEER!
EXCITE YOUR- SELVES MORE!!
THE LOUDER YOU SHOUT, THE MORE TERRIBLE THE SILENCE WILL BE.
IT'S COMING...
IT'S COMING SOON, MOTHER...

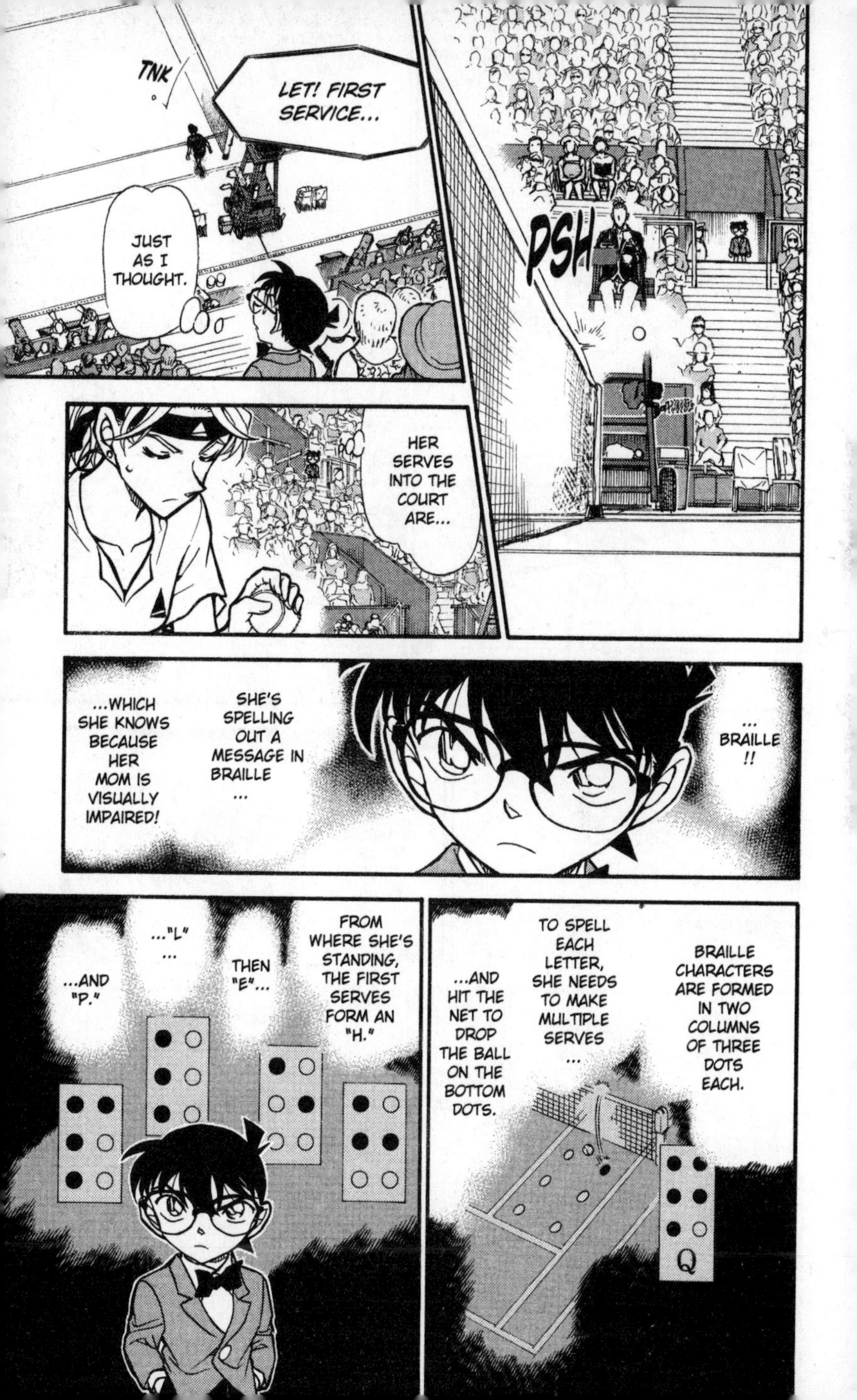
PSH
TNK
LET! FIRST SERVICE...
JUST AS I THOUGHT.
HER SERVES INTO THE COURT ARE...
... BRAILLE !!
SHE'S SPELLING OUT A MESSAGE IN BRAILLE ...
...WHICH SHE KNOWS BECAUSE HER MOM IS VISUALLY IMPAIRED!
BRAILLE CHARACTERS ARE FORMED IN TWO COLUMNS OF THREE DOTS EACH.
TO SPELL EACH LETTER, SHE NEEDS TO MAKE MULTIPLE SERVES ...
...AND HIT THE NET TO DROP THE BALL ON THE BOTTOM DOTS.
Q
FROM WHERE SHE'S STANDING, THE FIRST SERVES FORM AN "H."
THEN "E"...
..."L" ...
...AND "P."

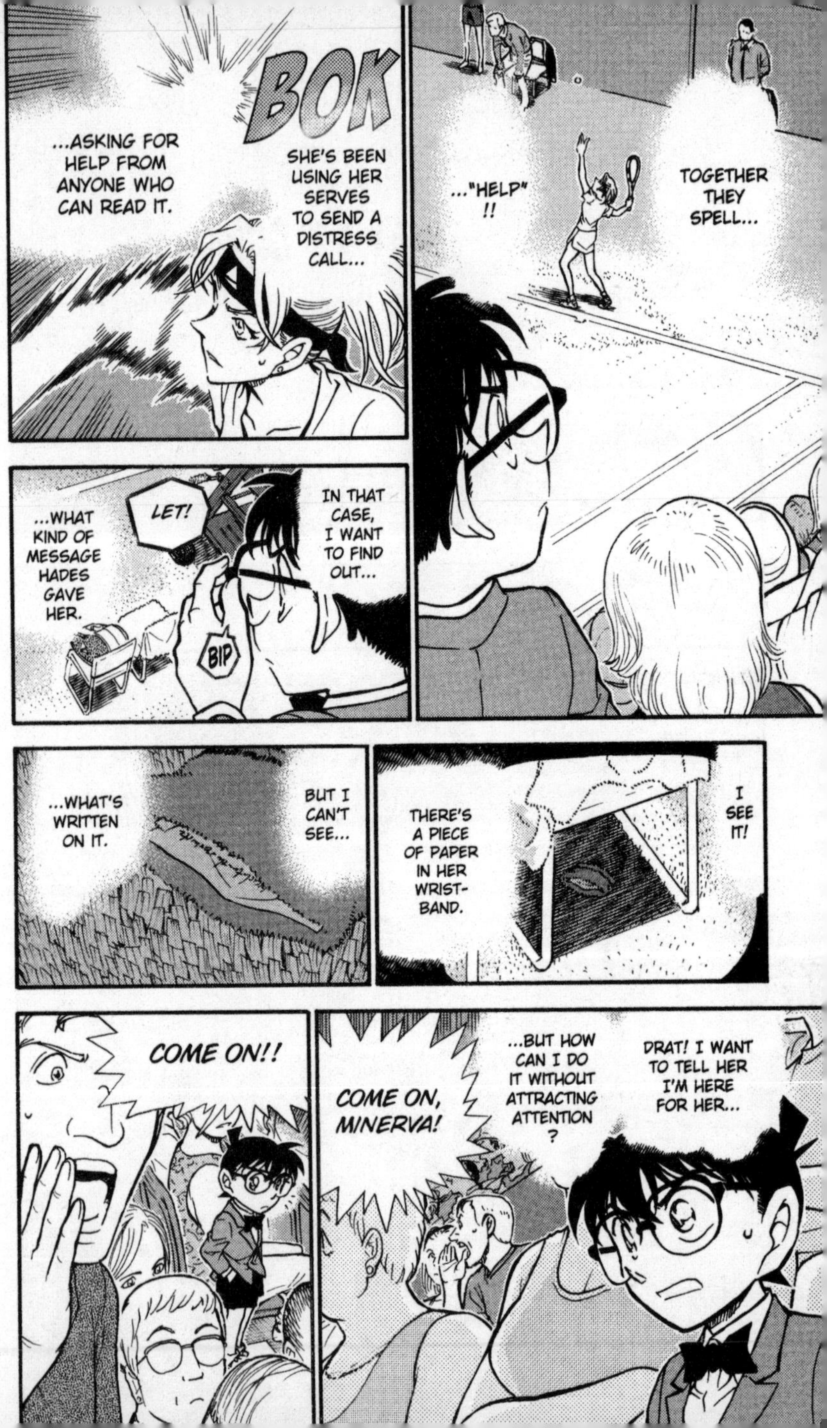
TOGETHER THEY SPELL...
..."HELP" !!
BOK
SHE'S BEEN USING HER SERVES TO SEND A DISTRESS CALL...
...ASKING FOR HELP FROM ANYONE WHO CAN READ IT.
LET!
IN THAT CASE, I WANT TO FIND OUT...
...WHAT KIND OF MESSAGE HADES GAVE HER.
BIP
I SEE IT!
THERE'S A PIECE OF PAPER IN HER WRIST-BAND.
BUT I CAN'T SEE...
...WHAT'S WRITTEN ON IT.
DRAT! I WANT TO TELL HER I'M HERE FOR HER...
...BUT HOW CAN I DO IT WITHOUT ATTRACTING ATTENTION?
COME ON, MINERVA!
COME ON!!

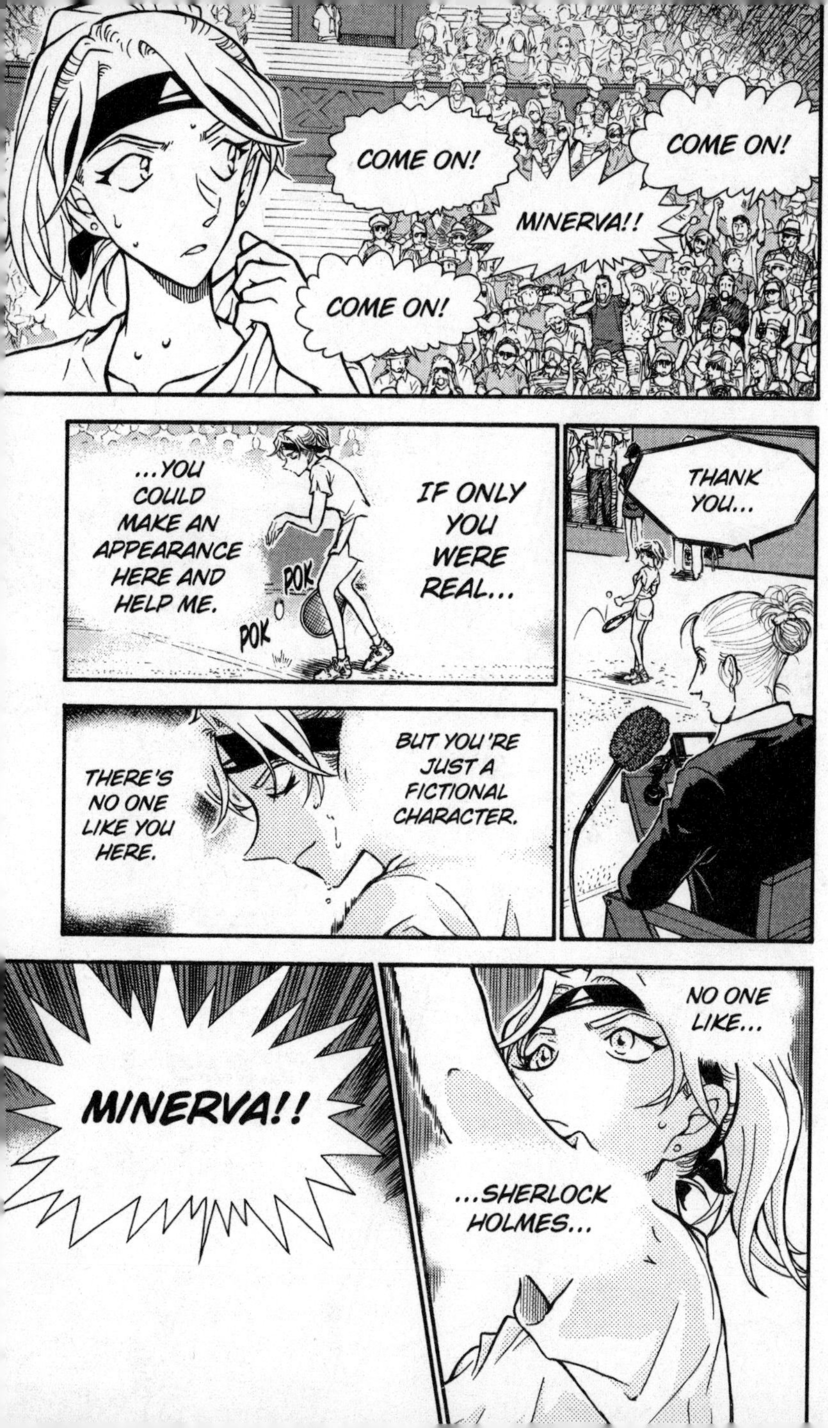
COME ON!
COME ON!
MINERVA!!
COME ON!
THANK YOU...
IF ONLY YOU WERE REAL...
...YOU COULD MAKE AN APPEARANCE HERE AND HELP ME.
POK
POK
BUT YOU'RE JUST A FICTIONAL CHARACTER.
THERE'S NO ONE LIKE YOU HERE.
NO ONE LIKE...
...SHERLOCK HOLMES...
MINERVA!!

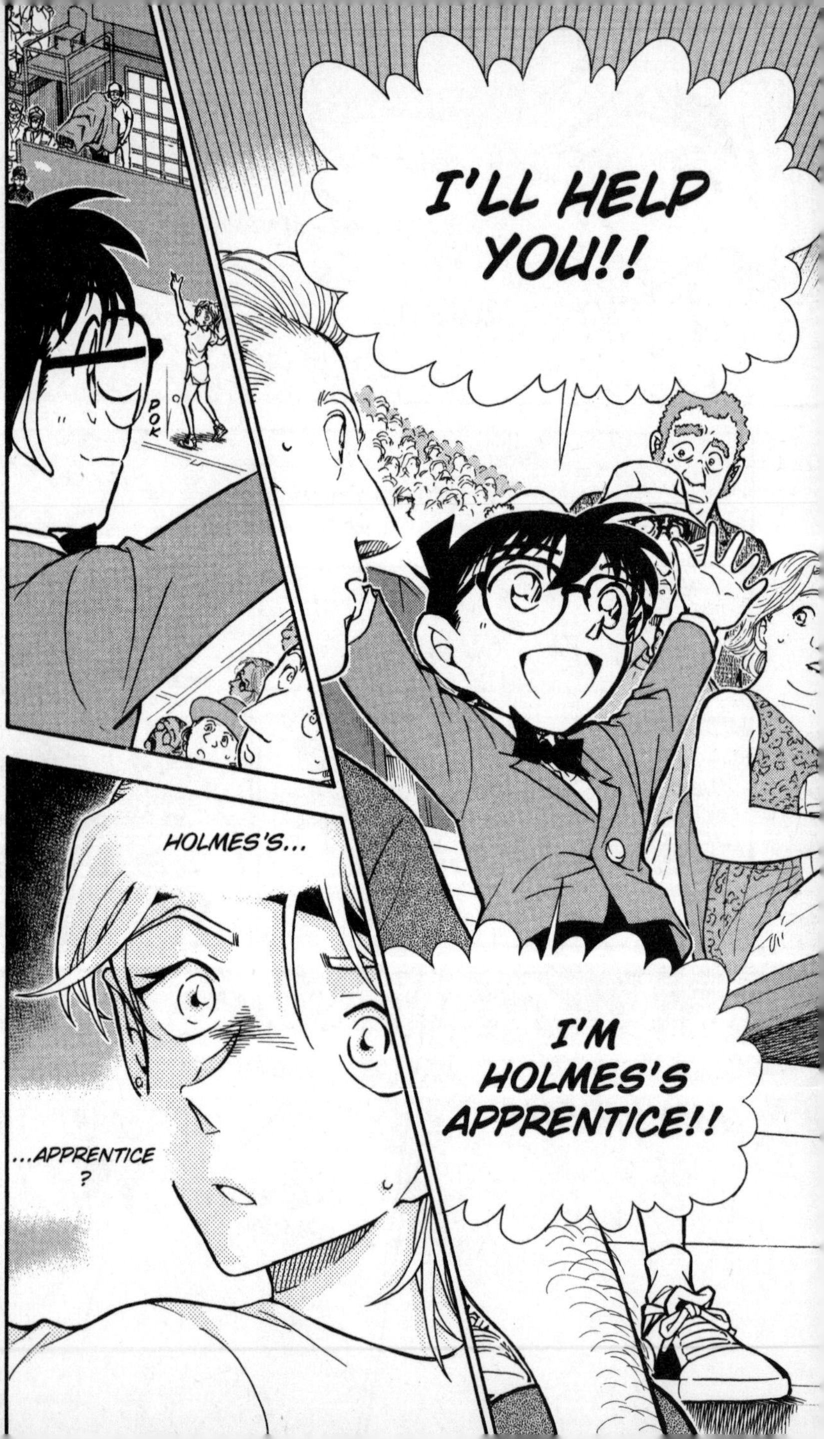
I'LL HELP YOU!!
I'M HOLMES'S APPRENTICE!!
POK
HOLMES'S...
...APPRENTICE ?

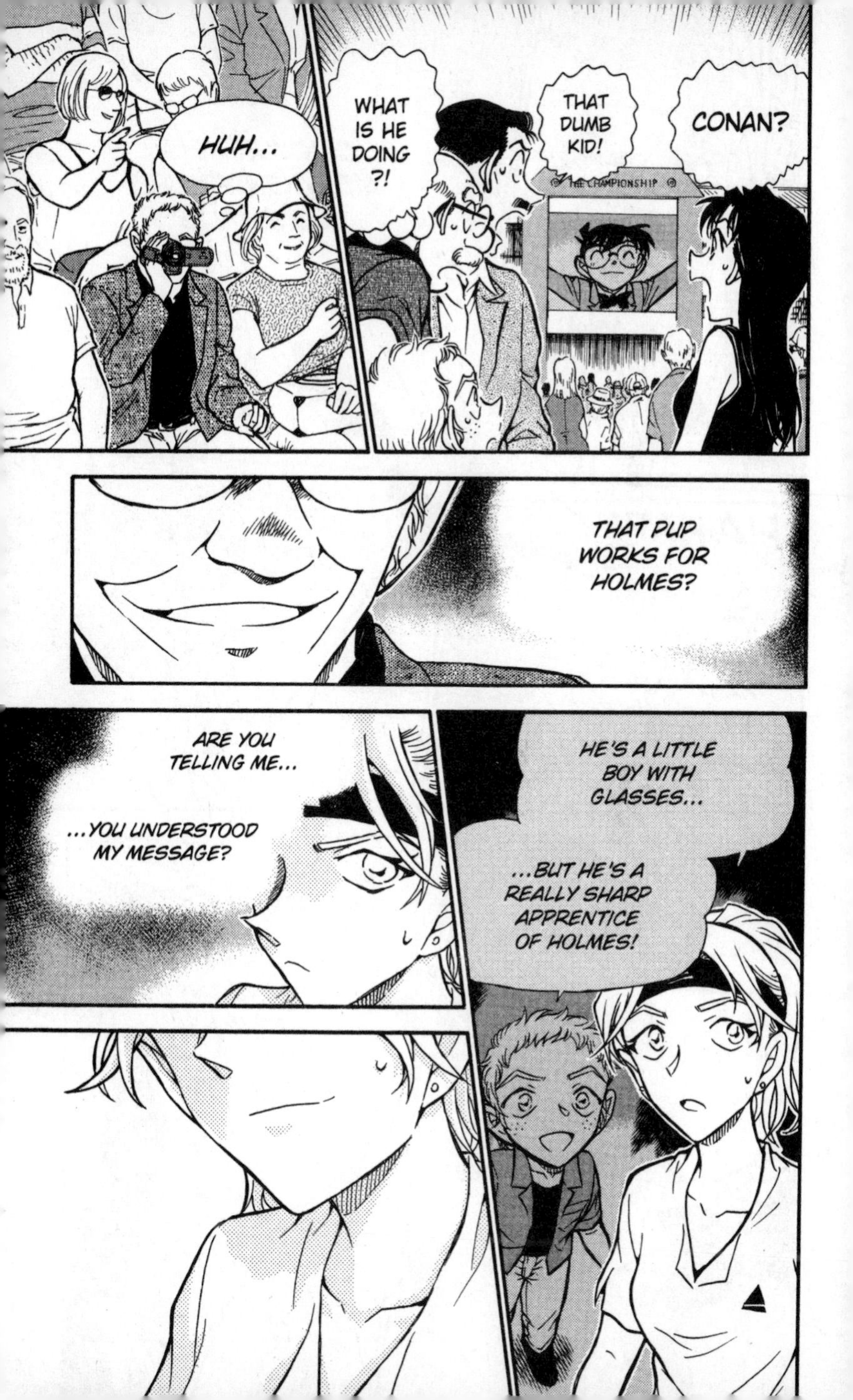
CONAN?
THAT DUMB KID!
THE CHAMPIONSHIP
WHAT IS HE DOING?!
HUH...
THAT PUP WORKS FOR HOLMES?
HE'S A LITTLE BOY WITH GLASSES...
...BUT HE'S A REALLY SHARP APPRENTICE OF HOLMES!
ARE YOU TELLING ME...
...YOU UNDERSTOOD MY MESSAGE?

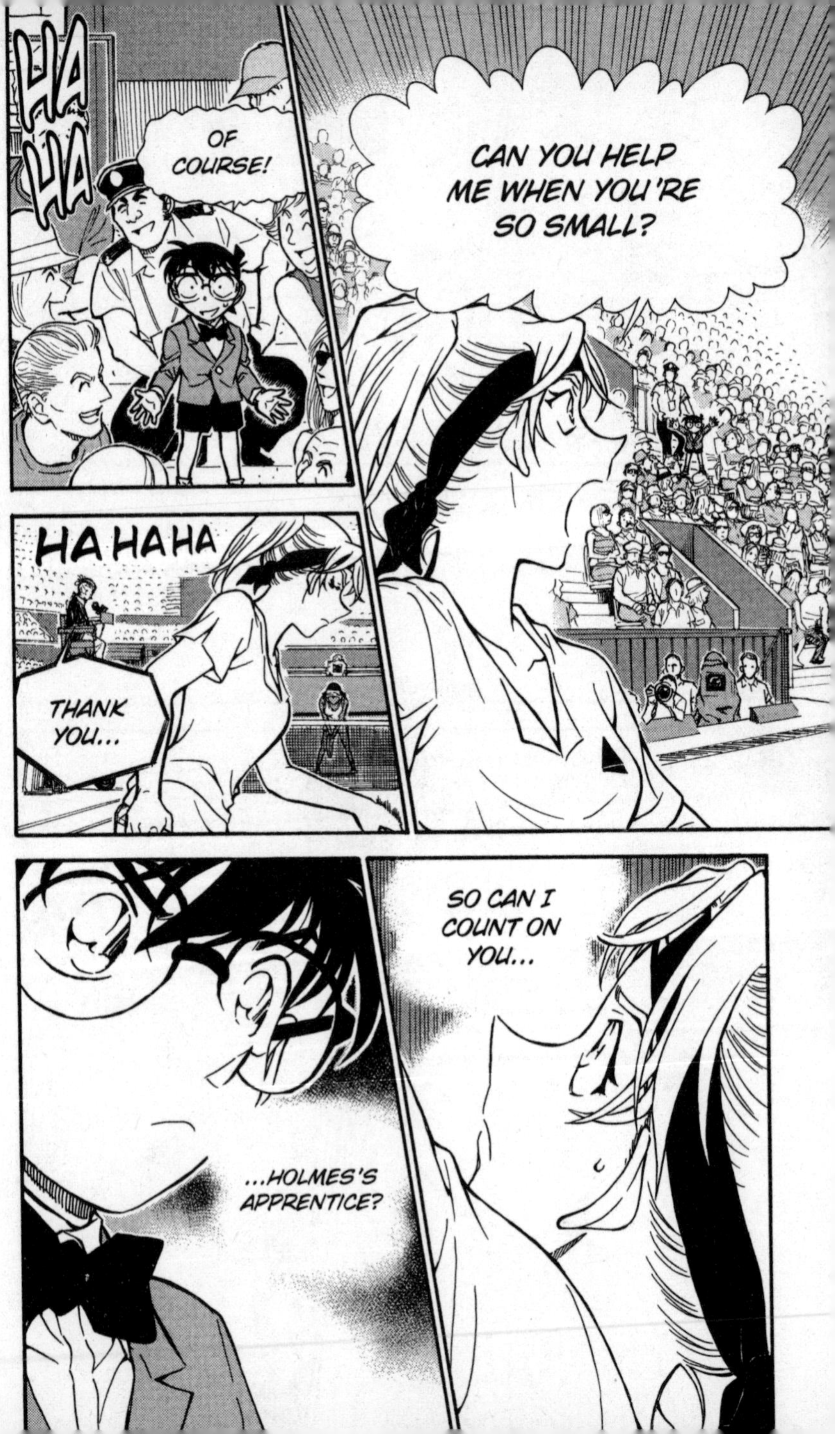
CAN YOU HELP ME WHEN YOU'RE SO SMALL?
HA HA
OF COURSE!
HAHAHA
THANK YOU...
SO CAN I COUNT ON YOU...
...HOLMES'S APPRENTICE?

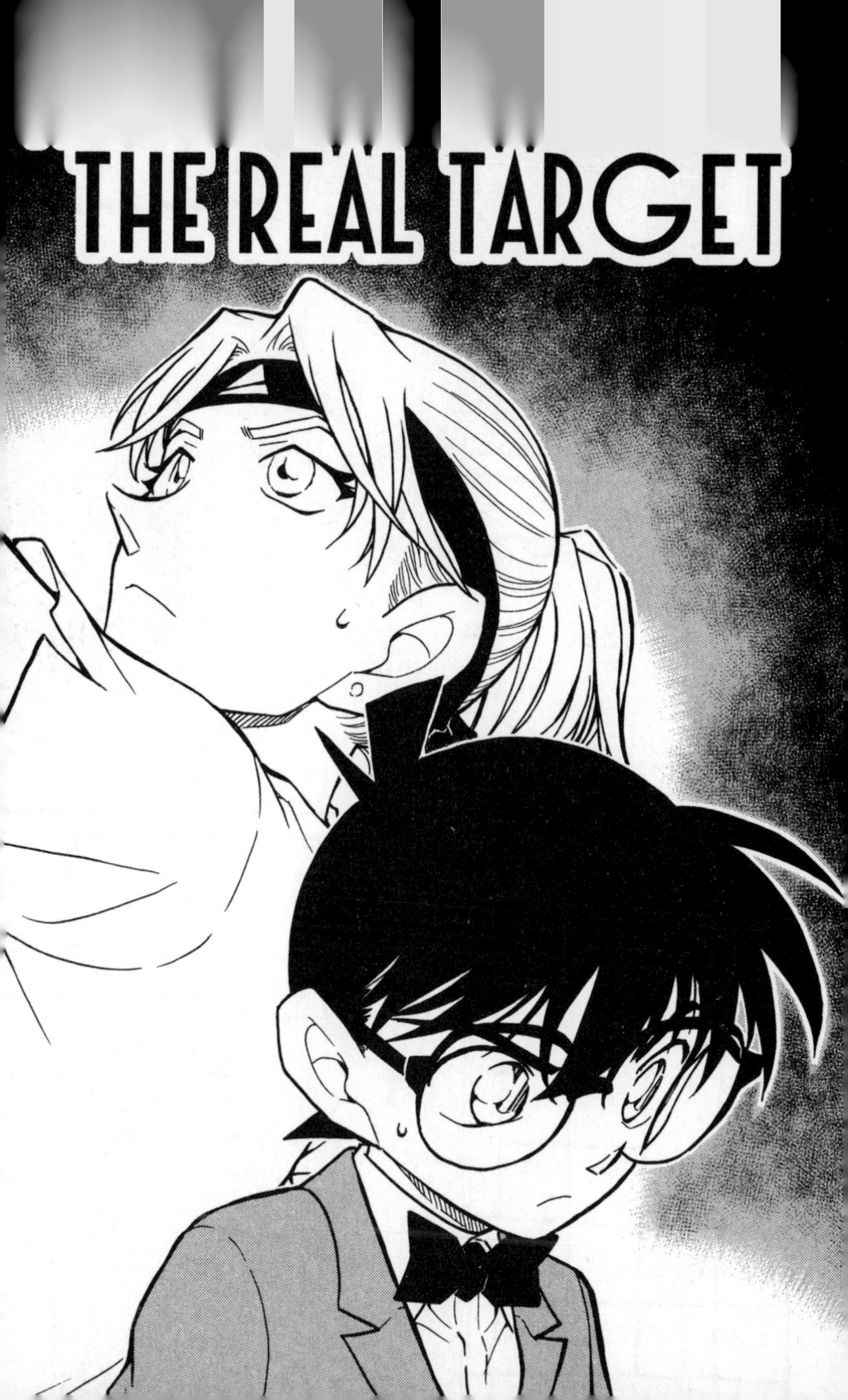
THE REAL TARGET

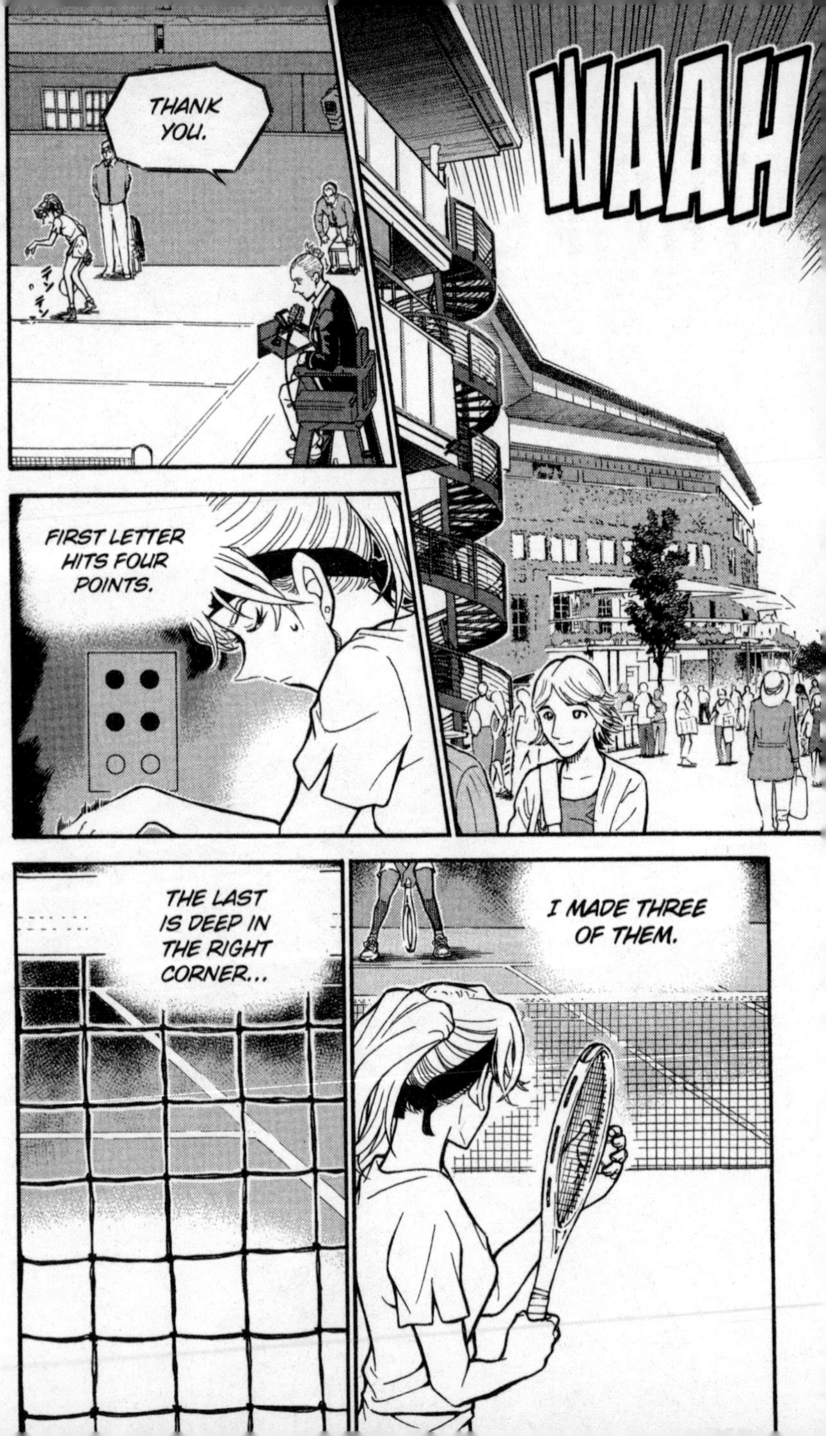
WAAH
THANK YOU.
テン テン
FIRST LETTER HITS FOUR POINTS.
I MADE THREE OF THEM.
THE LAST IS DEEP IN THE RIGHT CORNER...

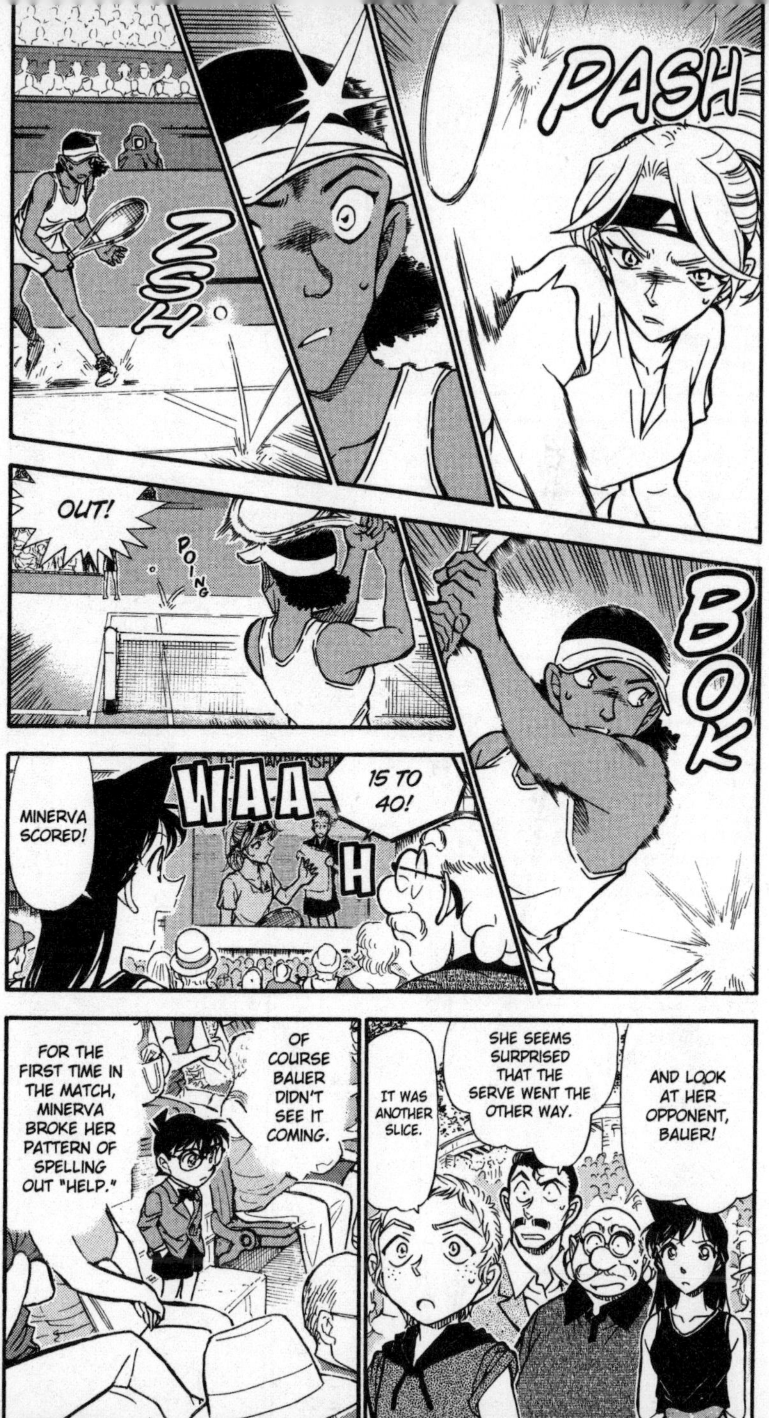
PASH
ZSH
BOK
OUT!
POING
15 TO 40!
WAAH
MINERVA SCORED!
AND LOOK AT HER OPPONENT, BAUER!
SHE SEEMS SURPRISED THAT THE SERVE WENT THE OTHER WAY.
IT WAS ANOTHER SLICE.
OF COURSE BAUER DIDN'T SEE IT COMING.
FOR THE FIRST TIME IN THE MATCH, MINERVA BROKE HER PATTERN OF SPELLING OUT "HELP."

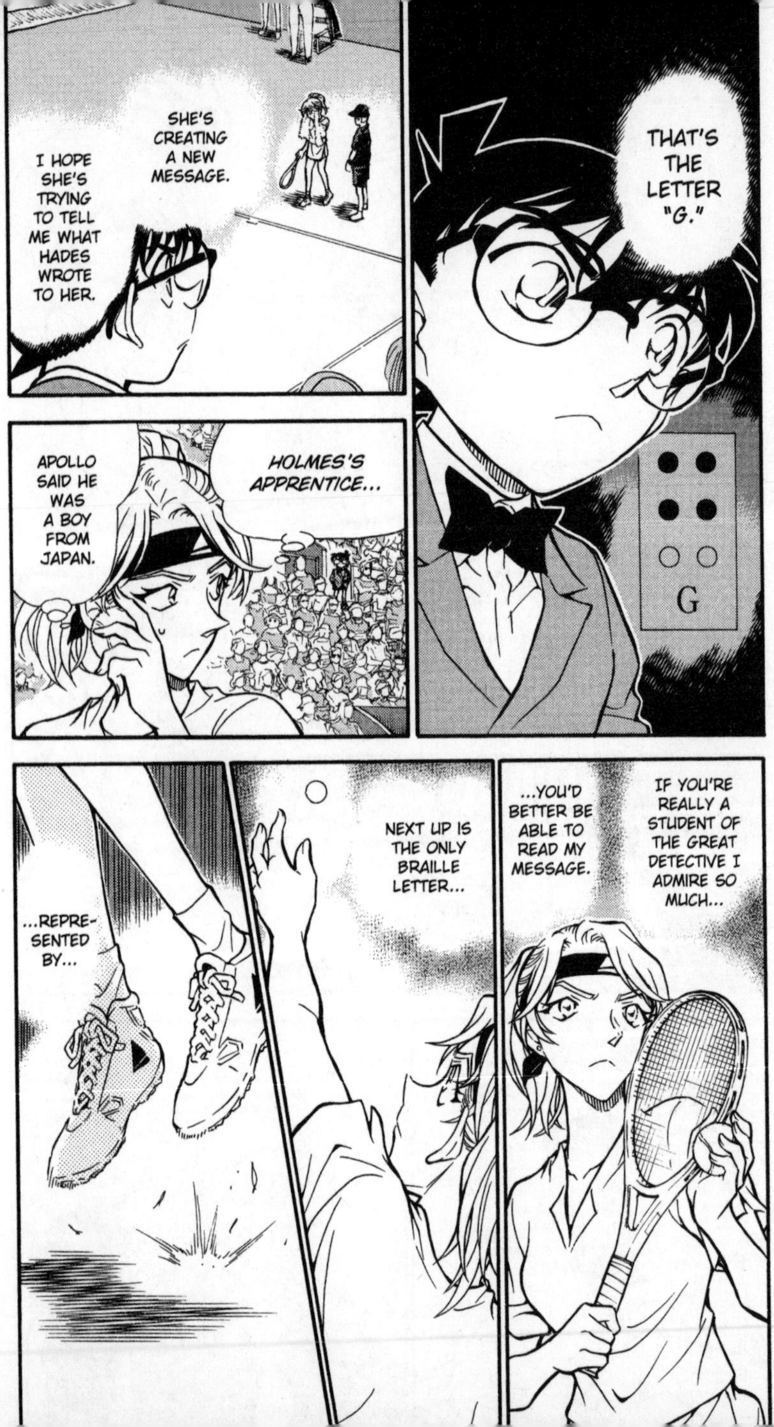
THAT'S THE LETTER "G."
G
SHE'S CREATING A NEW MESSAGE.
I HOPE SHE'S TRYING TO TELL ME WHAT HADES WROTE TO HER.
HOLMES'S APPRENTICE...
APOLLO SAID HE WAS A BOY FROM JAPAN.
IF YOU'RE REALLY A STUDENT OF THE GREAT DETECTIVE I ADMIRE SO MUCH...
...YOU'D BETTER BE ABLE TO READ MY MESSAGE.
NEXT UP IS THE ONLY BRAILLE LETTER...
...REPRE-SENTED BY...

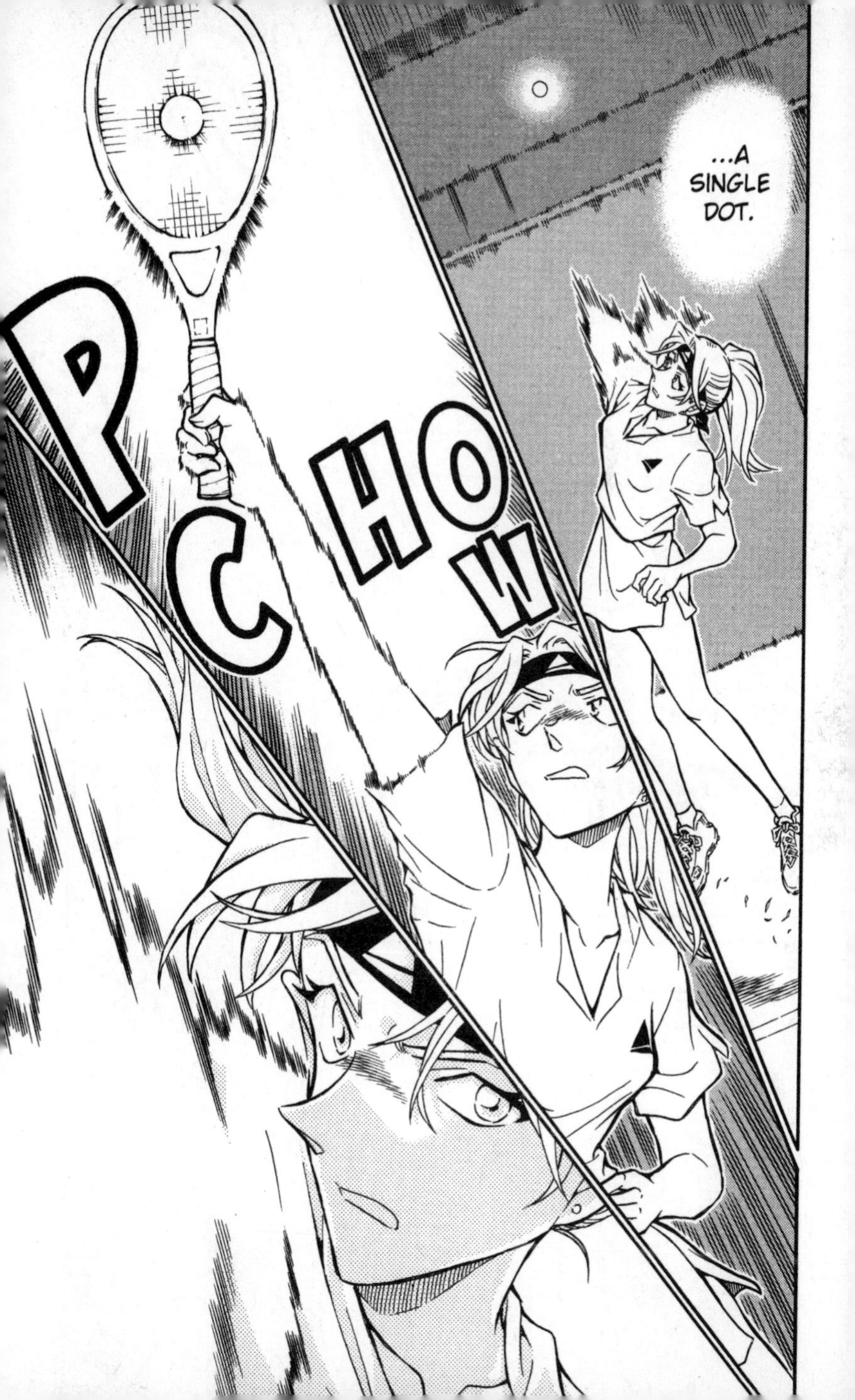
...A SINGLE DOT.
PCHOW

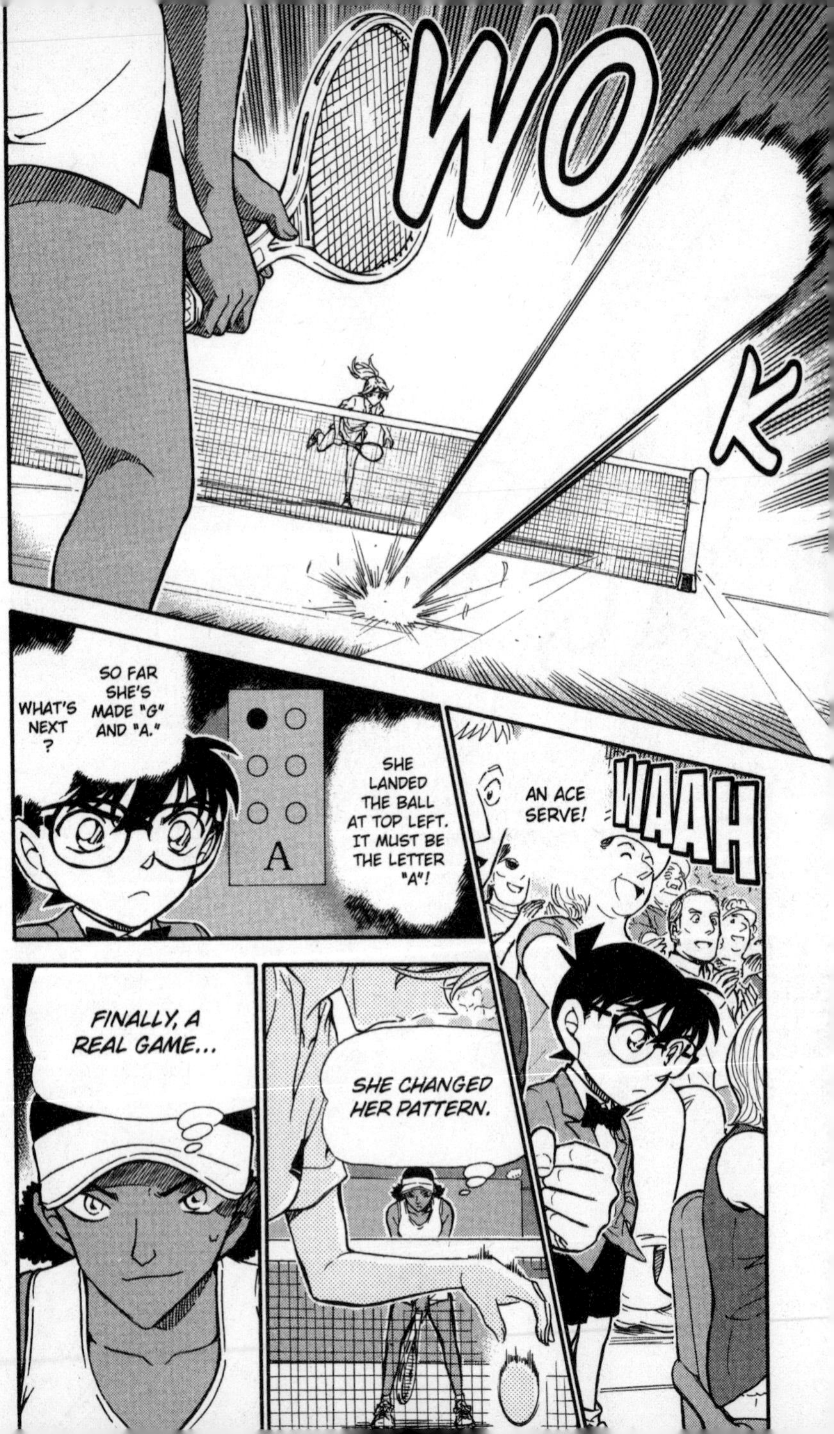
WOK
AN ACE SERVE!
WAAH
SHE LANDED THE BALL AT TOP LEFT. IT MUST BE THE LETTER "A"!
A
SO FAR SHE'S MADE "G" AND "A."
WHAT'S NEXT?
SHE CHANGED HER PATTERN.
FINALLY, A REAL GAME...

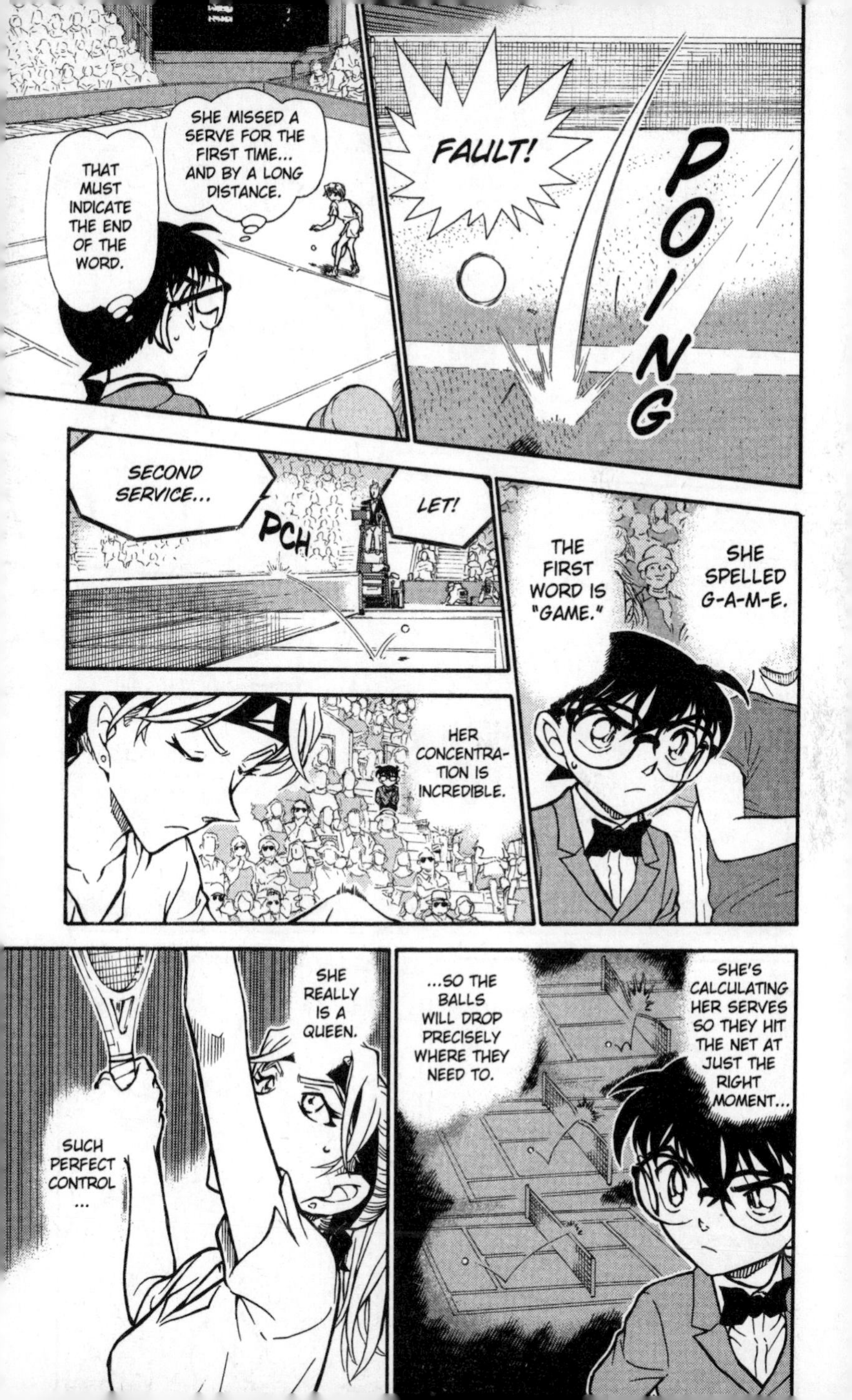
FAULT!
POING
SHE MISSED A SERVE FOR THE FIRST TIME... AND BY A LONG DISTANCE.
THAT MUST INDICATE THE END OF THE WORD.
SHE SPELLED G-A-M-E.
THE FIRST WORD IS "GAME."
LET!
PCH
SECOND SERVICE...
HER CONCENTRATION IS INCREDIBLE.
SHE'S CALCULATING HER SERVES SO THEY HIT THE NET AT JUST THE RIGHT MOMENT...
...SO THE BALLS WILL DROP PRECISELY WHERE THEY NEED TO.
SHE REALLY IS A QUEEN.
SUCH PERFECT CONTROL ...

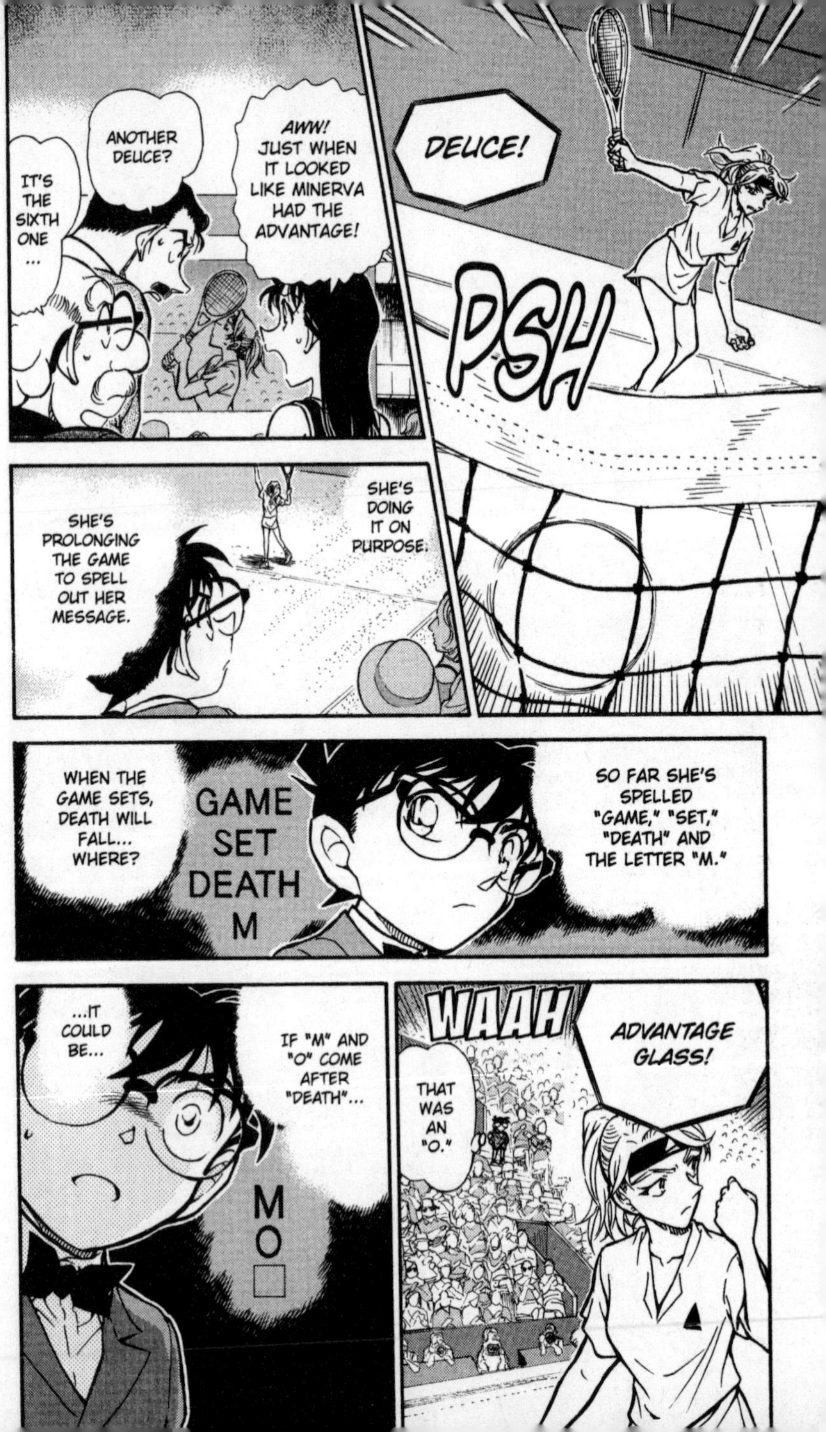
DEUCE!
PSH
AWW! JUST WHEN IT LOOKED LIKE MINERVA HAD THE ADVANTAGE!
ANOTHER DEUCE?
IT'S THE SIXTH ONE ...
SHE'S DOING IT ON PURPOSE.
SHE'S PROLONGING THE GAME TO SPELL OUT HER MESSAGE.
SO FAR SHE'S SPELLED "GAME," "SET," "DEATH" AND THE LETTER "M."
GAME
SET
DEATH
M
WHEN THE GAME SETS, DEATH WILL FALL... WHERE?
ADVANTAGE GLASS!
WAAH
THAT WAS AN "O."
IF "M" AND "O" COME AFTER "DEATH"...
...IT COULD BE...
M
O
□

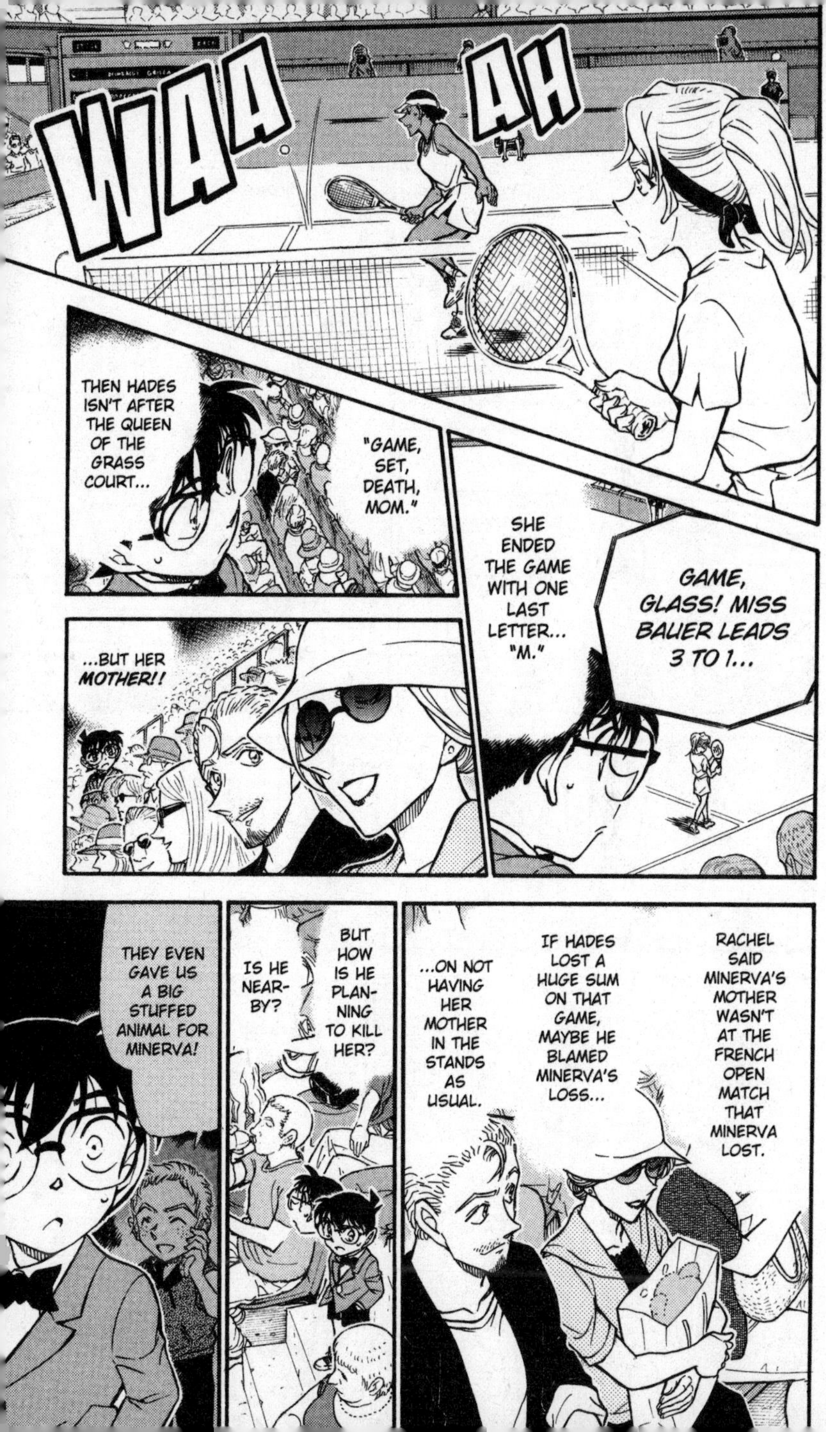
WAA AH
GAME, GLASS! MISS BAUER LEADS 3 TO 1...
SHE ENDED THE GAME WITH ONE LAST LETTER... "M."
"GAME, SET, DEATH, MOM."
THEN HADES ISN'T AFTER THE QUEEN OF THE GRASS COURT...
...BUT HER *MOTHER!!*
RACHEL SAID MINERVA'S MOTHER WASN'T AT THE FRENCH OPEN MATCH THAT MINERVA LOST.
IF HADES LOST A HUGE SUM ON THAT GAME, MAYBE HE BLAMED MINERVA'S LOSS...
...ON NOT HAVING HER MOTHER IN THE STANDS AS USUAL.
BUT HOW IS HE PLANNING TO KILL HER?
IS HE NEARBY?
THEY EVEN GAVE US A BIG STUFFED ANIMAL FOR MINERVA!

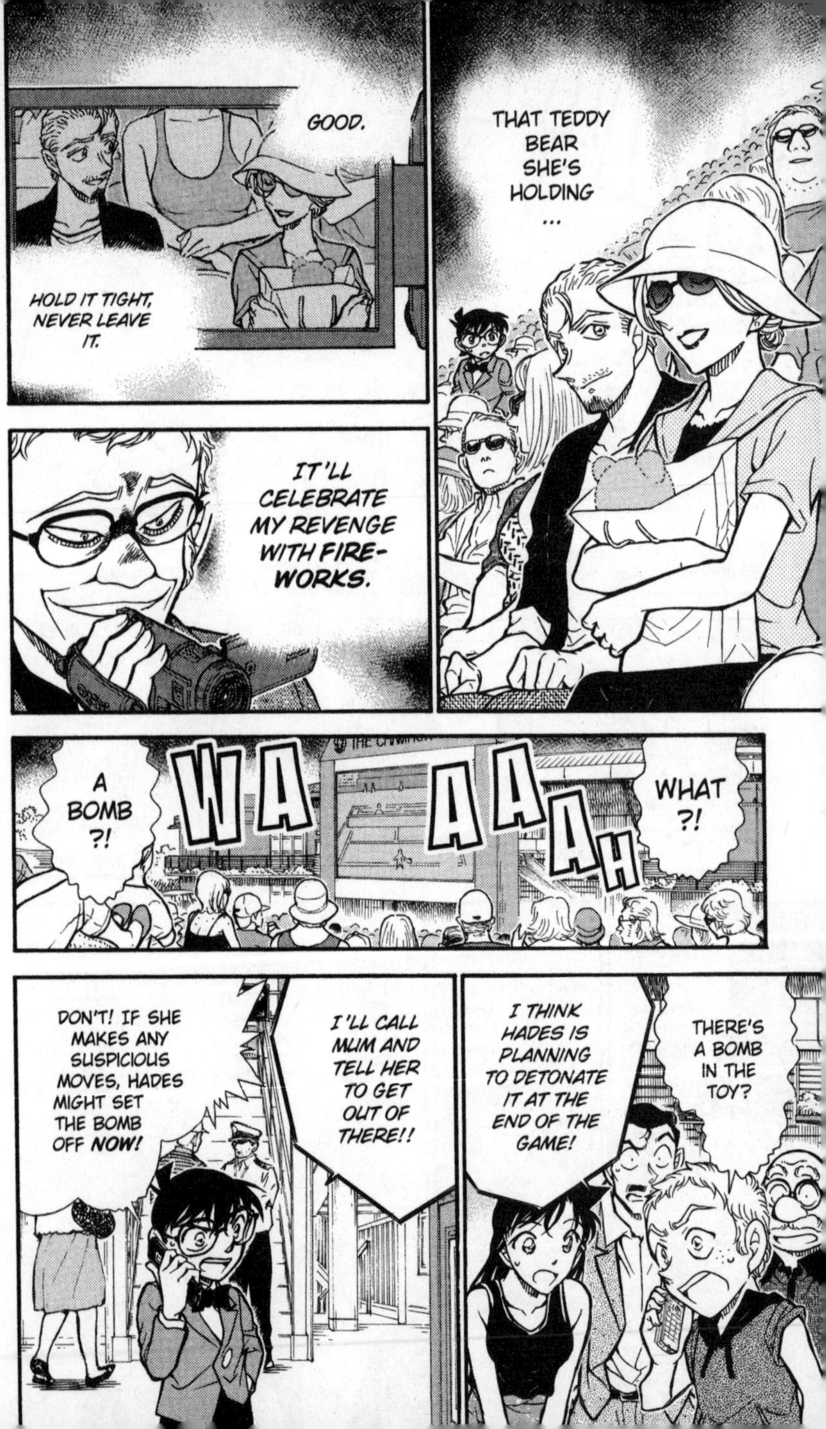

THAT TEDDY BEAR SHE'S HOLDING ...
GOOD.
HOLD IT TIGHT, NEVER LEAVE IT.
IT'LL CELEBRATE MY REVENGE WITH FIRE-WORKS.
WHAT ?!
WAAAAH
A BOMB ?!
THERE'S A BOMB IN THE TOY?
I THINK HADES IS PLANNING TO DETONATE IT AT THE END OF THE GAME!
I'LL CALL MUM AND TELL HER TO GET OUT OF THERE!!
DON'T! IF SHE MAKES ANY SUSPICIOUS MOVES, HADES MIGHT SET THE BOMB OFF NOW!

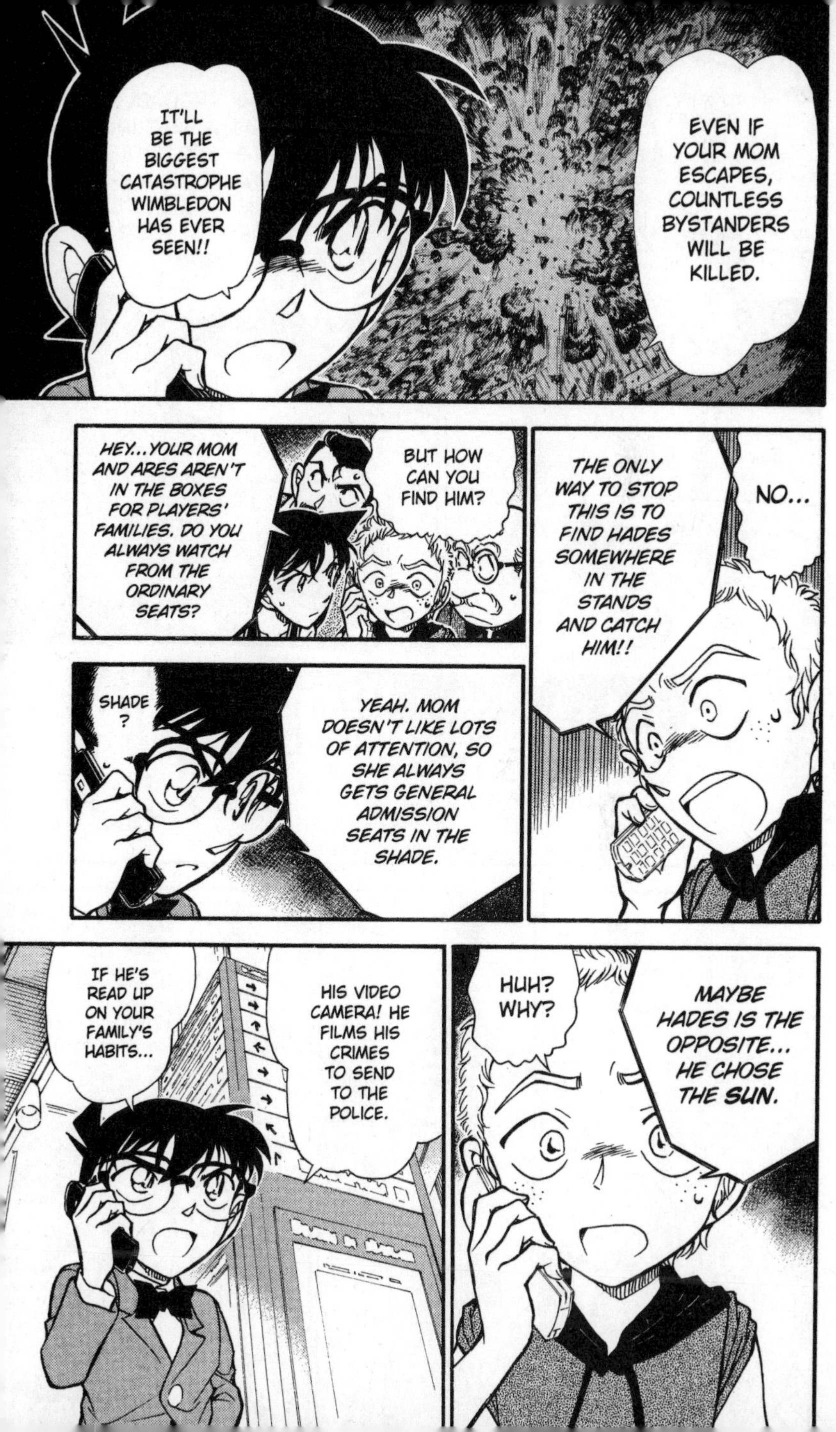
EVEN IF YOUR MOM ESCAPES, COUNTLESS BYSTANDERS WILL BE KILLED.
IT'LL BE THE BIGGEST CATASTROPHE WIMBLEDON HAS EVER SEEN!!
NO...
THE ONLY WAY TO STOP THIS IS TO FIND HADES SOMEWHERE IN THE STANDS AND CATCH HIM!!
BUT HOW CAN YOU FIND HIM?
HEY...YOUR MOM AND ARES AREN'T IN THE BOXES FOR PLAYERS' FAMILIES. DO YOU ALWAYS WATCH FROM THE ORDINARY SEATS?
YEAH. MOM DOESN'T LIKE LOTS OF ATTENTION, SO SHE ALWAYS GETS GENERAL ADMISSION SEATS IN THE SHADE.
SHADE?
MAYBE HADES IS THE OPPOSITE... HE CHOSE THE SUN.
HUH? WHY?
HIS VIDEO CAMERA! HE FILMS HIS CRIMES TO SEND TO THE POLICE.
IF HE'S READ UP ON YOUR FAMILY'S HABITS...

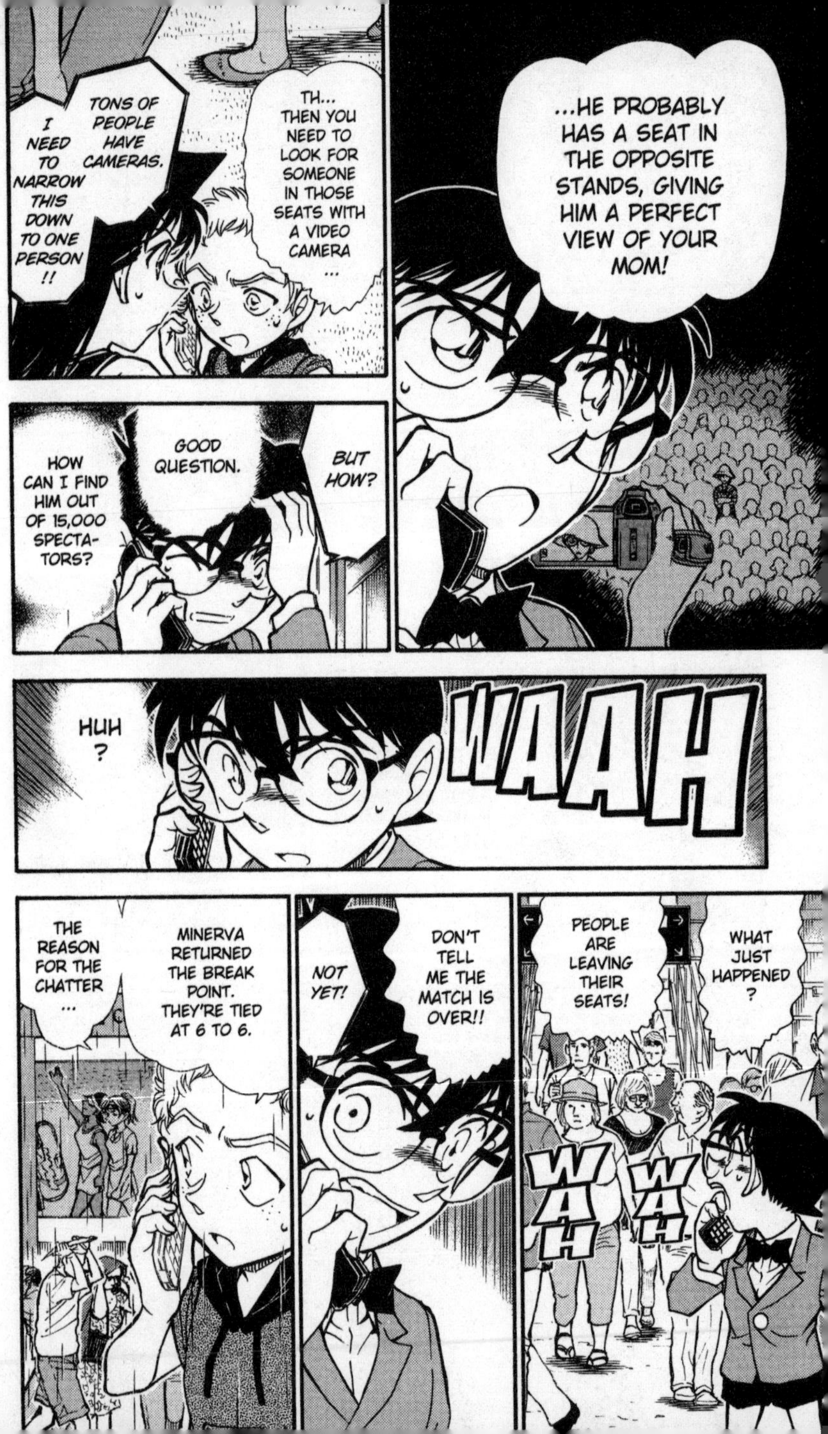
...HE PROBABLY HAS A SEAT IN THE OPPOSITE STANDS, GIVING HIM A PERFECT VIEW OF YOUR MOM!
TH... THEN YOU NEED TO LOOK FOR SOMEONE IN THOSE SEATS WITH A VIDEO CAMERA ...
TONS OF PEOPLE HAVE CAMERAS.
I NEED TO NARROW THIS DOWN TO ONE PERSON !!
BUT HOW?
GOOD QUESTION.
HOW CAN I FIND HIM OUT OF 15,000 SPECTATORS?
WAAH
HUH ?
WHAT JUST HAPPENED ?
PEOPLE ARE LEAVING THEIR SEATS!
WAH
WAH
DON'T TELL ME THE MATCH IS OVER!!
NOT YET!
MINERVA RETURNED THE BREAK POINT. THEY'RE TIED AT 6 TO 6.
THE REASON FOR THE CHATTER ...

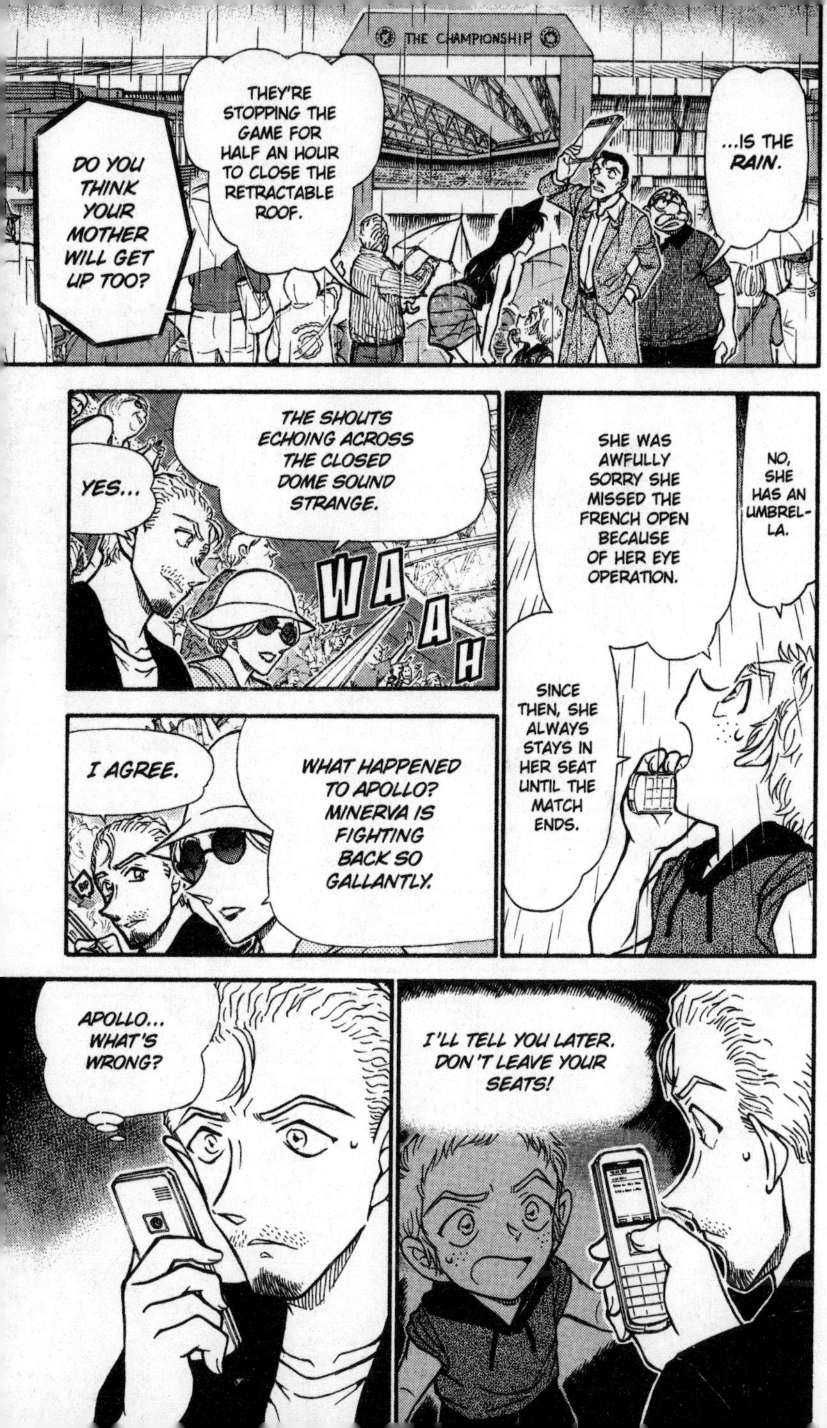
THE CHAMPIONSHIP
...IS THE RAIN.
THEY'RE STOPPING THE GAME FOR HALF AN HOUR TO CLOSE THE RETRACTABLE ROOF.
DO YOU THINK YOUR MOTHER WILL GET UP TOO?
NO, SHE HAS AN UMBREL-LA.
SHE WAS AWFULLY SORRY SHE MISSED THE FRENCH OPEN BECAUSE OF HER EYE OPERATION.
SINCE THEN, SHE ALWAYS STAYS IN HER SEAT UNTIL THE MATCH ENDS.
THE SHOUTS ECHOING ACROSS THE CLOSED DOME SOUND STRANGE.
YES...
WAAAH
WHAT HAPPENED TO APOLLO? MINERVA IS FIGHTING BACK SO GALLANTLY.
I AGREE.
I'LL TELL YOU LATER. DON'T LEAVE YOUR SEATS!
APOLLO... WHAT'S WRONG?

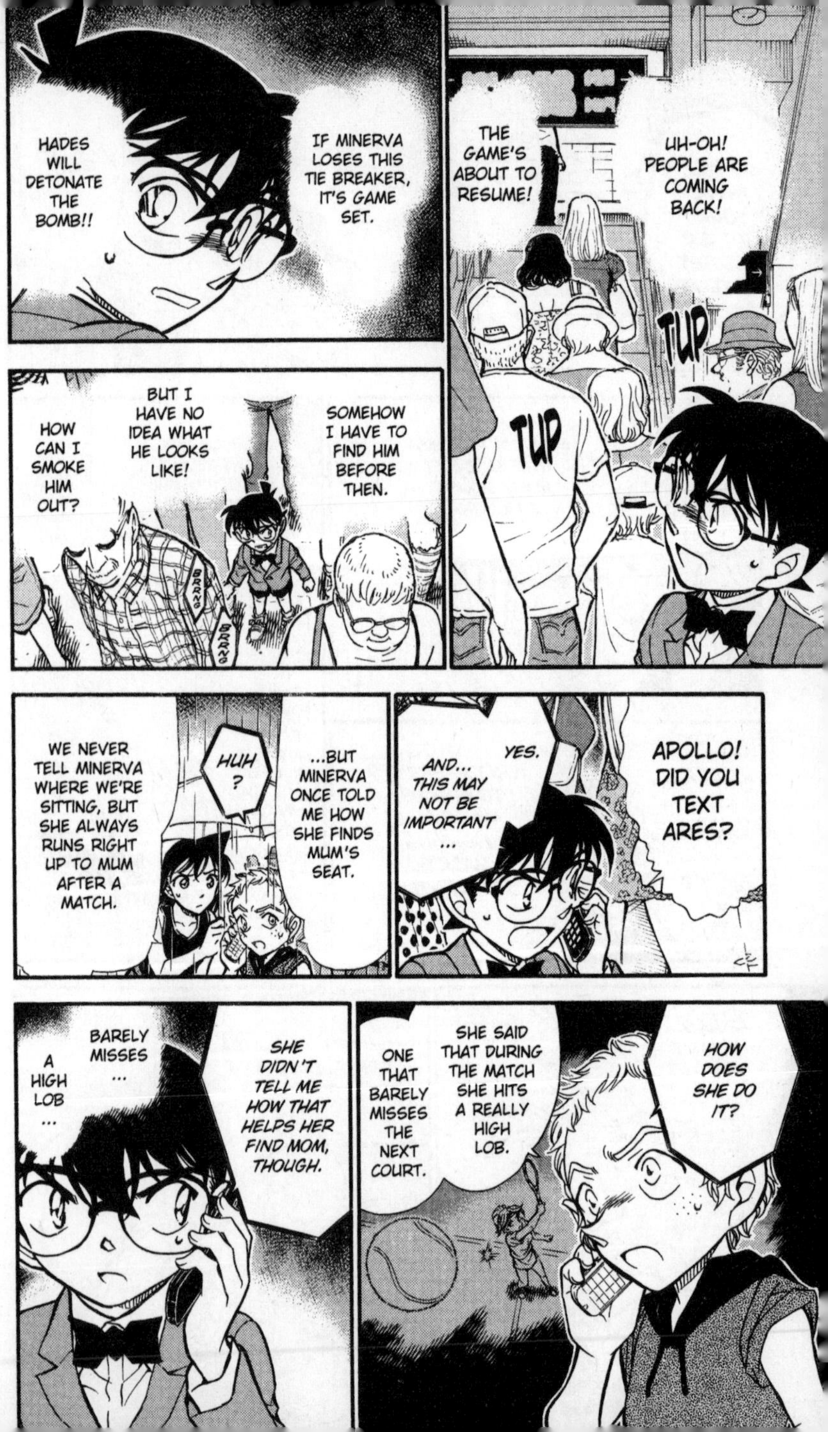
UH-OH! PEOPLE ARE COMING BACK!
THE GAME'S ABOUT TO RESUME!
TUP
TUP
IF MINERVA LOSES THIS TIE BREAKER, IT'S GAME SET.
HADES WILL DETONATE THE BOMB!!
SOMEHOW I HAVE TO FIND HIM BEFORE THEN.
BUT I HAVE NO IDEA WHAT HE LOOKS LIKE!
HOW CAN I SMOKE HIM OUT?
BRRNG
BRRNG
APOLLO! DID YOU TEXT ARES?
YES.
AND... THIS MAY NOT BE IMPORTANT...
...BUT MINERVA ONCE TOLD ME HOW SHE FINDS MUM'S SEAT.
HUH?
WE NEVER TELL MINERVA WHERE WE'RE SITTING, BUT SHE ALWAYS RUNS RIGHT UP TO MUM AFTER A MATCH.
HOW DOES SHE DO IT?
SHE SAID THAT DURING THE MATCH SHE HITS A REALLY HIGH LOB.
ONE THAT BARELY MISSES THE NEXT COURT.
SHE DIDN'T TELL ME HOW THAT HELPS HER FIND MOM, THOUGH.
BARELY MISSES...
A HIGH LOB...

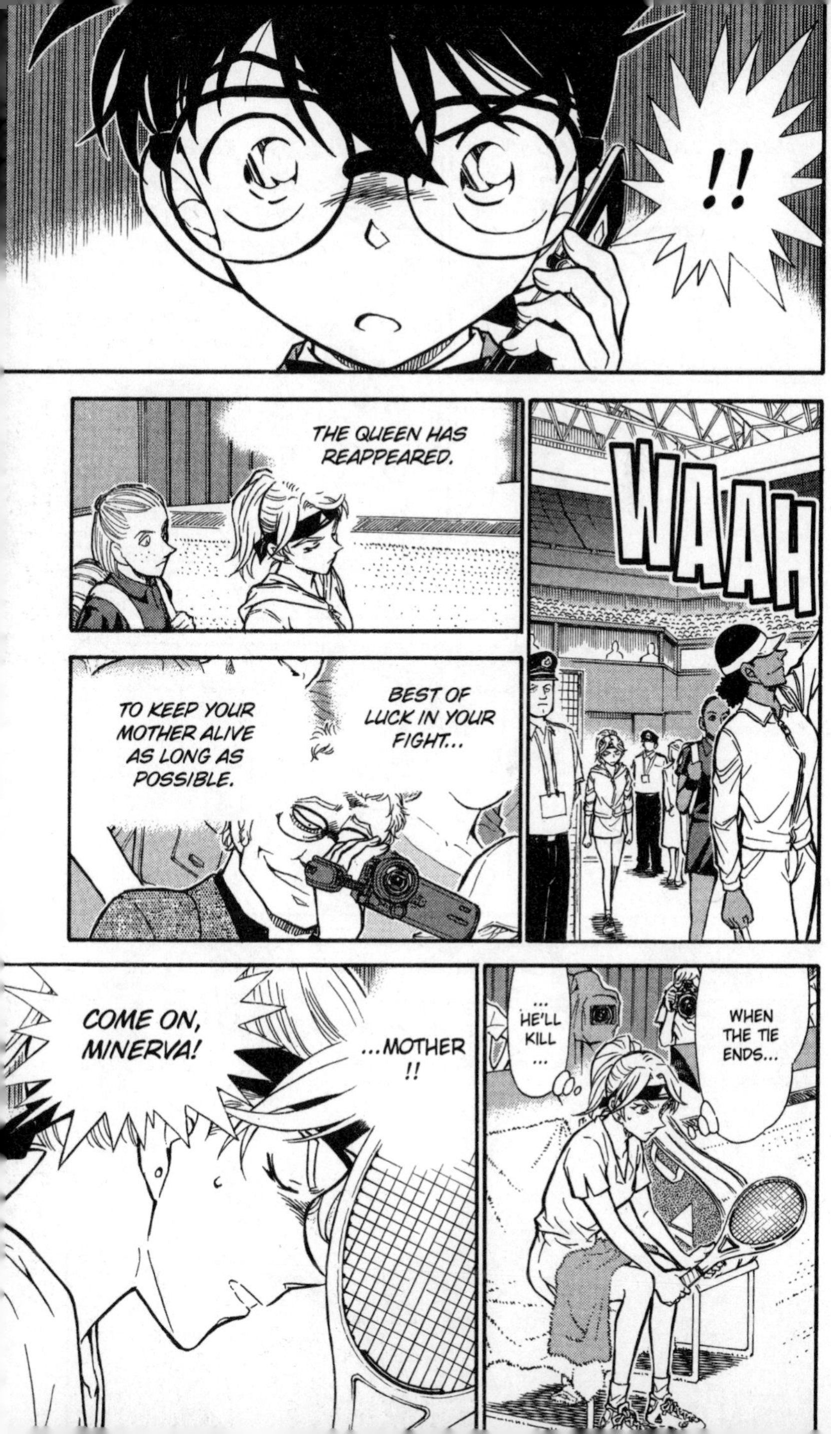
!!
WAAH
THE QUEEN HAS REAPPEARED.
BEST OF LUCK IN YOUR FIGHT...
TO KEEP YOUR MOTHER ALIVE AS LONG AS POSSIBLE.
WHEN THE TIE ENDS...
...HE'LL KILL...
...MOTHER !!
COME ON, MINERVA!

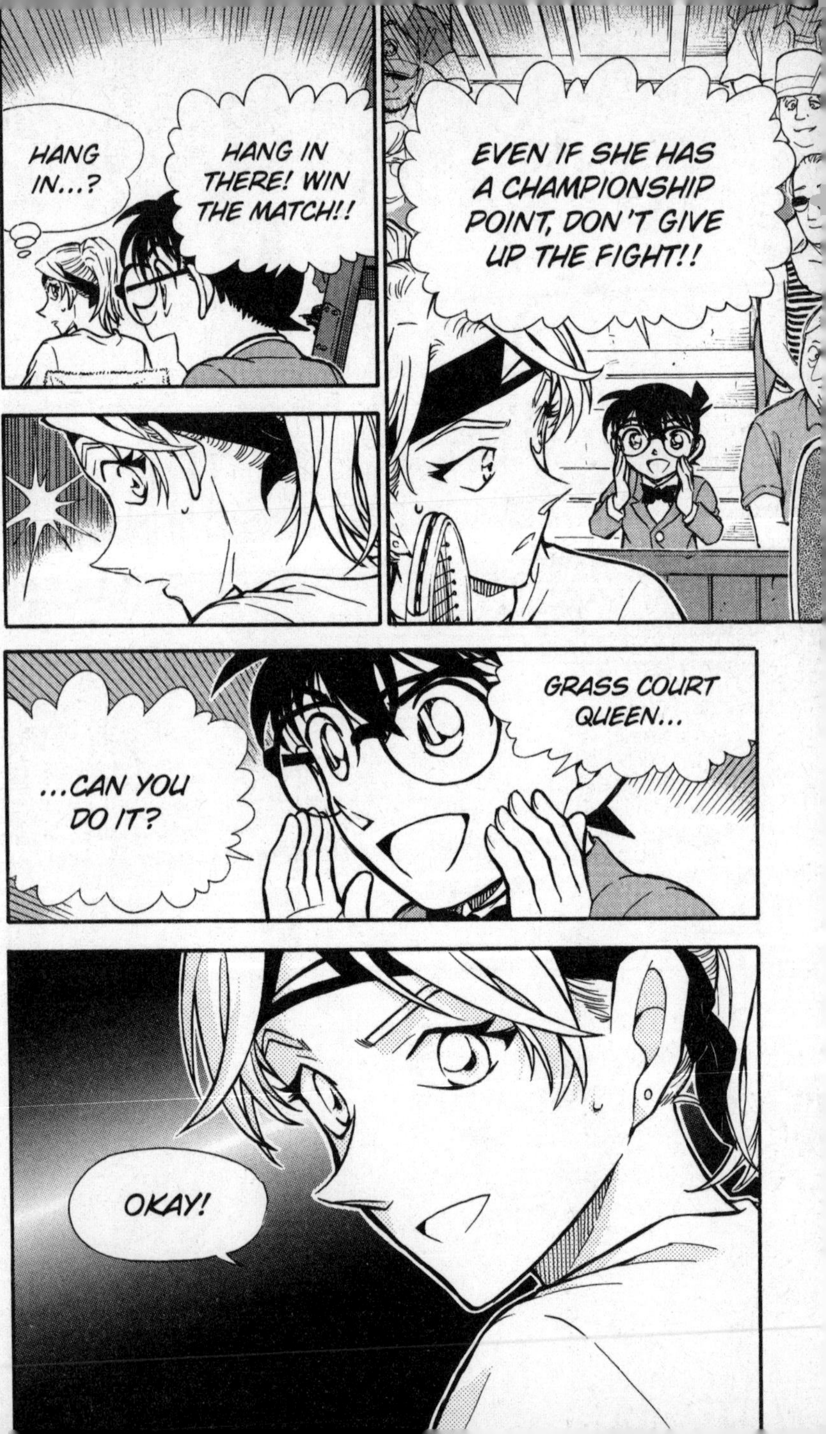
EVEN IF SHE HAS A CHAMPIONSHIP POINT, DON'T GIVE UP THE FIGHT!!
HANG IN THERE! WIN THE MATCH!!
HANG IN...?
GRASS COURT QUEEN...
...CAN YOU DO IT?
OKAY!

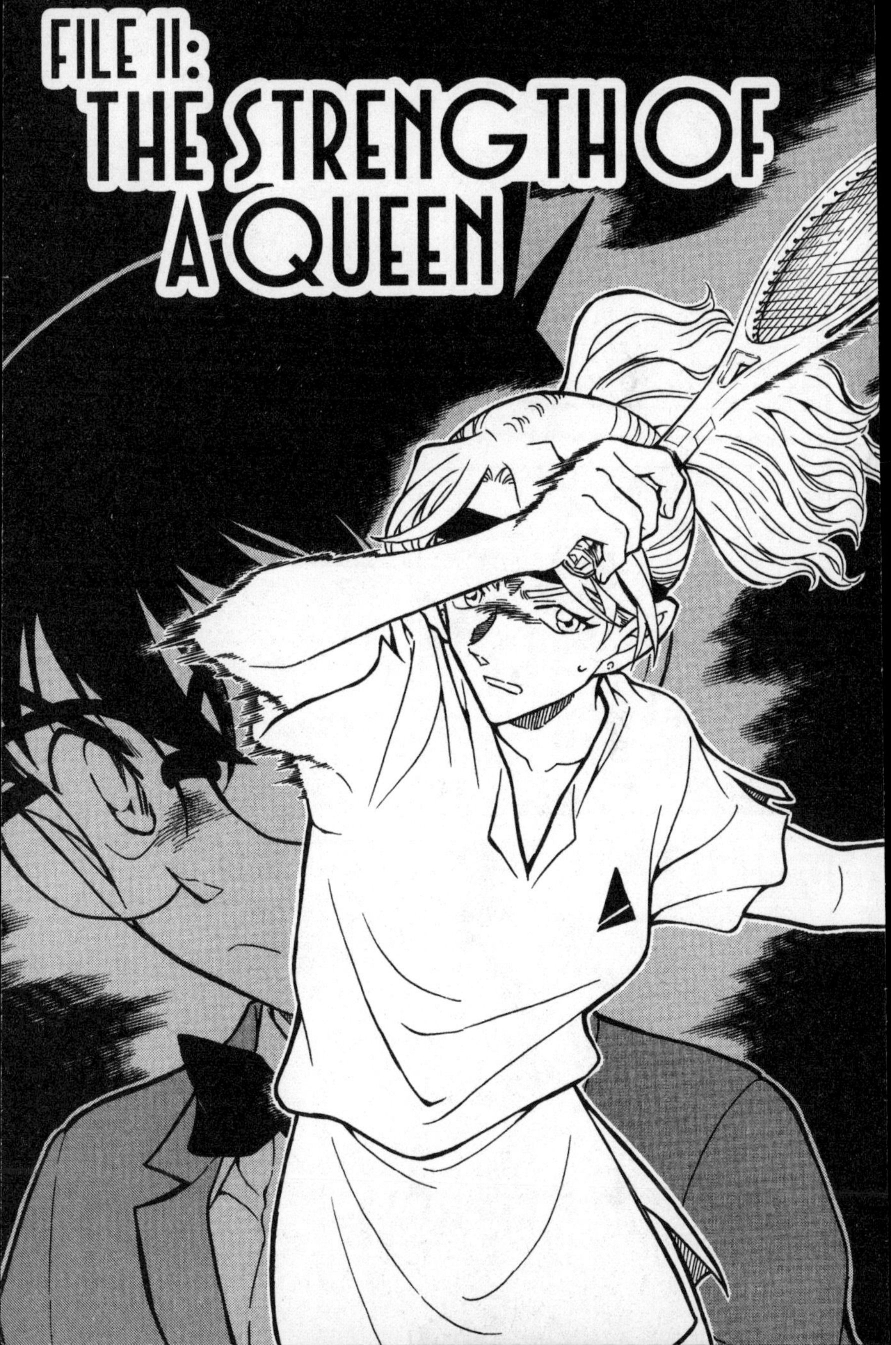
FILE 11:
THE STRENGTH OF A QUEEN

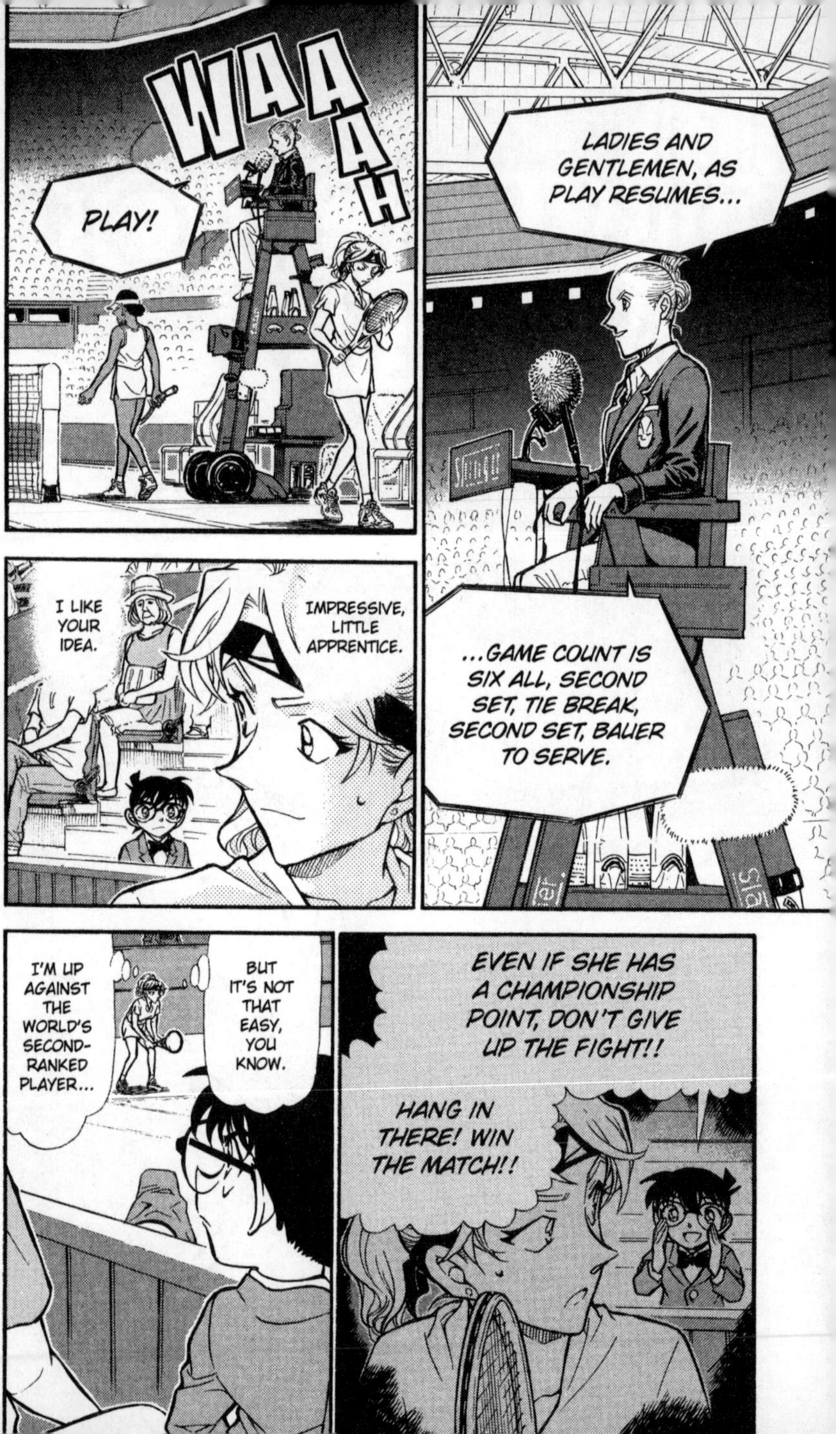

LADIES AND GENTLEMEN, AS PLAY RESUMES...
...GAME COUNT IS SIX ALL, SECOND SET, TIE BREAK, SECOND SET, BAUER TO SERVE.
WAAAAH
PLAY!
IMPRESSIVE, LITTLE APPRENTICE.
I LIKE YOUR IDEA.
EVEN IF SHE HAS A CHAMPIONSHIP POINT, DON'T GIVE UP THE FIGHT!!
HANG IN THERE! WIN THE MATCH!!
BUT IT'S NOT THAT EASY, YOU KNOW.
I'M UP AGAINST THE WORLD'S SECOND-RANKED PLAYER...

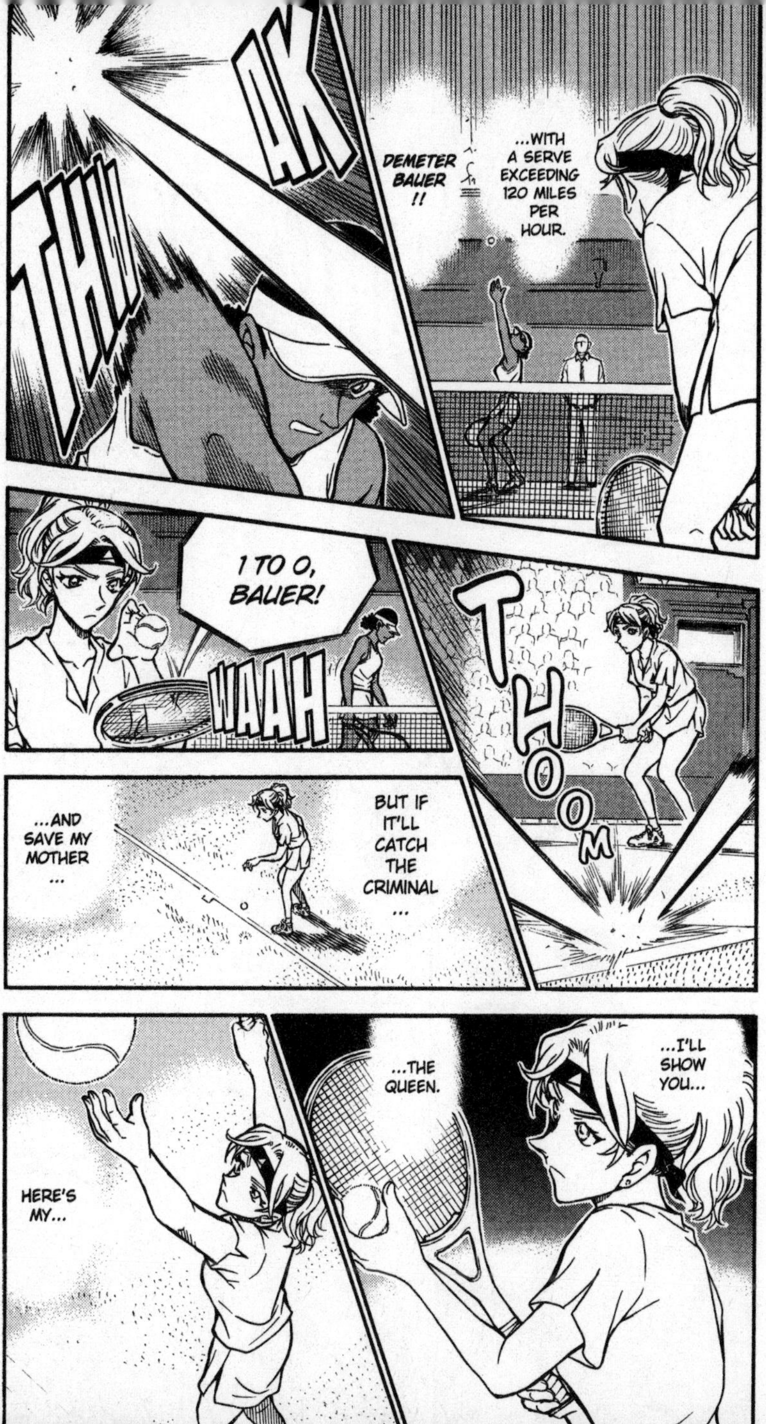
...WITH A SERVE EXCEEDING 120 MILES PER HOUR.
DEMETER BAUER !!
THWAK
THOOM
1 TO 0, BAUER!
WAAH
BUT IF IT'LL CATCH THE CRIMINAL ...
...AND SAVE MY MOTHER ...
...I'LL SHOW YOU...
...THE QUEEN.
HERE'S MY...

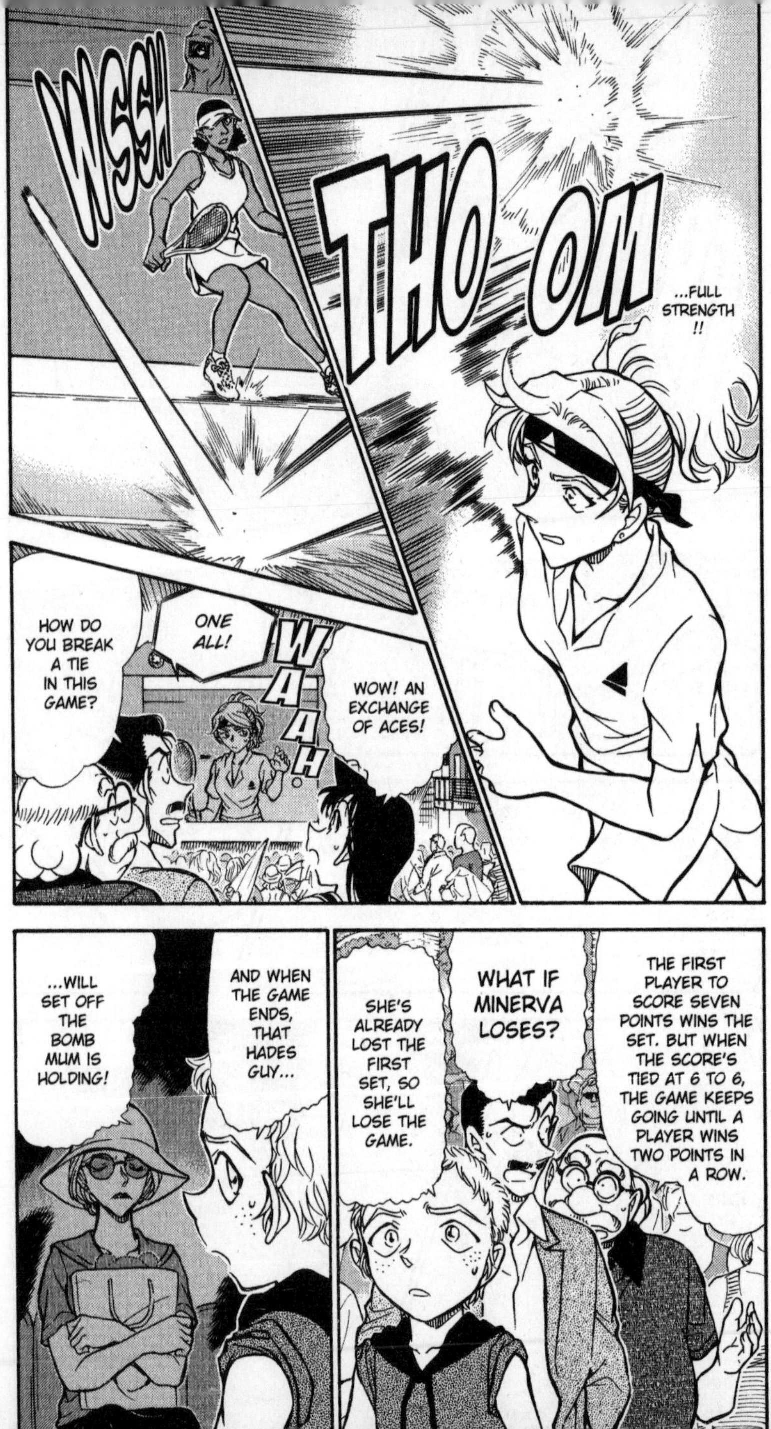
THO-OM
...FULL STRENGTH!!
WSSH
ONE ALL!
WAAH
WOW! AN EXCHANGE OF ACES!
HOW DO YOU BREAK A TIE IN THIS GAME?
THE FIRST PLAYER TO SCORE SEVEN POINTS WINS THE SET. BUT WHEN THE SCORE'S TIED AT 6 TO 6, THE GAME KEEPS GOING UNTIL A PLAYER WINS TWO POINTS IN A ROW.
WHAT IF MINERVA LOSES?
SHE'S ALREADY LOST THE FIRST SET, SO SHE'LL LOSE THE GAME.
AND WHEN THE GAME ENDS, THAT HADES GUY...
...WILL SET OFF THE BOMB MUM IS HOLDING!

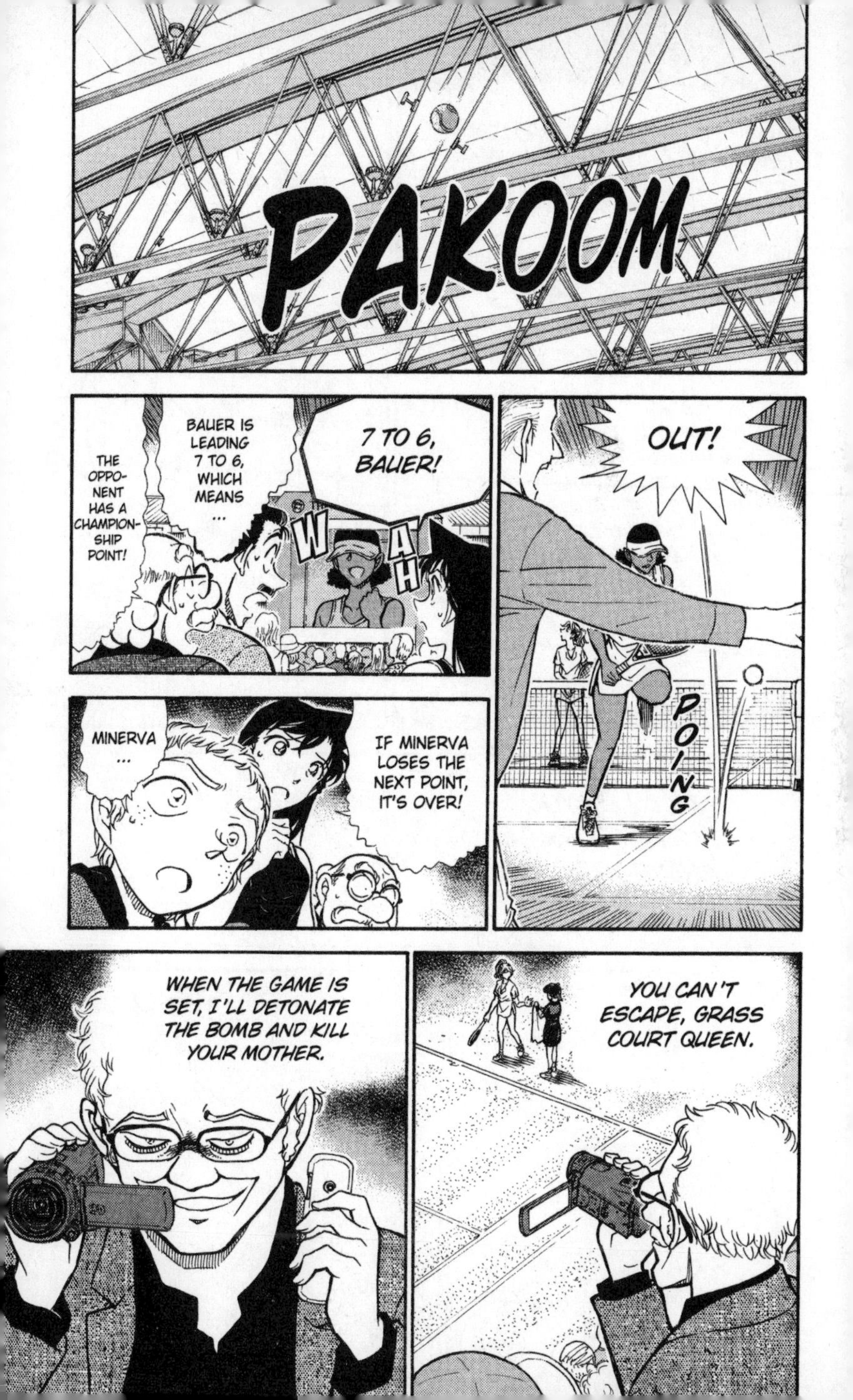
PAKOOM
OUT!
POING
7 TO 6, BAUER!
WAH
BAUER IS LEADING 7 TO 6, WHICH MEANS ...
THE OPPONENT HAS A CHAMPIONSHIP POINT!
IF MINERVA LOSES THE NEXT POINT, IT'S OVER!
MINERVA ...
YOU CAN'T ESCAPE, GRASS COURT QUEEN.
WHEN THE GAME IS SET, I'LL DETONATE THE BOMB AND KILL YOUR MOTHER.

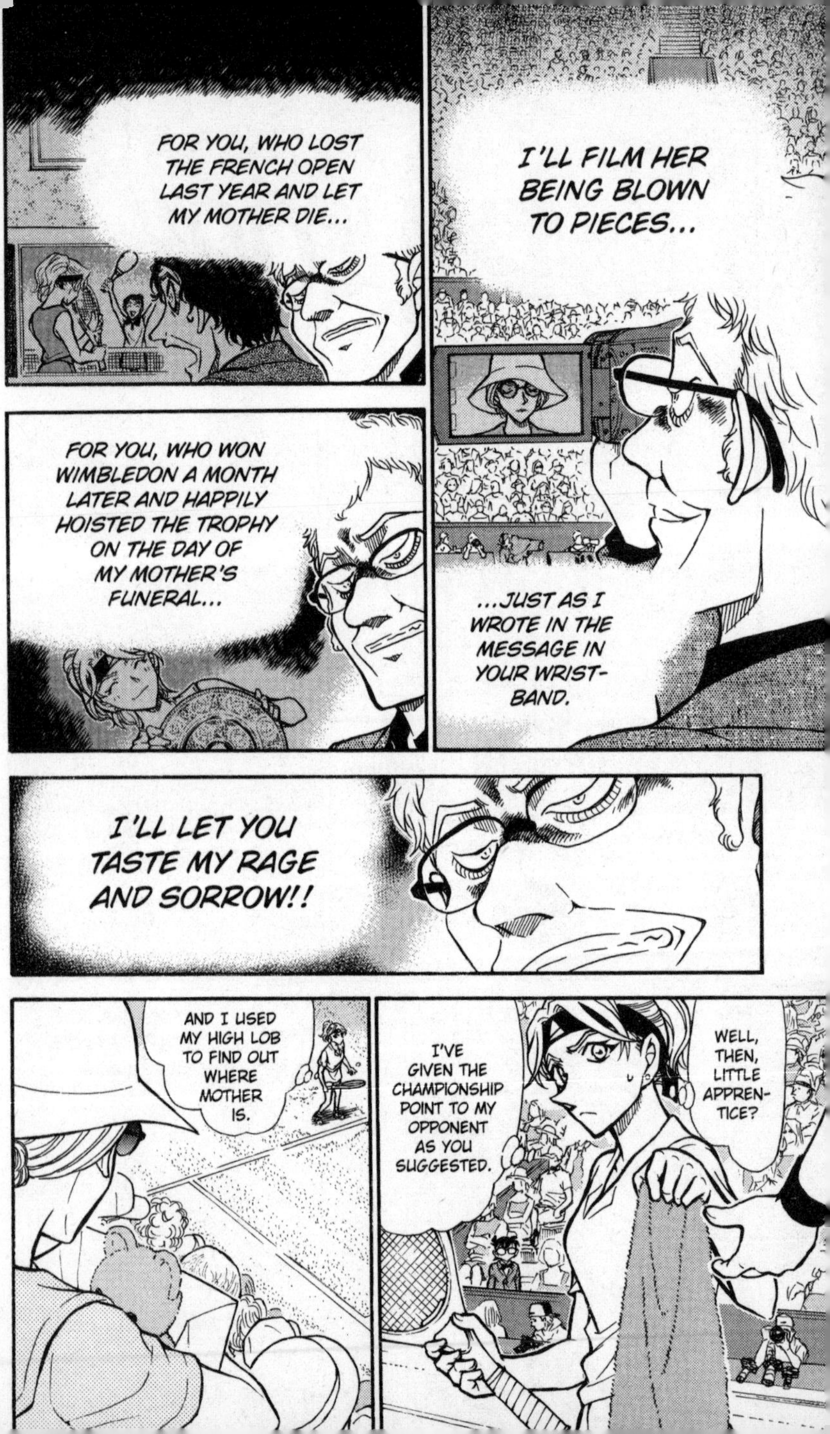
I'LL FILM HER BEING BLOWN TO PIECES...
...JUST AS I WROTE IN THE MESSAGE IN YOUR WRIST-BAND.
FOR YOU, WHO LOST THE FRENCH OPEN LAST YEAR AND LET MY MOTHER DIE...
FOR YOU, WHO WON WIMBLEDON A MONTH LATER AND HAPPILY HOISTED THE TROPHY ON THE DAY OF MY MOTHER'S FUNERAL...
I'LL LET YOU TASTE MY RAGE AND SORROW!!
WELL, THEN, LITTLE APPREN-TICE?
I'VE GIVEN THE CHAMPIONSHIP POINT TO MY OPPONENT AS YOU SUGGESTED.
AND I USED MY HIGH LOB TO FIND OUT WHERE MOTHER IS.

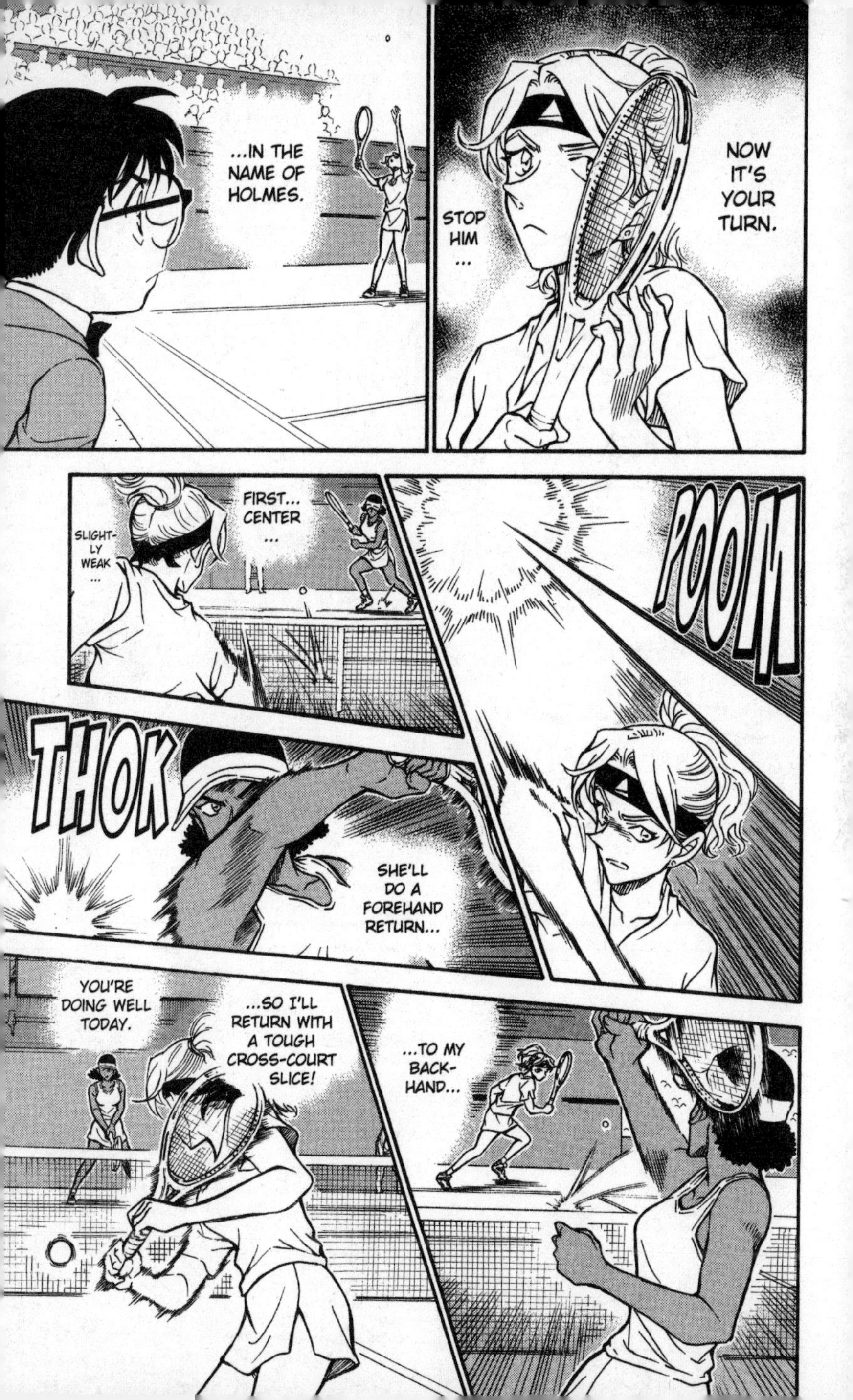
NOW IT'S YOUR TURN.
STOP HIM ...
...IN THE NAME OF HOLMES.
POOM
FIRST... CENTER ...
SLIGHTLY WEAK ...
THOK
SHE'LL DO A FOREHAND RETURN...
...TO MY BACKHAND...
...SO I'LL RETURN WITH A TOUGH CROSS-COURT SLICE!
YOU'RE DOING WELL TODAY.

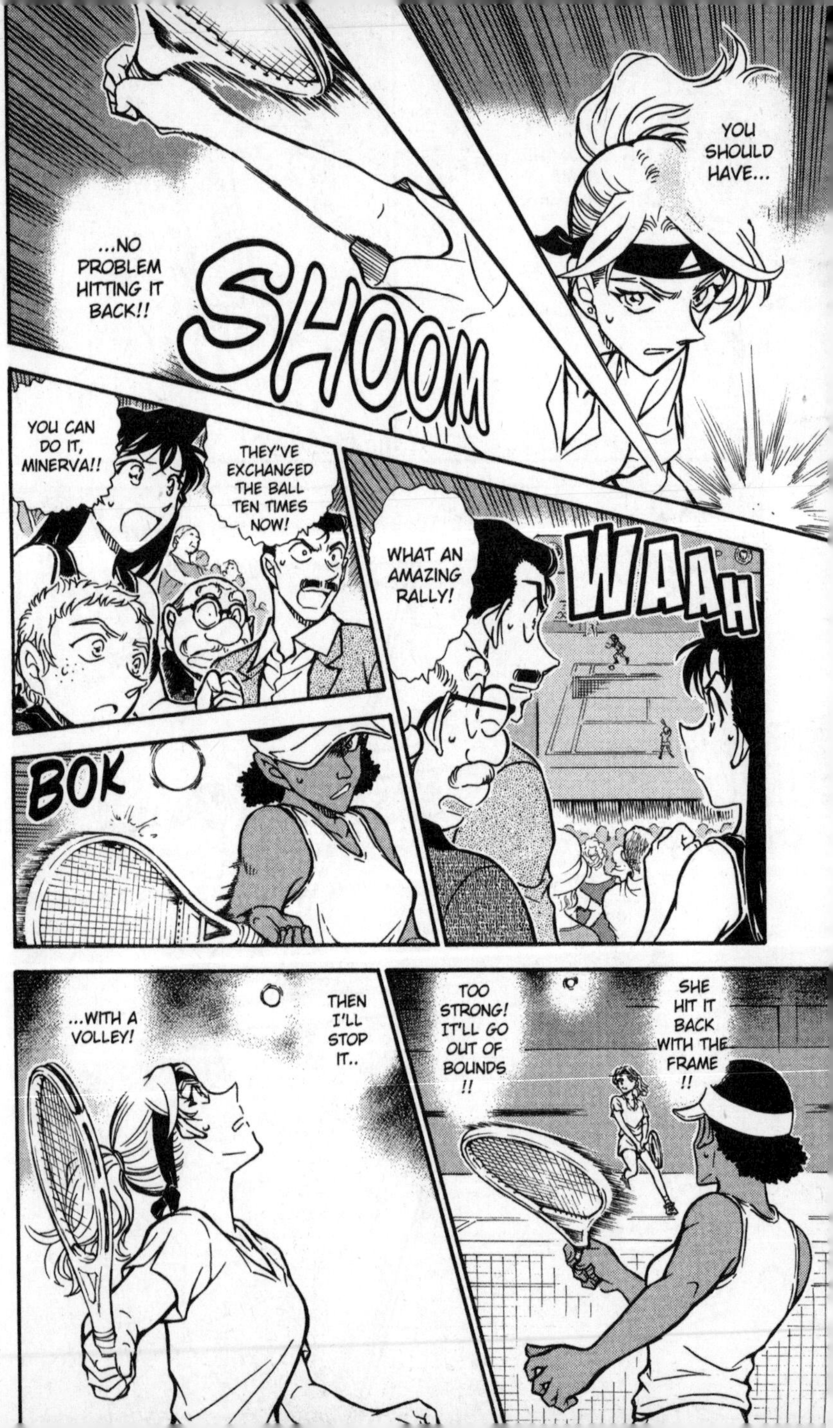
YOU SHOULD HAVE...
...NO PROBLEM HITTING IT BACK!!
SHOOM
WHAT AN AMAZING RALLY!
WAAAH
THEY'VE EXCHANGED THE BALL TEN TIMES NOW!
YOU CAN DO IT, MINERVA!!
BOK
SHE HIT IT BACK WITH THE FRAME!!
TOO STRONG! IT'LL GO OUT OF BOUNDS!!
THEN I'LL STOP IT..
...WITH A VOLLEY!

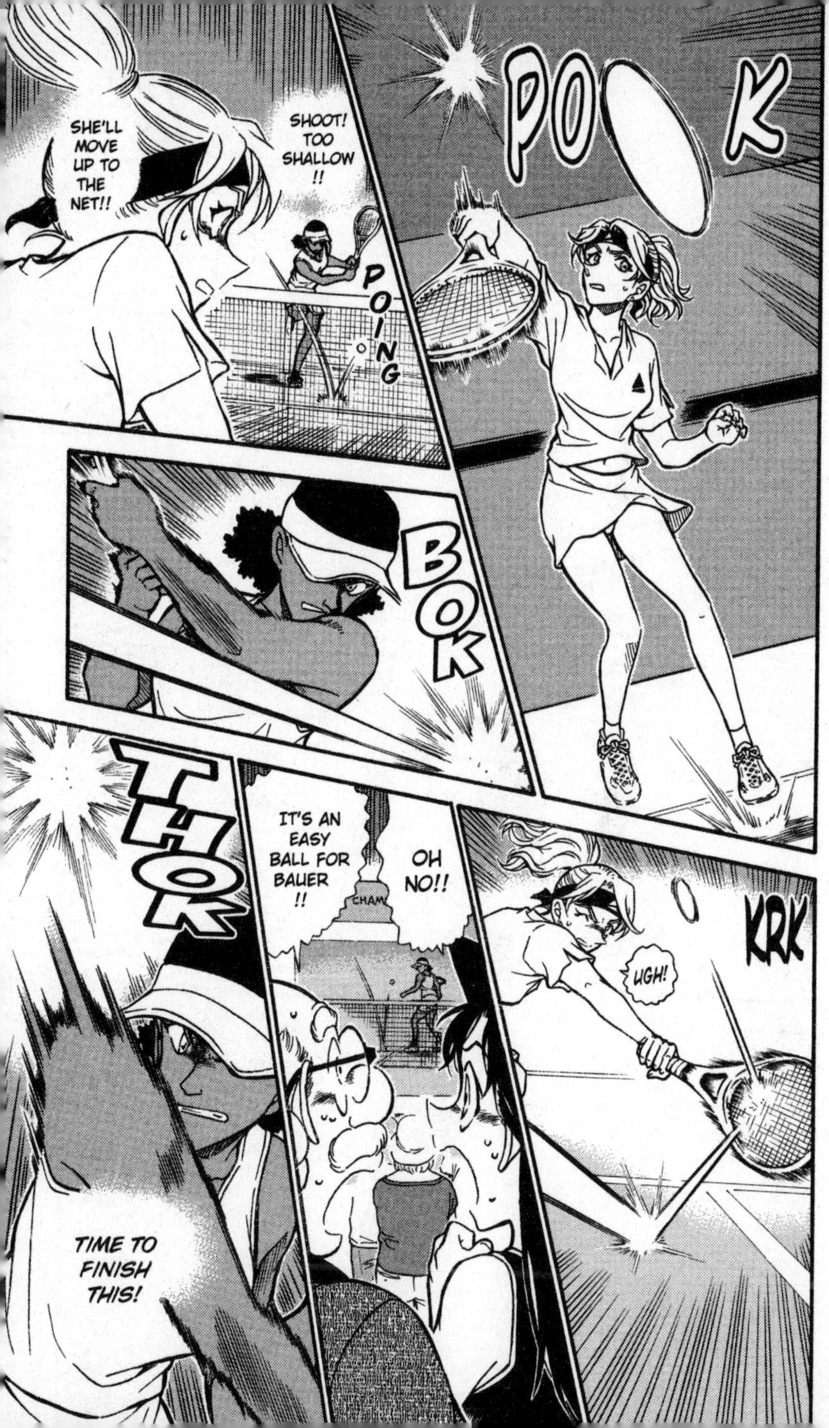
POOK
SHOOT! TOO SHALLOW!!
SHE'LL MOVE UP TO THE NET!!
POING
BOK
KRK
UGH!
OH NO!!
IT'S AN EASY BALL FOR BAUER!!
THOR
TIME TO FINISH THIS!

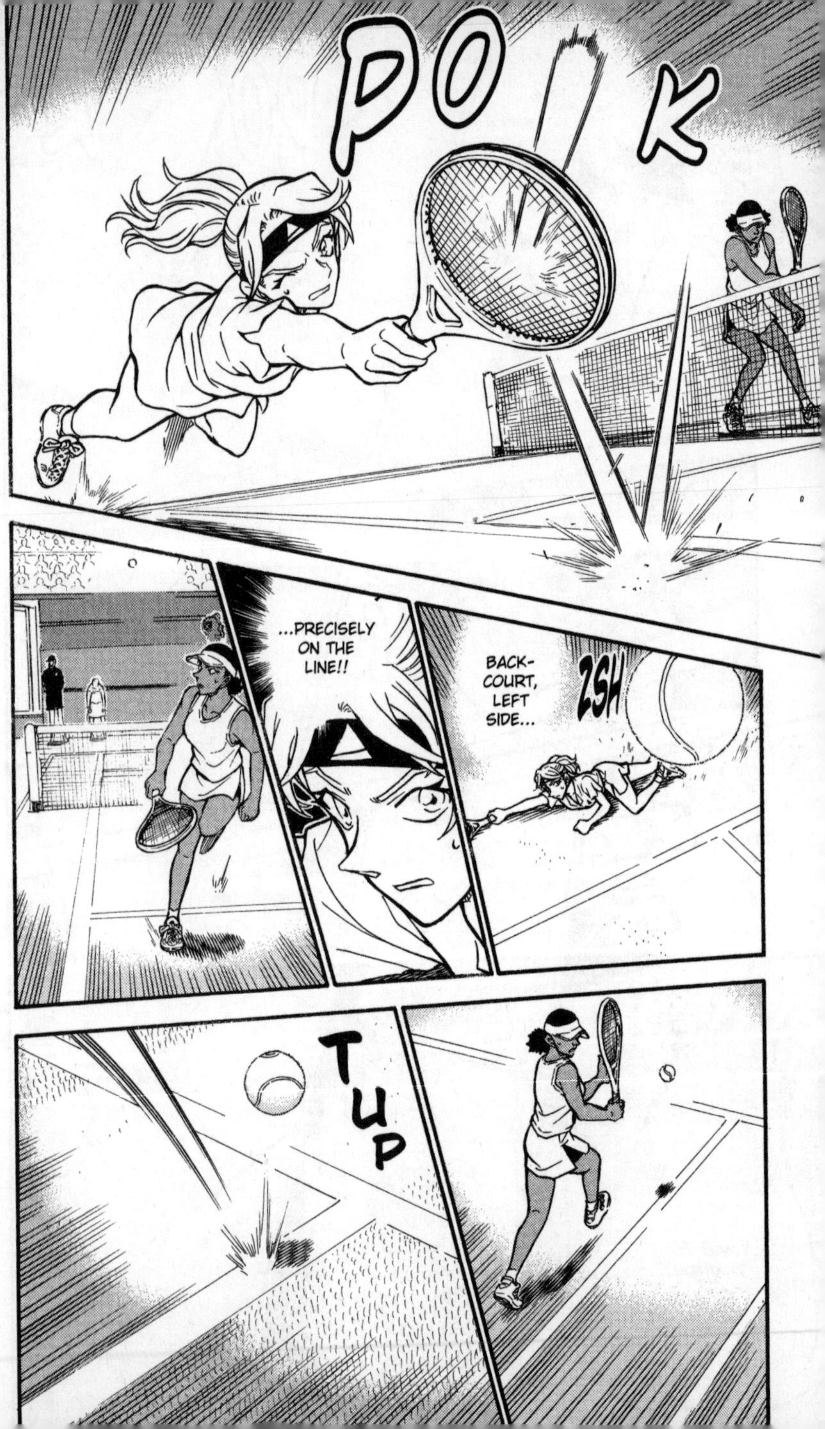
PO K
ZSH
BACK-COURT, LEFT SIDE...
...PRECISELY ON THE LINE!!
TUP

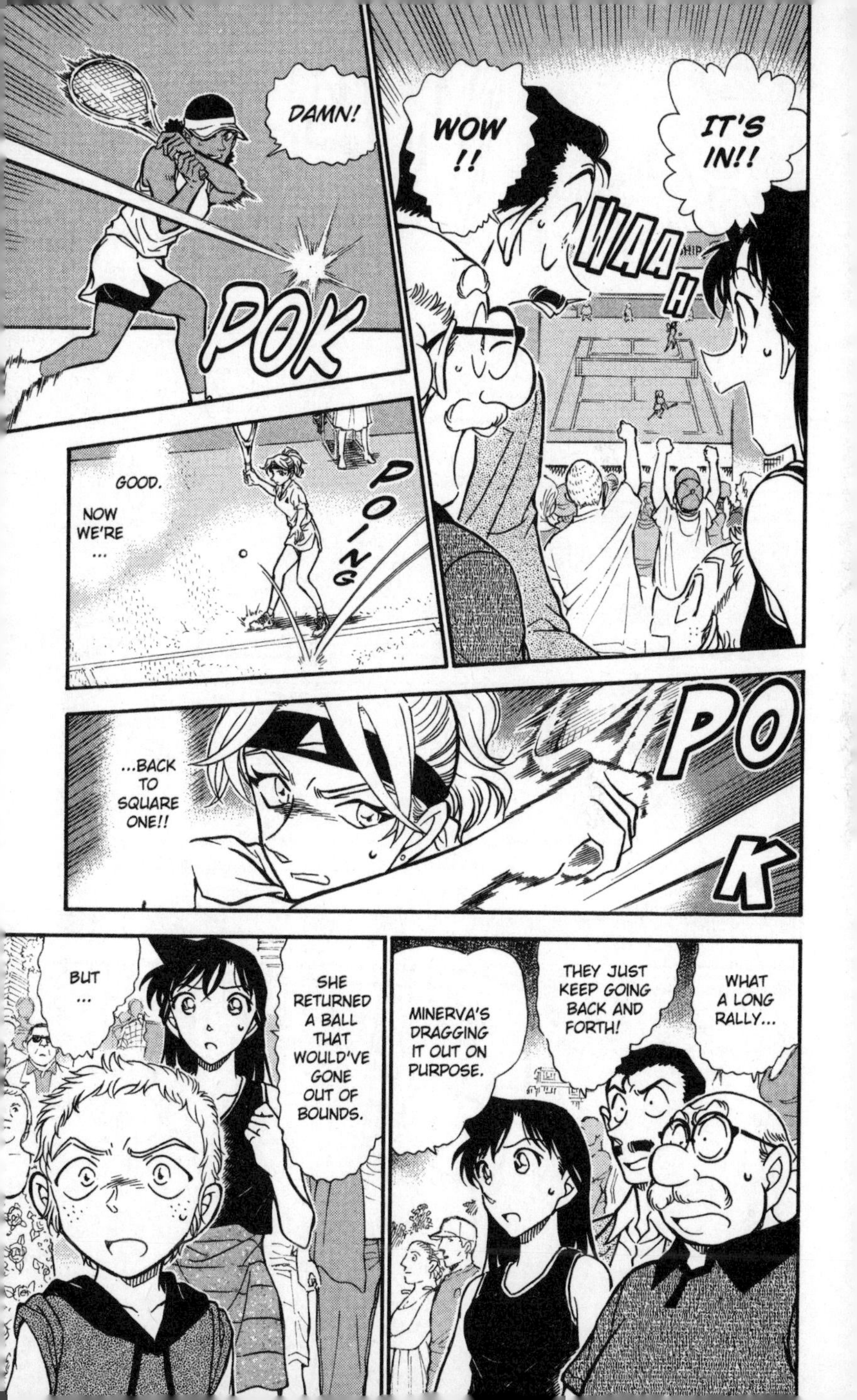
IT'S IN!!
WOW !!
WAAAH
DAMN!
POK
GOOD.
NOW WE'RE ...
POING
...BACK TO SQUARE ONE!!
POK
WHAT A LONG RALLY...
THEY JUST KEEP GOING BACK AND FORTH!
MINERVA'S DRAGGING IT OUT ON PURPOSE.
SHE RETURNED A BALL THAT WOULD'VE GONE OUT OF BOUNDS.
BUT ...

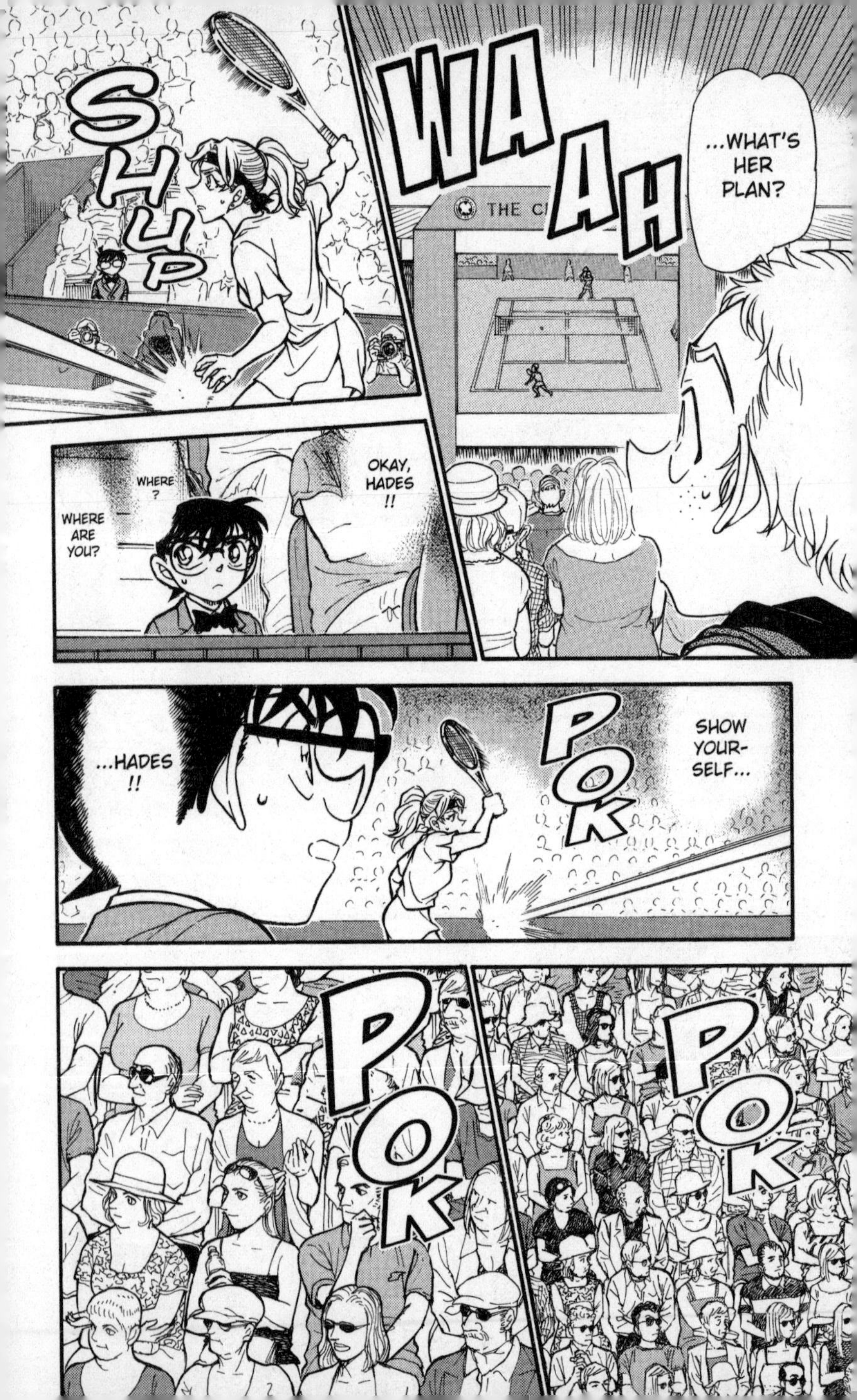
...WHAT'S HER PLAN?
WAAH
THE C
SHUP
OKAY, HADES!!
WHERE?
WHERE ARE YOU?
SHOW YOURSELF...
POK
...HADES!!
POK
POK

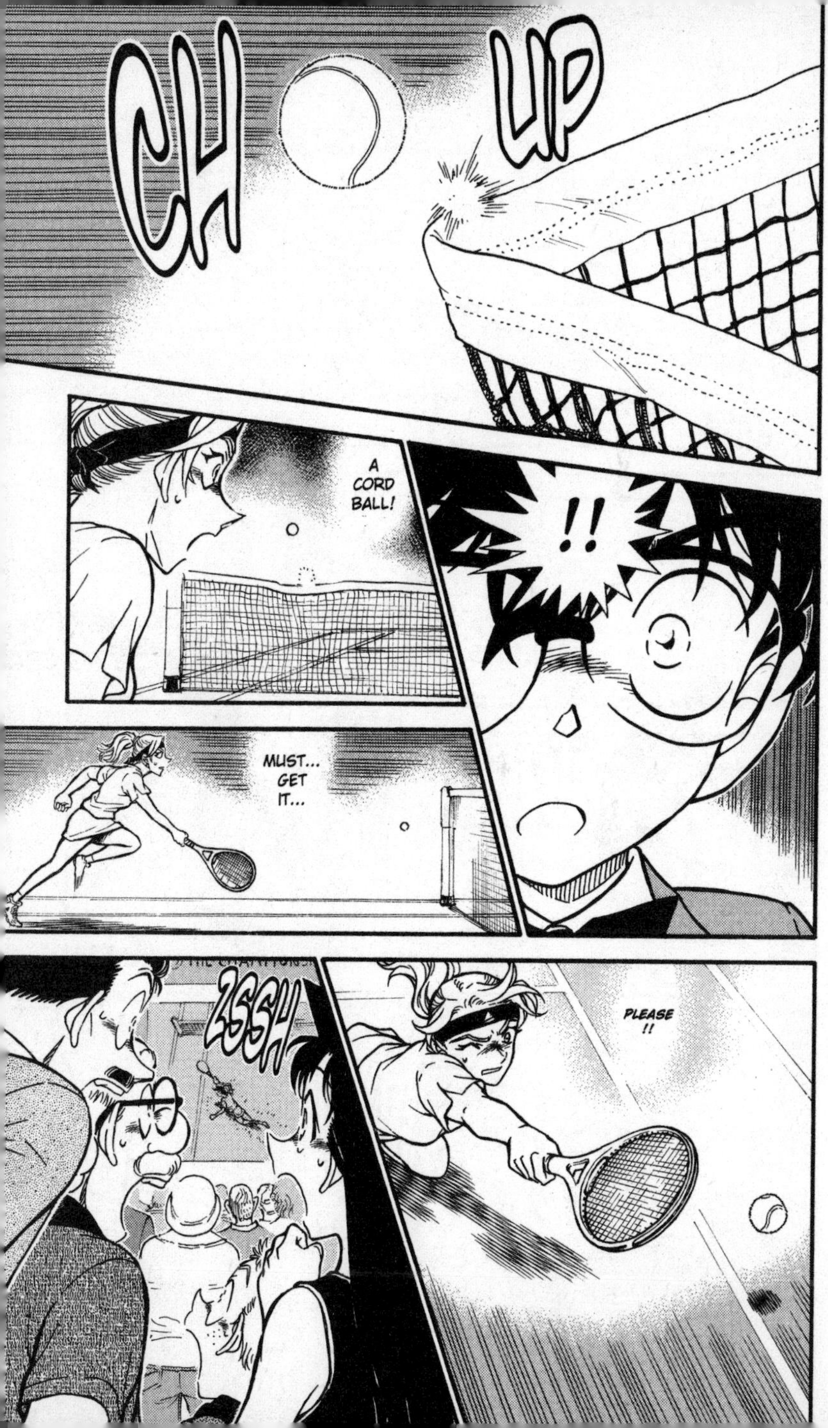
CH
UP
!!
A CORD BALL!
MUST... GET IT...
PLEASE !!
ZSSH

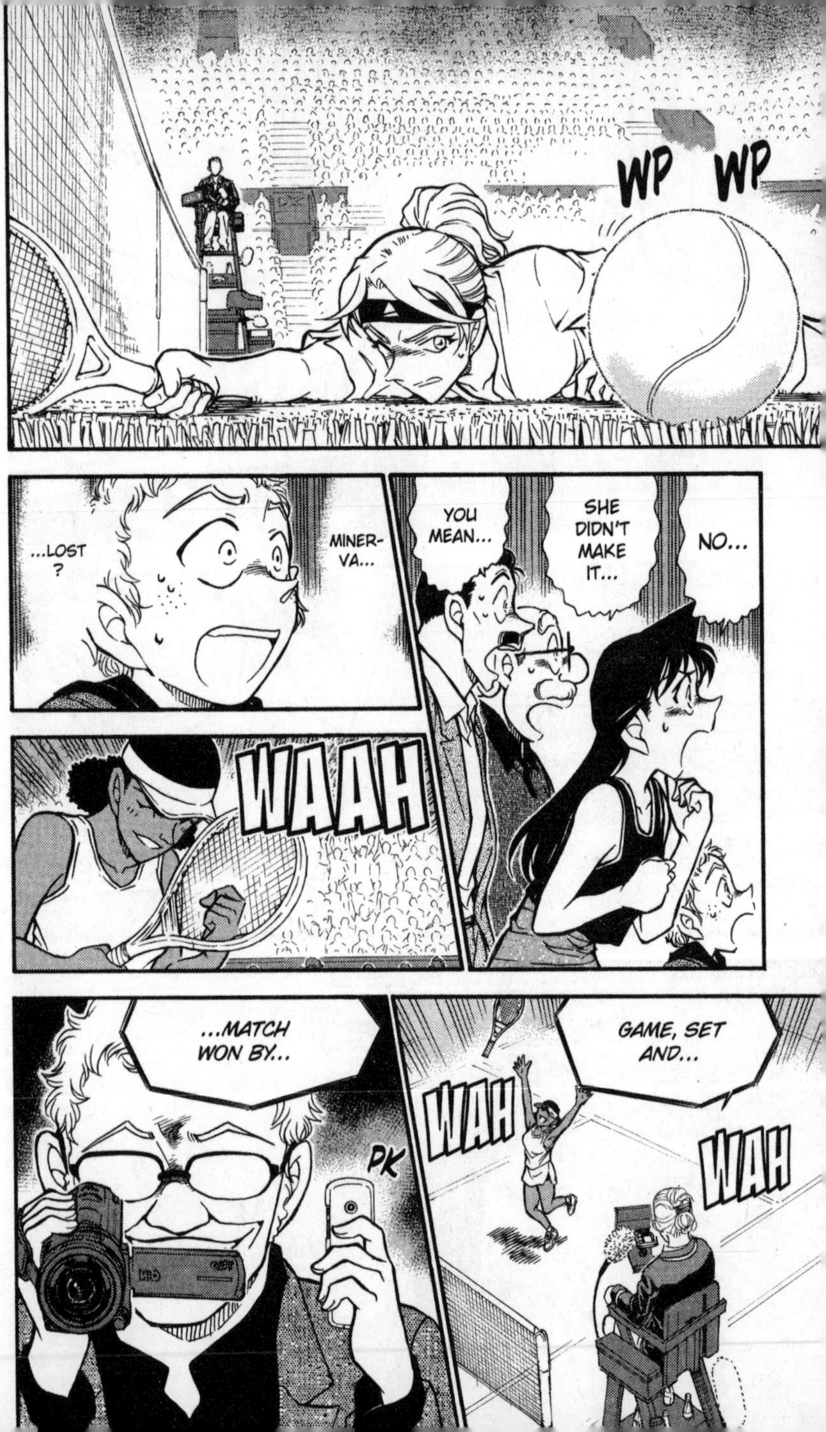
WP WP
NO...
SHE DIDN'T MAKE IT...
YOU MEAN...
MINER-VA...
...LOST ?
WAAH
GAME, SET AND...
WAH
WAH
...MATCH WON BY...
PK

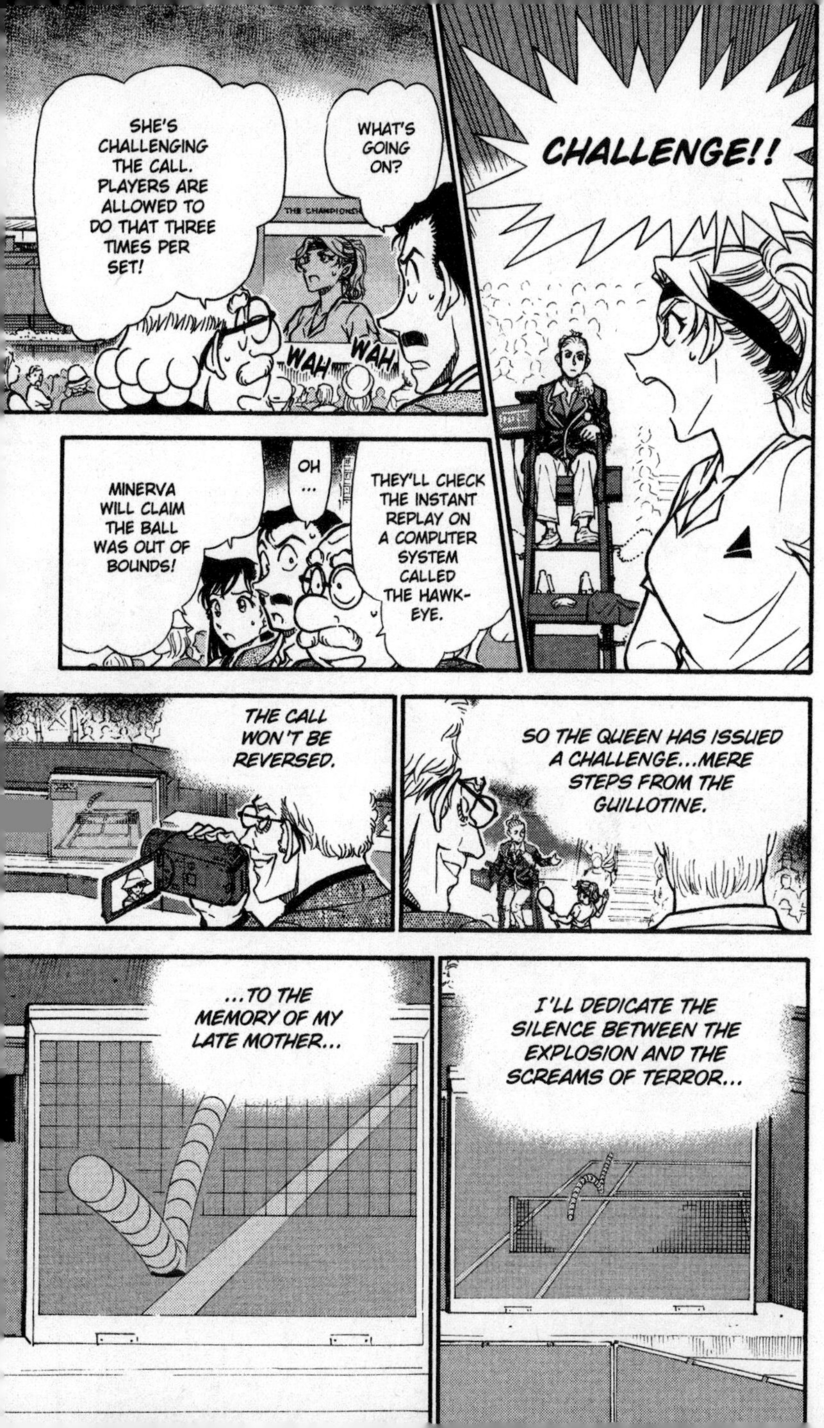
CHALLENGE!!
WHAT'S GOING ON?
SHE'S CHALLENGING THE CALL. PLAYERS ARE ALLOWED TO DO THAT THREE TIMES PER SET!
WAH WAH
THEY'LL CHECK THE INSTANT REPLAY ON A COMPUTER SYSTEM CALLED THE HAWK-EYE.
OH ...
MINERVA WILL CLAIM THE BALL WAS OUT OF BOUNDS!
SO THE QUEEN HAS ISSUED A CHALLENGE...MERE STEPS FROM THE GUILLOTINE.
THE CALL WON'T BE REVERSED.
I'LL DEDICATE THE SILENCE BETWEEN THE EXPLOSION AND THE SCREAMS OF TERROR...
...TO THE MEMORY OF MY LATE MOTHER...

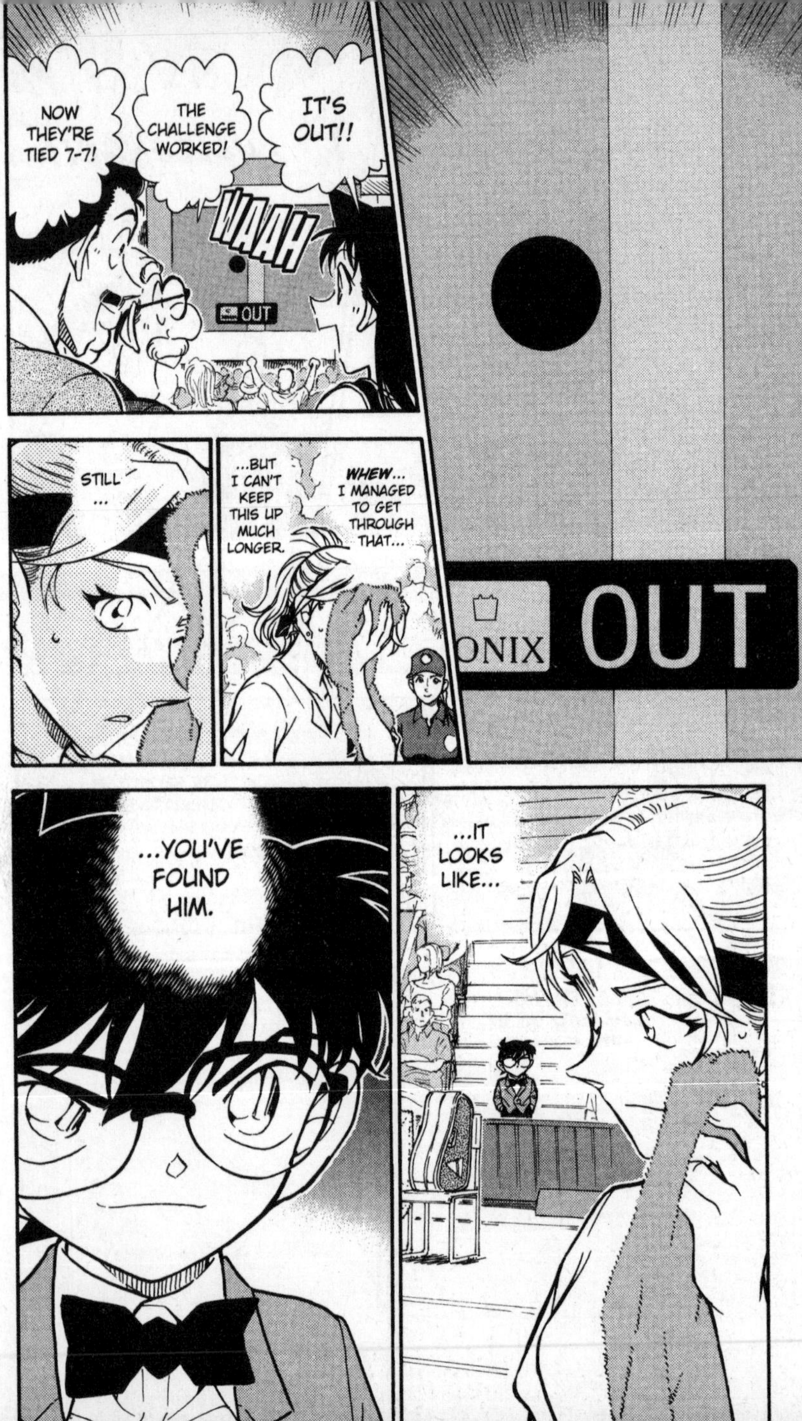
ONIX
OUT
IT'S OUT!!
THE CHALLENGE WORKED!
NOW THEY'RE TIED 7-7!
WAAH
OUT
WHEW... I MANAGED TO GET THROUGH THAT...
...BUT I CAN'T KEEP THIS UP MUCH LONGER.
STILL ...
...IT LOOKS LIKE...
...YOU'VE FOUND HIM.

Hello, Aoyama here!

My office has decided to computerize our manga work, so we visited the office of Kenjiro Hata, creator of *Hayate the Combat Butler*, who already works digitally. I hesitated at the sight of all the high-tech equipment lined up on his desk and thought, "Am I really going to go digital?"*

But then I noticed a hand-drawn cleaning duty chart! An old-fashioned paper chart with portraits of all the staff... Seeing that heartwarming item made me think maybe I could handle the change.

*Comment from original 2011 publication date.

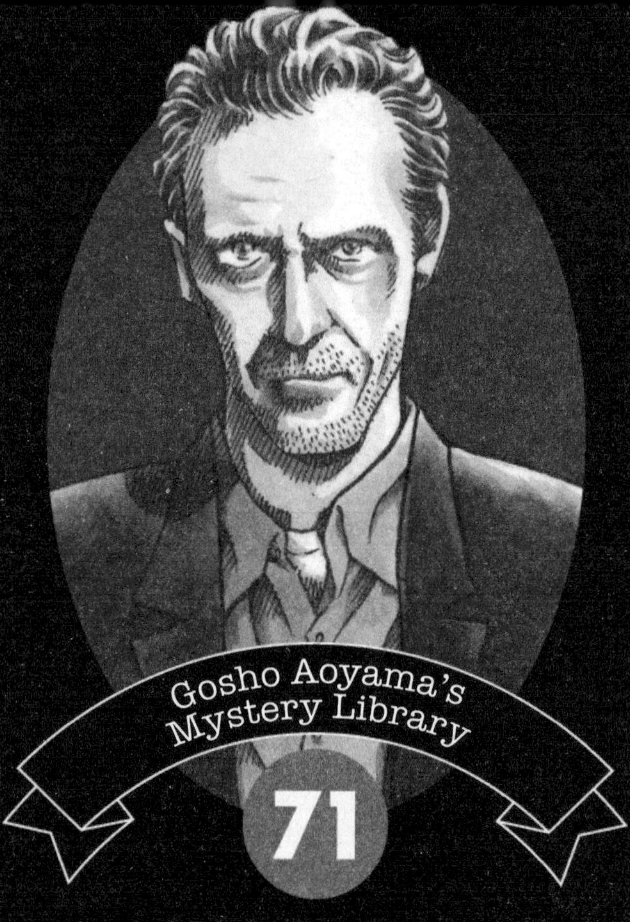
Gosho Aoyama's
Mystery Library
71

GREGORY HOUSE

The criminals this detective hunts aren't human. Parasites, bacteria, viruses... Yes, it's Dr. House, a genius who could be called a medical detective! Gregory House works at Plainsboro Teaching Hospital. A rather troublesome doctor, he wanders the hospital with his bad leg, ignoring the ordinary patients and taking an interest only in those with mysterious and unexplained symptoms. He's an arrogant man who often insists "Everybody lies." But he always saves the patient in the end with his skepticism, unparalleled medical knowledge and unconventional methods, so his friend Dr. Wilson and those who work under him trust him implicitly.

When Hugh Laurie, who plays House, first read the script, he thought, "How could a man like this be the main character?" It's the same with Holmes, but sometimes a sharp tongue is proof of a master sleuth! That's probably why Conan tends to be rude too. *Heh.*

I recommend the episode "Frozen."

Kidnapped by the Demon King and imprisoned in his castle, Princess Syalis is...bored.

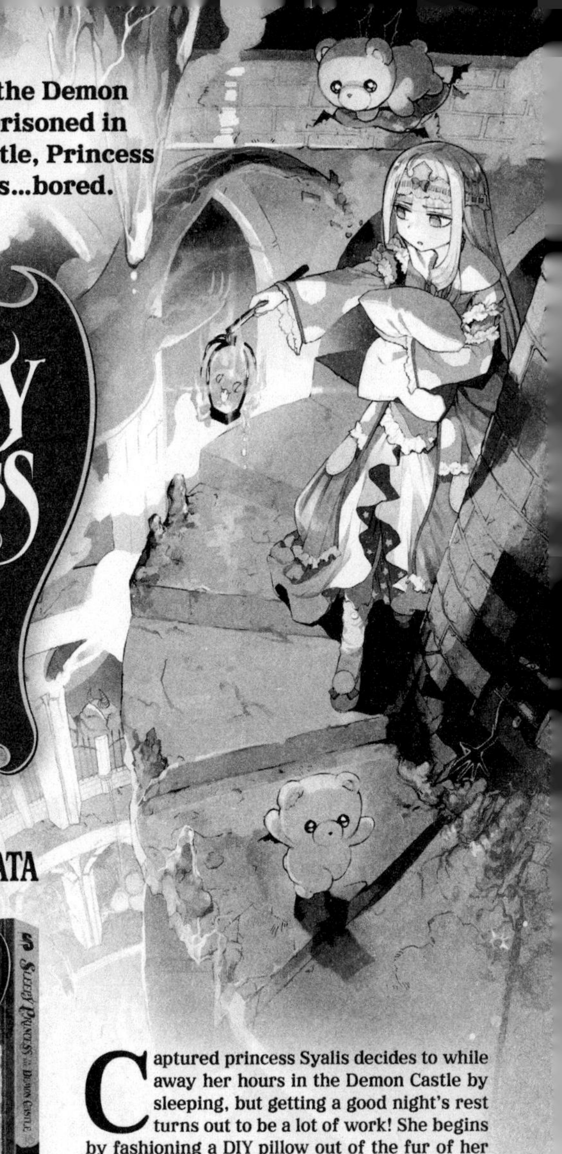

SLEEPY PRINCESS IN THE DEMON CASTLE

Story & Art by
KAGIJI KUMANOMATA

Captured princess Syalis decides to while away her hours in the Demon Castle by sleeping, but getting a good night's rest turns out to be a lot of work! She begins by fashioning a DIY pillow out of the fur of her Teddy Demon guards and an "air mattress" from the magical Shield of the Wind. Things go from bad to worse—for her captors—when some of Princess Syalis's schemes end in her untimely— if temporary—demise and she chooses the Forbidden Grimoire for her bedtime reading...

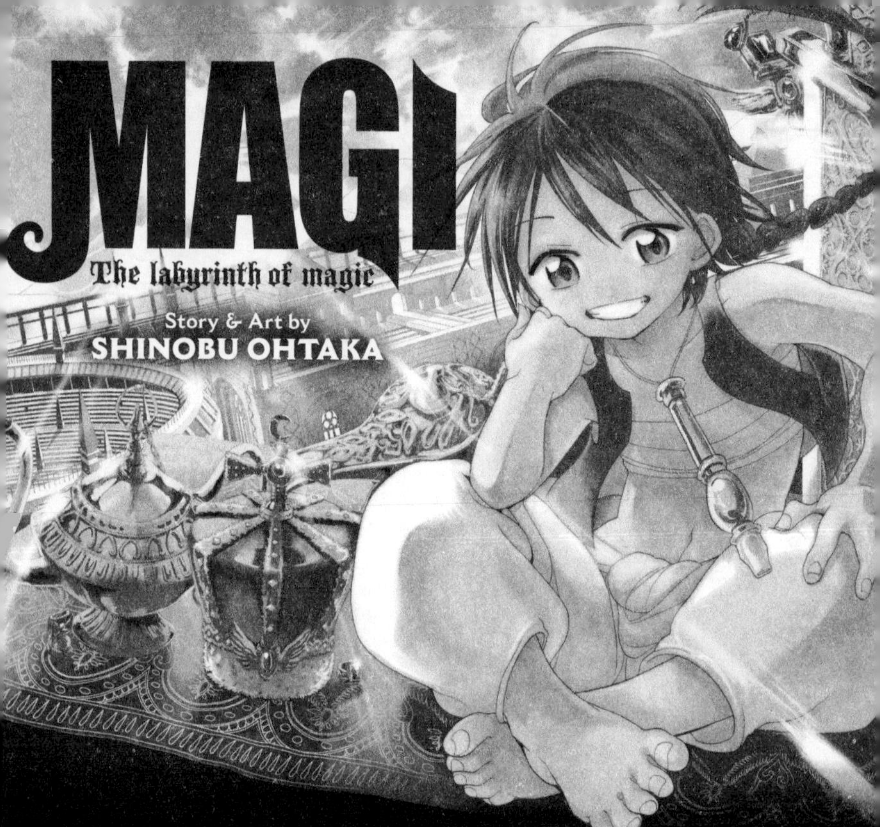
MAGI
The labyrinth of magic
Story & Art by
SHINOBU OHTAKA

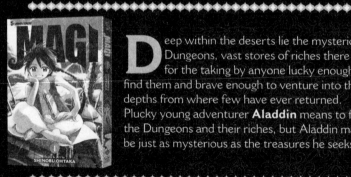